The
**Canadian Jewish
Outlook** *Anthology*

The Canadian Jewish Outlook *Anthology*

Edited by Henry M. Rosenthal and S. Cathy Berson

New Star Books
Vancouver

© 1988 by Canadian Jewish Outlook Society
All Rights Reserved

First printing August 1988
1 2 3 4 5   92 91 90 89 88

Canadian Cataloguing in Publication Data

Main entry under title:
The Canadian Jewish outlook anthology
ISBN 0-919573-68-1 (bound). — ISBN 0-919573-67-3 (pbk.)

1. Jews. 2. Jews — Canada. I. Rosenthal, Henry M. (Henry Michael), 1920- .
II. Berson, Seemah Cathline, 1931- . III. Canadian Jewish outlook.
DS102.95.C35 1988   909'.04924   87-091248-8

The publisher is grateful for assistance provided by the Canada Council
and the federal Department of Communications.

Printed and bound in Canada by Gagne Printing, Louiseville, Quebec

New Star Books Ltd.
2504 York Avenue
Vancouver, B.C.
Canada   V6K 1E3

Contents

In Memory of Ben Chud	9
Our Outlook	11
Introduction	13

I. The Canadian Jewish Experience

What is Canadian Jewish Outlook? / *Jack Cowan*	21
The Canadian Jewish Community and Zionism	24
Convention of the Zionist Organization of Canada / *Joshua Gershman*	35
Rags, Clothes, Bottles / *Ted Allan*	40
Jewish Communal Responsibility in Light of Government Cutbacks / *J. Torczyner*	43
Pea Soup / *Ida David*	49
A Stroll Down Spadina Avenue / *Rose Kashtan*	56
Transplants / *Rita L. Rosenfeld*	60

II. Secular Humanism

Is the Public School the Arena for Religious Education? / *Joseph Zuken*	69
Yiddish Culture and Anti-Semitism / *Moissaye J. Olgin*	71
Moses Mendelsohn / *Norman Massey*	74
To My Son on His Turning 13 / *Philip Resnick*	79
Son of Jeremiah / *Aaron Kramer*	80
The Getting of Religion / *Lanny Beckman*	84

III. Anti-Semitism and the Holocaust

With Embellishments / *George Lewis*	91
The Vulture Answers Their Call / *Walter Bauer*	98
Legacy for the Living / *Joseph Zuken*	103
I Knew Janusz Korczak / *George Scheinman*	105
Our Account With Nazi Collaborators is Not Yet Settled / *Joshua Gershman*	107
The Holocaust of Which Nobody Speaks / *Mike Cass*	112
Many Needed Saving, But "None" Was Too Many / *Joshua Gershman*	114
Anti-Semitism Considered "Respectable" / *Larry Haiven*	120
German Eyewitness in the Warsaw Ghetto / *Mike Cass*	123
Psychoanalysis in Nazi Germany / *Mike Cass*	125

IV. Peace and Disarmament

Vietnam is a Jewish Issue / *Jack Cowan*	131
Praying for Peace by the White House Fence / *Rabbi Abraham Feinberg*	133
Kampuchea / *Kathleen Gough*	138

The Question for World Jewry in 5743 / *Reuben Slonim*	142
The Shalom Committee / *John Mate*	147
Grenada / *Dionne Brand*	148
Mission to Nicaragua / *Ruth Herman*	150
Forty Years Later...	153

V. Israel and the Middle East

Voices of Reason / *George Lewis*	157
An Israeli Coup? / *Reuben Slonim*	162
Shadows of Lebanon / *Philip Resnick*	166
The Lebanese Tragedy / *Henry M. Rosenthal*	167
"Peace Now" is Needed Now! / *Eliezer Feiler*	172
Nahum Goldmann / *Mike Cass*	175
Chomsky, Israel and Nuclear War / *Norman Epstein*	178
On the Threshold of 1984 / *J. Lipski*	181
Report on the Geneva Conference / *Asher Neudorfer*	186
Mattiyahu Peled / *Asher Neudorfer*	190
Israel and the Rise of Zionism / *Zayed Gamiet*	194

VI. Yiddish Literature

The Negro in Yiddish Fiction / *Isaac E. Ronch*	201
A Poet of the Sweatshop Era / *Itche Goldberg*	204
Two Soviet Yiddish Poems / *Translated by Ben Chud*	208
A Vibrant Poet of the Sweatshop Period / *Sid Resnick*	210
Crazy Levi / *Rochl Korn*	215
Poet Radiates Compassion for His Fellow Man / *Sol Liptzin*	217
Melech Ravitch / *David Rome*	219
Kol Nidre / *Peretz Markish*	222
In the Quiet of the Morning / *Sholem Shtern*	223
Ber Green in Canada / *Aaron Kramer*	226
This is Not the Road / *Rajzel Zychlinska*	232

VII. Culture

"An Art of Anger..." / *Avrom Yanovsky*	235
Marc Chagall Pavilion at "Man And His World" / *Ruth Pressman*	238
In Siqueiros' Studio / *Samuel L. Kagan*	244
Enriching Introduction to Cree Culture / *Henry M. Rosenthal*	247
A Special Man, A Special Musician / *Edward Parker*	248
A Legacy to be Treasured / *Solomon Shek*	253
The Artist Speaks / *Margaret Ennenberg*	255
The Precious Legacy / *Riva Dolgoy*	257
Is Huckleberry Finn Racist? / *Paul Schmidt*	259
The Rediscovery of East European Jewry / *Michal Bodemann*	264

VIII. Women

Equality of Kibbutz Women / *S. Cathy Berson*	271
Being a Working-Class Jew / *Lilith*	279
Two Outstanding Women of Our Time	
I: Fania Fenelon / *Miriam Silver*	283
II: Bess Horowitz / *Hillel Schenker*	285
So That Another Generation Will Not Deny / *Lilith*	289
International Women's Day	291
Piece Work / *Mona Elaine Adilman*	292
Miriam Waddington / *Helene Rosenthal*	296

IX. Canadian Political Issues

Our Enduring Dilemma—1867 And All That / *Stanley B. Ryerson*	303
Observations on a Centenary / *Joseph Zuken*	307
Will Hunger Stalk the Land? / *Henry M. Rosenthal*	309
Lotusland / *Stan Persky*	315
What Happened to the "Just Society"? / *Ed Schaffer*	319
The Generic Drug Controversy / *Joel Lexchin*	324
The Shamrock Shambles	327
Human Rights and Civil Liberties / *Abraham J. Arnold*	328
The Macdonald Flim-Flam / *Daniel Drache*	332
Canada's Penal System Indicted / *R.S. Ratner*	338

X. Jews on the Left

Experiences of a Scientist / *Leopold Infeld*	343
"Never Let Them Change the Truth of Our Innocence" / *D.K. and R.K.*	349
The Death Kit of Irving Howe / *M.J. Granite*	355
Incisive Analysis of the Jewish Left / *Isaac E. Ronch*	364
The Decline of the Jewish Left / *Roz Usiskin*	367
Alejandro Lipschutz / *Bernardo Berdichewsky*	370
A True Man of the People	374
Rabbi Feinberg / *Henry M. Rosenthal*	376
The Contributors	379

November 1986

In Memory of Ben Chud
(1921-1986)

On the morning of the day he died, my father began this *Outlook* editorial on the recent meetings between Israel and the Soviet Union.

Israel-USSR

The "official" character of the two recent meetings between Soviet and Israeli representatives is an important component of their significance. After such a hiatus, during which all contact was at arms length, formal announcements about such gatherings mark a turning point. Nor should the level of contact be overlooked. At Helsinki we witnessed what might be called lower-level echelon discussions. In New York, at the United Nations, Peres met with the top ranking Soviet Minister of Foreign Affairs, Shevardnadze.

Little is known about the substance of these discussions except that each lasted for about 70 minutes. We do know that the Helsinki meeting was very abbreviated since it was slated to go for two days.

My father was not able to finish this article, but readers of *Outlook* do not have to guess at his conclusions. He would have applauded these tentative steps toward renewed Soviet-Israeli relationships. He would have called on peace-loving people around the world to encourage continued dialogue. And, always the optimist, he would have viewed these developments as part of his lifelong vision of a socialist world in which Jewish culture and humanist values can flourish.

—*Rita Chudnovsky*

We Shall Go On...

The loss of our beloved colleague Ben Chud came as a profound shock to all of us who worked with him. With the passage of the healing winds of time, the sense of shock is gradually dissipating. Even the pain can be expected to diminish as we cope with life and its problems. But the loss will remain with us for a very long time, as we continue to carry out our tasks toward a common goal without Ben's help and advice.

Let no one think that our efforts will diminish in any way. Rather, we are determined to intensify our struggle to provide an alternative voice for secular, progressive Jews. And we know that others will come forward to help fill the breach. Our greatest tribute to Ben will be continued growth of the magazine he held so dear.

—Henry M. Rosenthal
Editor

October 1963

Our Outlook
From the Inaugural Issue

We draw the curtain and put on the stage a *Canadian Jewish Outlook*. We will perform in a rapidly changing world, a world that must resolve its problems while at peace, seeking to prevent war—which is no solution at all.

We are fortunate that we begin our publication at a time when a partial thaw in the Cold War and a lessening of tension in the world is visible.

We selected our New Year to begin publication, as a portent of the health and happiness that all Jewish people dream of and wish for at this time... with a pledge that our pages be a force for making them a reality.

Peace and Security

Canadian Jewish Outlook was spurred into existence by the overwhelming need for developing and formulating a Canadian Jewish outlook which must today and in the tomorrows, together with all Canadians and all people of the world, ensure a life based on peace and security for all.

Stimulate Activity

We pledge to *reflect* the aims and desires of all peoples, and of the Jewish people in particular, who are a part of the whole, with a Canadian Jewish outlook for PEACE, DEMOCRACY, EQUALITY, SECURITY and EDUCATION for all—to *examine* high-points in general Jewish history, Jewish Canadian history, Jewish traditions, our contribution to Canadian culture, the contribution of Jews to the Canadian labor movement, life in Israel and of our people everywhere—and to *bring* to English-speaking Canadian-born Jews the treasures of Jewish culture, the works of Jewish writers and poets, past and present, the activities, both cultural and social, of Jewish organizations and institutions—and to *comment* on Jewish community problems and events, seeking to *stimulate* activity on all issues facing our people.

—*Editorial Board*

Introduction

The publication of this unique Canadian-Jewish anthology should be welcomed by Jews and non-Jews alike as a major contribution to a broader understanding of one of Canada's important ethnic communities. *The Canadian Jewish Outlook Anthology*[1] has a two-fold significance. First, it brings together for the first time a wide selection of the best writing to have graced the pages of *Canadian Jewish Outlook* during the past quarter-century: articles, editorials, poetry, debates and satire that continue to enlighten, strengthen and nourish secular Jews. Second, with this publication we proudly celebrate the 25th anniversary of the founding of the only Anglo-Jewish pro-socialist magazine in Canada.

In view of the fragility and high rate of extinction endemic among small Canadian periodicals, the survival over 25 years of a secular, progressive, ethnic magazine is indeed worthy of attention. It is not surprising that progressive newspapers and magazines have had, and continue to have, a precarious existence. As noted in a 1986 CJO editorial, "The ethnic press is a reflection of our general society and this means that progressive magazines and newspapers are the distinct minority among minorities. More than this, the progressive ethnic press is constantly struggling to stay alive financially." Along with the struggle to maintain its independence from commercial control, it has been the constant aim of this magazine to maintain a balanced ideological position. Notwithstanding these difficulties, we can say with pride after 25 years: CJO is alive, growing and better than ever!

It would be wrong to suggest that CJO appeared in a vacuum, without a history and without roots in a community. The magazine's evolution must be viewed in its larger historical context. The appearance of an English-language, left-wing Jewish periodical in the early 1960s was a natural outgrowth of the Yiddish progressive press which took root in the late nineteenth century in the U.S., and which dates from 1926 in Canada with the founding of *Der Kampf* (The Struggle). According to Paul Novick, veteran editor of New York's *Morning Freiheit*: "The history of

---

[1] The magazine *Canadian Jewish Outlook* was founded in 1963 and underwent a name change in 1986 to *Outlook: Canada's Progressive Jewish Magazine*. Since most of the articles in this anthology were originally published under the *Canadian Jewish Outlook* logo, that name, or simply CJO, is most commonly used.

the Yiddish press in the U.S. reveals that most of the language newspapers were founded as socialist papers or as sympathetic to socialism." It can be said that CJO continues to draw upon the proud traditions and wide experiences of its predecessors. It continues to carry forward its philosophy of Jewish radicalism which has been its anchor and its sustenance.

As a philosophy, Jewish radicalism has often been accused of being a hybrid, a strange amalgam of two irreconcilable factors: Jewish identity and socialist ideology. Strange or not, it was the synthesis of these two elements which provided the *raison d'etre* of the Yiddish progressive movement in North America and which remains its cornerstone today. As part of this movement, the Yiddish press sought to weave together the specific problems of Jewish workers with those of the general working class. Its aim was not the isolation or ghettoization of Jews but the incorporation of Jewish workers into the larger social process. Balancing particular Jewish needs with the project of radical social change became the key to the uniqueness of the Jewish radical experience in North America.

M.J. Olgin, one of North America's foremost Yiddish editors, expressed the essence of Jewish radicalism in this way:

> We wish to see a Jew who will not be a stranger in the country in which he lives, a Jew who will know how to link the progressive forces of the Jewish people to the progressive forces of all other people in the same country or other countries in the struggle for a better, more humane life and who will, at the same time, remain a Jew, a son of his people, a fighter for the future of our people.

This was much easier said than done, as one Canadian radical confirmed:

> Uneasy lies the head of that unique species of Jew who is committed to international socialism but still persists in retaining his ancestral ties. Such a political hybrid is apt to end up a political outcast, suspected by both sides of divided loyalties, or worse still, of being faithless to either creed.

Despite these difficulties, Jewish radicalism became embedded in the consciousness of the Jewish immigrant community in Canada. The Jewish radical movement evolved alongside a vigorous Yiddish radical press, the main connection to the larger world for thousands of Canadian Jews. Fraternal organizations like Arbeiter Ring in Montreal and Winnipeg, and the Labour League in Toronto, were a focus of political, cultural and social life in Jewish communities. Segments of the Arbeiter Ring and the Labour League merged in 1946 to become the United Jewish People's Order, the largest and most vibrant left-wing Jewish organization in Canada.

The nature of the Jewish immigrant community shaped the development of the Yiddish left-wing press and its English-language successor, *Canadian Jewish Outlook*. At the turn of the century, the first major wave of Jewish immigrants from Eastern Europe arrived in Canada. Fleeing pogroms, persecution and ghettoization, these Jews quickly became the dominant force in the hitherto small Jewish community, which had been composed primarily of West European Jews with an assimilatory bent and a middle-class orientation. East European Jews, on the other hand, came to North America as staunch Yiddishists and as part of the working class. Most were artisans, journeymen, apprentices and factory workers. A very small number were traders. By the turn of the century, 40 per cent of the Jewish population in the Pale of Settlement[2] had already been proletarianized. They were concentrated in six major industries: clothing, metal, woodwork, building trades, textiles and tobacco. However, it was in the needle trades, where they constituted 60 per cent of workers, that they played a major role in the development and unionization of this important industry.

After the failure of the 1905 Russian Revolution, thousands of young radical Jews came to North America where they began to make inroads into the Jewish community. By 1920, in each major urban centre where Jewish immigrants worked and struggled for survival, there existed a numerically small but very influential group of Jewish socialists who were dedicated to the needs of the working class, to the philosophy of Marxism, and to the creation of a Jewish working-class culture. Essential to these goals was the development of a Yiddish radical press.

In the struggle to survive in a society that was often hostile to Jews in particular and to East Europeans in general, the Yiddish press was to play an important role. For the first time, Jews in North America experienced a sense of freedom of expression hitherto unthinkable. They were able to publish, interpret and analyse events and experiences for the Jewish immigrant workers who were new to the political, social and cultural processes. The Yiddish radical press educated, encouraged and provided leadership to Jewish workers, many exposed for the first time to the industrial work process, to union formation, strike action and labour

---

[2] The term "Pale of Settlement" was coined in the reign of Czar Nicholas I (1825-1855) and referred to the territory within the borders of Czarist Russia where Jews were legally authorized to live.

politics. The Yiddish press, a source of news, culture, politics, entertainment and identity, aided the adjustment of the Jewish immigrant in a strange and foreign land. In return, the loyalty of the Jewish working class to the Yiddish press in Canada assured its survival from 1926 on.

From the beginning, the Yiddish progressive press has had a strong and sustained leadership. In Canada, Joshua (Joe) Gershman earned his credentials as a leader of the Yiddish/Jewish working class. In 1926 he became the editor of the first progressive Yiddish monthly, *Der Kampf*, later renamed *Der Veg* (The Road), and in 1940, the *Vochenblatt* (Canadian Jewish Weekly). During a span of almost 50 years, Gershman developed a truly magnificent journalistic career. On his 70th birthday, Gershman's lifetime contribution was summed up by Sam Carr in a 1973 issue of CJO:

> For many years now, it has been ungrudgingly recognized not only in Canada but in many countries where there are centres of Yiddish cultural life that Joshua (Joe) Gershman is one of the most outstanding publicists in the Yiddish language.

He was not only the writer, translator and editor of the Yiddish progressive press in Canada, but he made time to maintain his links with the Jewish communities across the country. Each year he toured Western Canada to help the local *Vochenblatt* committees in their fund-raising campaigns. His erudition, oratorical skills and insights into world events made his visit the highlight of the year in many communities.

Very early on, Gershman recognized the changing nature of the Jewish community and the need for "a new type of publication" that would address the needs of the growing number of English-speaking Jews in Canada. In 1963, after several unsuccessful attempts, he and a small group of dedicated supporters across Canada founded the *Canadian Jewish Outlook* in Toronto. The Anglo-Jewish monthly set out to "beam our message to the young English-speaking generation of Canadian Jews." It was to follow in the tradition of its predecessors in this fundamental way:

> What differentiated us was not only that we were not for the establishment, but that we were dedicated to the fundamental concept that Jews are first of all human beings, and thus the problems common to humanity are our problems—in addition to those of a specific Jewish character.

The progressive political developments of the 1960s and early 1970s provided fertile ground for CJO during its formative years. The relocation of the magazine to Vancouver in 1979 removed it from the centre of Jewish population and intensified the threats to its survival. However, it has survived, and for many reasons. A dedicated group of Vancouverites undertook the considerable responsibility of publishing the magazine. Their tenacity and commitment are reminiscent of the radical pioneers half a century before them. As co-editors, Ben Chud and Henry Rosenthal brought to CJO a collective determination and intelligence which gave the magazine its best chance of survival. Sylvia Friedman, a veteran of the Jewish left who trained with Joe Gershman, has been CJO's managing editor and, on a day-to-day basis, its backbone. As with numerous small magazines, the commitment of a few provides enlightenment for thousands.

The magazine has made a lasting contribution to the cultural, social and educational life not only of the progressive Jewish community but of the community as a whole. Its continuation has reinforced the fact that Jewish life in Canada never was, and is not now, a homogeneous entity. It encompasses a wide spectrum of social thought, class composition and ideology, with Jewish radicalism as one of its components.

It its 25 years of publication, the *Canadian Jewish Outlook* has always focused on local and national issues of concern to Canadian Jews. It has also consistently dealt with topics of a more global nature. For this anthology, the editors have selected articles, poems, graphics and reviews for their quality and representativeness, with the aim of presenting a panorama of our concerns and a reflection of the past 25 years. Included, therefore, are thoughts on Jewish education and culture, Jewish community life in Canada and abroad, and anti-Semitism. In reviewing articles on events in Israel we find that the problems of the past twenty years are still with us today. Included as well are topics of war and peace, civil liberties, the economy, national liberation struggles, labour conflicts and women's issues. These problems have not gone away. Faces, and sometimes places, may have changed; unfortunately, the struggles still go on. Therefore, it is our hope that this anthology not be viewed as merely documenting the past but also as presenting issues which are still very much alive for all of us.

Outlook today operates in a world of intense social, political and economic upheaval. Events in Israel, the rise of religious fundamentalism and conservative thought, and the resurgence of anti-Semitism demand a critical and courageous assessment of problems old and new. For 25 years *Canadian Jewish Outlook* has responded vigorously to this demand, as can be seen in the pages of this anthology. There is every reason to believe that it will continue to do so in the next 25 years.

I
The Canadian Jewish Experience

March 1969

What is *Canadian Jewish Outlook*?

Our Magazine in its Sixth Year

JACK COWAN

Publishing a monthly magazine that retains the interest of its readers in this age of capsule knowledge is difficult. Publishing a Jewish magazine is more difficult. The choice of material has to be narrowed to justify the special interests of its readers. Publishing a progressive Jewish magazine like *Canadian Jewish Outlook* is most difficult of all, for in addition to the usual problems of writers, deadlines and finances, there is on the editors the obligation of integrity in the selection of material, because the general objective is to convey a message or a guide to action on the issues of the day. The editors must make doubly sure that what the subscriber is to read will be helpful in moving society forward—including Jewish society.

What are the overall objectives? A world of peace, humanism, and economic and political security. This kind of world would not be a nirvana. There would still be challenges to meet: in science, in personal relationships, and in philosophy. But the framework would be present for the flowering of the human spirit.

We live in a world of uneasy co-existence between two social systems, capitalism and socialism. At the moment it is a standoff because the socialist system has managed to develop equal weapons of terror which capitalism is not prepared to challenge. But in our quiet and saner moments is it not relevant to ask whether the standoff cannot be expressed in terms other than weaponry? It has been estimated that present military budgets amount to over $200 billion annually. It is enough to make one tear his hair!

We would be naive if we believed that the weapons were developed and amassed only to be used by the two main protagonists against each other. Since the end of World War II there have been numerous examples of the employment of weapons for the purpose of suppressing freedom movements. The appeal of the *Canadian Jewish Outlook* to its readers is to support movements for social advancement. Since we cannot have "guns and butter," let us fight for more butter so that the amount available for guns will shrink.

A review of the *Canadian Jewish Outlook* over the past five and a half years since its founding in October 1963 indicates that the problem of disarmament and peace has occupied a leading place in its editorials and articles. This is not accidental. If there is a major military confrontation, the world will become a cinder-heap and all the problems that face us now would be irrelevant.

Our second emphasis has been on humanism. We regard all peoples as equals and do not subscribe to the theory that some are more equal than others. The *Outlook* has attacked infringements on civil liberties at home and abroad. We have not failed to express ourselves on the violations of socialist legality in those countries where such discrimination is practised. At the same time we have not fallen into the trap of condemning socialism as a system because of the regrettable bureaucratic administrative errors that do occur. We hope that time is on the side of freedom and justice for the mass of people.

A sincere effort has been made to give the *Outlook* a Canadian orientation. The bi-national character of Canada has received considerable attention because we felt that it was important for Jews to understand and sympathize with the aspirations of the Canadian citizens of French descent. We have dealt with the implications of the Auto Pact, the Fowler Report on Broadcasting, the Bi and Bi Commission Report, the Hall-Dennis Report on Education in Ontario, the hippie cult, etc.

We have dealt with problems that directly affect Jews at home and elsewhere. *Outlook* has devoted many articles to the dissemination of hate-sheets in Canada; to the guesting of Nazis on Canadian TV; to the protests of would-be Nazi fuehrers in Toronto parks; to the problems of Jewish parochial schools; to organized Jewish communal life in Canada; to profiles of Canadian Jews; to reviews of books by Canadian Jewish writers. Nor has *Outlook* confined its efforts to the examination of the purely local scene.

Long before the Six-Day War erupted we wrote about the critical situation that was developing. As the Arab threats mounted we pleaded for a settlement that would guarantee Israel's borders while Israel made some real moves to settle the Palestine Arab refugee problem. But the war did erupt and though in its wake came many difficult problems, most of which have not yet been solved, we are happy that Israel as a state and nation was not wiped out.

There is a strong progressive peace movement in Israel that opposes the Dayan annexationists and it is our hope that this movement will be strong enough to compel the reactionary leaders in the Israeli government to make all reasonable concessions at the peace table. This is no time for Jewish chauvinism. At the same time we reject the positions of some that because of the belligerence of this or that Israeli leader the entire nation should be wiped out. Israel has as much right as any other nation to have its share of political creeps. We feel the same way about the Arabs. The mass of people are exploited by their own exploiters and foreign imperialists; but there are signs of a growing movement for better living standards and political freedom. We hope that in this area the bellicose pronouncements of some Arab leaders will not be mistaken for the desires of the Arab peoples.

Outlook has published many articles on Jewish cultural questions, on Yiddish literature and, in "Scanning the News," a panorama of events the world over of interest to Jews. This reviewer fails to recall, however, a basic discussion of the "national" question which in progressive circles has come to the fore since World War II. Prior to that ghastly episode we didn't attach much importance to the question.

We assumed that the question would disappear as groups of nations polarized into blocs, and had some authority for such a position in the writings of Marx and Engels. Many believed that assimilation was inevitable anyway as far as Jews were concerned, but when the Holocaust occurred under Hitler, and when Jews were deprived of their constitutional rights, de facto if not de jure, in socialist countries, we awoke with a shock to the complexities of the "national" question. In the February 1969 issue of *Jewish Currents* of New York, a worthwhile contribution to the discussion of this question is made by Louis Harap in a review of a book, *Nationalism and Socialism*, by an American professor, Horace B. Davis. Dr. Moshe Sneh, a leader of the Communist Party of Israel, also makes a fine contribution to the discussion in a part of an address to the Sixteenth Congress of his organization in October 1968 under the title "On the Examination of the Problems of the Jewish People and Their Solution." I throw out a challenge and an invitation to our writers and readers to do some thinking about this vital problem and to write the results so that they may stimulate a discussion in the pages of *Outlook*.

Outlook has been quoted in the Jewish press of Canada, USA, France, Argentina and Israel (and perhaps in other countries as well). Considering its budgetary limitations, it has fulfilled its promise of October 1963 to be an Anglo-Jewish mouthpiece of and for Jews in Canada. Just a few more things are needed: subscribers, money and, above all, more writers. Each reader can contribute under one or more of these headings. Will you?

June 1985

The Canadian Jewish Community and Zionism
A Dialogue

On May 10, 1965, the public relations committee of the Toronto United Jewish People's Order held a public forum on the subject "The Canadian Jewish Community and Zionism." *Canadian Jewish Outlook*, in presenting excerpts from the two papers read and some of the questions asked and answered, hopes this is only a start on a long-overdue dialogue on all questions and problems confronting the Canadian Jewish community. The papers were delivered by Mr. Julius Hayman, National Secretary, Zionist Organization of Canada and editor of the *Jewish Standard*; and by Mr. Joshua Gershman, Editor, *Canadian Jewish Weekly*.

JULIUS HAYMAN: Before we go into our subject, my friends, I want to do two things. I want to define Zionism as I see it, and I want to give you an outline of the theory I hope to prove. Zionism is that movement in Jewish life which believes that this Jewish life can best be preserved and enriched through its tie with Israel. If you ask a rabbi how Jewish life may best be preserved, he would say *"through the Synagogue."* If you ask a Hebrew principal how Jewish life may best be preserved, he would say, *"through the Jewish school."* If you ask a Zionist how Jewish life may best be preserved, he would say, *"through our link with Israel."*

Now, many Jews, even Zionists, believe that Zionism began with Theodor Herzel and the first Zionist Congress at Basle in 1897. My theory is that Zionism is as old as the Jewish people itself. Until the fifteenth century, when the world was organized mainly along religious lines, Zionism expressed itself in religious terms, as a religious movement. When nationalism became the dominant force in the world, Zionism developed into a nationalist, secular movement. When it seemed as though political action might bring the re-establishment of a Jewish state, Zionism became a political movement. When the important thing was the practical rebuilding of the state to enable it to absorb the hundreds of thousands of Jewish refugees clamoring at its gates, the emphasis was on practical

Zionism. We are now entering a new stage in the development of the Zionist idea, a cultural Zionism which is spending every effort to work with Israel to the end that Jewish life may be strengthened and enriched. And because Zionism has gone through all the above phases, religious, national, political, practical and cultural, it has within it the power, if it is rightly used, to be the major centralizing force in Jewish life, appealing to the religious Jew, the nationalistic Jew, the politically oriented Jew, the practical Jew whose chief interest is Israel's physical growth, and the cultural Jew.

And now to the further development of my thesis.

My friends, just last week the Jews of the world celebrated an event which stirred the minds, and hearts and souls of all Jews, wherever we may be, whatever political faith we hold, whatever ideology we profess. Scattered as we are over all the countries of the earth, living as we do in every sector of the globe, we united in paying tribute to the gallant people who brought to pass one of the most significant events in our history, the establishment of the State of Israel. In the modern, gaily lit cities of the Western Hemisphere, in the dark, depressing, disease-infected mellohs of North Africa, in dynamic, confident Israel, yes, even in the communist and socialist countries of Eastern Europe, Jews uttered a grateful *shehecheyanuh*, and affirmed anew the indestructibility of a centuries-old dream of redemption and return.

We may all agree that over the past seventeen years, Israel has given us Jews reason to be proud. It has shown in the highest degree its ability to measure up squarely to the heart-rending problems which have plagued it since its creation. It has demonstrated its capacity to meet the demands of economic struggle, political pressure and military invasion, and yet emerge, strengthened and hardened by its ordeal of suffering, to meet the challenge of its destiny. And we in Canada paid tribute to this nation, small in area but great in courage and in spirit, to which we are bound by bonds of common peoplehood, and common ideals, and common hopes for a secure and peaceful future.

As we celebrated, joyously, this twentieth century miracle, no less marvelous than our miracle of Chanukah some 21 centuries ago, or the miracle of Passover 3,400 years ago, we allowed our minds to linger over the stirring events leading up to this incredible achievement. We recalled the idealism of the pioneers, who settled in Palestine over seven decades ago, dedicating themselves to its hot and arid soil. We remembered the vision of Theodor Herzel and the faith of the Zionists of the first few years of the twentieth century. We lived again through the crushing disaster which ground Europe's Jews under the heel of the unspeakable Nazis, and which forced a desperate Jewry to seek salvation in the land of its fathers. We thought again of the fierce struggle with the mandatory power during the 1930s and the 1940s and, finally, we thrilled again to the memory of those days of great courage and high resolve, when the haughty Arab armies crossed Israel's borders in 1948, boasting arrogantly that they would drown the stubborn handful of Jews in the Mediterranean and were themselves hurled back in shameful defeat. And as we saw Israel plucking the rose of victory out of the thornbush of disaster, we Jews, in the lands outside of Israel, felt ourselves one with our brothers in that distant land, and we shared with them the exciting, stirring, historic years—as partners in Israel's joys and sorrows, its defeats and victories, its tragedies and triumphs.

But to the Zionists, who had helped to mould the forces of history which brought Israel into being, the creation of the Jewish state was not the end but a new beginning. They saw their Zionism not as a transient influence in Jewish life but one of the great historic forces which had shaped its destiny over the ages. It is this concept of Zionism that I hope to place before you, a Zionism which, as I suggested, met the religious needs of a religious world, satisfied the nationalist drives of a nationalist world, took up the challenge of a political world and now, finally, is facing up to its latest challenge—the task of fulfilling its cultural purpose in a swiftly changing Jewish world.

The credo of the modern Zionist is this: Jewish identity is worth preserving, Jewish life is worth developing. In the weakening of religion and nationality as the constructive, unifying force in Jewish life, we offer them Israel. At best the Jews in the State of Israel, free of the heavy pressures of non-Jewish influences, have an opportunity of developing fuller, richer and more rewarding Jewish lives than do we here. And we Zionists try to ensure that the Jews outside of Israel, the Jews of the Diaspora, shall have a share in this better Jewish life to come. The Jews of the Diaspora, too, have a unique contribution to make to Jewish life and we Zionists accept the responsibility for ensuring that the spiritual and cultural exchange with Israel be a process in which the benefits flow not only in one direction, but in two. The Israelis, especially the native-born Israelis, are proud of their achievements. But we sense in many of these Israelis an impatience with the Jews of the Diaspora who have not chosen to live in Israel, we sense in them a contempt for the Jewish history of the past 2,000 years, years which have left on us the mark of the ghetto but which have also given us a spirit of understanding and compassion which belongs only to those who have known the anguish of suffering. It is a part of the Zionist purpose to make the Israelis understand that while *we* accept the centrality of Israel, we insist upon *their* acceptance of the importance of the role that Diaspora Jewry must play in the development of

Jewish life. And so, Zionists work for the realization of the ideal of a single Jewish people, one and indivisible, including both the Jews of Israel and the Jews of the Diaspora, each influencing and helping to develop the other.

What does this involve in practical terms? It involves us Zionists in certain functions we share with all Jews—or at least most of them. We help raise funds for Israel, in partnership with other agencies in the community. We sell and purchase State of Israel Bonds. We stimulate investment in Israel. We try to develop a favorable climate for Israel among our non-Jewish fellow-Canadians. But most of us Zionists in the Diaspora believe, deeply and sincerely, that our Zionist movement was not merely an instrument for the creation of a Jewish state but a vital force in Jewish life, with the power to release Jewish spiritual and cultural energy. Zionism, to us, is not only a means of helping to maintain a Jewish homeland in Israel for those who wish to migrate there, but a vital force in Jewish life which will help us, here in Canada, to resist the powerful non-Jewish influences which surround us and which urge us to accept a dilution of our Jewishness, to the point of outright assimilation. To us, Israel is not only a home for Jews, but a home for Jewishness, however we define it. If Israel is to fulfill its full purpose in Jewish life, it must constitute a cultural and spiritual centre from which currents flow to enrich, and invigorate, and unite Jews everywhere in their search for meaning in their Jewish heritage. And, as I have suggested, this involves the right, and the responsibility for us, in the Diaspora, to insist that *we* have a stake in the development of Israel, and that we therefore have a right to influence the shape of its future.

And so we Zionists accept *more* than a financial responsibility towards Israel. We accept the task of making Hebrew our common language, in which we can carry on a cultural and spiritual dialogue. We accept the task of stimulating personal contact between the Jews of the Diaspora and the Jews of Israel—and I don't mean *"study missions"* of millionaires but rather missions of students, who will bring the best of Diaspora Jewish culture to Israel and, in return, bring the best of Israeli culture back to the Diaspora. And the Zionist movement is facing up squarely, at long last, to the challenge of *aliyah*, the migration of Western Jews to Israel, so that there may be a true mingling of Jewish life, so that the Jews of the Diaspora and the Jews of Israel are one, not only in spirit and culture, but in ties of family and blood. And encouraging our young men and women to take a part, at least, of their education in Israel institutions, so that they may understand these fellow Jews, who live thousands of miles away, under such different conditions.

This is the Zionist ideal. We have fallen far short, of course, of its realization. But as I look about me I see no other instrument in Jewish life with the historic background, the breadth of vision, the universality of appeal, or the passionate conviction, to do the job. The synagogue has its place, of course, a unique and indispensable place, based upon the religion of the Jew. The Jewish schools, too, have their role, preparing their pupils for participation in Jewish life, in one or another of its various aspects. Congress has its place, in Canada, developing local institutions, fostering a richer Jewish life in the nation and working towards the safeguarding of Jewish political, economic and social interest. But there is, I believe, no other philosophy of Jewish life which includes as many shades of Jewish thought as does the Zionist philosophy, no other instrument in Jewish life except Zionism to make us—in Israel and in the Diaspora—a single people, one and indivisible, dedicated to the one supreme goal, a richer and more meaningful Jewish life for us all.

JOSHUA GERSHMAN: Friends, I too believe that the subject for tonight is not too clear, but I do not think Zionism as it has been discussed by Mr. Hayman is so far off the topic that we are all interested in. It is true that I do not intend to go into the history of the Zionist movement tonight, important though that history might be and which is a part of the history of the Jews. I prefer to come down to earth, and to present here problems of the day and the perspectives, primarily because I do not consider that the establishment of the State of Israel is a miracle. Zionism certainly made its contribution to the establishment of the State of Israel, but if it would only have been because of the existence of Zionism through all these various stages, there would never have been a Jewish state. This state came into being as a result of a bitter struggle, especially during the Second World War, a struggle against imperialism, a struggle led by the Israeli people and others. It was the fruits of a victory over fascism that made possible the establishment of the State of Israel with the assistance of all the anti-imperialistic forces throughout the world, including, and possibly with the most aid and assistance of, the Soviet Union and other socialist lands. Therefore, I will try to limit myself to problems that have to do with the contribution made tonight by Mr. Hayman.

From the various conversations with Mr. Hayman, I know that there are no disagreements with a man of my political views regarding the ills and weaknesses in our Jewish community life. Our disagreements stem from the ways and methods of healing the ills that beset us. They are based on the ideology and instrument that would provide the necessary values in the changed character of the Jewish community of today. It's clear Mr. Hayman believes, as you have heard tonight, sincerely so, that Zionism is the ideological weapon and that the new slogan, "facing the

Diaspora," adopted at the 26th Zionist Congress that took place in Jerusalem, is the remedy. I respectfully submit and I will attempt to prove wrong the concepts of this slogan and their unworkability. There can be no other conclusion, as the congress and the discussions on its eve and since it was held have proven. This slogan stems not from deep concern for the many and complicated problems but rather as a result of the serious crisis in Zionism itself, especially since the establishment of the State of Israel. (This does not imply any reflection on the sincerity and honesty of many Zionist leaders and especially my opponent of tonight, Mr. Hayman.)

I intend to show that the whole concept of "the centrality of Israel" is not acceptable for the overwhelming majority of the Jewish people the world over and, furthermore, it is harmful for Jewish continuity in the Diaspora as well as for the State of Israel.

Notwithstanding the affinity of Jews, of every walk of life, to Israel, the Jew in Canada, as in all other countries, considers himself a Canadian, or an American, British, French, etc. Even Mr. Samuel Bronfman in his speech in Jerusalem on May 11 found it necessary to recognize the fact that "the Jews of Israel are Israeli citizens, that the Jews of the United States are American citizens of the Jewish faith and likewise Canadian Jews are Canadians of the Jewish faith, etc." Most of the aid for Israel comes from non-Zionist and even anti-Zionist people. Aid and concern for the security of Israel in the mind of the average Jew is not associated with Zionist ideology at all and inasfar as Israel itself is concerned, assuming more and more sovereignty, entering a period of being capable of standing on its own feet, economically, culturally, politically, etc., the concept of that country will assume a distinct, independent Israeli character, and the little bit of Zionism still existing, mainly because most of its leaders are adherents of Zionist ideology, will evaporate to a point of complete disappearance. This is particularly true judging the thinking, the feelings of the Israeli people, not only of *Sabras* young and old but of many of the new arrivals. So writes M. Tzanin, editor of *Letzte Neis*, who said, "Zionism became [for the young generation] a word repugnant as 'ghetto yid' and why deny it—also the older generation in Israel, the generation that was brought up in the spirit of complete negation of the *galuth*, is also infected with this Canaanistic disdain. When one desires to say to a friend in the jargon of a *Sabra, hak mir nisht kain tchainia*, he says, '*Al tedaber tzionith*' (do not speak to me about Zionism)."

This also holds true concerning the attitude to other phases of Jewish life, including religion. In his very interesting article in *Conservative Judaism*, Winter 1965, Elizzer Whartman, discussing realities of life in the State of Israel, especially the Israeli youth, states, "the *Sabra* has come to regard the one great tie uniting the Jewish people throughout the world—religion—as something alien and repugnant." E. Whartman uses this fact to set off an alarm to the consequences of such an estrangement on the future of Israel-Diaspora relations. In plain words the Israelis in the main are not concerned with the Jews in the *galuth*.

In face of this and many other factors, which I cannot deal with now, the slogan "facing the Diaspora" as a weapon especially forged to bring back and enrich Jewish life in the Diaspora is no more than a dream and does not correspond with realities in the Diaspora any more than in Israel.

Jewish leadership in our country as well as in the United States is divorced from the Jewish masses and so is the Zionist movement. In the formerly mentioned periodical *Conservative Judaism*, Rabbi Joseph P. Sternstein, a friend of Zionism, discussing the deepening crisis in the Zionist movement states, "...the Zionist movement has divorced itself from current issues of life here"—and he gives examples and goes on to state: "the American Jew is caught up in the contemporary currents of public life," and that "Zionism said nothing to him about these issues," and he concludes, "if this means that Zionism has nothing to say about these bread and butter programs, the American Jew will simply turn his back on it. And this is precisely what has happened."

This has been strongly illustrated at the 26th Zionist Congress, especially by the utterances of the younger delegates of various countries. The congress was a great disappointment to them. One delegate, M. Shatner from France, expressed doubts about Dr. Goldmann's cry of assimilation and Dr. Goldmann's remedies. He stated, "the youth in every land can easily come to the conclusion that joining the communist movement for instance is much more important than to belong to the Zionist movement"; and the Zionist journalist Samuel Shnitzer in writing about the ideological emptiness of the Zionist Congress does not find any fault with the youth; he finds fault with the Zionist and Jewish leadership. Permit me to quote what this Mr. Shnitzer had to say.

"Yes, we have a good Jewish youth for whom ideals are a life tonic but he seeks content in his empty life in other places. He sacrifices himself for the rights of Negroes to vote in Mississippi, he goes to jail in South Africa, he goes to the revolutionary movements in South America, he lets himself be beaten up by police in demonstrations against nuclear weapons, he fights the battles with fascists and racists and he revolts against every adopted lie everywhere, where he meets up with it."

This kind of Jewish youth, though they may be a minority, constitute the life line for Jewish survival. Since Jewish leadership, including Zionist leaders who dominate in the main all major national Jewish organizations, does not meet the desires and aspirations of the Jewish people, the slogan "facing the Diaspora" will boomerang.

In conclusion you will notice that I have not indulged in a historical analysis of political Zionism, nor of its reactionary period, nor of other stages in the years of its existence. I do not believe that from the point of view of perspectives this is necessary. History will judge *all* movements. I am more interested, and *all* Jews should be interested, in differentiating between Zionists and Zionists, between leaders and leaders of various movements. The critical time that we live in requires, above all, Jewish unity on a minimum program, on points that unite us all and not those which divide us. The Zionist movement, with all of the criticism that I have always held, has been one of the movements that made its contribution towards the development of Jewish values as well as many other movements. Yes, including and particularly the left-wing in all countries. We on our part, as a secular Jewish movement, will continue to transfer a secular *Weltanschauung* and our point of view to the younger generation, to all Canadian-born Jews and strive for Jewish unity around basic issues on whose very existence the Jewish people, and for that matter, all of humanity depends.

In my opinion the answer will not come by Zionist ideology, by its new instrument of "facing the Diaspora" that Israel shall become the centre of Jewish life, because it simply does not correspond with reality and it is not going to be accepted by the Jews.

QUESTION ADDRESSED TO MR. HAYMAN: *Do you think that the Canadian Jewish Congress is sufficiently militant in the light of today's problems?*

MR. HAYMAN: The answer to that very simply is no. The Canadian Jewish Congress is not militant enough. It is not militant enough because it is actually reflecting the desires not of a segment of the Jewish population but the broadest element in the Jewish population and the broadest element in the population is an element of Jews that have become smug and complacent, and self-satisfied and simply don't want congress to rock the boat. Congress is in fact representing the broad view of the whole Jewish community, not my view, because as Mr. Gershman said, I am a "maverick"; but let us understand that congress in its lack of militancy is actually expressing the desire of a smug, satisfied, contented, fat Jewish population in Canada. I believe that the elements that are trying to stimulate congress—and I don't agree with all of what they are trying to do—are performing a very, very valuable function. Congress will respond to stimulus because congress leadership is worried about nothing more than that it should lose the confidence of its constituency. Don't think that the top leadership of the CJC is not worried about what we think or about what other Jews think. It is very, very sensitive. Just let me write an editorial criticizing the establishment in Jewish life and there will be a response... but unfortunately, the stimulus of the community is the stimulus of smug, self-satisfied Jews...

Now let me say something about Jewish leadership. It is true that Jewish leadership is woefully lacking. There are no good Jewish leaders anymore either in Canadian Jewish life or in American Jewish life or for that matter in Jewish life anywhere in the world. If there were Jewish leadership, we who attended the World Zionist Congress wouldn't have witnessed the fiasco in the Zionist organization where political ward heelers were determining the policy of the World Zionist organization; not philosophers, not idealists, but political ward heelers. What does that mean? It means that the Jewish world is as lacking in leaders as is the non-Jewish world.

QUESTION ADDRESSED TO MR. HAYMAN: *Don't you feel that the Jewish community should be more active than they are in peace activity and especially in reacting to present American policies in Vietnam and the Dominican Republic?*

MR. HAYMAN: I believe that there are many places that the Yankees are now that they have no place in.

MR. GERSHMAN'S SUMMARY: On many questions there are no disagreements between my point of view and Mr. Hayman's, especially on those confronting the Jewish community now. This is the important essence of our dialogue tonight, for it is this unity of aims that can begin to resolve many of the problems we are faced with today in the Jewish community.

Montreal Street Scene (oil) by Meyer Ryshpan (January 1978)

Tailor (oil, 1940) by William Gropper (January 1982)

Jewish Immigrants Arriving on the Prairies by William Kurelek (September-October 1982)

January-February 1973

Convention of the Zionist Organization of Canada
Selling a Counterfeit Bill of Goods

JOSHUA GERSHMAN

In a Toronto hotel on Saturday evening, November 18, I attended the official opening of the 40th National Convention of the Zionist Organization of Canada.

The opening session was dedicated to the 25th Anniversary of the State of Israel. It was perplexing to witness the absence of any festive spirit on this great occasion. The small measure of joy conveyed by the youth song and dance groups, who entertained before the session opened, was soon erased by the crude propaganda speeches, replete with worn-out cliches, which followed.

The reason for this joyless celebration became amply apparent soon after the top leaders, together with the Israeli Consul-General Shmuel Ovnat and the guest speaker of the evening, Mr. Arieh L. Dulzin, treasurer of the Jewish Agency and president of the World Zionist Organization, took their seats at the head table.

The introductory remarks by the evening's chairman, Mr. Eric Exton, were both formal and spiritless. The greeting by the Israeli consul-general lacked all that one expects of an inspirational message. In presenting the main report, Daniel Monson, Q.C., president of the Zionist Organization of Canada, a very able man and a fine speaker, somehow managed to maintain the level of dullness set by those who preceded him.

It is not my purpose, at this point, to dwell on the reasons for the serious crisis in which the Zionist Organization of Canada finds itself, although this situation undoubtedly affected the evening adversely. (And it should be borne in mind that the Canadian Zionist Federation, which held its convention in Ottawa prior to the ZOC convention, is in a not much better state, in spite of the purported "life-giving injection" represented by the election to the presidency of the "fresh-from-the-oven ardent Zionist," the former Toronto mayor, Mr. Philip Givens.)

Rather, I wish to devote myself to some examination of the speech delivered by the guest speaker, Mr. Dulzin. The essence of his message was that 75 years of Zionism and 25 years of the State of Israel represent "only the beginning" of the fruition of Zionist ideology. It is the sacred duty of the Zionist movement to make Israel the centre of Jewish life everywhere in the world.

Here Mr. Dulzin chose to ignore completely the fact that Jews in various lands are citizens of their countries, countries in which they rear their children and where they fully intend to reside for generations to come. Mr. Dulzin apparently did not consider it to be his task to call upon Jews in the world to actively participate in solving the problems faced by each country where Jews reside nor to struggle for justice for all mankind and, above all, for peace in the world.

He maintained that, while it is a fact that the State of Israel came into being as a result of the 1947 decision of the United Nations, the map originally delineated was unjust to Israel. He claimed that this is so since, when the Jews began "their return" to the land of Israel some 50 to 75 years ago, Palestine was uninhabited. If there were any people in the land, he declared, they were a mere handful.

According to Mr. Dulzin, the Arabs who lived in the land in 1947 were not "Palestinians," but people who filtered into the country from other Arab lands, especially during the years of the British Mandate. Therefore, the speaker asserted, 60 per cent of the Arabs who were in Old Palestine were in fact themselves "immigrants," and "there never was and there is not today such a national entity as Palestinians."

Need we remind the reader that this position is in essence a repetition of the claims made by Golda Meir, General Dayan and their cohorts, the annexationists in the government of Israel? They categorically refuse to recognize the existence of a Palestinian nation and maintain that in all territories under the Israeli flag, the only nationality which is a reality is the Jewish one.

Mr. Dulzin went on to inform his audience that only with reluctance did Israel accept the 1947 map as drawn by the United Nations. However, he claimed, the miracle visited upon the Jews came as a result of the war the Arabs waged in 1948, which resulted in a considerable expansion of Israel's territory.

This, Mr. Dulzin declared, was only *the first phase* in the struggle to free *all of Israel*.

Conveniently, the speaker then vaulted from 1948 to 1967. He apparently forgot to mention the aggressive attack launched by Israel against Egypt, in a nefarious partnership with France and Britain, in 1956—the so-called "Sinai action." This caused untold harm to Israeli relations with the Arab world.

Mr. Dulzin termed the Six-Day War of 1967 the second phase. It was, he said, as a result of this that "we liberated" practically "all of Israel." He went on to stress "the unquestionable right" of the Jews to what he calls "all of Israel." To him, the territories occupied in 1967 are in fact "liberated areas of Israel."

While making these reprehensible statements, Mr. Dulzin assured his listeners that he "does not deny the rights of the Arabs [Palestinians—J.G.], but let Jordan become their state."

What did the speaker have to say about the possibility of peace in the Middle East? Peace will come, he maintained, when the Arabs recognize that "Israel is here and will be here forever." His contention was that such a recognition will come about simply by the persuasive force of ever-greater Israeli power. According to the Dulzin method, a militarily strong Israel will "teach" generation after generation of Arabs, until they agree that all occupied territories must forever remain part of Israel. The boast "we are strong" was repeated by the speaker ad nauseam.

Mr. Dulzin told his listeners that since the establishment of the State of Israel some 1,600,000 Jews, half of them former residents of Arab lands, migrated to Israel. Instead of describing both the great achievements as well as the thorny problems of the state, the speaker proceeded to describe some sort of near-paradise. He considered that all problems that may have existed have been solved and "without resorting to communism or socialism." According to Mr. Dulzin, all Israelis enjoy the great benefits of the "welfare state." There are no rich or poor, no exploiters or exploited, apparently. Well, what about the Arabs in Israel? They live well, we were told again and again.

We would like Mr. Dulzin to read the opinions of Mr. M. Tsanin, editor of the Tel Aviv *Die Letste Nais*, who wrote in the New York *Forward* of November 22 of the uneasiness that permeates the people of Israel, arising out of the immorality of casting the Arab workers in Israel into the role of "hewers of wood and drawers of water" for Jews—yes, for rich Jews, at that.

History teaches us that occupiers of other people's territories remain occupiers no matter how well they treat the people whom they have conquered by the violence of military force.

Can anyone honestly deny the many oppressive measures suffered by the Arabs at the hands of Israeli military power in the occupied territories? Occupation engenders resistance, resistance results in oppression, no matter how good the intentions.

The final part of Mr. Dulzin's oration was devoted to the influx of

Soviet Jews into Israel. He denied vehemently all universally recognized achievements of socialism. He set out to "prove" that communism and socialism "are bankrupt," especially when compared to the glories of the welfare state in Israel.

(This is a serious, false accusation, but unfortunately it cannot be dealt with adequately in the short space of this article. It will be the topic of a future, longer discussion.)

Such a speech could not enthuse an intelligent audience. We know the adage "people are not fools." Mr.Dulzin's listeners have been to Israel, they have read reports and they undoubtedly resented being served such a rosy picture of the life of the average Israeli while no attempt whatever was made to deal realistically with the most urgent issue—peace with the Arab people.

People who are seriously interested in Israel and who study the realities of the Middle East situation are aware of the fact that not only among Israeli people at large, but even in government circles, there is an active questioning of the present policy of "might is right" as advocated by Meir and her associates.

Many of Israel's foremost academics, themselves ardent and life-long Zionists, are taking an active part in the struggle against the annexationists. One of these, Professor Jacob Talmon, wrote recently:

> Those who claim that might will solve all problems live from day to day, and fail to concern themselves with the future. The success of the policy of might at the moment appears in their day-dreaming as the last word in the development of history. They cannot comprehend that the book of history is a living, open phenomenon and that the angel of history elevates the downtrodden and denigrates the arrogant...

Professor Talmon, citing the history of many nations, declares: "Those who depend entirely on their might must set out to conquer the world, and they resemble the rider astride a tiger who no longer has the choice when he wishes to dismount."

The opposition to the holding of the conquered Arab territories is expressed by many influential Israelis. Thus, Professor A. Rubinstein, himself an active Zionist, reminds his people in his recent writings that in his book *We and Our Neighbors*, published in 1930, David Ben Gurion wrote:

> We have no intentions of robbing the Arab people, grabbing their

land, and settling in their places. . . . We have no right to cause harm to even one solitary Arab child—even if at such a cost we could realize all of our dreams.

It is essential to remember the assurance of the late prime minister of Israel, Levi Eshkol, given on the eve of the Six-Day War, when he stressed again and again that Israel did not covet one single inch of Arab territory, that all it sought was peace and security.

True friends of Israel must realize that Mr. Dulzin's unbridled boasts of Israeli might, as well as his contention that everything can be achieved by such might, are replete with most dangerous consequences not only for peace in the Middle East and the security of Israel, but also for the very peace of the world. Apart from the avowed annexationists there are not many people in Israel today who seriously deny the existence of a Palestinian people. The knotty problem of the refugees, the Palestinians, will have to be solved on a democratic basis, on the basis of self-determination.

Mr. Dulzin's euphoric report shows little respect for the intelligence of his listeners. Any serious student of Israeli life knows that Israel, a capitalist country, in a sense boils like a kettle with many class contradictions—strikes by the underpaid, a growing resentment against the growing number of millionaires (especially since the Six-Day War), the clearly apparent polarization of rich and poor with workers struggling to live on low wages and unable to obtain decent housing—all these are, alongside great achievements, part and parcel of the totality of the Israeli scene.

It is obvious that Mr. Dulzin's presentation of Israel and its life cannot be accepted as a reality by sensible people of all persuasions, not even by ardent Zionists.

For all Jews, the very fact that Israel has existed for 25 years is in itself a great and historic event. All Jews wish Israel to grow as a nation in a Middle East at peace. To achieve this attitude among Jews the Dulzins need not embark on "selling us" a counterfeit bill of goods.

True friends of Israel must see the realities as they are. In appreciating achievements one must not ignore the difficulties and even evils existing in Israeli society.

The Jewish community in Canada, in common with other Jewish communities outside of Israel, suffers from the Dulzin type of pseudo-patriotism in relation to Israel. The communities are victims of the Dulzin-type purveyors of super-patriotism and chauvinism, who understand so little of the true feelings of the Jews for the people of Israel that they believe that only an Israel which is perfect will merit support.

Professor Talmon, whom we quoted earlier, points to real patriotism when he writes:

> Not as invaders and as all types of imperialists will we build a fatherland, but with the sweat of our brow and without forcing out or oppressing others.

It is clear that Mr. Dulzin and the other spokesmen for the Meir ideology do not have this type of Israel in mind.

January 1981

Rags, Clothes, Bottles
A Short Story

TED ALLAN

"We are the chosen people," the old man said. "Whenever someone is wanted to be beaten, they choose us. When they want to indulge themselves in hate, they choose us. When there is a fire, a pestilence or a famine and they need someone to blame, they choose us."

David, to whom the old man spoke, was four and a half years old so he did not understand everything his grandfather was saying. To David, Zaida was the most wonderful thing that had ever happened. And if Zaida frightened people sometimes with his big, booming voice he did not frighten David. They understood each other.

The old man liked to show him off to his cronies at the synagogue each Sabbath.

"Tell them who is Solomon," Zaida would say.

"The wisest of them all, almost as wise as Zaida."

The old men would cackle and Zaida would caress his head and say softly, "You're my treasure. You're my life."

It was when he sat beside his Zaida on the wagon that Zaida would talk to him of many wonderful things; of how the Jews had marched through a sea which had opened up on both sides, how walls had fallen at the sound of a trumpet, how water had been changed to wine; and then also the terrible things, which the boy hardly understood—stories of people burned in furnaces, "millions, millions, millions of us." It was on the wagon that Zaida had spoken of the chosen people and then had told him, "You are Jewish and you must learn to speak Hebrew. Repeat after me..." Then the old man would say a prayer in Hebrew and the child would repeat it.

Sometimes the old man would forget he was driving a horse and wagon through the streets and back alleys of Montreal and raise his voice, singing some ancient hymn, and the boy would sing with him, with the same tone of anguish. The old man felt the anguish. The boy dimly sensed it.

When the word of God or Jehovah was mentioned, David had a clear picture of what He looked like. He looked just like Zaida, with piercing black eyes and a long grey beard with streaks of white and streaks of chicken soup on it. And He sounded like Zaida, with a voice like thunder, making the glasses ring on the shelves when he shouted.

"One alone of my progeny has a soul!" he would shout at his wife, or his daughters or his sons-in-law. "David! One alone of my fruit has a brain! David."

"He's spoiling the boy," David's mother would complain.

"The old crab is a ham actor," David's father would say.

For saying things like that about his Zaida, David did not like his father.

Zaida's horse was called Ferdeleh, which means "little horse" in English. Its belly hung very low and its ribs showed. Sometimes the bigger boys of the street would take a stick and play it across Ferdeleh's ribs shouting, "It's a harp. It's a harp!"

"Pigs!" Zaida would yell at them, waving his whip. "Goyem! Ganovim!" David would pat Ferdeleh's ribs gently, asking the old horse if it hurt. But it never seemed to hurt and Ferdeleh didn't seem to mind.

David knew the other boys were jealous of him, for what other boy had a Zaida with a horse and wagon, and what other boy played the game David played with Zaida every Sunday when it didn't rain? When it didn't rain he would go with Zaida on a ride through the back lanes of Montreal and every Saturday night before going to sleep the boy would pray for sunshine on Sunday so that his mother would let him go with Zaida. If it rained he could not go. His father objected to his going, sunshine or not. "That horse will collapse in a heap one of these days and there'll be an accident," his father said.

His father made jokes about Ferdeleh. He called it a nag, a cross between an elephant and a dog. "It's dead and doesn't know it," he would say whenever he saw it. His father also complained that the smell of the stable, which was in back of the house, smelled up the house. Zaida would reply in an angry voice that the smell of a horse was the healthiest smell there was. His father would shout back, "In the old country maybe, but not here. Here it stinks!"

"Your father, I am sorry to say," his Zaida told him once, "has the brains of an ox."

"Is that much?" David asked.

"It is practically nothing," his grandfather answered.

"Is that why he talks so foolish?" David asked.

"That, my dearest one," replied his grandfather gravely, "is exactly why he talks so foolish."

Once, when his father made some slighting reference to his Zaida, David said, "You have the brains of an ox."

He did not understand why his father burst into laughter. His mother, trying to control her smile, told him it wasn't a nice thing to say to his father.

"Did Zaida tell you that?" his father asked.

"He did—and he knows," the boy said. His father went into Zaida's room and there was some loud talking. Later Zaida took David aside and said, "Your father has the brains of an ox, but he feels bad when you tell him so, so don't tell him."

"But he laughed when I told him," David said.

"He really is an ox," the old man said, shaking his head.

But the wonderful game they played each Sunday morning, when it didn't rain! They would feed Ferdeleh, hitch her to the wagon, listen to the admonitions of grandmother and mother telling them to be sure and be back in time for lunch, and be off. When they were out of sight Zaida would give him the reins and sometimes would let him wear his derby hat which fell over the boy's ears and covered one eye.

When he wore that hat people would laugh and he would laugh too, feeling that everyone was as happy as he was. And then the game would begin. His grandfather would cup his hand to his ear and shout, *"Regs, cloze, bottles! Regs, cloze, bottles!"* David would do exactly the same, shouting, *"Regs, cloze, bottles!"* in the same loud, sing-song voice. Then women would appear on back balconies and beckon to them. David would run up with five cents, or a dime, or a quarter and get all kinds of colored rags and old clothes and bottles, and dump them onto the wagon. And every Sunday, if it didn't rain, Zaida would take him to play that wonderful game.

Many such Sundays passed and the boy lived for them from week to week. He would be up first, rush to the window to see if the sun was shining, run into the backyard and give the horse its feedbag, getting everything ready for Zaida. Then he and Zaida would eat breakfast prepared by grandmother and say a prayer in Hebrew for each plate.

One Sunday when he awoke to the sun's rays across his bed, he was told by his mother that Zaida was sick and would not be going out with Ferdeleh that day. When he started towards Zaida's room he was told that he could not go in because Zaida was very sick. Later that day his Zaida called for him. He looked very strange, very white. He didn't say anything. He just looked at his grandson and his lips moved but nothing came out. David was taken from the room...

Sunday morning was bright with sunshine. David ran into the shed and then into the stable. Ferdeleh was not there. He felt bad thinking that Zaida would have gone off without him. Then he went to look in Zaida's room. It was empty. The boy walked into his own room and stood by the window staring out into the street. He heard someone come in. It was his father.

"Zaida's gone to heaven," his father said. "With Ferdeleh?" David asked.

"Yes" his father answered.

He didn't cry, but he knew that somehow life had changed for him. This was the first sunny Sunday morning that his Zaida had gone out with Ferdeleh and not taken him.

March 1982

Jewish Communal Responsibility in Light of Government Cutbacks

J. TORCZYNER

To ask about the Jewish community's responsibility in light of government cutbacks is both pressing and timely. The primary question, however, is: What is the Jewish community's responsibility to its poor regardless of what this or future governments may or may not do and regardless of past patterns of support for various Jewish agencies.

I intend to suggest a revitalization of our communal decision-making process, a redirection of our political energies and styles, and reevaluation of all agencies—their mandates and the services they provide—guided by one central concern: their impact on the Jewish community in general and particularly on the Jewish poor.

I have deliberately chosen to focus on the poor while fully aware that the Jewish community has always had and will continue to have a broad mandate which promotes the welfare of the entire Jewish population. But since the community should have as a priority to support its people who cannot support themselves—our elderly, our handicapped, all people linked together by hardship and fear—the way in which we conduct ourselves in these matters would portray our approaches to other issues as well.

To protect our neediest has in our tragic moments meant to defy government and put in peril the lives of our communal leaders rather than to seemingly promote the community's welfare by not protecting those least able to help themselves. This fact was starkly demonstrated in the Ghetto of Kovno in November of 1941. Under the ruse of increasing benefits for some and generally promoting the community's welfare, the Jewish community council was ordered by the occupying Nazis to distribute white cards to its most accomplished artisans. As it became known that only those holding white cards would survive, the Jewish community council ordered that all cards be returned rather than aid in a selection process which would compromise those least able to fend for themselves.

Comparable? Perhaps not. After all, today's issues are one of government cutbacks in service, and not of genocide. But the principle is one of justice. I use the word justice because we, as Jews, have no concept of charity. There is no word for it because charity suggests something you do for others at your own expense. And as far as a principle of justice is concerned, let me state unequivocally that when the going gets rough, we get tough and do our utmost to assist our weakest regardless of the cost.

The fact that government does provide benefits, the fact that we live in a democratic society wherein we have the right to make demands on government, suggests to me an opportunity and responsibility to persuade and challenge government to restore its supports to its previously inadequate level and then to increase these benefits.

To be most effective in the political arena, however, we must adopt a stance which is very different from our past patterns. During the Liberal reign in Quebec, the Jewish community had cultivated excellent links with government and had courted favors through various forms and channels of private influence. With the election of the Parti Quebecois the Jewish community has sought to create such links where none existed by placing a representative in Quebec. This approach, a continuation of traditional patterns where Jewish community leaders sought to beseech governments on behalf of its members, ignores possibilities and potentials which exist for us here and were unavailable to us in Europe.

We do have the possibility of aligning ourselves with non-Jewish groups to fight for the welfare of all elderly, of all handicapped, and of all the poor. We can and must put aside our differences and find common ground when it comes to these shared principles. We must join forces and protest government indecency and disrespect for its poor in all legal ways. We must demonstrate in behalf of our poor. Let AJCS [Allied Jewish Community Services] put aside its differences with Centraide and let these two powerful organizations lobby for change in government policy.

There is no contradiction between fighting to raise government levels of support and maintaining Jewish services which are necessary and important. This is a necessity because Jewish federations are unable to solve the problem of poverty through service and income supplementation. Were AJCS to extend its financial supplementation program to all of its poor Jews, it would cost the community $20 million a year. This expenditure of funds would preclude programming in any of the other vital areas of concern. This point is particularly important. The costs of AJCS services are likely to increase more quickly than contributions to the Combined Jewish Appeal. Professionalization, specialization, inflation, and the rapid growth of an elderly Jewish population will spiral service costs over the next decade. It is only government which has the financial capacity to ensure that all people will have adequate shelter, health care and sufficient food. We must continue to supplement poor government policy and provide services which have a distinct Jewish component, and we must begin to challenge government to change its policies.

We must make certain that our poor can take full advantage of their government entitlements. Many people, because of a lack of information, of transportation, fear of government bureaucracies or language difficulties do not attain their benefits. We need to advocate for them and to make these services more accessible. There are still Jews who live and die alone, whose resources are few, and who are often afflicted by disease and despair, abandoned and forgotten, who receive none of the benefits of Jewish or government social services. Current economy and government policy will worsen their situation and swell their numbers.

This is a partial answer to what is the Jewish community's responsibility in light of government cutbacks. A second direction is to make certain that we get the best use of our funds by evaluating our current agencies and services. We have contented ourselves, to date, with program descriptions and general statistics without seriously examining what these programs do and what their impact is on consumers. It is well documented in the social service literature that agencies which do not undergo systematic re-examinations, which are assured of their funding, and which have no mechanism for consumer participation, do not adapt or change readily and may continue to service needs which are no longer priorities and provide programs which are no longer suited to current realities.

In actual fact, the current crisis need not generate retrenchment and conservatism. It can be a call for unity, creativity and innovation. Ninety per cent budgeting is a small step in the right direction, but in itself is insufficient. It has come to mean that if an agency gets 10 per cent less one year, it gets 20 per cent more the next—without evaluating how effective these services are.

My concern is not with staff security, although this is important. Nor is my concern the maintenance of organizations—even ones which I helped create. My concern is the effect that agencies have on those who need us most, and the likely effects that cutbacks will produce.

I suggest that AJCS review each and every one of its expenditures and ask what are the essential Jewish components; are these services a substantial improvement over government programs, are government programs nonexistent, and to what extent do the poor benefit from services available to the entire community? I am quite certain that a serious examination of this nature would reveal that we are not doing as much for the poor as we claim, and that substantial parts of the budget ought to be reallocated.

A closer examination of AJCS spending would show that a lot less is spent on direct, essential relief costs than would appear at first glance. The essential items of food, cash, shelter, health and home care account for only $860,000 of the $4,675,000 spent in Montreal in 1975. Adding Montreal's contribution to JIAS, which is a national agency and does provide direct relief for immigrants, and considering the total funds raised by the Jewish community in Montreal, approximately $1,700,000 of more than $18,000,000 dollars raised in 1978 was spent on these direct, essential relief costs. Public relations and statistical gymnastics aside, slightly more than ten cents of every dollar went to support these essential needs of the Jewish poor in Montreal in the year 1978.

Many of our services are important and helpful to those they reach. Unfortunately, they do not touch the lives of the vast majority of the Jewish poor. Our agencies are simply not accessible enough or accountable to the people they service. Very little outreach is conducted, and many consumers, especially the elderly poor, are intimidated by the bureaucratic structures, lavish offices, and professional styles which most social service organizations have developed. This problem is not peculiar to AJCS organizations. What is peculiar is the little that has been done about it. Rather than taking cutbacks and limited communal responsibility, we need to redeploy our budgets, improve our services, and then if necessary, increase our funding.

An important ingredient in these efforts is participation by the recipients of service in agency and AJCS decision-making. Because policies are developed and programs implemented without the participation of the people who need and use the services, many important programs which are priorities to the Jewish poor and are not funded by government go unmet. Moreover, by doing this AJCS has by and large ignored the self-help capacity of our community.

In this regard, I can point with pride to the work of the Project Genesis. Some 40 volunteers working hand in hand with four staff will help 4,000 people this year. Golden Age and Baron De Hirsh among others also have volunteers who participate in service delivery. The elaboration and proliferation of this concept enables us to help more with less, generates self-help potential, and frees up social workers to provide more specialized service and catalyze others to actualize our finest instincts—the service of others.

These proposals require at least a reaccreditation of our sacred cows. This can only occur through a continuing debate, and a full opening up of the decision-making process. While many opinions are represented and indeed these opinions and the decisions which prevail may be the very best ones, there is a serious credibility gap and questionable legitimacy concerning communal leaders and their decision-making process. At best, the current practice of community decision making suffers from a lack of input by many segments of the community. A handful of appointed leaders in close collaboration with their executive staff decide the communities' priorities and directions.

If the decision is the wrong one, and indeed it is quite possible for AJCS to make a wrong decision, there is no systematic community mechanism through which the people affected by these decisions are fully informed and have recourse. Nor is there a mechanism through which errors can be corrected and the leadership held accountable.

The community, it is claimed, is apathetic. We welcome participation and few people who want to assume a role in Jewish communal life are turned away. The doors are open, but people do not want to put in the effort.

This argument presupposes that these portals provide avenues to healthy structures. The door, even if it is open to all—which I seriously doubt—is clearly not as an entrance to the only possible structure. Certainly there are examples in Montreal Jewish communal life of more democratic decision-making and vehicles for participation. But there are 100,000 Jews in our community who are really not represented in AJCS. This population is comparable to the fifth largest city in Quebec. No one here would support a government of this scale whose officials are neither elected nor accountable. No matter what decisions are made, they certainly cannot be the right ones because of the ways in which they are made. What the Jewish community's responsibility is in light of government cutbacks ought to be debated, discussed and decided by as many Jews as possible in public meetings and open forums and not only in the closed boardrooms of AJCS.

These proposals may appear radical but be that as it may, I think our task might be made easier by these eight recommendations:

1. To assert the Jewish community's responsibility to its poor in times of economic prosperity and to increase its support during times of economic malaise.

2. To open up decision-making and planning bodies to include representation of all segments of the Jewish community in general and the Jewish poor in particular in order to generate a full elaboration of communal priorities.

3. To promote more outreach services in order to assist low-income Jews to make full use of both public and private services to which they are entitled.

4. To develop more community organization programs among the poor to assist them in defining their priorities and to help them help themselves.

5. To make alliances with non-Jewish groups in order to convince federal and provincial governments to develop more adequate legislation.

6. To carefully evaluate all agencies and their services in view of client impact, their essential Jewish quality, and in light of government programs, and to implement these in ways which will be more accessible and have greater impact on those who need the services.

7. To ensure that government services are physically and psychologically accessible to the Jewish poor.

8. Lastly, to renew and instill volunteer activity in areas of social justice and social service to carry forward our tradition that we are one people.

January 1980

Pea Soup
A Short Story

IDA DAVID

Goodbye... goodbye... heartrending sobs tear at the small, narrow chest. Goodbye, mama 'n auntie and uncle... goodbye, Hana, Nessa, Mirra, Sroolik... goodbye, all my friends... goodbye to my beautiful dollandcarriagethatpapaboughtjustbeforehedied... never will I see you again, Haya weeps... never... never... never....

The ambulance has stopped. Slam goes the door. Here comes that stinky doctor again. Haya gets ready for more humiliation at the hands (it was his hands that smelled so bad, she remembers) of the husky, young, French medic who had, much earlier on this sunny, Sunday afternoon, bounded up their stairs and into their house.

After a rough probing of her throat, he had rudely flung back the bedcovers to check her belly rash. Grunt. Yeah, she had the scarlet fever, all right. Quickly, he'd bundled her into the harsh blanket that dangled from his shoulder and out of the house, racing crazily, trailed by the tearful family, all the way down the winding, outside staircase onto the street, where already, half the residents on the block surrounded the dread vehicle. At the wheel, the driver made growling noises.

"Stand aside," came the doctor's gruff command. With one muscular hand he opened the double doors and, in a neat toss, to the mixed accompaniment of admiring gasps and disapproving murmurs, deposited Haya on the waiting cot with the other.

Now, in front of the sprawling, grey stone structure, he leaps into the van and grabs the quivering patient. Fully expecting to be hurled to her death, Haya shuts her eyes for the last time.

She is in someone else's arms. Someone running. Haya opens one eye as the red-faced nun who is galloping through the drafty corridors with her rounds a bend. They skitter to a stop in a sky-lit vestibule, where two, small, snotty, caterwauling children occupy a miniature, iron bench, their patches of spotted, naked flesh gleaming in the afternoon sun as though painted.

The nun plunks down her latest charge, snatches the blanket and gallops off. "Shush!" she roars back as Haya begins to howl.

"Go way, you... go way, go way," one sobbing creature, face contorted, shrills, pushing at the newcomer with both hands. Haya stops, furious. She checks out genders, quits yanking at her own brief nightshirt, resumes her howling.

What's this? The nun is back... reaching out for a victim. Haya ducks, evades her. Not so the other two. Gathered up, they are raced off, shrieking as they go, bare feet skimming the slippery stone floors, their sweaty captor yelling the same incomprehensible words at them, over and over again.

Before the commotion fades into the distance, other voices have joined in, heavy doors have slammed and now, billowing clouds of steam swirl down, fill the hallway. With a final clang, what sounds like ponderous gates swing shut, cutting short the ear-splitting screams that have begun to filter through. Silence.

Please, oh, please, God, save me, Haya blubbers. Her voice reverberates. No use. Why, why is she always late? Late... late... always too late...

Just one more chance, she begs... I'll be good for the rest of my life ... honest, she snivels. I swear... give me one more chance... I'll never be bad again... I swear it! Oh, God, please! Echoes.

Hands wrapped about her neck to squeeze an aching throat, she plops forward in choking, skinny misery. Body twisted, head dangling loose like a slaughtered chicken, she slumps there, sobbing and whining and promising to be good forever. More echoes.

Haya has been well prepared. But not that well. No previous contact with French Canadians, divided as they are from the Anglos, the Anglos from them and both from all "the others" in this divided city of Montreal—no shaky rapport with the next-door Gauthiers, who regularly threaten their rascally young with "the Jews'll getcha!"—no egg-shell relationship with Aline and Madeleine Brisebois, whose doors are anyway barred to "Christ killers"—not even the rough and ready street alliance (home visits *verboten*) with the young Desjardins which had last winter cost her a good slice of scalp; not to mention endless lectures from the family (stay away from them!) for getting klonked with a chunk of ice by their New Brunswick import maid, whom her "friends" egged on to zap Jewish kids too foolish to flee—nothing in her entire albeit brief life has ever remotely prepared Haya for this present, altogether too close encounter.

Why, oh, why did that Protestant hospital for contagious diseases, the Alexandria, have to be full up? But it was. And the Catholic St. Vincent de Paul was not. Even Dr. Leavitt looked leery about sending her there.

For not only was St. Vincent's a Catholic hospital, its very location, way down east in the heart of Montreal's French section, was so far away and so inconvenient as to seem almost an affront; at least, to Jewish families. Worse still, French-Canadian doctors staffed it and, worst of all, Catholic nuns ran it. Yes, precisely those black-robed daughters of the church whom one encountered mainly in eerie, sombre groups and from whom the offspring of Jewish immigrants had early decided to run like hell. Not only run like hell, but backwards, cursing and spitting as they ran.

Faced with such odds is it any wonder that Haya, aged eight and burning with fever, should feel unequal to the task?

Still, when caught, she manages to acquit herself with some degree of honor. Throat feeling sliced into little pieces, she nevertheless thrashes about and screeches her head off, just as the other two had done before her.

First thoroughly boiled and raked over with a spiked brush in a fiery lake of a tub, she is then mercilessly scrubbed with what looks and feels like a large building brick instead of the pumice it is. After that, a floursack towel having rubbed her sore, an equally delicate hospital shift is dropped over her head, a horse blanket onto her shoulders, and her splotchy, throbbing body is dumped onto a cot and shoved out for pickup.

Before she can raise her leaden head, a multiple-chinned novice pads over, acres of flesh straining at her shiny, new, grey habit. Panting and snuffling, large feet splayed out in a pair of outlandishly garish slipper socks, she now proceeds to tear through miles of corridor, the cot slipping and sliding in her casual grasp. None of which boded any good to anybody at all, in the opinion of one slack-mouthed, swollen-eyed, undersized, dazed, somewhat terror-stricken, little girl.

At length, arrived at a cavernous room, Haya is trundled therein and bounced out, face down, like newly baked bread onto what feels like a steel slab with a sheet glued on. A rock of a pillow stands guard at its head.

Now left to reflect on her sins, Haya flops over to do that. What, she asks herself, hands gripping the cold bedrails, rolling eyeballs pressed against tightly closed lids, what, what, what have I ever in my whole miserable life done to deserve such a miserable end. No answer.

...Cheeks aflame, blue eyes popping, her freckled skin all-over irritated, too scared to lie there, too weak to sit up, our frazzled heroine now leans on a gelatin elbow to inspect her quarters.

No longer does she believe the initial reception was meant to finish her off. Too primitive. Much too primitive. From what she has gathered, from sources fictional and otherwise, more refined tortures are yet in store. So, with eyes darting from door to door, breathing in noisy, little gasps, Haya leans and awaits her doom.

The room, shaped like some gigantic ship's cabin, four ceiling to floor bay windows at one end, is crammed with bodies. All girls. All shapes and sizes. Some seem quite ill, others are livelier, some lie abed and dream, while still others sit up, talk, read, play games. The room is dimly lit. Appears to be the quiet hour. And from the distance somewhere, comes a far-off clatter—sounds of food in preparation by a kitchen staff in full swing.

Haya has ears for only one—the sound of her poor heart beating. Already, alien odors have begun to drift into the room, plaguing her kosher nostrils. Already, she feels a little sick.

All at once, at the ping of a distant bell, hundreds of figures glide in. Nuns. As in a dream, they appear, out of nowhere, lining the walls and billowing between beds, filling the room with dark shadows, their snowy, starched wimples swaying, rustling as they move into place.

A hush. Another ping. Onto their knees the nuns drop, begin to count their beads. Tenderly, they finger the rosaries that dangle from shapeless waists. All face the wooden Christ figure, whose ivory blood drips in exquisitely carved splatters onto the large, golden cross which dominates the far wall and from which Haya has for some time been having difficulty averting her hysterical gaze.

To her dismay, she realizes that with the exception of those too ill to do so, every single child in the room, apart from herself, is kneeling, on their knees, somewhere, on something—a bed, a piece of rug, a pillow on the floor, the bare floor itself—all hard at prayer.

"I can't! You can't make me! I'm Jewish!" she gets ready to squawk as soon as someone approaches. No one does. Uneasy, ignored, she leans back, awaits developments. Within seconds, to the steady drone and peaceful click of Ward C's (C for *contagieuse*) twilight prayers, Haya is fast asleep.

...A hand on her forehead awakens her. The hand is cool, light. She looks up, opens a dry mouth for the outthrust thermometer. Her pulse is being checked too. Haya examines the nun's face. It is an ordinary face, nothing special, but very young, very cross looking and very pimpled. Haya has never before seen a pimpled nun. But then, neither has she ever before really looked at a nun, certainly not straight in the eye. She detests this one at once and yearns for home.

The nun goes out, returns with a tiny glass of what looks like a rare, two-layered, brown and white potion. Drink, she says, in French, drink. Haya shakes her head. The nun shakes hers, stalks out, glass in hand.

Now Haya's heart manages the ultimate leap. Straight through her ribcage it goes. Now she is ready for home in earnest. How did uncle know she would need those cards so soon?

Carefully...she must be very careful...great tears cascading down her face, Haya casually slides down over one side of her bed, searching for her little valise. And is stopped dead by the sight of two pairs of black, Oxford shoes; one on either side. She slides back up.

You must take your medicine, a stern, older nun is scolding, in heavily French-accented English, as the young one, each pimple oozing in a separate, nasty smirk, holds out the same, tiny glass.

Oh, the devils! moans Haya...the mean, dirty, wicked devils! Trapped, she takes the glass and drains it, watching their faces every minute. Yes...it is...there is no question now...it's poison, all right ...much too sweet to be anything else. Oh, yes, it's poison for sure. Handed a huge, red pill she downs that, as well. Certainly are in one big hurry, she thinks, bitterly. Oh, please God, save me! Probably too late already. But at least, maybe mama'n auntie can come get my body before they start cutting it up.

She looks for her postcards again, finds one, begins to write. Hands trembling, she realizes with the first words that English will surely betray her. She tears up the card. Considers swallowing the pieces, reconsiders, stuffs them into her bag and starts another, this time in Yiddish.

Mein Tyersteh Fahmeelyeh, she writes, enormous, salt tears running into her mouth, My Dearest Family, they are trying to kill me. First they scalded me, burned me terribly, then they gave me poison. Just now. Come, I beg you, come right away and take me home. Maybe it's not too late—it was only a small glass. But they hate me and they'll try again ...come quick, and get me out of here! I kiss you and miss you all. Your loving Hayaleh.

By this time she is weeping uncontrollably and supper has begun to roll around. Enormous wagons race by in the corridor. Tray-laden carts racket into the ward. More poison! What to do? She will touch nothing. Eyes glazed, she sits there, ready for anything. Not a thing will she touch...nothing.

All around her, girls are digging in, exclaiming, eating, drinking, smacking lips and calling out to one another. She looks everywhere around the room, begins to feel faint. Surely, she thinks, they wouldn't...they couldn't...it is a hospital, isn't it? A place of healing? Doesn't make sense, she mutters.

Doesn't smell bad, either, she decides. From her own tray-stand the steaming dishes have been beckoning. What's wrong with her? How can she possibly be hungry? And for non-kosher food, at that!

She pulls the tray over. Just for a peek. And succumbs. She has just remembered—the sick are allowed! Important rule. To get well, especially when in the hospital, Jews, particularly children and the old, are permitted, indeed enjoined, to eat what they are served in order to get well as quickly as possible. That's the rule and she intends to abide by it. She drinks the cup of soup. Green pea with bits of something. Scrumptious.

Now she shuts her eyes and, with the one slice of white "English" bread, mops up every morsel of tasty meat chunks (don't ask, cautions her palate) mixed with vegetables and gravy on the platter. The prune, pear and raisin compote, the milk and the square of white-iced cake that melts in her mouth she devours with open-eyed pleasure, finishing her first hospital meal all too soon, licking her fingers, sighing and wishing there were lots more.

Practically the last to finish, Haya is now conscious of staring eyes. From the bed next to hers, radiating deep, brilliantly white smiles surrounded by deep, golden dimples, a curly-haired blonde calls out, "Was that ever good, or was it?" A shy nod from Haya.

In rapid speech, words tumbling out almost too fast for the pretty lips to form, her first hospital friend, name of Doreen, fills the newcomer in. Sister Felicia is their cook. Isn't she the greatest? She is Doreen's favorite Sister, is French-Irish, same as Doreen and, what's more, gives her favorite patient, Doreen again, all kinds of extra goodies all the time, which she, Doreen, then divides with her very special friends in the ward. So says Doreen.

See that girl, that one over there, dark straight hair with bangs? She's my partner, Dodo, Doreen now informs the new inmate. We're both twelve...in charge of the smalls. We help with breakfast, play games if they got no fever...like that. Hey, you're a small, ain't you? How old? she asks. Eight, replies Haya. Eight! Thought sure you're a six, says Doreen, disgusted. Too old for the group, she grumbles, radiance gone. End of friendship.

Haya doesn't understand. Not yet sure what exactly is expected of her, she keeps quiet. Thus launched, Haya slips warily into the intricate shallows of life as lived in Ward C Pour Filles, L' hospital St. Vincent de Paul, Montreal. Six absorbing weeks of it. At the end of which time she is to wish with all her heart that life in Ward C might never ever end.

Doreen heard from again. She has been mulling it over. "Say, how come you didn't pray before? You did not! I watched you! Didn't even kneel, don't tell lies, smartie...I saw...you didn't do one thing! What are ya anyway, some kind of dirty Jew or something?"

Here, out in the open at last is something Haya knows a thing or two about. She crawls deep into her blanket and covers her head.

...A small, round nun has set her small, round bottom on the bed. As she tugs at the blanket, she says, in English, leaning over to kiss Haya's cheek, I'm Sister Mary Angela, Marie-Ange...welcome to Ward C. An outburst of loud hiccuping tears is the response.

Cry, says the nun, stretching out on the bed and cuddling the heaving body. Go ahead and cry, get it off your chest. She strokes the spasm-ridden head, hugs the scrawny shoulders. I know, lovey, she soothes, you're sick and you're lonesome...Cry...you'll feel better, you really will...don't worry, love, everybody cries here...it's the rule! She nods, beams and smiles, all at the same time.

Haya has turned over to look at her. What a sweet face! Shivering, Haya stares at the little Sister, falls madly, irrevocably in love. She rubs cheek and chin against the soft-skinned hand, extends her own and, although shocked at her impulse, kisses back, lets herself be petted some more and turns onto her side, eyes shut, to be covered and tucked in, just like home.

A dream for a moment, she lies there, thinking of home and is up on her elbow with a start. Where is that card? Oh, God, where is it? Mustn't let them find it...can't read it but they might suspect...Oh, my God, it absolutely must not be mailed...they'd be worried sick at home!

To her great relief, she finds the crumpled card under her pillow. Getting under the blanket again, she shreds it, then stashes it away in her bag and takes out a fresh one. Postcard in one hot hand, pencil in the other, Haya struggles to sit up, leans against her pillow and promptly falls into a deep sleep. It's been a long day.

March 1986

A Stroll Down Spadina Avenue

SPADINA AVENUE by Rosemary Donegan, with an Introduction by Rick Salutin. Toronto & Vancouver: Douglas & McIntyre, 1985.

REVIEWED BY ROSE KASHTAN

Ms. Donegan has given us more than another color-plate coffee table picture book, filled with the landscape and changing seasons—but a picture book of people, people who created the street, who lived, worked and struggled; people who influenced their times.

Rick Salutin's introduction is rewarding for its summary of the development of the street from pre-survey days. Toronto is, after all, only 150 years old. His essay, Salutin's own interpretation of the history lived out on Spadina, is entertaining and informative. "Everyone takes his own walk along Spadina," says Salutin. In preparing to take my own, I decided to walk along with him.

I enjoyed Salutin's warmly personal but unsentimental reminiscing about his family's roots in the *shmata* business, and his description of working conditions in the needle trades from its beginnings. The strike of the garment workers against Eaton's in 1911, protracted and bitter, gives us background for the recently concluded strike of salespeople at Eaton's (also largely unsuccessful). So Salutin starts his walk at Adelaide St., describing almost brick by brick the buildings on both sides of Spadina, taking the reader inside Jewish-owned factories right to the Jewish workers at the machines.

I could wish that Salutin had tarried a while longer at Queen and Spadina, where the Workers Unity League and the Dressmakers Industrial Union had their headquarters. He could have told us what it was like to organize the unorganized in the twenties as compared to his own experiences as organizer for McGregor Hosiery in the seventies.

I could wish also that Salutin would have included the melding of the never-ending anti-war campaigns, the agitation against the threat of fascism with the economic battles of the thirties. The Spanish Civil War is not mentioned.

But this is not the definitive work on "Jewish Spadina" or Toronto from the twenties to the sixties; perhaps one of the leading personalities of the period will take us through those difficult times with them. A study of contemporary history should not be an indulgence in nostalgia only, but a search for the truth behind the facts, for some light on the future. It is accepted that those who have no past have no future.

What was the atmosphere surrounding life on Spadina? "In 1924 the Toronto *Telegram* wrote: 'an influx of Jews puts a worm next to the kernel of every fair city where they get hold. These people have no national tradition... They engage in the wars of no country, but flit from one to another under passports changed with chameleon swiftness, following upwind the smell of lucre.' " This was Tory, Orange Toronto. This is the background for Salutin's twinning of "industrial Spadina with Jewish Spadina"... the mix was volatile and creative. Indeed!

The photographs in the photosection are fascinating and varied. Readers of *CJO* may find themselves or their parents or even grandparents there.

Jews arriving at the turn of the century brought with them their cultural baggage, much richer than their worldly goods. They would find a shelter and a job, all on and around Spadina; then they started to create places where they could really live. Their hopes and dreams for a better life created the energy to build. The Arbeiter Ring (Workmen's Circle) was among the first (1907 in Toronto). Bundists, socialists and anarchists created this fraternal sick-benefit and burial society.

The 1917 Revolution in Russia burst upon the world. For the members of the Workmen's Circle it was a catalyst and divider. Supporters were expelled at the 1922 Toronto convention, and from then on Spadina was about "What Side Are You On?" The question was asked about everything from the development of craft trade unions, from often spontaneous strikes against demoralizing piecework, to the formation of industrial unions. The clash between right and left was felt in every phase of Jewish Spadina and the distancing process accelerated. The Labour League was created by those expelled from the Workmen's Circle.

The Labour Lyceum, 346 Spadina, built with the $5 shares sold to workers, became a right-wing stronghold. It was both complemented and challenged by left-wingers centred in Alhambra Hall, 450 Spadina.

The creative energies centred in Alhambra Hall and the actions flowing from it were truly incredible. It housed the Jewish Working Women's Association, The Workers' Sports Association (Toronto Jewish section), The Youth Division, The Young Pioneers, The Mandolin Orchestra, The Freiheit Gesangs Farein (forerunner of the Toronto Jewish Folk Choir), The Jewish Drama League. The Progressive Arts Club met there (producer of *Eight Men Speak*, with a cast of 25 at the Standard Theatre). The

Communist Party held public meetings, debates, lectures and concerts there. Avrom Yanovsky, artist and labor cartoonist, presented chalk-talks, a new art form in Toronto. The first copies of *Der Kamf*, edited by the late Philip Halperin, were welcomed at a gala concert meeting and sold at auction (sort of) to raise funds. This was the forerunner of *Vochenblatt*, edited by the nationally known labor leader Joshua Gershman. It was a most vital and vibrant community centre.

As the 1929 "crisis" developed into depression, people responded to radical leadership and organized to demand work, relief, unemployment insurance. That's the year the notorious Brigadier-General Draper became head of the Toronto police commission, and appointed a special "Red Squad" headed by Det.-Sgt. Wm. Nursey. An edict was issued banning all public meetings not held in English. The battle to lift the ban united many nationalities—Jewish workers, Ukrainians, Finns, Russians, British, Scots and others. Deportation was a weapon—between 1930 and 1931, 11,000 persons were deported, some after serving prison sentences—"back where you came from."

In 1931 eight Communist leaders were charged under Section 98 with "advocating the violent overthrow of the Government." Salutin notes: "The case became a touchstone for civil liberties activities across Canada." They were sentenced to five years in Kingston Penitentiary. They were released in 1934—by late 1936 Section 98 was finally repealed.

The struggle to "Make Toronto a Union Town" continued along with protests against the rise of fascism. In July of 1933, Hitler had come to power. A united front of over 50 Jewish organizations together with many other organized groups brought out 15,000 in a surge up Spadina and on to Queens Park.

May Day, 1938, a stronger united front including Communists, the CCF and the Trades and Labour Congress rallied 25,000 to Queen's Park.

September '39 saw Canada at war. "The Jewish population enthusiastically supported the war against Nazism... No-strike pledges were given to governments," writes Salutin. By 1941 it was total war.

In 1943 two Communists were elected to the Ontario Legislature—J.B. Salsberg from St. Andrews, which includes Spadina, and A.A. McLeod from nearby Bellwoods. Salsberg held the seat for twelve years until he was defeated by a Tory, Allan Grossman, in 1955. "The entire community divided in a vituperative campaign...Grossman won and went on to become a cabinet minister." Salutin summed it up.

The Jews were moving up, were leaving Spadina. There were new waves of immigrants. "Jewish-owned factories and businesses were still operated...but there were fewer and fewer Jewish workers in the factories." Some unions were still Jewish-led but members were often Italian, Greek or Portuguese. "The industrial Jewish era was ending on Spadina." Salutin's walk continued; of course he stops in at Grossman's and pays his respects to poet Milton Acorn. He notes the coming of the "hippies" of the sixties and then the arrival of American "draft-dodgers" protesting the Vietnam War, and witnesses the most recent wave of wealthy immigrants from Hong Kong as well as the "boat-people" from South Vietnam.

For the people whose lives centred on Spadina this book is living history and even a tribute. For younger people, it will help them understand that "the good old days" they hear about were really rough, that the freedom of speech and expression we enjoy today and the right to unemployment insurance and old-age pensions were dearly bought. People were beaten, people were imprisoned. We know from our daily lives that these rights have to be guarded and defended. The pictures, of course, progress historically to the present Spadina, now almost completely Chinese—the latest immigrants.

Ms. Donegan concludes with a reprint of the *Globe and Mail* highlight history of the Spadina Expressway project beginning in December 1953 and concluding in June 1971. "Cabinet rejects continuation of expressway..." (It stopped at Eglinton Avenue West.) That peoples' victory certainly had its roots in the battles of the first half of our century. But it may not be the last word. The cry for "redevelopment" is heard again—people will still have to be vigilant to ensure that any redevelopment benefits the many and not the few.

Acknowledgements list no less than 140 individuals. There is a useful index. This most unusual book would be an appreciated gift for young and old. It should be available in public libraries. May I congratulate Ms. Donegan for the concept and the realization. Thanks for the memories.

March 1981

Transplants
A Short Story

RITA L. ROSENFELD

Just after the turn of the century, Shmuel received a notice of conscription to fight in the Russo-Japanese war. He and his family lived in Lagov, Poland. Deciding to evade the draft, he fled to Canada, leaving behind his wife, Rayzl, two daughters and an infant son.

After a number of years had gone by he returned to Poland and said, "Pack, Rayzele. You are coming to Canada." Rayzl, not wanting to leave her family and friends, objected, "but where will we find a husband for Dvorele in such a strange land?" "What do you think, Rayzele," her husband scoffed, "that it is a land of savages? There are there, too, Jews."

The son, Chaim, was now ten years old and the younger daughter, a marriageable sixteen. An older daughter, who was herself a mother of several infants, stayed with her husband in Lagov.

Both youngsters were excited about removing to Canada; they had heard villagers referring to the country as the *"Goldene Medina"* —the land of gold. "And will we be able to pick up gold from the streets?" Chaim marvelled. His sister, though, thought of other matters, of young men more worldly than the ascetic Talmudists and timid tradesmen that inhabited Lagov.

The journey across the Atlantic was a joyless affair. They were forced to spend most of their time, ill, in the cramped and poorly ventilated steerage of the ship, along with other emigrants.

By European standards the family was a small one and they soon found living space in Toronto with another family, in rented quarters. Shmuel, they discovered, had become a chicken peddlar. He owned a horse and cart, and travelling on the perimeter of their new town, he visited a regular circuit of farming communities.

Before long other Lagovers emigrated to Canada, some to Toronto, where they formed a Lagover society, a group of people bonded together by a common past and an eager desire to succeed in the new country. From Poland they brought their concept of community life. Life revolved around the *shul* and the home.

After a few years had elapsed Shmuel and Rayzel bought a house on

Markham Street, just above Dundas Avenue, close to their *shul*. The house was red brick, two-storied, attached to a twin, with a wide wooden porch. On the front lawn stood a huge old Catalpa tree—its long finger-shaped pods littered the lawn in the fall. Behind the house stood a roomy barn with a woodshed attached. "There we can keep the horse," Shmuel said to Rayzel, "and in the back you can make for me a vegetable garden," she replied, happily.

Chaim began accompanying Shmuel on peddling trips. He learned from his father how to befriend the farmers, how to assess the weight of poultry, how to inspect a flock for illness. By handling a suspicious looking bird, Chaim learned to determine the manner of its illness, and to cull it from the herd. He was shown how to crate the poultry for transport to the co-operative which disposed of the poultry. His father was a shareholder in the co-op, like others of his fellows. "When you learn, when you have your own wagon and route, I will buy you shares," Shmuel promised his son.

Soon a robust young man came calling on Dvore. Her parents had seen his face before at the *shul*, and friends attested as to his family background. A wedding was discussed.

"But I won't shave my hair off!" Dvore warned her parents. They turned shocked glances on Moishe, her fiance. But he spread his hands good naturedly and said, "Here, in this country, it is not seen as an act of impiety."

Rayzele turned to her daughter. "You will shame your husband!"

"Mother," Dvore replied, "who will see me?—the cows?" for it was Moishe's aspiration to become a farmer, an occupation outlawed to Jews in Poland. And with the help of her parents, the young couple bought a farm near Kleinburg, Ontario, and there they began to raise their own family.

In time, apple-cheeked Dvore's hair turned gracefully grey, while her mother, with her deeply lined face, still wore the same brunette *peruke*.

"This Canada, this country, teaches Chaim bad ways," Rayzele wrung her hands. "Woe!" For his part, Shmuel took more direct action, beating his son for his absences from home. "Cur! I'm told you like to gamble! How is this, a son should stray so far from custom?" But the boy was growing up, he became fond of expensive clothes, developed a taste for hard liquor and began to avoid synagogue attendance. His absences were a cause for anxious gossip. Shmuel mumbled excuses.

Then a young woman arrived from Poland, with her sister and brother-in-law. The couple started a small kosher butcher business, living above their shop, and the young woman, Sara, roomed in Rayzele's house. The house was convenient to the sister's place and not far from where the young woman worked, at a garment factory on Spadina Avenue.

It wasn't long before Chaim began spending more time at home. The old couple hoped that marriage would reform their wayward son.

"I want a place of my own," Sara said, soon after their marriage. "Your mother watches me all the time. I have no privacy. And anyway, we will need more room soon." Delighted with the news, Chaim rented a set of rooms at Kensington Market, just across the street from where he generally played pinochle, in the back room behind a delicatessen.

Now Shmuel and Rayzele lived alone, without any of their children. They rented out the whole upstairs and kept their front room for entertaining. Dark furniture glistened from constant polishing and antimacassars lay on the arms of the sofa. When their daughter's children came to visit, they would enjoin them to "study and learn!" "With education comes everything," they told the children, convinced of the unlimited opportunities in this land.

Shmuel was now the "Zayde" and Rayzele was the "Bubbe" and so they were addressed by their grandchildren. The Zayde continued to go to *shul* every day, twice a day. And the Bubbe would prepare his tea in a glass with sugar cubes and sliced lemon, served with sugar cookies to refresh him. As his beard grew wispier and whiter, he continued to use a horse and wagon despite the growing use of motor vehicles. As the neighborhood slowly changed, and a new flood of immigrants took the place of the old, she kept more and more to her house.

By correspondence the old couple learned that their older daughter lived now in Warsaw and her husband had a small mercantile business there. Their children were grown and had graduated from a gymnasium and the boys prepared to enter their father's business. They had felt no interest in emigrating to Canada at the urgings of the old people.

Then it was too late, and the war years permitted little concrete news outside Europe.

Although Chaim worked hard, had bought a truck and developed his own chicken peddling route, Sara found it hard to make ends meet. She often borrowed money from her sister, and her brother-in-law, the butcher, gave her meat from his store. Chaim refused to eat poultry. "I hate it," he growled. "I ate so much of it at my parents' house I thought I'd grow feathers and cackle!" But the loans also became gifts; Sara could never manage to pay them back.

Sara never did learn that her husband visited his parents from time to time whining that bills were due, that his wife overextended the family's finances. The old couple kept giving their son temporary loans which were also never repaid.

Soon after the birth of her son, Sara took a job, leaving the boy in the care of an old woman who lived downstairs in the same building. The old woman would chew up food with her hard gums, then place it in the little boy's mouth. "Eat, my little darling," she would croon to the infant. "Eat, my little orphan."

After a few years, the child, Itchele, learned the short route to his grandparents' home, and from the time he was four he came daily to stay with them, keeping them company. His mother was usually at work and when she was home, had no time for him. He had quickly sensed that Chaim had no use for him. "Out of my way!" was what he heard most commonly from his father.

Entering the house on Markham Street, the little boy would come across his grandmother rolling dough for egg-noodles, in the kitchen. "Hi Bubbe," he'd kiss her, and ask for his Zayde. She would indicate with her flour-covered hands the door leading to the cellar. On his way downstairs, a disembodied voice floating upward would call, "Itchoo are you there?"

Itche watched his Zayde shovel coal into the flaming mouth of the furnace. He'd watch the old man turn a spigot on one of the barrels lining a cellar wall. "Don't you do it, Itchoo, just watch Zayde." He'd watch his Zayde drain off a small amount of the bright liquid and "test."

Zayde loved to dig in the backyard, to feel the lumpy dirt in his hands, and Itche dug with him. Zayde enjoyed fresh radishes just pulled out of the dirt, and Itche, wrinkling his nose, tried to eat them too, but Zayde said fresh rhubarb sprinkled with sugar was better for little boys.

Rummaging around in the boxes of metal scraps in the shed, Itche would hear the Zayde's horse banging about in its stall. "Itche, be careful, sonele. Don't go behind the horse, no? He might kick you."

Sometimes the old man would encourage Itche to take snuff from a small horn snuff box, its top pulled by a metal ring. "Take! Go ahead, like this—take a little bit—here on your hand." He would show Itche how, saying "it's good to sneeze. It will help you to think better."

The boy went to *shul* with his grandfather and there the Zayde's *landsmen*, other old men with long wispy beards and gnarled hands, wearing capel and tallis, would playfully tease the child's cheek. "A sweet child!" They would ruffle their dry hands through his hair and offer him candy.

When the war came to an end, rumor became fact. The rubble of war yielded a relative handful of Jews; former inmates of death camps were removed to displaced-person camps. There were long waits while enquiries poured in from all over the world; people searching for their relatives and friends.

The Bubbe and Zayde were told by the Jewish agency that there remained one member of the older daughter's family, the youngest son.

At last, a tearful reunion. Of course, no one recognized anyone else. But Bubbe knew her daughter's son. "You look just like your mother," she said, leaning on the painfully gaunt young man, water welling from her sunken eyes.

The refugee came to live with the old couple, his grandparents, and Itche had to adjust to the idea that he had to share their attentions. Bubbe was more demonstrative with the newcomer than anyone had ever seen her before. She stroked his poor thin face and asked him questions about his mother. He pleaded for patience; he wanted to forget his terrible ordeal first. She understood.

The young "greenie" found a job in the shipping department of a clothing manufacturer. He paid room and board and bought little gifts for the family's children and the Bubbe. They lived this way for years, the young man slowly improving his position, learning English, establishing himself as a garment cutter with the clothing firm.

Once, Itche, soon to be bar-mitzvahed, was scrounging about in the scrap boxes in the cellar. He was alone, had earlier heard his father come into the Bubbe's house. For that reason, he lingered in the cellar, unwilling to go up until his father left. For the first time, Itche overheard his father saying "I need money."

"What for?" his grandfather replied. "We gave you money only last week. From where will we get so much money? We are old people!"

Perhaps when Chaim had approached his father in the past for money the event had been less celebrated by voices raised in loud complaint. This time the refugee had overheard too.

That evening the greenie told the old couple he was not really their daughter's son. He tried to explain to the incredulous old people that all their family had perished; tried to talk beyond the anguish in their eyes.

"I met your grandson in Auschwitz. He died from starvation. We were part of a work crew." He told them in a barely audible voice that he had taken their grandson's identity and so had made contact with them through the Jewish agency.

"I needed a sponsor, don't you see?" he begged. "I couldn't stay there any longer! I felt I was going crazy, don't you understand? I wanted a chance to live!" He told them he loved them, he would do anything for them.

Silent at first, her grey face stricken, the Bubbe succumbed to a new grief. The Zayde had compassion, would have forgiven, but the Bubbe would not be moved. She hated the young man now with the burning passion she had reserved for her family's murderers. Her shrieking curses followed him out the door of her house.

No one was allowed to speak his name again.

Life carried on. Their backs became more stooped, their chests hollow. Their voices faltered; they were less likely now to smile, to laugh.

At Itche's wedding the old couple walked haltingly down the aisle, leaning on each other, to sit before the wedding canopy. The Zayde cut the huge *challah* with his trembling hands and the tiny pieces were handed out to all the guests, according to tradition.

When they could no longer look after their house, Itche drove them out to live on their daughter's farm. But because they were so frail, before long a family council decided they would be better off in a home for the aged. They were moved back to the city where they shared a room in a huge new building that housed aged residents.

One of the daily newspapers in Toronto did a cover story on the old-age home. A big photograph of the Bubbe and the Zayde headed the story. Her head lay inclined toward his chest. His arm hung protectively over her shoulder. Her wig was still dark, a kerchief was tied jauntily under her chin.

In the picture, they were smiling.

II
Secular Humanism

December 1963

Is the Public School the Arena for Religious Education?

JOSEPH ZUKEN

We invited Alderman Zuken of Winnipeg to comment on the controversy around religious instruction in our public schools, since prior to his election as alderman, he served for twenty years as a member of the Winnipeg School Board.

The controversy over the teaching of religion in public schools has flared up again in Canada. Two recent occurrences illustrate the never-ending pressure against the public school system to introduce or intensify religious education.

In Toronto, Rev. Gordon Hunter of the United Church recently denounced Jews as seeking to make Canada a godless country by being in the forefront of the resistance to religious instruction in the schools. To this accusation Mr. Hunter added the ominous warning that such activity of Jews invites anti-Semitism.

Mr. Hunter's blast is reminiscent of the angry charge made by a Catholic clergyman in Winnipeg this year—after the Winnipeg School Board rejected a petition of some 25 parents that religious instruction be instituted in the Daniel McIntyre High School—that the action of the school board was due to the pressure of Jews, communists and the Unitarian Church.

Mr. Hunter's position is, therefore, not peculiar to Toronto, or the Province of Ontario. Actions are stronger than words or threats and in Manitoba, the historic battleground of the religion-school controversy, some definite action has been taken to inject religious education into the public schools. The experience in Winnipeg is of interest and significance throughout the land.

The Public School Act in Manitoba contains a provision which gives parents the right to petition a school board that religious instruction be introduced in a particular school and that the school board must act upon a petition of 25 parents. Such a petition was presented in 1963 to the Winnipeg School Board signed by 25 Catholic parents whose sons and daughters attend the Daniel McIntyre High School.

It is significant that the Canadian Jewish Congress made no representations to the school board on this issue—and the silence of congress in Winnipeg was and is deplorable.

When the question came up for decision by the school board, the board's solicitor recommended that the petition be dismissed on the legal ground that the Public School Act was not clear on this point. Did religious instruction mean instruction in one religion or in all religions? Because of the unclarity in the act, and the fact that the petition did not specify the kind of religious education requested, the solicitor gave his legal opinion that the petition was not acceptable.

The debate at the school board dealt with the substance of the problem as well as the legal technicalities, and the result was that the petition was rejected by a decisive margin.

It may be of some comfort to Mr. Hunter, but not to the people of Winnipeg, that the only Jewish member of the school board, Dr. Wolch of the NDP, took the position that while he personally disagreed with religious education in the public schools, nevertheless, the Catholic parents had the right to petition under the Public School Act, and the school board was duty-bound to accede to the petition. He, therefore, voted to permit religious education in that high school.

The parents who petitioned refused to accept the decision of the school board and commenced a court action to compel the board to institute religious education. The outcome of this court action—and the question may possibly be carried to the Supreme Court of Canada—will be of tremendous importance to the future of the public school system not only in Manitoba.

The problem is deeper and more serious than the easy task of giving the lie to the words of Mr. Hunter. The Toronto *Globe and Mail* was correct in its editorial comment that "Mr. Hunter is not helping matters by dealing with the matter as one in which Jew is opposed to Gentile. Nor are those who answer him in his own terms. This is a question of principle to be answered by every citizen as a citizen."

The issue is not a campaign against religion. The fundamental principle is the historic separation of state and church or synagogue. The real issue is to protect the non-sectarian character of our public school system. Our public school system requires urgent reforms—but the injection or intensification of religious controversy in the public schools will split, divide and cause irreparable harm to public education.

The effective answer to Mr. Hunter and those who continue their religious pressure against public education is for a great democratic counteroffensive to be mounted by the teaching profession, parents' associations, the labor movement and Canadians of all national origins for the defence of the founding principle of separation of state and church. As part of that process the public school legislation of the various provinces should be reviewed and amended to guarantee the secular character of the public school structure in Canada.

November-December 1978

Yiddish Culture and Anti-Semitism

MOISSAYE J. OLGIN

The following abridged article first appeared in the December 1938 issue of *Yiddishe Kultur* published by the YKUF (Yiddish Cultural Association). In this article, as in others of that period, M.J. Olgin further elaborated his views on the Yiddish language, Yiddish culture, Jewish unity against fascism and anti-Semitism, Jewish identity and assimilationism. It is evident that the ominous situation faced by the Jews in Europe in the fascist-dominated countries and in the others threatened by fascism on the eve of the Second World War greatly preoccupied Olgin's thought in that period.

We believe the culture of every people possesses the wonderful power of uniting, elevating and stimulating the people if this culture's best and most progressive features are utilized. Whenever reaction extends its power it seizes not only upon the body, the material side of the life of the people, but also upon its spirit which is expressed in the best creations of its culture.

It is the misfortune and shame of Germany that fascism in its drive to enslave and brutalize the masses of the people took to burning the best books, and with reckless effrontery chopped down the magnificent edifice of German culture. However, where the people oppose the degenerating power of reaction they ask to quench their thirst at the living source of the people's culture. To a greater extent this is true of the Jewish collective because it has suffered more than all the others in modern times.

Consciousness is itself a great weapon. The enemy, in order to dominate, seeks to dull, to vulgarize and degrade the people's spirit. Culture in its better expression is the greatest antidote to this poison of oppression. A people which has to stand up against its enemies, a people which needs to understand who its friend and foe is, a people which needs to see a clear path for itself, must drink deeply from the source of its culture.

The great majority of the Jewish people speaks in Yiddish and lives its life in Yiddish. This majority has to drink from the source of Yiddish culture. But also those parts of the Jewish people that do not understand Yiddish must come to this source of consciousness in the languages in which they feel more comfortable. This effort needs to be encouraged and led by the activists of Yiddish culture.

Yiddish Culture and the People

A people which enters into a struggle with a powerful enemy requires the feeling of belonging together. Without this no people's front can be formed. The feeling of belonging together is nourished by various factors: historic, traditions, awareness of common origin, etc., but the most important factor which adds to the feeling of belonging together is the people's culture.

In the overwhelming majority of its products, Yiddish culture is a progressive culture whose tendencies completely contradict retreat and passivity. Yiddish culture and Yiddish theatre have almost never known moods that welcomed death. Despair, sorrow, anguish were frequently depicted by our best writers, but the writers themselves never idolized those feelings. Except for a very few, all of them were always so closely linked to the masses of the people that there could never be any question where they were concerned of the death of the people. The pulse of the people's life beats too strongly in their veins.

In his address to the World Yiddish Cultural Congress (in Paris, September 1937) the writer of these lines warned against the so often repeated view that the Jews bring or had brought their contribution to the cultural treasure of mankind. This view, he said, "assumes as axiomatic that somewhere there is a strongbox called 'the cultural treasure of mankind' to which each people must contribute as a justification and ransom for its right to live.

"Should it not make this contribution, it is not worth remaining upon this earth. This is a basically assimilationist concept and it is as slavish as is every assimilationist theory. Its premise is that the Jew must work for non-Jews and enrich the non-Jewish culture in order to justify the existence of the Jews."

It was indicated in that address that though the Jews do not reject having cultural ties with other peoples, and though they are prepared to create cultural values that can be used by other peoples, it must, nevertheless, not be forgotten that "not a single people is obligated to create for exchange with or directly for other peoples. Every people must strive, first of all, to satisfy its own cultural needs in its own way. The rest will come of itself."

Feelings of Cultural Inferiority Among Jews

In the context in which this view was placed in that address (in Paris) it was correct. However, there is another side to this question which needs to be stressed now. When the fascist desecrators of science come forth and declare that the Jews are "an inferior race" and when there is the danger that this idea will infect the minds not only of non-Jews, but also of certain Jewish groups that do not have a clear understanding of the spiritual labor of the Jewish people, it is necessary to emphasize the kind of cultural treasures that were created by the Jewish people, how they enriched world culture and on what a high level the national (Yiddish) culture stands.

At the present time this consideration is of quite great significance. This, too, the popularization of the achievements of the Jews through the generations in all fields of culture, is a task which rests upon the cultural activists of the Jewish people.

This brings us to a consideration of our assimilated youth, without which our people's front will never have enough strength or fighting ability. The Jewish youth was educated in the spirit of assimilation. Yet these assimilated sons and daughters of the Jewish masses are now also aroused. They are searching for a path, they are seeking a firm footing. Many of them have begun to refresh their Jewish knowledge which they acquired in their homes but which they neglected until now.

Many undertook to learn Yiddish and to become knowledgeable in the original sources of the Yiddish culture. However, there are hundreds of thousands who do not study Yiddish. Their language is English and will remain English. They, too, can be won for the Jewish collective if they could receive in English some knowledge of Yiddish culture, its achievements and its spirit. For them, too, Yiddish culture can become a means that will link them to the Jewish collective.

A beginning of such an effort was already made by the Yiddish Cultural Association, when its activists addressed large groups of Jewish intellectual youth. The result was truly astounding. In place of uncertainty there is now hopefulness, in place of doubt there is now faith in the forces of the Jewish people, in the place of lurking defeatism there is now pride and readiness to struggle for the Jewish future.

The tasks before Yiddish culture at the present time are great and breath-taking. Nobody should stand at a distance.

—*Translated from the Yiddish by Sid Resnick*

March 1985

Moses Mendelsohn
The Father of the Haskalah Movement

NORMAN MASSEY

In recent times, discussion has resumed on the phenomenon of the Haskalah movement of the eighteenth and nineteenth century. Extreme Orthodox Jews have always looked upon the Haskalah as a grave aberration. But then these are precisely the people who are continually calling for "a correction of a grievous error," urging, in the same breath, a return to Cheder and Yeshiva, and the jettisoning of all secular thought. In a word—a return to observance of ancient customs and traditions.

Haskalah denotes enlightenment. The word derives from the root *sechel*, meaning understanding, knowledge, scholarship. Simple though these words may sound, the movement represented a historic epoch in the saga of the Jewish people. This was the period of Jewish Renaissance—an echo of the *Sturm und Drang* period prevailing in the Europe of that day. The great struggle for freedom in France, which ultimately gave birth to the French Revolution, found European Jewry in an advanced state of decline, benumbed as it was by the dry formalism of rabbinic Judaism. Surrounded by hatred and contempt, Jewry very deliberately divorced itself from the outside world.

Jews in Germany and Western Europe, although ghettoized culturally and spiritually, nevertheless could not escape the influence of European enlightenment and its political side effects. A process of "Europeanization" began to make inroads amongst the Jewish upper classes. Its leading figure was the great Jewish philosopher Moses Mendelsohn.

This article will not dwell on Mendelsohn's enormous contribution to the study of philosophy. Rather it will describe his role in the founding and development of the Haskalah movement in Germany, and its subsequent spread beyond into Eastern Europe.

The "Century of Enlightenment" in Western Europe was sparked by such intellectual giants as Jean Jacques Rousseau, Diderot, Voltaire, Montesquieu, Holbach and others. These were the founders of that group of intellectuals known as the "Encyclopedists." And it was Mendelsohn who transmitted this "Century of Enlightenment" to the Jewry of Western Europe. From its origins here it spread rapidly to all the rest of European Jewry.

Until the advent of the Haskalah movement, there existed tremendous pressure on the Jews from Christian reactionary elements. And amongst Jews themselves, the forces of reaction were fed by sundry Jewish clerical elements. Christian obscurantists were locked in a struggle with Jewish obscurantists. It was against these Jewish forces of darkness that Mendelsohn prepared to take issue. And encouraged by his friends, the Encyclopedists, he went on to make his great contribution to the struggle waged by the progressive elements in Europe.

Fuelling the advent of this "Century of Enlightenment," and of the Haskalah, were the burgeoning economic and social developments sweeping European society. Europe had entered a period of bourgeois revolt against feudalism. The years between 1572 and 1576 marked the bourgeois revolution in Holland, then the most democratic of European nations. Sixteen forty-nine saw a similar revolt in England. King Charles lost his head in its wake.

The climax came in 1789-93, when the great French Revolution rang the death knell of European feudalism. It proclaimed a "Spring to all Nations" with its call for *"Liberte, Egalite et Fraternite."* And, for the first time in history, Jews were offered equal rights as citizens. Moses Mendelsohn was the first Jew in Germany who called for a parallel revolt in Jewish life. Just as the Encyclopedists provided the intellectual basis for the French Revolution, so Mendelsohn and his followers prepared the groundwork for the great Jewish Revolution against the domination of the clerics and obscurantists.

The Haskalah movement lasted a hundred years till the seventies of the nineteenth century—the greatest revolt in all of Jewish history. A great number of Haskalah activists—thinkers, writers, poets and scholars—spearheaded the struggle to lead European Jewry out of its intellectual darkness. From Germany, under Mendelsohn's leadership, the movement spread eastward to Poland, Russia, Austria, etc.

While the Haskalah movement had an enormous impact on Jewish life in Europe, it had its negative aspects, such as its assimilationist ideology and its antagonistic attitude towards the Yiddish language. Conversely, not all Maskillim (Haskalah proponents) were assimilationists, nor were they all opponents of Yiddish.

Mendelsohn was born in 1729 in the German city of Dessau. His father was a great Jewish scholar and became his first teacher. Very early on, Mendelsohn Sr. recognized his son's brilliant mind, and enrolled him in the Yeshivah of the Chief Rabbi of Dessau, David Frankel. Under Frankel's tutelage the young student became deeply engrossed in the ideas of Rabbi Moshe ben Maimon (Rambam). When Frankel moved to Berlin, his student Mendelsohn followed. Mendelsohn quickly mastered the German language and was chosen to edit all correspondence between the Jewish Kehillah (community council) and the German government.

At this time Mendelsohn befriended one Moshe Zamoscz. Zamoscz came to Berlin to escape the hounding of the Jewish clerics of his native Poland. Dr. Abraham Kisch, an eminent scholar living in Berlin at that time, also exerted a powerful influence on him, instructing him in Latin, French and English. He became fluent in all three.

Later he met Dr. Ahron Gusferz, an adherent of Voltaire. Gusferz made Mendelsohn aware of the ideological fabric of the French Revolution and the philosophical doctrines of Leibnitz, Wolff and Spinoza. He introduced Moses to one of the eminent progressive thinkers of that period, Ephraim Lessing, as well as many other like-minded Christian progressives. Lessing was much attracted to Mendelsohn and they became great personal friends.

Thus, Mendelsohn acquired a reputation as a respected thinker. A competition, organized by the Berlin Academy of Sciences, posed the question, "Can metaphysical truths be as clearly demonstrated as mathematical truths?" Only two dissertations won the prize, the first being the one submitted by Mendelsohn. The second—Emmanuel Kant.

Moses Mendelsohn has earned the role in Jewish history of the great Maskil, the pioneer ideologue of the Haskalah movement. He strove to free Jewry from its hermetically sealed caste existence. In his book *Jerusalem*, he counsels: Adjust to the laws of the country you live in, but—maintain your commitments to the faith of your fathers, even though this double responsibility is not an easy one.

Mendelsohn, as opposed to the Encyclopedists, was neither atheist nor wholly a rationalist. The essence of *Jerusalem* was a call to the Jewish

Kehilla and the rabbis to observe humane practices, act with tolerance, outlaw the use of the *Cherem* (excommunication) and encourage desegregation. Unfortunately, these liberal ideas of his were abhorred by those elements who wanted Jewish life enshrouded in perpetual darkness.

He went on to translate the *Tanach* (Old Testament) into German, accompanied by his own overview. Discarding ancient scholastic piety, he brought a fresh interpretation to biblical critique based on scientific data. This was a far cry from the earlier translation done by Martin Luther several hundred years earlier. Sadly though, to this day his translation is regarded as anathema by all shades of orthodoxy.

Shortly thereafter, the Jewish clerics in Germany, Poland and Russia raised a hue and cry against this "heretic" from Dessau. Every rabbinate in Europe banned this translation. Nevertheless, it was avidly studied clandestinely by young people in many of the Yeshivas of Germany, Poland and Russia.

Mendelsohn and his friends hoped that Jews would increasingly speak German, and thus contribute to the solution of the *Yudenfrage*. In this, however, he was to be greatly disappointed. Other *Maskillim* yearned for Hebrew to become the literary language of Jewry, and were instrumental in founding a magazine of literary reviews called *Ma'asef* (compilation). Many of Mendelsohn's students and friends became its contributors or supporters.

The great Jewish historian, Simon Dubnow, formulated Mendelsohn's role thus: "He was a writer whose personal charisma exerted far greater influence than his actual writing. As a leader of men he was much more effective than as a literary figure. He could inspire people, and direct them to participate in positive communal activities. Two main objectives prevailed amongst his disciples and colleagues—"restructure the Jewish educational system and develop a dynamic literature in the Hebrew language."

The foundation for these goals was laid during his lifetime. Thus, in 1778 there was founded the first Jewish Free School, where subjects were taught in German. These included current general studies, Hebrew grammar, as well as bible study (*Tanach*). The new school was meant to correct the drawbacks of the traditional Cheder where curriculum consisted of one main subject—the Talmud. This was a revolutionary innovation in that period.

No encyclopedia published in Europe fails to identify Moses Mendelsohn as one of the great philosophers and thinkers of the eighteenth century. He was a giant of the Jewish Renaissance. He takes his place in Jewish history as the great *Maskil*, the pioneer and most prominent ideologue of the Haskalah.

It is well to remember that Mendelsohn, adventurous in his theories though he was, was nevertheless distant from the radicalism which swept through France of that day. He really reflected the frightened German bourgeoisie of the time which was fearful of the possible consequences of the revolution in France.

The most important function of Haskalah, as he saw it, was to sound the death knell of rabbinic dogmatism. And he was able to incite many Jews to think, rationalize and question the hitherto unassailable rabbinic traditions. German-Jewish youth studied his translation of the *Pentateuch* and his interpretation of its obscure passages. German, alongside Hebrew, became the important language of the Haskalah.

Moses Mendelsohn died in 1786 at the age of 57. His funeral was the occasion for a demonstration by the German intellectual elite. Scholars, writers, poets and many cultural personalities from many lands came to pay their last respects.

Mendelsohn once wrote, "Differences in one's faith must not bar one from enjoying his civil rights to the fullest. Governments must be on guard always to maintain the principles of tolerance, freedom of thought and convictions." Mendelsohn the rationalist had this to say—"I do not wish to recognize any eternal truths other than those that the human spirit can conceive." He fused distinctly Jewish traits with those of non-Jewish society. The struggle the *Maskillim* waged was a dramatic one. It was a passionate battle, and the costs were high—but in the end it shook the very foundations of Jewish life and changed the course of its history.

—*Translated from the Yiddish by Irvin Rivkin*

October-November 1985

To My Son on His Turning 13

PHILIP RESNICK

As you have learned, for the Hebrews
this marks a turning point.
We are not quite sure from where the custom derives,
and why 13, not 16 or 12,
would not have done as handsomely.
But there it is,
a number chosen from a hat,
and adhered to by reformed, conservative, and true-believers.
You, of course, are none of these,
with your mixture of almond eyes,
straight nose, thin lips, chestnut hair.
More of the Hellenic than of Judea,
your home one from which the superstition of old-world religions
has been studiously effaced,
for all the echoes that from time to time come your way.
Yet you, rebellious,
have taken from the Old Testament chain
an amulet or two.
Wear them well as you grow older,
knowing that Abraham was a smasher of idols,
and Amos, the goatherd,
one who spoke truth to power
when such things were neither chic nor fashionable,
and all the great ones who followed,
Spinoza and Freud and the Karl we partly named you after,
intrepid explorers climbing Jacob's ladder to the stars.

January-February 1986

Son of Jeremiah: Sol Funaroff

AARON KRAMER

Early in the McCarthy period Joy Davidman—formerly poetry editor of *New Masses*, formerly wife of an Abraham Lincoln Brigade veteran—found religion, High Episcopalian that is. She shat on her past, won C.S. Lewis' aged hand in marriage, and penned a page one series for the Hearst press, "I Was a Girl Communist," which proclaimed, among much else, that with one or two exceptions, the poets of the left amounted to nothing. Who would dare challenge her? Certainly none of those poets.

Shortly thereafter, more prudent than his by-now thoroughly blacklisted fellow anthologist Alfred Kreymborg, Louis Untermeyer discreetly omitted from the new edition of *Modern British and American Poetry* his lifelong comrades Genevieve Taggard, Maxwell Bodenheim, and Kreymborg. How many noticed?

Afterward the tyrannies of time and taste gradually deposited a thick layer of dust, not only over the entire lyric left-wing except for Kenneth Fearing, Langston Hughes and Muriel Rukeyser, but over many major figures who merely leaned leftward, such as Millay, Sandburg and the brothers Benet. By 1969, when the phenomenally influential Irving Howe dismissed without exception all the proletarian writers of the thirties "both in English and Yiddish" as "middle-class intellectuals engaged in poetic slumming," he seemed to be beating a dead horse. The possibility that Howe, a dedicated Trotskyite from youth, might in fact be merely getting back at the Stalinist arch enemies who had dominated American campuses during his City College days was raised, as far as I know, only by me.

Even if I were not myself a child of the thirties, familiar with and owing much to that vibrant, variegated group, I hope I would be imprudent and saucy enough to compel here in Hartford at least a modest focus on two of its most neglected voices. One can make a busy career of disinterring unjustly buried reputations—there have been so many, and the process never ends.

Sol Funaroff was born in the Near East in 1911. His parents had fled from Russia and were penniless. His father died in Palestine. His mother brought her young sons to New York's Lower East Side and worked in a sweatshop. At four Funaroff nearly died in a tenement fire. He had a short but active career, helping edit the *College Student Review*, 1932, *New*

Masses, 1933, *Partisan Review*, 1934, *Dynamo*, the same year, and *New Theatre Magazine*, 1936. He published some important poets for the first time. In 1933 he co-authored *We Gather Strength*. *The Spider and the Clock*, his first solo collection, appeared five years later. He died in 1942. *Exile from a Future Time* was issued the following year.

Genevieve Taggard, a somewhat older and still occasionally mentioned member of the group of left-wing poets, wrote of Funaroff: "He was Jewish, and aware of his people's experience." Yet it is veritably impossible to detect a trace of Jewishness in his early poems, often published under such desemitized pseudonyms as Charles Henry Newman, Steve Foster and Sil Vnarov. His first volume is proletarian and internationalist to the core. Its sole Jewish reference is in the title poem: "Oh here's a Joshua set to tame the sun!/Blow your horn Joshua!/Blow!" But this is merely part of an ironic political commentary followed by "Congress will open with a prayer," as in another poem, "The radio voice intones the Sunday Prayer" and "the religious merchants" are "death's dealers."

Two passages seem to inherit the imagery and feeling of the Yiddish sweatshop poets of the 1890s; in "Time is Money," he sings:

> Tick-tock. Scabshops of starvation...
> Oh we work, work, work,
> time, time and overtime,
> until the dawn is feverish in our faces
> like the flush of a consumptive;
> and our thin fingers ache with needles stitching
> pain.

Very close to the music and atmosphere of his Yiddish contemporaries, the Proletpen poets, is "Dusk of the Gods, Part II":

> I toiled twelve hours,
> they took the work of ten,
> I toiled ten hours,
> they took the work of eight.
> They took my bed
> and they took my books,
> the clothes from my back
> and the crust from my table
> and I walked, holes in my shoes,
> on the damp pavement.

But how Jewish are these lines? They certainly applied equally to and were equally welcomed by the non-Jewish poor of the thirties. Further, if Funaroff was influenced by the Yiddish revolutionary poets of his own and earlier times, it should be pointed out that in the main their work avoided specifically Jewish subjects; they managed to be Yiddish but not Jewish. Nor was this accidental. In a 1982 interview, the Proletpen leader Ber Green recited his group's unswerving program throughout the twenties and thirties: *"Mitn ponem tsum haint, mitn ponem tsum arbeterklas, mitn ponem tsu America!"* (With our gaze fixed on the present, on the working class and on America!)

To be truly Jewish a poet should decry wickedness in the prophetic tones of Isaiah and Jeremiah. This, Funaroff does:

> I made of the truth
> my sword of need,
> I made of my anger
> a battlefield.

It took the unfolding Holocaust to Judaize the Proletpen poets and their then huge audience. By 1942 Sol Funaroff was dead of what a slum doctor had diagnosed as a "poverty heart." But his posthumous collection, *Exile From a Future Time*, reveals that in his final years he too was moving toward public identification as a Jewish poet. One of his "Negro Songs" alludes to the Towers of Babylon, the Jordan River, the Children of Israel, and the Angel Gabriel. "Iron Calf," an unfinished poem, modernizes the golden calf legend:

> The flock in fold
> bow and pray
> to an iron god...
> Iron that governs the soul
> with iron laws.

Of his "Prose Poems," the most powerful is "Medieval Jew":

> My soul is a tall, dark-haired medieval Jew in a long, black cloak. And his face is powerfully featured and inquisitioned with strong emotions. And he chants *Kol Nidre* in a rich bass voice through a profound black beard.
>
> And his mourning is my soul crying like the dark wind and waters flooding the silent rich black mountain of midnight with their awesome weeping.
>
> And this my song, my soul, becomes full-throated, stronger, more tortured, until, as I listen, alone, trembling in a cold black

wind that whirls fear about me, I hear rushing loudly upon the night
that surrounds me,
stronger, stronger!
the song of a stormy
river surging, beating, tearing—
O woe is me!—O woe is my world!

"My Winter Coat on the Battlefield," commemorating the Spanish Civil War, is a translation by Aaron Kurtz, a leading Proletpen poet. "Song of Fatigue" has the most astoundingly Yiddish tone, syllable by syllable, I have ever come across in an English poem:

The meal's long over. The room is strangely silent.
My child sleeps. My wife is thinning thread,
Her gaze is sharpened upon the needle;
Upon her lap the frugal cloth's outspread.

We once walked in the cool streets at evening.
Now I sit at the window, stars overhead.
The dark tenement walls are before me.
My mind is numb, my body chill, my day is dead.

Hitherto anti-fascist in a strictly international sense, Funaroff finally became a great anti-Nazi Jewish poet in his biblical cantata, "The Exiles," choreographed by Anna Sokolow:

The beast is in the garden
the beast with claws of iron,
the beast with breath of fire,
the brown pestilence in the land.

The walls of the garden are fallen,
swine feed in the ruins...

The branches are slashed with swords,
the limbs are lopped with terror,
there is burning instead of beauty,
there is no green thing

Awake and sing, you that dwell in the dust.
Gather yourselves together,
gather together, o people not desired,
blow the trumpet.

Blow the trumpet,
cry, gather yourselves and go,
gather yourselves in troops
against those who besiege you.

The brown beast shall perish,
the cities of his pestilence crumble,
you shall rise in the dust of their cities
as a people of grass,
as roots out of dry ground.

Awake and sing, you that dwell in the dust,
take root in the earth,
O people of grass,
and rise again.

Set up your banners...

wave them in the fields,
gather in the hills,
roll in the valleys,
from the crevices of earth
go forward
march.

September 1986

The Getting of Religion

LANNY BECKMAN

The Sunday morning west coast downpour was partly brightened by the glow radiating from the television screen. Most of it shone from the face of Pat Robertson, host of the born again TV show the *700 Club* and head of the Christian Broadcasting Network. Robertson is gearing up to run for the U.S. presidency in 1988, which explains why I've added myself to his millions of viewers.

He doesn't stand a chance of course and neither did Ronald Reagan, Jimmy Carter or Richard Nixon. In a few years Americans may be paying their taxes through the *700 Club* phone bank. Bowing and scraping might emerge as the country's chief form of mass transit.

With heaven on earth imminent, the laws of God and man are likely to converge, and the Rev. President Robertson will be the official representative of both constituencies. We Canadians may be the first to discover that the Lord, like U.S. foreign policy onto which He will be grafted, is no respecter of national boundaries.

The prospect of living next door to or in or under a nuclear-armed theocratic state inspires meditation on ultimate questions of life and death (and reminds me to refill that Valium prescription). Paradoxically, the anticipation of having religion shoved down my throat has started me chewing on the subject myself. A vaccine of sorts.

I've given little thought to theological matters since undergoing a profound secular conversion at the age of ten. It was brought on in the way that such transformations often are, by a man who earned his living interpreting the Word of God. Still, it was quite easy to pick up where I'd left off 30 years earlier, an example of the old cliche about falling off a bicycle—once you learn how, you never forget.

The quest began at the beginning, with the primordial question of God's existence. Is there a God? Is there evidence of His existence? Fortunately, social science suggests an answer. God does exist, by a margin of about 75 per cent according to public opinion polls of recent years. However—and this explains vice-presidential hopeful Jerry Falwell's special calling—God's existence has been steadily slipping in the polls since about 1940, or, to be more precise, since 1600. In those righteous days, disbelievers and undecideds were unheard of, at least by the time their cries of agony died away.

Whence, then, came the Lord? How was He created? Philosophers of religion postulate three main possibilities: 1. God has always existed; 2. He created Himself; 3. He was created by man. The human mind is unequipped to understand the meaning of the first two theories and they are therefore quite popular. The third theory, that of God as a human invention, is comprehensible and is backed up by plentiful evidence. Accordingly, no one has ever been known to subscribe to it, at least not on television.

There is a fourth theory—a non-theory really—which views God's origins and His ways as mysterious and inherently unknowable. Here, blind faith rushes in to fill the black void of ignorance. Belief grows and shrinks in proportion to the dimensions of the void. By this logic, irrefutable proof of God's existence would instantly turn believers of this type into atheists.

What of God's nature? What is He like? The rainbow of the world's religions (which are really jigsaw puzzle pieces magnetized to repel each other) has endowed Him with all the possibilities of the human imagination. At one extreme He is seen as loving and merciful. At the other, as despotic and evil. As is rarely the case, the true answer lies somewhere in the middle: God is loving and merciful between bloodbaths. Former rabbinical student Woody Allen takes a less cynical view. He denies that God is evil, and claims that the most we can say is that He is an underachiever.

One nice thing about religious immersion is that you can do all your immersing at home. They make housecalls. The old-fashioned door-to-door salesmen from various Christian sects still appear on Sunday mornings, always in pairs and decked out like the Blues Brothers minus the hats and glasses. And the more modern Christian sects appear around the clock on television. Other religions, if they still exist, are hard to find. (Appearing on the news in blood-splattered airports or amid the rubble of bombed civilian neighborhoods qualifies as only a weak case for existence.) The miracle of evangelical marketing is turning the rainbow of religions monochromatic.

Now, instead of arguing, I practise active listening as the messengers at the door enlighten me on God's position on abortion, gay rights and the distinction between authoritarian and totalitarian dictatorships.

One peripatetic servant of the Lord said there was only *one* important question I had to face: Was I prepared to be raptured? If I'm not prepared to accept "impacted," "accessed" and "backburnered" as verbs, I'm certainly not prepared to accept "raptured"—but I kept this thought to myself because I could imagine this guy down the road as the federal Minister of Holy Revenge with a long memory.

"Raptured," I was informed, is a kind of heavenly milkshake, with God sucking His few darlings up through a straw to His eternal side before turning the soda shop and everyone left in it into nuclear dust.

Sensing it was time to part company until next Sunday, I graciously accepted the young men's pamphlets and headed upstairs to catch Pat Robertson, who seemed like a pillar of only mild insanity by comparison.

They were already Praising The Lord when I tuned in. The ritual begins with a single Praiser Praising and then, in a sort of chain reaction, everyone joins in like waterfowl responding to an ancient instinctual urge. As the quacking subsides, Pat says "Praise The Lord" in a tone genetically coded to inform the others that this round of Praising is over and an Appeal For Money is coming up.

Then, out of a clear blue sky, God Himself appeared before me in what seemed like a vision (though it could have been a television). Close encounters with the Lord happen regularly to Pat's once-lost now-rich guests (especially to ex-convicts turned best-selling authors), so why not me?

Battling the cacophony of the *700 Club*, God and I sat on the sofa and had a talk. I liked Him. He gives you straight answers to straight questions, unlike certain Eastern deities. God genuinely didn't seem to care whether I knew what happened to my fist when I opened my hand.

I asked Him what He was really like. "Basically decent," He said, "but humble too...powerless...Do you know what depersonalization is? A psychiatric condition causing you to seriously doubt the reality of your own existence..."

"And what I don't like is sycophants," God said, giving me a straight answer to a question I hadn't asked. "All that begging and adoring, it's embarrassing. It emphasizes my sense of impotence. Goddamit, it consumes me with guilt. From the beginning of time, I've only been able to answer one prayer successfully—a black boxer fighting a white opponent, split decision. Do you know what I'm saying?"

I did, and I was also thankful that I'd gotten my credentials as a semi-professional therapist.

"What about heaven?" I asked. "Is that really where Your believers go?"

He seemed to lighten up. "I'm like Groucho," God said. "He wouldn't belong to any club that would have someone like him for a member, and I wouldn't admit anyone into heaven who would believe in a God like Me. Well, their version of Me. You know what I mean."

"So there's no heaven."

"Sure there is. It's a little cramped but it's filled with a few decent souls who leave Me alone, who don't 'believe in Me.' " God's gnarled fingers described quotation marks in the air.

Atheists. "Only atheists go to heaven?"

He smiled. "That's why you don't find them in foxholes."

As Pat rolled down a wall map and pointed to Nicaragua, I sensed that God was slipping away.

"Just one more question," I said. "Will there be a nuclear war in the next 30 years?"

"Not if I can help it," said God, "but of course, I can't. Anyway," He added, pointing to Pat, who was now pointing to Cuba, "why ask me? He's the guy with the answers."

With that, God kissed me on the forehead, begged my foregiveness

and was gone.
  The rain continued to pour.
  Pat said, "Praise The Lord."

III
Anti-Semitism and the Holocaust

May 1964

With Embellishments

GEORGE LEWIS

In the course of the recent weeks a veritable storm of worldwide protest gathered momentum in connection with the publication of a booklet by a hitherto unknown author.

The booklet, *Judaism Without Embellishments*, written by one T.K. Kichko and illustrated by M.O. Savchenko, appeared last fall in the Soviet Ukraine as a publication of the Ukrainian Academy of Science.

The furor caused by this booklet is understandable when one bears in mind that, irrespective of one's opinion of the economic and political system of the USSR, for two generations now men and women of goodwill everywhere always assumed that racial discrimination and anti-Semitism were alien to the very fundamentals of Soviet philosophy.

The Kichko booklet is one of a long series of publications designed to combat religion and promote atheism. The suggestion by some irresponsible writers that *Judaism Without Embellishments* marked the singling out of the Judaist religion for attack is false. No religion is immune from atheist publications in the USSR. It suffices to mention such recent publications as *Popular Lectures in Atheism*; *Conversations About Religion*; *From God to the People*; *Christianity and Humanity*; and *Catechism Without Embellishments*, all of which subjected religion to criticism from the point of view of Marxist philosophy.

The Kichko book, alas, is not a scientific tract against Judaism. Hence it called forth a veritable deluge of condemnation, not only in publications with a constant, militant anti-Soviet bias. This booklet was denounced by progressive, pro-socialist Jewish and non-Jewish organizations; it was also condemned as anti-Semitic by a number of Communist parties in countries such as the United States, Canada, England, France, Italy, Sweden and Norway.

The booklet was the subject of a most critical review in the authoritative Kiev journal *Radyanska Kultura* (Soviet Culture); it called forth a special statement by the Soviet news agency Novosti, and it was discussed in an address to the Paris Diplomatic Press Association delivered by Alexei Adzhubei, editor of the official organ of the Soviet government, *Izvestia*. Finally, the booklet provoked an official statement by the Ideological Commission of the Central Committee of the Communist

Party of the Soviet Union.

Ugly Illustrations

Until this writer had an opportunity to examine the Kichko booklet, he was under the impression that the most objectionable part of this now notorious effort was the anti-Semitic nature of the caricatures used profusely for illustration purposes.

It is often suggested that we Jews are "too sensitive." However, as other intelligent people, we know that political caricatures are a legitimate weapon in the arsenal of moulding public opinion. We do not and cannot object if a prominent figure in public life, be he or she a Jew or Gentile, is the subject of a caricature. We cannot object if the facial characteristics of a specific person are used, even with some distortion, to convey criticism and disapproval. But the Kichko booklet illustrations are not in the category of legitimate caricatures. On page after page, Jews as a group, as a people, are portrayed as beak-nosed, ugly individuals, all endowed with short fat necks and grasping skeleton-like hands—grabbing one thing only—money.

The caricaturist, Savchenko, a Soviet citizen, presumably educated in the spirit of socialist humanism, should have known that to represent a people by stereotyped, identical facial characteristics is *racism*, irrespective of the origin of such work, be it of Stuermer or Academy of Science manufacture.

In criticising the booklet, *Radyanska Kultura* declares: "Many drawings in the book, as well as on the cover, are pretentious and are of a low artistic standard and can only insult believers."

While we agree with much of the criticism advanced by this journal, the above contention must be decisively rejected. There is nothing pretentious about the Savchenko caricatures. They consistently convey one idea, the idea that Jews are despicable and hateful. This idea is not only an insult "to believers," *it is an outrage against humanity, an outrage against believers and atheists, against Jews and Gentiles.*

The suggestion that the caricatures are bad because they are of "low artistic standards" is not acceptable as a euphemism for the essential proper description of these cartoons as racist and anti-Semitic. As a matter of fact, from a technical point of view, Savchenko presents his poison most effectively.

A Diatribe Against Jewry

As we stated earlier, the "art" in the booklet, bad as it is, can only be considered as a small part of the total crime involved. Under the guise of presenting a scientific atheistic work, published under the most respectable auspices of an Academy of Science, Kichko in fact produced a most irresponsible diatribe against the Jewish people, with very little legitimate, knowledgeable and effective critical examination of Judaism in the content of the booklet.

Judaism Without Embellishments ignores a basic tenet of scientific examination, one insisted upon by the philosophy of historical and dialectical materialism. Kichko does not examine Judaism, its origin, its development and its contribution in the historic setting of the origin and development of this religion. He completely confuses the simpleton pastime of "god-killing" with scientific investigation and conclusion. Kichko certainly does not follow the example of Soviet historians who, examining history and movements in their proper setting and perspectives, find it necessary to recognize that not only Peter the Great, but even Tsar Ivan the Terrible made constructive contributions to the development of their nation.

Occasionally, as if awakening to Soviet realities, Kichko finds some good words for some "good Jews," but this is quickly drowned in the deluge of indictment.

His refusal to admit that the Jewish people have in their history created any lasting moral values leads Kichko and his artist Savchenko to present an illustration of the Tablets with the Ten Commandments being "amended by former Premier Ben Gurion" so that the first commandment calls people to "lie," the second to "kill" and the sixth to "steal."

The Jews a Sterile People

Warming to his subject, Kichko soon foregoes the pretext that what he is writing about is a religion rather than a people. On page 19 of his opus he categorically proclaims:

> It is not surprising that these people did not produce anything outstanding in either the fields of industry, farming, thought or lasting cultural values. This exposes completely the unfounded claims [about] some exceptional history of the Jewish nation, and about its particular role in the creation of the culture of the world.

This type of "scientific finding" hardly needs any rejoinder. Kichko, however, being consistent, follows this learned analysis by devoting some twenty or more pages of his booklet to a concrete portrayal of Jews as he sees them. Setting aside any pretense of scientific examination of

Judaism he in fact devotes his full attention to piling up "evidence" amounting to nothing less than villification. As if the sinning against a belief makes the belief invalid, he bombards the readers with concrete examples of Jewish amorality and perfidy which to him is the best evidence against the philosophy of Judaism.

Here is one of the many examples of this scientific data:

> Citizens, believers and atheists in Novograd Volinsk, in the district of Jitomir, refer with resentment to Abraham Ivankovitzer, a member of the Board of the Novograd Volinsk Community [we assume the Jewish community—G.L.]. He is 65 years old *but he received no pension because he never worked and did not earn one.* A "believer" of long standing, he is in the produce business... he fattens and sells pigs, although the Judaist religion forbids Jews the consuming or the owning of pigs. "Abraham," believers ask him, "Have you no conscience?" "Yes," he answers, pointing to his pocket, "this is it."

Page after page is devoted to stories of the above type, describing in detail Jewish behavior until a crescendo of anti-Semitic expression is reached in the following definitions of the role of the synagogues and what the Jews permit it to be:

> Speculation in matzo, pigs, thievery, deception, debauchery. These are the real characteristics of many synagogue leaders. Shrewd operators convert synagogue from religion into their own personal feeding grounds. They make free with the contributions of the believers and become wealthy from them.

We Jews are aware that just as among any other people, among us there are also some thieves, speculators and debauchers. At the same time we know what Kichko chooses to ignore and that is that our people have, not less than any other people, produced a considerable quota of truly great men and women who made a lasting and recognized contribution to humanity.

The Macabbeans, the heroes who stood firm under the tortures of the Spanish Inquisition, the immortal 40,000 Jews who rose against the Nazi beast in the Warsaw Ghetto, the tens of thousands of Jews who fought as partisans shoulder to shoulder with their Ukrainian, Russian, Byelo-Russian and Polish brothers, as well as the many Jews in the resistance in France, Belgium and in the armies of the world who fought the Nazis are all Jews, whom Kichko, blinded by the poison of racism, cannot see.

Kichko should at least think of the 99 Soviet Jews upon whom a grateful government conferred the greatest accolade for heroism, the title of "Hero of the Soviet Union." It is painful though gratifying to see that *Radyanska Kultura* finds it necessary to call Kichko to recognize:

> The great sacrifices of the Jews in the Second World War and consequent plague of illness, loss of family and dislocation of living conditions which befell them.

The State of Israel Also Attacked

Kichko's booklet makes Judaism and the State of Israel synonymous. In the very introduction to the booklet, written by two men, the first of whom introduces himself as a "Doctor of Historical Sciences," Professor Vedenski, we are informed that in Israel: "Fooled by misleading promises of bourgeois agitators, people from 74 countries foregathered here. Although they are all of Jewish origin, *they have nothing in common* apart from Judaist beliefs" (my emphasis—G.L.).

This professor of historical sciences has apparently never heard of the centuries of persecution of the Jewish people culminating in the destruction of six million Jews in the fire of the Hitlerite crematoria. This professor apparently does not know what Jews have in common, apart from religion.

We should inform Professor Vedenski that only ten per cent of the people of Israel cast their votes for the religious parties and that tens of thousands of young and old, men and women, went through hell and high water to get to Israel, not only in order to assure their personal survival, but also to prove that Hitler failed in his avowed purpose to obliterate our people. Kichko and Vedenski can read in the Israeli religious press the bemoaning of the atheism of the young.

Radyanska Kultura, in taking to task Kichko's booklet, properly tells him:

> We cannot agree with the author who when criticising the Zionists as a bourgeois nationalist movement carries this criticism over to the internal life of the State of Israel. It is known that in addition to Zionists, there are in Israel, democratic, progressive organizations of working people, who take their stand for peace, and for peaceful co-existence, for democratic freedom, against colonialism and imperialism. Generally it seems to us that in a book devoted to criticism of religious ideology there is no room for evaluation (and at that, often false ones) of the activities of Israel as a state and its

role in international relations.

The "Jewish Question"

It is not surprising that in the USSR, a land where the constitution makes anti-Semitism a crime against all people, the Kichko book, even though belatedly, should result in official condemnation. The statement of the Ideological Commission of the Communist Party of the Soviet Union thus declares:

> The mistaken positions in the booklet contradict the Leninist position of the party in the religious and national questions and only serve to feed anti-Soviet insinuations by our ideological opponents, who try under all circumstances to create a so-called "Jewish Question." It is precisely because of this that the mistakes in the Kichko booklet could not but call forth disagreement on the part of the Soviet people.

As we would say in this country, the statement is fine but it does not cover the waterfront. Should not the Soviet authorities ask themselves some very pertinent and most disturbing questions? Should they not ask: How is it that 47 years after the October Revolution, and nineteen years after the termination of the war against Hitler's racists, there can in a land of socialism appear a booklet such as *Judaism Without Embellishments*? How is it that not only did a professor and his assistant deem the booklet worthy of a flattering introduction, but how is it that the leadership of the Academy before publication, and Soviet authorities once the booklet was out, found no need for decisive action until world public opinion arose in fury against it?

The constantly repeated assertion of the Soviet authorities that there simply is no "Jewish Question" in the USSR does not solve any existing problems. The establishment of the economic basis of socialism does not ipso facto change man. If this were so the Soviet authorities would not be plagued by economic crimes and other manifestations of anti-socialist behavior. Old prejudices and hatreds die hard. Hitler's occupation of the Ukraine obviously left behind some of the racist poison which continues to plague not only the Ukraine but the world at large, including our own Canada.

We must regret that the absence during the past years of an active campaign against anti-Semitism in the USSR obviously made possible the obnoxious weed which sprouted into the Kichko book.

We know that Soviet Jews, in their tens of thousands, are in the sciences, the arts, the professions, the government and the army. We also know that there are in the Soviet Union religious Jews and that as long as they wish to practise their religion as law abiding, constructive Soviet citizens, they are entitled to be supplied with matzos, talleism or prayer books on the same basis as candles, bibles and other religious articles are made available to religious people of other persuasions in the Soviet Union.

The right of atheistic propaganda is provided for in the Soviet Constitution, so is the right of the believer to continue practising his religion.

It would greatly help the struggle for peace the world over if the problems connected with the requirements of the relatively small group of religious Jews in the USSR would be satisfied without constant uproars such as the recent furor over matzos in Moscow. It would help the struggle for peaceful co-existence if the enemies of socialism would not constantly be afforded material for their purposes by the slowness and the lagging of a re-establishment of the facilities for cultural expression of the people of the USSR whose mother tongue, according to their own choice, is still Yiddish. A wider development of socialist culture in the Yiddish language as well as ample care for the religious minority would be in the spirit of Lenin's teachings. While trying to change man, man's dignity must be respected and his beliefs neither ignored nor ridiculed.

This writer believes that T.K. Kichko and M.O. Savchenko should be placed on trial by the Soviet authorities in the Ukraine. This is asked for not in the spirit of revenge. We think that such a trial could mark the beginning of a struggle against the vestiges of racist and anti-Semitic poison in the Ukraine and elsewhere. Such a trial would be a contribution to the struggle for a better world.

January 1967

The Vulture Answers Their Call

WALTER BAUER

They keep still
their brown hands
in their pockets.
When the arms stretch out to salute,
how many will follow?

Is it a fact
that for certain Germans
the Hitler salute
is an inherited trait?

You do not need
to raise your arm
to pay your respects to "German honor."
Look into those steely eyes
and you get the point:
They've gotten the whole kit back out of hock.

Weak, indeterminate faces
look forceful under a steel helmet.
They deal regularly
with the arch-enemy
who may not be the same one from day to day:
it all depends on the situation.

"German grandeur"
is the spark
in their glazed eyes.

Thoughts of "the Reich"
still live on
in their dough-like brains.

They are trying to conjure up
the German Eagle.
It is the vulture that answers their call.

They raise every war casualty
to the rank of hero.
The men of the 20th of July
are traitors.
"Whoever opposes will be shot."
Not today. But in the foreseeable future, because
"We have faith in Germany."
Faith, thy name is gullibility, and
gullibility is powerful.

The concentration camps are being erased.
They never existed.
Underneath a beech tree, dedicated to Goethe,
the Buchenwald Male Choir
sings in naive innocence,
"O beautiful forest, who created thee?"
No scream was ever heard here. No one
was ever beaten to death. No smoke.
All the old slogans were justified.
Back then, "in the good old days."

"Dough-heads, all of you,
rally to our standard.
Everyone with undefined ambitions
belongs in our ranks.
If you hate your neighbor
because he thinks differently from you,
we look forward to seeing you.

With sarcastic cynicism
we insist on democratic treatment
to ensure our rights.

"In any case
there are lots of people
making too much fuss about 'German grandeur.'
Who are they trying to fool?
Gentlemen, please
define your terms."

My Canadian friends
say to me, "How come...?"
Sick at heart,
I make them no excuses.
With a ray of hope
I point to the courageous individuals
who comprehend.

I must have recourse
to my friends.
But those others
I must reject.
Their language is not my language.
Their country is not my country.
I never knew them.
I will cut the tablecloth in two.

—Translated from the German by Humphrey Milnes

Warsaw Ghetto Uprising Mural (1959) by Arnold Belkin; photo: Searle Friedman (April 1981)

Woodcut by Frans Masereel (February 1981)

The Ghetto in Attack (etching) by Maurice Mendjizki (April 1978)

Above: Monument at the entrance of Treblinka death camp (May 1978).

Left: The Last Walk by H. Ostrzega (January-February 1973)

April-May 1973

Legacy for the Living
Guest Editorial

JOSEPH ZUKEN

It has been well and truly said that a people that forgets its past may be condemned to repeat it. This thought haunted me when in 1950, as the delegate of the United Jewish People's Order to the World Peace Congress in Warsaw, I visited the desolate site of the Warsaw Ghetto. There, in the rubble of that historic battle ground, stood the magnificent monument to the immortal heroes of the Warsaw uprising who fought for the honor of the Jewish people and the Polish nation and the freedom of the world. Nearby, as a grim reminder to the living, was what remained of the headquarters of the *Judenrat*—hated symbol of Nazi collaboration.

In the dying days of the ghetto, two contending philosophies —resistance versus abject surrender—reached a climax and resistance won. Out of that struggle there was forged the united Jewish anti-Nazi front whose heroic deeds against impossible odds won everlasting fame in Jewish and world history.

This was our and your Stalingrad and Vietnam. Had there not been resistance there would "only" have been the horror of the Holocaust. Had there not been anti-fascist unity of the entire political spectrum in the ghetto there would not have been the glory of the Warsaw Ghetto which triggered and inspired revolts in other ghettos. There would not have been the legacy for the living.

Today, on the threshold of the 30th anniversary of that historic watershed in the history of our people, that legacy remains as valid and as challenging as ever. Those in the Canadian Jewish community who blur and distort those fateful events by decrying their real meaning and wrapping them in mystique are guilty of criminal injustice to the ghetto heroes. Never to forgive, never to forget—these are more than great slogans. They are a battle cry and guidelines for action by the living. Applied to the 1970s this means vigilant action against war, neo-Nazism and racism. It means never forgetting that it was finance capital in and beyond Germany which brought Hitler to power and enabled him to unleash war, Auschwitz and other murder camps, ghettos, unbridled racism and the Holocaust. It means recognizing the vicious and dangerous role of the

CIA in bringing to power the contemporary dictators in South Vietnam, Greece and elsewhere in the name of the thesis perfected by Hitler—anti-communism.

True observance of the 30th anniversary of the historic ghetto uprising also demands an accounting by the establishment in the Jewish community in Canada and the USA as to why the behest of the ghetto fighters of all-inclusive unity remains scorned and unfulfilled. Far from being obsolete, that vital lesson of unity is relevant today and in the future.

In 1959 when I revisited Warsaw, reconstruction was amazing in contrast to the war destruction so evident in 1950. One shared a feeling of socialist pride in the magnificent cultural achievements of the Jewish survivors in Warsaw and Lodz, many of whom had been partisans in the anti-Hitler struggles and had contributed with great dedication to the building of a socialist Poland. How tragic it is that so many thousands of them have in the past few years felt compelled to leave their homeland because of anti-Semitism. Perhaps the tragedy which has struck the socialist Jewish life in Poland is best exemplified in Lieb Domb (Trepper), the heroic, almost legendary anti-fascist revolutionary who was the chief of the "Red Orchestra," an amazingly effective intelligence service against Hitlerism. There is a vivid description in Gilles Perrault's book, *The Red Orchestra*, of a great mass meeting attended by delegations from every land assembled at Auschwitz in 1965 to celebrate the twentieth anniversary of its liberation:

> The Polish prime minister was there. Also present was the Soviet general who had opened the gates of Auschwitz in 1945. Sitting before him was Lieb Domb, president of the Jewish community in Poland. He stood up to address the eighty thousand people gathered in front of the platform. Listen to him: he is speaking on behalf of the Red Orchestra's dead to the dead of Auschwitz and the living throughout the world. It is fitting for his voice to ring over Auschwitz, for it is precisely to prevent the unspeakable crimes committed there that the members of the Red Orchestra had fought and died; they were of every nationality, every race, every outlook, but their abhorrence of Nazism had united them during the battle and forever after it. It is fitting that a place which had witnessed the slaughter of so many defenseless women and children, of so many Jewish men unable to fight back, should re-echo with the voice of the Jew who must surely have dealt the Third Reich its deadliest blows.

Today, Lieb Domb, ailing in health, is prevented by the Polish government from leaving Poland to rejoin his family, Why? Why? To be silent in the face of this injustice is a crime.

In 1959 when I visited the Jewish Historical Institute in Warsaw, I saw there among the archives of the uprisings in the ghettos the appeal of a young Jewish ghetto fighter, Gele Sackstein, who before she died wrote: "Make sure that such atrocities will never happen again."

Let us listen to and implement the legacy of the bold heroes of the ghettos to help make certain that there shall be no more war, no more cursed racism, no more Maidaneks, no more ghettos.

April-May 1973

I Knew Janusz Korczak

GEORGE SCHEINMAN

Janusz Korczak was known and loved by thousands of children by his real name of Dr. Henry Goldsmith.

Dr. Goldsmith came from a middle-class academic family. He was a distinguished man, tall, slightly bald at the forehead, and wore a neatly trimmed beard and moustache. He wore a mandarin-style smock and always seemed to have his hands tucked into his belt.

Warsaw was confronted with the tragic situation of thousands of orphans who were the victims of wars, pogroms and starvation. Dr. Goldsmith, who dearly loved all children, could not bear to see these children left to a plight of poverty and extinction. He felt compelled to save them. So, with great personal sacrifice, he began his orphanage.

Krochmalna was a plain, ordinary street in Warsaw amid factories, a few working-class homes and a very big brewery across from which was Krochmalna 92. This was Dr. Goldsmith's dream turned reality. It was a beautiful and well-designed building with a front garden and a playground in the back.

Due to lack of funds Dr. Goldsmith could not employ too much help so the responsibilities were divided among the children. He introduced a constitution and developed a democratic self-government within the home. The children elected their representatives to parliament and senate and appointed judges. There was full participation. The children even had their own newspaper to report all activities.

Dr. Goldsmith was a very mild, tender man. When he would smile his approval at the children's progress, they would drape themselves around him laughing, and he would rejoice knowing that it was a sign of their good health. If a child lost a tooth, Goldsmith would tell him in all seriousness that this tooth was needed for his studies. The child would be very proud to contribute to science.

Dr. Goldsmith created an atmosphere in his home where each child's potential was developed to the fullest in music, poetry, drama, writing and art. Great interest was shown by many distinguished artists who gave their time voluntarily to work with the children. Dr. Goldsmith watched with pride the success of his children in all their cultural activities.

These children had something many did not have—the love and understanding of a great man who was able to bring out the best in each child. From this they learned a sense of justice and fair play, assisting each other when in need.

The children needed a summer home badly. The doctor picked the site of Waver Anin, about twenty miles from Warsaw, and there pitched tents. Hiking, swimming and other games were carried on for the summer.

One day the happy procession went for a hike with the doctor in the lead. A youngster picked up a handful of wheat. A guard noticed it and arrested the child for smuggling. (This was under German occupation.) Dr. Goldsmith demanded his release and the boy was freed immediately.

Upon their return to Krochmalna 92 at the end of the summer, the sad news circulated that Dr. Goldsmith was being called to the war. The children were shocked and the home was filled with sadness.

Miss Stepha Wilchinska took over the supervision of the home while the children hoped and waited for the doctor's return. On his homecoming Dr. Goldsmith was able to transform the senseless butchery of the war into stories for the children—one in particular of a horse who refused to go to war.

Dr. Henry Goldsmith wrote under the pen name of Janusz Korczak. In his small room in the attic he wrote many children's books including *King Mathew the First, Jushki Jaski Frankie* and *The Child from the Street*.

He also published a national weekly paper for young people called *Maly Pszeglad* or Little Chronicle. Youth from all over the world contributed to this paper.

Janusz Korczak received many awards for his outstanding literary works. His lectures on children were very popular, and people would come from far and near to listen, learn or just to see this great humanitarian.

Having known Janusz Korczak, I consider him the greatest human being that ever was. He saved so many lives and in the end he gave his own.

November-December 1976

Our Account With Nazi Collaborators Is Not Yet Settled

JOSHUA GERSHMAN

Thirty-one years after the end of the Second World War, the pursuing of Nazi collaborators and war criminals is still considered by many countries and peoples as a major task. This is in compliance with the slogan "Never to Forget! Never to Forgive!"

According to a Soviet news report of November 4, 1976, a military court in Moscow sentenced seven Russians to death by firing squad for their betrayal of 1,100 Soviet partisans who were murdered by Nazi occupiers during the Second World War.

Interviewed in Toronto recently, Gideon Hausner, the former Israeli Attorney General who in 1962 successfully prosecuted Eichmann in Jerusalem, stated that "primary evidence shows" that about 70 Nazi war criminals are living in the United States. Recently, two Latvians and a Lithuanian became the first resident aliens in the United States to face deportation in more than twenty years on the grounds of concealing war crimes to enter the country.

Joshua Gershman, editor of the *Canadian Jewish Weekly*,

and Peter Krawchuk, prominent Ukrainian-Canadian writer, contributed introductions to the new Canadian edition of *Lest We Forget.*

Mr. Gershman, in his introduction, exposes the consequences of the fact that "our account with Nazi collaborators is not yet settled."

These important factors emphasize the need, now more than ever, for a book such as *Lest We Forget,* and we reprint here in its entirety, Mr. Gershman's significant introduction.

When I read the first edition of *Lest We Forget* by the New York journalist Michael Hanusiak (in 1973) I was very moved and appreciative of the courage shown by the writer, himself a Ukrainian, to expose publicly so many facts about the brutality perpetrated by Ukrainian nationalists, collaborators of Hitler, during the Nazi occupation of the Ukraine, and during the Second World War in general. However, I was even more impressed with the third edition (September 1975) as the author of the book proves himself an uncompromising hunter of Nazi collaborators, even today, more than 30 years after the military defeat of Nazi Germany.

The third edition is strengthened by the addition of further authentic documents and photographs. Michael Hanusiak deserves credit for making further on-the-spot explorations by visiting the Western Ukraine to gather additional material from the Regional State Archives in Lviv and personally interviewing reliable individuals, Jews and non-Jews, about the brutal deeds of the OUN (Organization of Ukrainian Nationalist Police) who placed themselves, willingly, at the disposal of the murderous Nazi occupation forces.

It is of historical importance that Mr. Hanusiak corroborates that "Long before the Second World War started, the OUN leaders had begun the anti-Semitic indoctrination of the rank-and-file Ukrainian village lads, whom they dominated" (page 8, third edition).

One shudders upon reading the details of how the Ukrainian overseers went about liquidating the Lviv Ghetto and the Yanivsky Camp, as related to him by the lawyer, Falek Weiser, and in the eyewitness account of Sofia I. Odvak-Pliusnina, both survivors (pages 47-72).

Thousands of people perished at the hands of these barbarians: Jews and non-Jews, anti-Nazis, Communists, elderly men, women and children alike.

On reading *Lest We Forget,* one is impressed with the necessity of such well-documented books in English about the atrocities committed by the Nazi collaborators in Lithuania, Latvia, Estonia, not only in their respective countries, but also carrying out their brutal activities on order of the

Hitlerites on Polish soil.

To me, what is most distressing is the fact that the leaders of the Jewish establishment on this continent have chosen to go along with the position of their respective governments, aware that many of those who committed this mass murder are allowed to enjoy full freedom in our two countries, as well as in the European capitalist countries, to say nothing of the many Latin American countries where these unspeakable elements have found a haven.

However, it should be mentioned that the Canadian Jewish Congress did intervene in this problem with the government, but in the main, agreed to go along with the government decision not to extradite war criminals. On one occasion, the Canadian Jewish Congress called for the annulment of citizenship granted to those who obviously lied about their past in order to gain entry into the country.

What is despicable is that in numerous cases, so-called Jewish leaders collaborate with these same bloodstained murderers in their reactionary campaigns. It is particularly evident in their combined hatred of the Soviet Union and other socialist countries.

It is no secret that leaders of the capitalist political parties in Canada—including Jews—are often honored guests at celebrations of the Ukrainian nationalists and other chauvinist ethnic community organizations, particularly at the time of elections. They express solidarity with the misleading slogans calling for the "liberation" of the Ukraine and other Soviet Republics.

These reactionary organizations gained tremendous strength immediately after the Second World War when the United States and Canada opened their gates indiscriminately to war criminals. By doing so, our governments violated the Potsdam and Yalta Agreements, which pledged all the Allies to seek out those who participated in the annihilation of millions of innocent victims and bring them to justice.

The Canadian government, as well as all governments harboring these criminals (many of whom are named in Mr. Hanusiak's book), have been supplied with authentic documents, facts and figures, names and addresses of war criminals, by the Soviet government and the governments of Poland, Czechoslovakia, Yugoslavia and others. Not only has the Canadian government rejected the request for extradition to the countries where the atrocities were committed (using the flimsy argument that there is no extradition treaty with these respective countries), thus ignoring the International Potsdam and Yalta Agreements, but the federal government has granted full citizenship to those whose hands are stained with the blood of millions of innocent victims. Unbelievable as it may sound, one such war criminal (Kupiak) was allowed to stand as a Tory candidate in Toronto for public office.

Such an attitude on the part of Canadian governments, at all levels, helps to strengthen the reactionary forces in the ethnic communities in our country, particularly among the Ukrainian nationalists. It spawned such groups as the Edmund Burke Society in Canada (now known as the Western Guard) and the John Birch Society in the U.S., which may change their name, but not their racist ideology.

Progressive organizations in Canada, Jewish and non-Jewish, since the end of the war have continually demanded that the Canadian government heed the request of the Soviet government, so that justice be meted out to those who have committed the crimes.

One is forced to ask why the governments in all capitalist countries reject the just request of the Soviet government and why so many war criminals in the Federal Republic of Germany have never been brought to trial; and why those numbers who have been tried, got off with extremely light sentences or were released, thus making a mockery of justice. If one follows the events closely in the so-called "free world" you can only draw one conclusion: the answer lies in the Cold War policies emanating from Washington. This, incidentally, is also the opinion of Simon Wiesenthal, Director of the Documentation Center in Vienna, the untiring hunter of Nazi war criminals, as explicitly charged by him during his appearance on the Dick Cavett television program.

Much to our regret, many leaders of the Jewish establishment place their loyalties to the Cold War above the task of fulfilling their pledge to their martyred six million brethren murdered by the Nazis: "Never to Forget! Never to Forgive!"

Thus we witnessed in Canada, in 1971, during the official friendship visit of Soviet Premier Kosygin, the ugly collaboration of Cold Warriors among the Jewish, Ukrainian, Hungarian and other ethnic groups, demonstrating against the Soviet Union. It reached its horrendous peak when a Hungarian emigre threatened the life of the Soviet Premier. The leader of the fascist-minded Jewish Defense League, one Milton Eugene, boasted about the co-operation they got from other ethnic groups and the anti-Semitic Edmund Burke Society. The anti-Kosygin demonstrations were organized against the advice of the Canadian government, at a time when a poll showed that 67 per cent of Canadians, of all points of view, favored the improvement of Canadian-Soviet relations.

Traditionally, the "official" Jewish leaders in Canada slavishly follow government policy (Tory or Liberal). With the Kosygin visit, they, for the first time, rejected the written advice of the government, sent by the then minister of foreign affairs, Mitchell Sharp, to the Canadian Jewish

Congress requesting them to abstain from any anti-Soviet demonstrations.

Let me state at this point that the leaders of the Jewish establishment rationalized their actions under the pretext of their so-called "concern for the fate of Soviet Jewry." However, we have yet to see them demonstrate against neo-fascism and war. Furthermore, they have never shied away from accepting the co-operation of the Petluras and Banderas (so judiciously exposed by Hanusiak) in their endeavors.

Of late, we hear of requests to work even more closely with the Ukrainian nationalists in particular. In the *Canadian Jewish News* of Toronto (April 18, 1975), one Avraham Shifrin, formerly of the USSR, rebuked Jewish leadership for not working closely enough with the Ukrainian nationalists. He argued: "The Soviets are more opposed to Ukrainian nationalism than they are to Jews... They see the rise of Ukrainian nationalism as the greatest danger to communism. We must cooperate with other national liberation movements living in or originating from the USSR, so that we can fight communism together. It will serve all our purposes, if Russia is divided."

This Mr. Shifrin, and he is not the only one, boasted that while living in the Soviet Union he had contact with Zionist underground groups, as well as with Ukrainian nationalists. The *Canadian Jewish News* further elaborated that "Even today, he maintains contact with Ukrainian nationalist leaders in different parts of the world."

I wonder how many of his Ukrainian contacts are among those who participated in the atrocities exposed by Mr. Hanusiak in his book.

The very fact that the editors of the *Canadian Jewish News* displayed this article without any editorial comment proves that the Jewish establishment condones this attitude.

The book *Lest We Forget* is of extreme importance. It serves to remind us of the warning given by the famous Spanish-American philosopher George Santayana at the turn of the century: "Those who do not remember the past are condemned to relive it."

Millions of people will never forget, and will truly appreciate the expose which Michael Hanusiak so faithfully describes in his *Lest We Forget*.

No, our account with the Nazi collaborators is not yet settled, even 31 years after the military defeat of Hitler Germany. As a Jew, an anti-fascist, I consider this book as substantial evidence of the fact that the Jewish masses have powerful allies in the struggle against neo-fascism, racism and war among the progressive Ukrainian and other Slavic and Baltic peoples, in the labor movement of our country and among all peace-loving peoples.

It is the duty of every anti-fascist to read this book and to participate in the struggle to assure that fascism shall never again raise its ugly head.

As Canadians, we must continuously demand that the government live up to the International Agreements and the verdicts of the Nuremberg Trials, which stand as a model for the treatment of war criminals.

June 1980

The Holocaust of Which Nobody Speaks

MIKE CASS
CJO European Correspondent

The extermination by the Nazis of between 500,000 to 800,000 European Gypsies, gassed, shot and butchered to death in the same way as the Jews were exterminated, is the Holocaust of which nobody speaks. It follows the same trail of anguish, through the ghettos of Lodz and of Warsaw, to annihilation in Treblinka and Auschwitz.

The Gypsies—our brethren in suffering and in death, our brethren in prejudice, in discrimination and vilification. They are guilty of loyalty to their tradition, their clan and their families. *Therefore they are tainted by every libel: they steal, they are lazy, they rob children.* In truth, a folk gifted in handicrafts, natural born fiddlers and merry makers who have inspired many a European composer and poet such as Liszt, Bizet, Pushkin; they have been, and still are, persecuted as rabble and outlaws because of their longing for freedom and independence, for dance and music and the laughter of children.

Is conscience and justice a function of publicity? Obviously yes. How else could it be possible that 35 years after the Holocaust there is still no restitution for these victims of the Nazis? These survivors of the concentration camps are treated not as victims, but as potential criminals, against whom the Nazi state *had* to take preventive measures. Worse still: in West Germany the Gypsies are *still* hunted, they are looked upon as

stration outside the German embassy in Paris. A member of the West German parliament went to meet them and promised action on their complaints. On Good Friday, April 4, twenty German Gypsies began a hunger strike on the site of the former Dachau concentration camp. At a press conference of the "Sinti-Union" (the German Gypsy association) Klaus Thüsing, Social Democratic Member of Parliament, said: For 30 years German politicians have neglected to deal with the Gypsy problem. The legalized brutality against the Gypsies is a continuing scandal. He promised that the Social Democratic parliamentary caucus would deal with this subject and would propose legal steps to meet the demands of the Gypsy Nazi victims.

March 1983

Many Needed Saving, But 'None' Was Too Many

NONE IS TOO MANY by Irving Abella and Harold Troper. Toronto: Lester & Orpen Dennys, 1982.

REVIEWED BY JOSHUA GERSHMAN

Those of us who have been following Canadian immigration policies closely are aware of the fact that it has always been reactionary, discriminatory and in certain periods of time, openly anti-Semitic. In April of 1981 I published an article about this in which I pointed out that if Mackenzie King, who was prime minister of Canada, had eased up on the stringent immigration laws of that time, several hundred thousand Jews might have been saved from the Nazis. But in that article of 1981 I made use of the more generalized and limited knowledge then available.

Today, due to the work of the two well-known Jewish academicians, Irving Abella and Harold Troper, we now have the facts and figures

outlaws and are subject to special legislation that denies them their human rights.

In 1956, a West German court ruled that the deportation of Gypsies to the ghettos and camps of Poland had been necessary to protect the security of Germany and counter criminality.

A Nazi "security" unit on Polish territory reported to headquarters: "We do not waste our time here. We carry out three to four encounters every week. We vary them between encounters against Gypsies, against Jews or against partisans and other rabble."

Following is a sample of the so-called protecting the security of Germany and countering criminality:

> A group of 28 Gypsies is brought to Tarnograd and locked up in jail. When the gendarmes find out that the arrested Gypsies are gifted musicians, they have them play for many hours by day and night, whilst the Nazis are wining and dining. On the fourth day the Nazis show their gratitude to the musicians by offering them food and drink. Afterwards, the Gypsies are ordered to strip. Then they are led to the Catholic cemetery and shot to death. A newborn baby and two infants are not shot however—in order to save bullets their tiny heads are smashed against some trees.

Illiteracy, lack of organization and lack of spokesmen made it easy, until recently, for German bureaucracy to deny the Gypsies their rights and justice. It was impossible for anyone known to be a Gypsy to lead a normal life. Many Gypsies who did well, or managed to study and become professionals, cut all ties with their people and kept their origin well-hidden. (Some Jews saved themselves under Nazi rule in the same way.)

This situation is beginning to change. The Gypsies have formed a world organization and national centres. President of the world organization is Dr. Jan Cibula, a physician living in Switzerland. Dr. Cibula remembers the words of his father: "You will study. You will be successful. You will be better off than we are. When this comes to pass don't forget your people. They will need you."

On March 2, 1979, Dr. Cibula achieved a first step towards recognition of the Gypsies as a people. The Romani-Union (as the world organization is called) was given consultative member status in the UN economic and social council.

In the past few months a number of activities of Gypsy bodies and their spokesmen have met with some success in getting the publicity that is needed as a lever to make justice perform. On March 27, 1980, 200 French Gypsies who survived deportation to Germany staged a demon-

which irrevocably substantiate the case. In their recently published book, *None Is Too Many*, the authors have produced a work which is the most definitive volume yet published on the immigration policies of the Canadian government, particularly as they affected Jewish people. The Abella-Troper book is without doubt the most important and authenticated effort of its kind. I hasten to add that *None Is Too Many* is well written and thoroughly interesting.

Aided by the new Freedom of Information Act and despite the still-existing restrictions contained in the act, Abella and Troper were able to delve into the archives of the federal government dating back to Hitler's rise to power and the pre- and post-war years of World War II. Thus, while the book is replete with facts and figures, it is further enhanced by direct quotes from the mouths of the prime minister, his aides and advisers.

The authors not only sought out and used material from civil servants and Jewish spokesmen, but effectively managed to escape the dryness of "scholarly works" by using the highly personalized material gathered from survivors of the Holocaust, some of whom are still alive. There is little doubt that this helps to account for the impact and popularity of the book among Canadians, Jews and non-Jews alike.

Abella and Troper effectively link the anti-Semitic immigration policy to the ongoing and overall discriminatory immigration policies of the government during that entire period. Everything was then built on the so-called argument of "national self-interest of Canada." Based on that assumption Canada followed a policy of highly "selective" immigration even during the "good years" and this was applied so rigidly that it even affected prospective immigrant farmers.

Mackenzie King, who was then prime minister, was constantly preoccupied with his own re-election and always considered immigration policies as one ploy which could be artificially foisted on the populace to heighten fear, especially during the economic crisis of the thirties, that fear being the danger of being flooded by foreigners, "undesirable elements" and Jews.

Many of those responsible for Canadian immigration during these fateful years were, as the authors clearly demonstrate, out-and-out enemies of the Jewish people, including the Minister of Mines and Resources Thomas Crerar, who was also responsible for immigration. Canada's High Commissioner to London, Vincent Massey, played a particularly sinister role in all of this. But it was Director of Immigration Frederick Charles Blair, who implemented the immigration policies during the period 1936-43, who looms very large in this regard. No less culpable was A.L. Jolliffe, who succeeded Blair in that position.

Space does not permit quoting chapter and verse regarding the nefarious activity of Blair and his cohorts. But one example is indicative: The Avion Conference of 1937, which was concerned with saving refugees, had Canadian representatives and they expressed "sympathy" with the plight of the refugees, but Blair, with the endorsation of Mackenzie King, proceeded to shut the doors to immigrants even more tightly, even barring Jews who were well to do. A case in point is a refugee family with about a million dollar fortune for investment in Canada which found their application refused.

How ironic that Crerar and his anti-Semitic associates rationalized their position with the argument that the admission of Jewish refugees would "play into the hands of the anti-Semites." Such sentiments were expressed at a time when the King government was encouraging the spread of anti-Semitic propaganda, and maintained a veritable silence when the Duplessis government of Quebec utilized the semi-fascist press to spread the rumor that Quebec was on the verge and in danger of being flooded by 100,000 Jewish refugees.

Mackenzie King, who paraded as a liberal, was, in truth, an anti-Semite and on more than one occasion voiced his sympathy for Hitler. It was he who warned of the "danger of mixing bloodstreams." King held that the question of refugees to Canada in 1938 constituted a larger danger than did Hitler.

At one point he wrote, "The truth is, Hitler and Mussolini, while dictators, have really sought to give the masses of the people some opportunity for enjoyment, taste of art and the like and, in this way, have won them to their side." Indirectly, King takes a swipe at the Jews in Germany for he goes on to say, "The dictatorship may have been necessary to wrest this opportunity from the privileged interests that have previously monopolized it."

Further evidence is supplied by the secretary of the American Legation in Ottawa, who attended an informal dinner arranged by Mackenzie King only one week after the Avion fiasco. In a report to his government the American diplomat recalls how King spoke proudly about his meeting with Hitler the previous year. The diplomat wrote that King "described Hitler as being, in his opinion, a very sincere man. He even described him as being 'sweet.' He said that he [Hitler] had a face...of a good man... He [King] intimated that he had asked Hitler some very frank questions and that he had been satisfied with Hitler's answers."

Abella and Troper write that even one year before Canada declared war on Germany, King had mixed feelings about Hitler and his methods. King declared that Hitler "might come to be thought of as one of the saviors of the world." It is clear that the Blairs, Crerars and Jolliffes would not have dared to be so open and crude about their anti-Semitism if they did not feel that they had the backing of the head of the country.

The authors document King's preoccupation with his re-election at the time of federal elections. And there is, in fact, a great deal of truth that among many Canadians, and particularly in Quebec, there was strong opposition to immigration in general and to Jewish immigration in particular. But instead of fighting against these sentiments, both the bourgeois parties, the Liberals and the Tories, encouraged and fanned the flames even further. Unfortunately, Abella and Troper fail to point this out although they do make mention of a number of liberal-minded non-Jewish Canadians who voiced opposition to the discriminatory and anti-Jewish immigration policies.

With Mackenzie King at the head of the government the stench around immigration emanated from the head.

Documentary evidence provided by the authors of this book proves that the immigration policies of the United States government were not very much better. The role of the U.S. at Avion and later in Bermuda in 1938 was only somewhat more positive. This was no doubt due to the pressures brought by Rabbi Stephen Wise and others. Because of this pressure and despite continued restrictions, the United States did allow more Jewish refugees to enter the country.

Jewish immigration figures in the period 1933-45 reveal that the United States, under Roosevelt, accepted 200,000 Jewish refugees, England 70,000, Bolivia—a relatively poor country—accepted 14,000 and the relatively well-to-do country of Canada a grand total of 5,000.

Several years after the end of the war when the urgent situation of displaced persons was high on the agenda, Canada continued its shameful policy and this was especially so as it applied to Jews who were still in displaced persons camps. At an informal gathering with journalists in 1945, an anonymous but highly placed Canadian government representative was asked about the number of Jews Canada would accept after the war. His spontaneous answer was, "None is too many." It was this response which provided Abella and Troper with the title of their book.

Efforts made by Jewish organizations in Canada aimed at bringing victims of Nazism to these shores also encountered overt and covert discrimination. This was based on the Blair/King Jew-baiting which expressed itself in statements about European Jews who "maintain strong root ties" and upon arrival in Canada "dragged their relatives over" and besides "they are generally undesirable."

One example of a Jewish organizational effort and its consequences is illuminating. A number of Jewish clothing manufacturers formed a partnership with the needle trades unions with the objective of bringing several thousand clothing workers to Canada. The project partners informed the government that they (the partners) would assume all the responsibility for money spent on travel of the refugees and also that none of the immigrants would be a burden on the state. Officially, the government agreed to the project, but the immigration authorities placed obstacles in the way of its realization and very suddenly a new regulation was introduced which stated that only 50 per cent of such immigrants could be Jewish.

It is extremely revealing that the government demanded the co-operation of the unions and the manufacturers in "screening" of immigrants for political backgrounds. This "screening" would be "not of Nazis but Communists." The results of such a policy are now clearly evident; hundreds of Nazi criminals entered Canada unhindered, while tens of thousands of Jewish refugees had the doors of this country shut in their faces.

The inescapable conclusion from all of the above is that Canada's immigration policy contributed to the extermination of hundreds of thousands of Jews at the hands of the Nazis. It shall forever remain a black spot on Canada's history.

Abella and Troper make a further contribution by examining the activity of the official Jewish leadership of this country. The picture which emerges underscores the sinister and dangerous role of those who engage in servile intercession. After a lapse of some fifteen years the Canadian Jewish Congress renewed its activity in the year of 1934. At that time the Canadian Jewish Congress relied heavily on the three Jewish parliamentarians, Samuel Jacobs of Montreal, Sam Factor of Toronto and Abe (A.A.) Heaps of Winnipeg. Their advice was to inhibit and restrain the mass of the Jewish people who were enraged by the events of those days and who were demanding mass action. It was only after the tactics of these three parliamentarians proved to be completely bankrupt that real struggles were undertaken by large numbers of Canadian Jews despite the advice of the Jewish leadership.

To their credit, Abella and Troper dared to do what others hesitated to undertake—namely, they present a critical analysis and point to the negative results which accrue from an attempt to intercede in a servile way with government.

While giving the authors their due in this regard, there are nonetheless some serious omissions. Abella and Troper fail to analyse the underlying reasons for the inner struggle in Jewish organized life and this is especially so as it relates to the congress leadership and the Union of Polish Jews, which organization was demanding mass action. A similar lack of clarity is to be found in the struggles in and around the Jewish Immigration Aid

Society (JIAS).

Almost at the beginning of their book the authors very correctly point to the fact that there were many Jewish organizations which did not go along with the policies of the Canadian Jewish Congress. They write about the birth of the "Folks Komitet Kegn anti-Semitizm" (People's Committee Against Anti-Semitism) and designate that organization incorrectly as "a front for the United Jewish People's Order which had remained outside of the umbrella of Canadian Jewish Congress." It was this People's Committee that sent a deputation to Ottawa in order to express the sentiments of the Jewish population. At that time the committee represented more than 10,000 Canadian Jews and at a meeting with Minister Crerar the refugee policies of the government were strongly condemned and positive action was demanded. Needless to say this deputation and its demands upset the congress leadership which had committed itself to the dangerous tactics of the three Jewish parliamentarians.

In the Abella-Troper book the People's Committee Against Anti-Semitism "fades out of the picture" much too quickly. It was the activity of this very committee and its protest delegation to the government which acted as an inspiration and finally led to a mighty outcry on the part of the Jewish *landsmanshaftn* and societies. Incidentally, it was the demand on the part of the societies and *landsmanshaftn* which in 1943 resulted in the inclusion of the United Jewish People's Order into congress. (The UJPO was expelled from congress in 1952 because that organization (UJPO) insisted on a campaign against German rearmament and the freeing of war criminals.) The significance of that historical fact cannot be overlooked since it substantiates the role of the progressive left-wing Jewish movement in Canada which throughout the years and since the rise of Nazism was embroiled in all kinds of struggles both in and outside of the congress against the immigration policies of the government and the inherent dangers of the back door dealings of the top leadership of the Jewish community. Despite the general objectivity of Abella and Troper they nevertheless have somehow lost the significance of the progressive Jewish movement.

Despite these gaps, *None Is Too Many* represents an honest and very important contribution which adds to our knowledge about one of the most tragic periods in Jewish life. During this time a democratic country such as Canada undertook policies which resulted in the murder of hundreds of thousands of Jews whose lives might otherwise have been saved. The book is a severe indictment of the Canadian government and, yes, also of the servility which characterized the activity of the established Jewish leadership. Both must be indicted.

June 1983

Anti-Semitism Considered 'Respectable'

LARRY HAIVEN

A recent spate of anti-Semitic incidents in Alberta had focused the attention of Jews in Canada and around the world on this Canadian province. And the weakness of the response from provincial authorities and other public bodies has raised fears that 40 years after Alberta found itself on the map as a centre of anti-Semitic feeling, that sentiment may still run deep here.

So high are emotions among Edmonton's 5,000-strong Jewish community, that over 1,000 people, practically one representative for each family, crammed into the Jewish Community Centre recently to hear community leaders explain the history of the controversy and their reaction to it.

First, a social studies teacher who was also the mayor of a small town 150 kilometres southwest of Edmonton was dismissed for having taught his students, over a period of fourteen years, that there is an international Jewish conspiracy to take over the world and that the Holocaust was a "fabrication" of history.

Jim Keegstra, teacher and mayor of Eckville, Alberta, characterized capitalism as a Jewish concept which makes use of usury to enslave the masses; at the same time he accused the Jews of attempting to introduce communism to the world.

The appeal of his firing was dismissed by the court of Queen's Bench. However, subsequently it was discovered that many of his former students and colleagues still agree with him.

Shortly after the Keegstra affair became news, a member of the provincial legislature in the ruling Conservative party told a reporter from the Edmonton *Journal* that the Holocaust had been "blown out of proportion" and "I haven't seen anything in terms of documentary evidence to prove to me that they [the Jews] were necessarily persecuted."

The statements unleashed a huge outcry from the Jewish community, which demanded the expulsion of Steven Stiles from the provincial Tory party. The Conservatives refused. Stiles was forced to issue an apology in the legislature and the government House leader "dissociated" his party from Stiles' statements. But Premier Lougheed, who was out of province when the statements were made, spoke out only after a month of requests that he do so (including one from famed Nazi-hunter Simon Weisenthal in Vienna).

Critics of the government pointed to the fact that Lougheed had no hesitancy some years ago about expelling MLA Tom Sindlinger from the party because Sindlinger did not agree with the Tory line on the new Canadian constitution.

Lougheed did make a formal address on the subject on May 12 in which he pledged his government to "reduce if not eliminate the possibility of the recurrence of the recent situation wherein a certified teacher in the province's school system was able to transmit. . . views that were unequivocally racial, religiously prejudiced, historically inaccurate and distorted."

Nevertheless, he said he does not believe that there has been a resurgence of bigotry and prejudice in Alberta.

Lougheed was presumably referring to the situation in the 1930s when Alberta was governed by the Social Credit Party, one of whose founders, Major C.H. Douglas, wrote considerable material on the idea of a "Jewish conspiracy." Until Premier Ernest Manning purged them some years later, the party and even the provincial government were full of people who believed in these theories. According to one Edmonton businessman, Alberta was regarded by Nazis in the 1930s as one of their potential power bases outside of Europe. The Social Credit Party was swept out of power by the Conservatives in 1971 after more than 35 years in office. But it was not until the last election in the autumn of 1982 that the Social Credit Party was eliminated from the provincial legislature.

It would seem that the party still harbors a large number of anti-Semites. Keegstra was vice-president of the federal party until he was suspended recently. When party president Martin Hattersley asked for his resignation in April, several prominent party members jumped to his defence.

Said Tom Erhart, second vice-president of the party's national council, "We're tired of listening to this Holocaust, six million Jews that never were. It was totally impossible for six million Jews to die in the concentration camps."

When Hattersley subsequently suspended Erhart and another Social Credit Party official at the same time as Keegstra, calling them an "isolated minority," first vice-president Jean-Marie Noel objected. "I think freedom of speech is the issue. . . We've let three fine Christian gentlemen down." The suspensions will be reviewed by party members at a June 18 convention.

Hattersley admits that the party's constitution does endorse "the philosophy and system of social and political reform originally written by

Major C.H. Douglas."

Reporters and others covering the Keegstra affair thought at first that the Jewish community here was blowing the thing out of proportion. They were soon proven wrong. In his May 5 column in the Edmonton *Journal*, respected columnist Don Braid wrote:

> Wrong, wrong. The man actually has *support* from his school principal in Eckville, certain knot-heads in the Social Credit Party, and people who write letters so prejudiced our editor won't print them.
>
> This poisonous movement is so entrenched that Keegstra can say exactly what he thinks and still keep his friends.
>
> His views are *respectable*. That's the chilling thing that frightens anyone who gets too close.

Braid quoted CBC reporter Linden MacIntyre, who made a short documentary about Keegstra and who admitted he was shocked by the "breezy anti-Semitism" he found in Eckville. (It appears that Eckville has no Jews.)

"I never really expected anyone to go on camera and say these things," claimed MacIntyre. "I nearly fell out of my chair when they did."

Despite the disturbing support for Keegstra in his community, it was one of Eckville's residents, Mrs. Susan Maddox, who blew the whistle on him. Upon hearing the kind of material Keegstra was teaching, she withdrew her son from his class and made a formal complaint to the school board. She also spent hours preparing to appear at a meeting of the board to refute Keegstra's claim of an international Jewish conspiracy.

Herb Katz, chairman of the community relations council of the Jewish Federation of Edmonton, calls Maddox "a genuine hero," and members of the Jewish community have proposed awarding her a prize for her humanitarianism.

Some other Eckville parents also helped Mrs. Maddox in her campaign and now that the controversy has filled the newspapers across the country, Eckville's Chamber of Commerce is calling for Keegstra's resignation or a by-election to determine whether he still has support.

But Keegstra, proud and unrepentant, refuses to resign, claims that he is being persecuted and that his enemies have the wrong reading of history.

Obviously, the issue is far from over.

April 1984

German Eyewitness in the Warsaw Ghetto

MIKE CASS
CJO European Correspondent

Joe Heydecker was seventeen when the Nazis came to power. For two years he had been apprenticed to a photographer in Frankfurt. His father disliked the Nazis. "I do not want to live in such a country," he said. His mother had a child from her former Jewish husband. The parents left Germany in 1933 and Joe Heydecker decided to break from his apprenticeship and join them. From 1933 to 1938 he lived in various European countries, including one year, 1937, in Poland. Heydecker was in Austria when the Nazis occupied it. He was conscripted into the German army and later was sent to the western front in the war against France. In January 1941 he was ordered to Warsaw as a lab technician for the photo laboratory of the German army there.

Heydecker wanted to find out what had happened to Jewish friends he had made during his stay in Warsaw in 1937. Since the city registry still functioned, even for Jewish residents, Heydecker got the address, a house in the ghetto, and even though it was a grave offence for an unauthorized person to enter the ghetto, he managed to sneak in in February 1941 and meet his friends. Heydecker was shocked by the misery he saw, the starvation, the overcrowding, and by what his Jewish friends told him.

In his army photo unit, Heydecker had two friends, anti-Nazis like himself, in whom he could confide. When he told them where he had been and what he had seen, they refused to believe him. Heydecker returned to the ghetto, in uniform, this time taking his camera along. His motive was "to conserve the outrage, to conserve the scream I should have cried out into the world," and "my fear that a time could come when the truth of all this might be doubted." The film that he took inside the ghetto was clandestinely developed with the help of his two friends and hidden by his wife who had also been drafted into an auxiliary army unit and had volunteered to go to Warsaw, to be near her husband.

The Warsaw Ghetto was established under Ludwig Fischer, head of the Nazi administration of Warsaw on October 16, 1940, and declared liquidated by General Stroop on May 16, 1943. The normal population of this district was 160,000-180,000 Jews and 80,000 non-Jews. Due to the war another 160,000 Jews from Nazi-occupied Poland had fled to this Warsaw district. On October 16, 1940, the 80,000 non-Jews were ordered to move out of the ghetto and 160,000 Jews living in other parts of Warsaw to move into the ghetto. They were given a fortnight to move. There was no transportation for such a mass exodus available, and most Jews had to abandon even their personal belongings. Accommodation for the newcomers in the overcrowded ghetto district was another problem, and many had to stay in the streets for weeks and months.

In May 1941 the ghetto was inhabited by 430,000 people. A room was on the average shared by thirteen people. Starvation was rife. Officially there was a bread ration of two pounds a week, but in reality, the handed-out ration did not amount to more than an ounce of bread a day. When Heydecker took his pictures in February and March 1941, the extermination policy of the "final solution" was not in force yet. But death took its toll. In 1941, 45,000 people died in the Warsaw Ghetto; they mainly starved or froze to death. Warsaw's Nazi mayor Fischer cynically remarked: "The Jews will succumb to starvation; what will remain of the Jewish problem will be a cemetery."

In 1960 Heydecker moved to Brazil. In 1981, after 40 years, his photos appeared in print with the help of Jewish organizations, published in Sao Paulo with a commentary in three languages: Portuguese, English and German. In 1983, a paperback edition was published in West Germany.

Heydecker disproves the argument that everything was done so secretly that the Germans did not know what was going on. Hundreds of thousands, he says, watched the brutalities that were committed by Germans against Jews at the ghetto gates between 1941 and 1943, among them the large numbers of German soldiers who passed through Warsaw. Again, when the Nazis invaded the Soviet Union in June 1941 and began mass executions of Jews in the course of their advance, they were not yet concerned about secrecy, but committed their crimes in full view of the German armies. Some soldiers were revolted by what they saw, which prompted General Field Marshall Walter von Reichenau to issue the following army order on October 10, 1941: "The main aim of the military campaign against the Jewish Bolshevik system is the extermination of the Asiatic influence on the European culture. This creates tasks also for the troops that go beyond the traditional one-sided soldiering. Therefore the soldiers must have full understanding of the necessity for the hard, but just, atonement for the Jewish sub-humans." This should do away with the legend of the "innocence" of the German army and its leadership because the crimes were supposedly only committed by Gestapo and SS.

June 1986

Psychoanalysis in Nazi Germany

MIKE CASS

CJO European Correspondent

Again psychoanalysis has come under attack—not a new phenomenon since the turn of the century. It has become fashionable to "prove" Freud's theories wrong, unscientific, outdated (the same accusations as against Marxism). Accused is not the Freud who erroneously tried to substitute psychology for the social sciences, but the Freud who based his exploration of the mental processes, conscious and subconscious, on scientific and rational methods. The new attacks on Freud and his teachings are part of the current offensive of irrationalism by neo-conservative forces. What lends itself better to irrationalism than psychology, dealing with the "soul"? It is no coincidence that E. Zimmer, the banner bearer in popularizing the refutation of Freud, is an adherent of the philosophy of the new right in France and of the Anglo-American "discoveries" that white I.Q.s are superior "by nature" to Blacks'.

Psychoanalysis as a humanist social science (Herbert Marcuse stated that social criticism is inherent in Freud's psychoanalysis) has had to face enemies from without, like the Nazis or the new irrationalists, but it is equally subject to dangers from within its own group.

Psychoanalysis and Nazism—is there another relationship feasible between the two than mutual enmity? German psychoanalysts thought they could "save" Freud's teaching in Nazi Germany by concessions and opportunistically adapting themselves to the circumstances—and lost their soul in the process.

Right after the Nazis had come to power in January 1933, the psychoanalyst Carl Mueller-Braunschweig took well-meaning but politically and morally disastrous steps to "save" the "German Psychoanalytic Association" and psychoanalysis, by voluntarily bowing to the Nazi lords. He published an article, "Psychoanalysis and Ideology (*Weltanschauung*)," in which he stated that psychoanalysis was a dangerous instrument only in the hands of a destructive spirit but that it could be turned into an instrument for the Third Reich by, for instance, turning weaklings into heroes. In 1935 Mueller-Braunschweig suggested that to save the association, Jewish members should "voluntarily" withdraw, and the Jewish members complied "voluntarily." One "Aryan," Bernhard Kamm, protested this decision, and also withdrew. He was followed by

"Aryan" Richard Sterba, who left Germany saying as a non-Jew he felt all the more in danger of falling into the Nazi trap. A few members became active in the resistance.

All honor to John F. Rittmeister, who joined the "Red Orchestra," the most successful of the anti-Nazi groups that managed to penetrate the Nazi High Command and to supply the Red Army with invaluable information. (Head of the organization was the Polish-Jewish Communist Leopold Trepper.) Rittmeister was executed in May 1943. Freud was not happy about the concessions to the Nazis but refrained from laying down rules for German "Aryan" analysts. Ernest Jones, the English head of the International Psychoanalytical Association, accepted and actively assisted the changeover.

In spite of concessions, the German Psychoanalytical Association had to give up its identity and join the "German Institute for Psychological Research and Psychotherapy," called the "Goering Institute." It was headed by M.H. Goering, a cousin of the Nazi leader. The psychoanalysts became "Working Group A." The outpatient department was headed by John Rittmeister and was a haven for psychoanalysts and their patients till his arrest in 1942. Rittmeister was succeeded by Kemper, also a "resistance" member. The department succeeded in saving lives of psychotic patients, doomed to be killed in accordance with Nazi practice, by treating them as "neurotic." M.H. Goering, who obtained his position through his family ties, was eager to turn psychoanalysis into a tool for the new rulers, increasing the work-efficiency for the Nazi war effort by psychological means. Personally he acted decently, protecting the psychoanalytical group from persecution.

After Rittmeister's arrest the group lost the privilege of being identified as "Group A." The price for "saving" psychoanalysis by concessions was high. Step by step they slid deeper into the Nazi net to become a tool in Hitler's war machine. The action of the Dutch contrasted with that of the Germans. When the Dutch Psychoanalytical Association was faced with the demand to "Aryanize," it decided to save its honor and not permit the separation of the Jewish members, and dissolved the association! Secretly they kept up contacts and concentrated on helping and hiding their Jewish colleagues.

Actually Freud was not guiltless in the failings of the German Psychoanalytical Association. There was no doubt that personally Freud was courageous. After the invasion of Austria when Nazis entered his home he frightened them off with his dignity and stern looks. Before allowing him to leave Austria, the Gestapo wanted him to sign a paper that he had in no way been molested or hampered. When Freud read the document—pen in hand—he was told that he was not allowed to cross out

Anti-Semitism and the Holocaust 127

anything. "But am I allowed to add something?" he asked—and he wrote on the document: "I can warmly recommend the Gestapo to everyone." But—as the political crisis in Europe unfolded, Freud pursued a questionable path. He declared his teachings "neutral" and demanded political abstinence from his followers.

In the early stages, Freud and psychoanalysts were critical of existing society. This would appear only natural—the basis of psychoanalysis is materialistic; it strives after truth, disregarding "authority" that is not legitimized by reason, rejecting mysticism and metaphysics. When Freud realized that repression was the cause of mental disorder, be also realized the role of suffering through repression caused by existing social taboos. Freud wrote: "[It is] impossible to carry out an isolated reform without changing the basis of the system in the same way in which you cannot restore a suit torn to pieces with a single silken patch." But by 1929 Freud had changed, and said it was not the task of psychoanalysis to change or improve society.

Willi Reich, the favored pupil of Freud, became a Marxist and recognized the explosive potential inherent in psychoanalytic theories. Formerly a therapist of the well-to-do, he now addressed himself to the ordinary people and succeeded within a short time to create a proletarian mass movement involving hundreds of thousands. Freud denounced the "Bolshevist" Willi Reich. A remarkable incident occurred in 1933. A Scandinavian journal reprinted an article of Willi Reich that had appeared five years earlier in a psychoanalytic journal in Vienna. The editor was taken to court, accused of pornography. Reich implored Freud to explain in a letter that the article was not pornographic but serious scholarly research. Freud refused—and the editor had to go to jail. (It is like a joke of history: Writings of Willi Reich sparked the French students' uprising of 1967. What became known as the "bedroom revolt" in Nanterre University based itself on just rediscovered writings of Willi Reich. And the bedroom revolt sparked the 1967 uprising.)

When, after the socialist uprising in Austria of February 1934, democracy was abolished, it was forbidden for members of the Austrian Psychoanalytic Association to be politically active (leaving only underground activity) or to treat patients who were so active.

But political abstinence did not save psychoanalysis. It only helped to pave the way with concessions to complete surrender to the Nazis and to create problems in the aftermath of Hitler rule: By a process of memory repression, the German psychoanalysts "buried" their unheroic twelve years from 1933 to 1945 in the same way in which the German people repressed and buried the twelve years of Nazi rule. The German Psychoanalytic Institute was reconstituted as if nothing had happened. The twelve years of shame became taboo. A characteristic example: Max Eitington, an outstanding psychoanalyst, was president of the German Psychoanalytic Association until, as a Jew, he was forced to resign under Hitler. In memory of his 100th birthday in 1981, the German Psychoanalytical Association published a paper on his life and work. It says not a word about Eitington's forced resignation or his emigration to Palestine. It refrains from explaining why Eitington had to give up his life's work and the practice of psychoanalysis.

But the fate of psychoanalysis under the Nazis, as well as the problem of political abstinence and what it leads to, as exemplified by Sigmund Freud's political shortsightedness (not to mention the continuing attitude of the conservative trend in psychoanalysis) is more than past history. The issues and problems are still alive, as evidenced by the following:

Frankfurt just celebrated the 25th anniversary of the "Sigmund Freud Institute," an important centre of teaching, training and healing. The institute was headed by Alexander Mitscherlich with the assistance of his wife Margaret. The Mitscherliches never forgot the Nazi era. Two of their important books are *The Inability to Mourn* (on the millions of victims slain by the Germans) and *Science Without Humanism* (on the barbaric abuse of science by Nazis). The Mitscherliches did not shy away from politics. To them, psychoanalysis can only help people if it does not close its eyes to the social and political problems of the day. Alexander Mitscherlich died in 1982 and the institute is now reverting to "neutrality"—to "pure therapy." For the anniversary celebrations the Sigmund Freud Institute "overlooked" Margaret Mitscherlich and invited as guest speaker an analyst from abroad who is not in favor of the Mitscherlich trend. Margaret Mitscherlich stayed away from the celebrations, and in the resulting scandals, the issue of political abstinence versus engagement became again a topic for discussion.

Horst Eberhard Richter, psychoanalyst, professor of psychosomatics, president of the German section of Physicians for Peace, author of many widely read and discussed books, involved in many public issues, has just published his autobiography, *The Change of Conscience*. In analysing his experiences of the Nazi era and the post-war era in West Germany, he comes to this conclusion: "It is not enough to critically interpret dehumanizing structures, but a physician as a political citizen has to recognize his co-responsibility and thus make his contribution—no matter how insignificant—to bring his influence to bear on the situation."

This applies not only to physicians and psychoanalysts.

IV
Peace and Disarmament

May 1967

Vietnam is a Jewish Issue

JACK COWAN

Because of the length of the war in former Indo-China, now Vietnam, probably more has been spoken and written about it than about any other war in history. The words, whether diplomatic, justifying or searing condemnation, will continue until the suffering of the Vietnamese people and the mounting casualties of the USA and its "allies" come to an end.

In the past, support for one's own side has grown as wars continued. This time opposition to the escalation is sharpening, especially in the USA. American boys are publicly burning draft cards. Some are serving prison terms rather than be inducted. Protest demonstrations are spreading and expanding. Universities—a few so far—are refusing to supply the draft boards with information on student standings. More and more protest meetings! More and more protest petitions and full-page advertisements!

Emil Mazey, the respected secretary-treasurer of the United Auto Workers Union, said recently at a Chicago peace rally: "In Vietnam, our country [the USA] is participating in its greatest tragedy. Our country got involved in the dirty Vietnam war by assisting the French to maintain their colonial domination over this unhappy country, beginning in 1950.

"Our nation should have been on the side of the Vietnamese people in helping them to obtain their freedom and independence. We should have supported the right of self-determination of the people of Vietnam in seeking their own future path."

T.C. Douglas, NDP leader, says: "United States President Johnson is shooting craps with the survival of the human race if he continues to escalate the war in Vietnam."

Philip H. Klutznick, a former president of B'nai B'rith and a former United States representative at the United Nations, speaking at a governors' luncheon of the B'nai B'rith, said:

"The Johnson administration should earnestly re-examine its political motivations in Vietnam and determine whether the war serves the national interest. If it doesn't," he said, "it should either escalate its efforts at negotiations or drastically and unilaterally reduce its military role in Vietnam. To those who say, 'but we can't quit now,' I must ask: If it is in our national interest, why not?"

Rabbi Arthur J. Lelyveld, president of the American Jewish Congress, told a banquet session of the National Women's Division convention of congress in New York that the American Jewish Congress regarded Vietnam as a "Jewish issue."

Rabbi Lelyveld said: "We are proud to be the cutting-edge of every forward movement of self-respecting Jews who take both their identity within the Jewish people and their covenant role seriously. This is why we of the American Jewish Congress have spoken out on Vietnam—because we are loyal Americans and because we are faithful Jews."

The Jewish Congress leader said that "everything in our tradition prompts us to believe that there are times when silence is immoral. 'Thou shalt not stand idly by the blood of thy neighbor' is a primary demand of Jewish ethics recorded in the Book of Leviticus.

"We call upon our own government to take the initiative by ending the bombing in the North and by holding itself open to other initiatives likely to bring about a standstill truce."

Canada is not directly involved in the war in Vietnam, but it is not indifferent. On the one hand, our "industrial-military complex" is making profit out of the weapons of death that are being supplied to the American war machine. On the other hand, we are a member of the International Control Commission that is supposed to supervise the peace in Vietnam; and in a hundred ways our people have spoken up for peace—through meetings, demonstrations, petitions, medical aid and even knitting for the war victims. There is no reason why the protests of Canadian people should not be as loud and clear as those of the American people.

How do we explain the silence of Canadian Jewish leaders on this issue? Are they not concerned because it is Vietnamese children that are being burned and not Jewish children? Some of the Canadian Anglo-Jewish press have not even had the doubtful sense to keep quiet. They have editorialized viciously against Rabbi Abraham L. Feinberg, who had the courage to visit Hanoi during the period immediately following the commencement of the bombing of that city, and to bring back to the Canadian and American people a first-hand report of the ghastliness of the war and a plea for peace. Rabbi Feinberg has spoken to scores of thousands of people in Toronto, Winnipeg, Vancouver, Detroit, Chicago, San Francisco and other places—a heavy program even for a strong young man, but a grave burden on a retired rabbi who is practically blind.

It was the editor of one of these same papers who eulogized the new "democratic" Federal Republic of Germany (West Germany) before the storm broke over the resurgence of neo-Nazism that has been documented by scores of writers and journalists since 1946. (This editor asks, "Who sponsored Rabbi Feinberg's trip to Hanoi?" It is fair to ask this editor: Who sponsored and paid for his trip to the Federal Republic of Germany?)

The United Church of Canada has voted $50,000 for aid to Vietnamese civilians and has appealed to the Canadian government to develop a vast program of medical aid and hospitalization for the civilian victims. The generosity of the Jewish people is a byword among men. Instead of official silence and Jewish newspaper attacks on supporters of peace in Vietnam, the Jewish people of Canada should match any grants in aid for the innocent victims of a war which they did not start and do not want. And while they are doing this, they should with one voice join U Thant and other world figures, including American Jewish leaders, in demanding a stop to the bombing of North Vietnam and an end to the attacks on the people of Vietnam.

July-August 1970

Praying for Peace by the White House Fence

RABBI ABRAHAM FEINBERG

Friday evening May 8, on the sidewalk facing the White House in Washington, I conducted a Jewish peace fellowship candlelight Sabbath Eve service as a memorial to the four martyrs of Kent State University and as protest against President Nixon's Indo-China war.

Only the whir of autos, the chanting and reading of our prayers and whispered inquiries from Gentiles about the meaning of Hebrew words broke the leaden ribbon of silence. Even the youngsters who fixed candles on the iron spikes of the White House fence did so without a word.

Then a small knot of Kent State students came to us from a nearby

Peace Poster by Azriel and Irene Awret, Safed, Israel (October 1986)

End the Arms Race Peace Walk, April 25, 1987

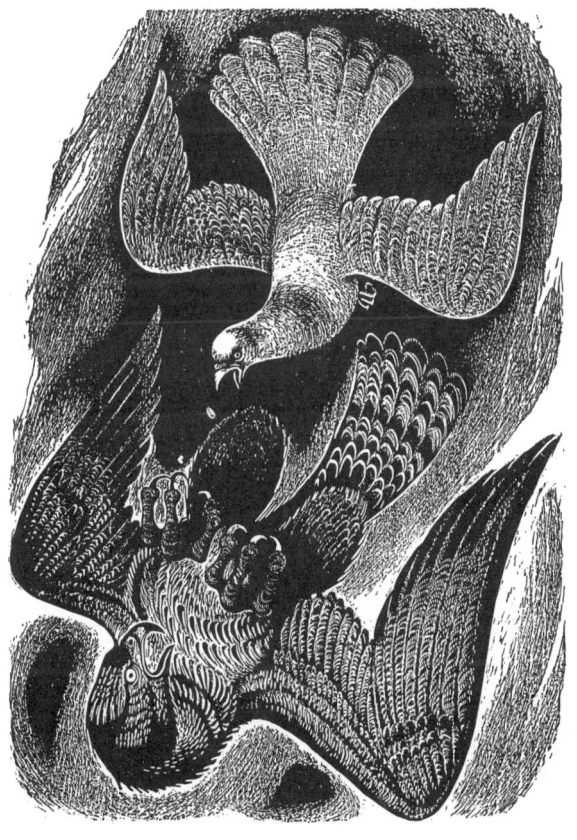

The Dove and the Hawk (engraving, 1969) by Fritz Eichenberg (July-August 1987)

church. A Kent boy asked us to lock arms with them and sing "We Shall Overcome." There was little, then, of defiance in our voices. Suddenly, at my side, appeared Russell, junior brother of Jeffrey Miller, whose coffin had been borne by 4,000 mourners from a funeral chapel in New York. The stricken youth and I turned our faces toward the president's mansion and wept together.

The four we mourned were not flaming revolutionaries. They could not even have been targets for the artfully structured rhetoric of Spiro Agnew, much less for the bullets of National Guardsmen sworn to defend law and order. They had no greater value as human beings than the million peasants and workers and their children, and the 50,000 American GIs killed in Vietnam. No one is unimportant.

We grieved for many things beyond Kent's campus: for vanishing hopes that the Nixon administration would be moved to common sense and compassion; for the dishonor of the American people who, like the slugging hardhat construction workers and the applauding white-collar warriors of Wall Street, permit themselves to be gulled by archaic appeals to national honor; for all the dead, of every nation, offered up in massive holocaust to the stinking idols of avarice and empire; for the hard cold men of the Pentagon who dare not view young American males except as inanimate card-indexed items in global strategy; for Richard Nixon, the most powerful human being in all history, yet powerless to be truly human.

Richard Nixon's inevitable retreat into the rarefied aura of unprecedented power has been reinforced by all-consuming obsession with the presidency. A man with a mania to occupy the White House can hardly be expected to relate to his fellow men save insofar as they are useful. He is captive of a dream.

A successful aspirant for office must cultivate men of wealth and power who can provide financial sinews in the war for votes. Only a minority of college students have reached 21; a negligible number can spare money for campaign contributions, particularly at a time of growing campus contempt for the electoral process. They are therefore expendable citizens. To this formula for alienation from the young add Nixon's intellectual mediocrity, total lack of charismatic posture in language or ideas (in contrast with the two Kennedys), a high threshold of sensitivity to suffering, characteristics that his staff, I am told, define as "arithmetically political, administratively mechanical, but lacking in antennae and imagination"—and the iron barrier around the White House becomes insuperable.

After the closing recitation of the prayer for the dead (*Kaddish*), a group of us walked toward the only gate open to the White House grounds. The president would soon begin his heralded press conference. Newsmen and television crews were being admitted.

"Civil disobedience!" Suddenly the words came forth. It had been agreed upon as a possibility if the police prevented us from meeting at the White House fence. I held debate with myself.

The kids with guns who shot the kids with rocks at Kent were shaped by reverence for the flag and the presidential office, obedience to "higher" authority and the chain of command, and by "respectability," favorite establishment method of emasculation. Reverence, as taught by organized religion, begins with the "sanctification" of rabbi's robe, bishop's mitre, and (years ago) the "divinity that doth hedge a king." Obedience, as taught in the schools, when unchecked by individualism, spawns a race of literate, potentially militarized sheep. Respectability, when dominant, suffocates... All three are counter-productive, if not a downright surrender to evil, when a president who vowed to end the war in Vietnam escalates it to Cambodia, when innocents are slaughtered for being on a college campus at the wrong time.

Our authority issues from the Hebrew prophets who challenged the seat of temporal power. *Our* tradition is anti-military, *our* prime concern is man, *our* law the will of God, above all laws of earthly governments... Thus I rationalized civil disobedience on the president's doorstep.

Soon a transistor radio brought the president's "apologia," his bid for peace with a rebellious minority that could expand into a non-silent majority openly questioning his judgment.

His audience on the sidewalk detected no real concessions or change. Perhaps the military quick-step, jaunty tilt of head, imperious clipped speech of a commander-in-chief were gone; the hawk remained. Perhaps the mood had turned inward, unsure, almost pathetic in anxiety to win friends among those whom the engineers of war and the paladins of "stability" had been pushing aside.

Gasps of disbelief swelled into a near-chorus at the end of the president's news conference when he asked for a moment of silence in tribute to a recently deceased journalist. "He didn't even think of the four kids from Kent!"

Saturday: the march with Ben Spock, dedicated movie stars, peace leaders and diverse activists, in a shapeless line flanked by marshals clasping hands, to a towering speakers' platform in the Ellipse behind the White House.

There, while speech followed speech, I listened instead to one of the youngsters with whom President Nixon had conversed on the steps of the Lincoln Memorial at 4:30 that morning. "He didn't seem to know what this is all about. He spoke of surfing and football and travel in many countries like a kind of tour and told us to try to understand people in other lands. He wasn't with it. He gave us a little lecture, a pat and told us to have a good time. Like a picnic!" Not a hint of derision or complaint in her voice, only bewilderment and profound sadness.

The future program of the United States peace movement was merely intimated from that podium May 9. It clearly forecasts a shift of emphasis from White House to Capitol Hill and the voters. The campus thrust against war, poverty, racism, pollution, urban blight will be geared to political organization, not polemical demonstration. The kids are reunited with faculty and administrators.

A Smith College senior told an alumnae group in Toronto recently how the job is to be done. A steady, continuous campaign, employing every resource of intelligence, research, dynamic young energy for a congress that will heed the summons to change. There will even be courses in the art of lobbying. And some far-out males will cut their hair in deference to squares. The classroom advances to the place where the history not only of America but the world will be written.

If the non-violent campus bums and the young in general fail to evoke support and understanding from as yet unpersuaded middle America (and timid Canadians), or falter through discouragement, the future of America, and the "free world" it heads, is bleak indeed. If they "turn things around," the monument to the four who died at Kent may well be the redemptive revolutionary ardor kindled by their martyrdom.

June 1982

Kampuchea
Second Holocaust

KATHLEEN GOUGH

Mass murder on a scale equalled only by Hitler occurred under the Pol Pot regime in Kampuchea from 1975 to 1978.

As is well known, Kampuchea was governed by Prince Sihanouk as a neutral kingdom in the 1950s and 1960s. Sihanouk was overthrown in 1970, Lon Nol came to power with American backing, and United States forces invaded the country to try to eradicate Vietnamese communist sanctuaries together with a growing Khmer Rouge (Red Kampuchean) movement. After the American public forced President Nixon to withdraw his troops, a bloody civil war with saturation bombing continued until April 17, 1975, when the U.S.-backed government capitulated and the Khmer Rouge took the capital, Phnom Penh.

Scattered in revolutionary groups in different parts of the country, the Khmer Rouge formed at least three factions. One, led by such figures as Heng Samrin and Hun Sen, the present president and foreign minister, favored a gradual transition to socialism on the Vietnamese pattern. A second faction under prominent leaders like Hou Youn and Hou Nim was Maoist and, unlike the Vietnamese communists, supported the Chinese cultural revolution. A third group also thought of itself as Maoist and had support from China, but combined its belief in "instant communism" with a strong admixture of racism and chauvinism. It was this group, led by Pol Pot, Ieng Sary, their wives, Khieu Samphan and Son Sen, who took power in Phnom Penh and soon wiped out most leaders and thousands of troops and followers of the other two factions.

Under Pol Pot the population was divided into old people, new people and enemies. The old people, some 4½ to 5 million, were peasants living in areas already under Khmer Rouge control. The new people, about 3½ million, were urbanites who had lived in Phnom Penh and the smaller provincial towns under Lon Nol. These people were evacuated at gun point to the countryside and forced to work as agricultural slaves of the new state. Within a few months, the distinction between old and new people became blurred; all Kampucheans except the Pol Pot troops and cadres came to occupy villages that were really concentration camps and to work under conditions amounting to slavery.

The "enemies" were initially all those who had served the Lon Nol government and all from the cities who had more than seven years of education, that is, had attended high school. These people were to be killed. Most of them, in fact, *were* killed. They were summoned to offer their services to "Angkar" ("the organization"), and then they were spirited away at night and murdered.

The "enemies" quickly came to include other large categories. These were chiefly Vietnamese, Chinese and Cham-speaking minorities in Kampuchea, tribespeople in the mountains, Buddhist monks and nuns, rival communist factions, district and village headmen or cadres of Pol Pot who came under suspicion of treason, and any hapless citizen who disobeyed some trifling rule of Angkar. I was told, for example, that if a person stole a chicken or a mango from the common stores, tried to leave his village, wept for a dead relative, refused to marry a partner chosen for him by Angkar, spoke a foreign phrase, read a book, wore spectacles, or in some way revealed that he was educated, he was likely to be taken away at night and executed. Altogether, the present government estimates that some three million out of 8½ million Kampucheans were killed by the Pol Pot regime or else died of neglected disease or starvation. When the country was liberated in January 1979, only 500 out of 82,000 Buddhist monks remained, only 195,000 out of 750,000 Muslim Chams, 69 out of 645 doctors, pharmacists, and dentists, and 121 out of 1,241 writers and artists. Four-fifths of the primary and secondary school teachers died. Almost all the college teachers and all the veterinary surgeons were exterminated.

The executions required special death camps. The largest was the Tuol Sleng prison (formerly a high school) in Phnom Penh in the centre of a Pol Pot army camp. More than 16,000 prisoners were tortured and killed there, their dossiers, confessions and photographs being preserved. Several thousand were buried in pits in the back yard; the rest, in a field 14 kilometres away, where 8,982 skeletons have been unearthed, and it is thought that up to 30,000 more may be buried. Every one of Kampuchea's 127 districts contains one or more similar mass graves.

For those who survived, life was a nightmare of hunger, fear and overwork—a twelve to sixteen hour work day with, at best, half an eight ounce can of rice with a little salt and vegetable. The "surplus" food, which surviving scholars estimate was about five-sixths of the total produce, was shipped to China in return for weapons or stored for use by the army in preparation for a long-term campaign to conquer South Vietnam. Thousands died of hunger, and many women, perhaps a majority, were so malnourished that they lost their menstrual cycle and were unable to bear children.

In addition to a large part of the population, the economic infrastructure was almost totally destroyed. Trains, buses, cars, banks, factories, post offices, power plants and a hydroelectric dam were dynamited, as well as schools, hospitals, market buildings, mosques, churches, pagodas, about one million houses and libraries.

In 1978 rebellions broke out in several parts of the country. At the same time, the government stepped up both the internal killings and the invasion of South Vietnam. It was widely believed that Pol Pot intended to kill all the Kampucheans except his most trusted followers, and bring in Chinese to replace them. Although I myself can scarcely credit it, the mass executions in the latter half of 1978 gave substance to this belief, which is still held by many Kampucheans today.

Fortunately, Kampuchean liberation forces who had fled to Vietnam, together with some 200,000 Vietnamese allies, arrived in time to stop the slaughter of more millions, and in 21 days put to flight the Pol Pot forces. The present government of President Heng Samrin is formed from the small, pro-Vietnamese communist group that was able to flee the massacres, and from the 10,000-odd intellectuals of varying political persuasions who survived.

Kampuchea's recovery since January 7, 1979, has been remarkable. When I spent three weeks travelling about the country in February 1982, I found that although the towns and cities are still largely blasted, the people are fairly prosperous and much of the economic structure has been restored. In spite of floods and droughts, Kampuchea is almost self-sufficient in food again. An estimated 65 per cent of the adult population are women, up to 80 per cent in some villages. The families, mainly headed by widows, form mutual aid teams of ten to twelve households whose members cultivate, build houses, and construct roads, wells and schools in common. On weekends they are joined by Vietnamese soldiers, Kampuchean liberation army fighters, government servants, foreign diplomats, and members of international aid agencies, who help them to plough, transplant rice seedlings, or bring in the harvest. Factories, banks, hospitals and schools have been restored. Most of the thousands of orphans have been adopted by families whose children had been killed, but in Phnom Penh there are four orphanages for about 2,000 children who are well cared for and educated. Once a week, the orphans in their blue and white uniforms direct traffic in Phnom Penh's now crowded streets.

When Pol Pot fled the country he took with him about 60,000 troops and a kidnapped population of some 100,000 villagers to the mountains bordering Thailand. The present Pol Pot forces are conscripted from this population or from cadres, many of whom are already guilty of massacring their countrymen. Thousands of the Pol Pot forces have surrendered and gone home, but about 30,000, armed by China and aided by the CIA, still harass the border regions. The Pol Pot troops who were captured or who surrendered were granted amnesty. After a few weeks in detention they were returned to their villages, where they are kept in line by the local authorities.

I went to Kampuchea without my Vietnamese friends because I wanted to enquire privately how Khmers felt about the Vietnamese troops' "occupation" of their country. I visited seven out of twenty provinces and talked to 50 Kampucheans of all classes. All said that the Vietnamese had saved them from destruction and were their chief friends and allies, and that their troops must not leave until the Pol Pot forces are banished, until China, the USA and Thailand stop trying to subvert the new government, and the Khmer liberation army is strong enough to defend the country. I asked several people if they thought the present set-up was "irreversible" as the Vietnamese and the Kampuchean government claim. "We do hope so!" was the gist of their replies. The government faces mountainous problems; it is short of everything, but in three years it has shown that it can administer the country, command respect and affection and effect a remarkable revival.

It is tragic that our own government still upholds the Pol Pot gang's right to a seat in the United Nations and refuses to recognize the government of Kampuchea. Even the postal service to Kampuchea has been suspended. But we should help Kampuchea and Vietnam. They deserve it.

September-October 1982

The Question for World Jewry in 5743

REUBEN SLONIM

The major question for Jewry in 5743 is whether we are prepared to recognize the rights of the Palestinian Arabs and take the initiative in making an accommodation with them.

Without a Palestinian-Israeli understanding, Israel, in spite of its victory over the PLO in a devastating war which has turned out to be a common disaster for victor and vanquished alike, will find no security and achieve no prosperity. And Jews who are concerned for Israel will continue to be in turmoil and crisis.

Jews and Palestinians are adversaries refusing to meet head-on, one set of protagonists unable to see the other for what it is. Each group regards the other as monstrous trouble-makers who will not go away as they ought to. Each side believes the other to be mindless, rootless, dead but without the grace to lie down.

How do we go about healing this blurred vision?

The first step is to recognize the failing in ourselves, in the spirit of the penitential theme of Rosh Hashanah and Yom Kippur. Traditionally when the Jews faced a problem they first examined themselves: "Because of our sins we were exiled from our land."

The natural tendency is to avoid such self-examination. But being a Jew has never meant making life easier. This is not a year for tired people, least of all for tired Jews. Nor is it a time to wait for the Palestinians to make the first move, to start healing themselves. By the time they get to it, they may be too late for themselves and us. We must take the initiative, since we have no alternative.

Zionist Dysfunction

The fact is that myopia toward the Arab has been a Zionist dysfunction from the beginning. The drive to make and maintain Palestine as a Jewish land has been at the root of the liberal Jewish dilemma.

Theodor Herzl, founder of political Zionism, must have known that Palestine in the late nineteenth century was peopled. It had been the subject of numerous travel accounts, most of them widely known, by Chateaubriand, Flaubert, Lamartine and others.

As a journalist he could not have been unaware of Baedeker, who ascertained that Palestine was inhabited in the 1880s by 650,000 people, mostly Arabs. Yet in his diary he says that the mass of poor natives were to be expropriated, adding that "both the expropriation and the removal of the poor must be carried out discreetly and circumspectly."

This was to be done by spiriting "the penniless population across the border, procuring employment for it in transit countries while denying it any employment in our own country." Herzl predicted that the small class of large landowners could be "had for a price," as indeed later they were.

Even Chaim Weizmann, president of the World Zionist Organization in the decades leading to the birth of the State of Israel, who grasped the heart of compassion and justice, was unable to see that the Arab had the same capability of devotion to Palestine as did the Jew: "It seems as if God has covered the soil of Palestine with rocks and marshes and sand, so that its beauty can only be brought out by those who love it and will devote their lives to healing its wounds."

While the Arabs had the land, Weizmann appeared to be saying there was no love in it or for it. The native inhabitants were curiously believed to be out of touch with history and, it seemed to follow, were not really present.

Growing Blind Spot

The blind spot grows as we come closer to our own time. On Carlebach Street in Tel Aviv stands a building that houses the offices of *Maariv*, Israel's most popular newspaper. The late Dr. Eliezer Carlebach was founder and editor of the paper. I interviewed him in the spring of 1955. His view that Palestinian Arabs were shaped by Islam, and were therefore to be shunned, bordered on racism, and my editor advised against publishing the interview. Later that year, *Maariv* carried an article with Carlebach's view summarized as he had presented it to me:

"Wherever Islamic psychology rules there is the inevitable rule of despotism and criminal aggression... The danger stems from the totalitarian conception of the world, the passion for murder deeply rooted in the blood, from the lack of logic, the easily inflamed brains, the boasting, and above all the blasphemous disregard for all that is sacred to the civilized world..."

This is a progression of the attitude that the Palestinian Arabs are nonexistent. They may exist, but they are not human in the sense that Jews and Europeans are. One man's opinion? Carlebach's article was cited by government officials as I made my journalistic rounds in the late 1950s. Even friends and relatives would haul it out on my return to Israel from Arab capitals.

It is just a short step from claiming a moral justification for ignoring the Arabs to an unabashed philosophy that we are better off without them. From 1932 on, Joseph Weitz was director of the Jewish National Fund. In December 1940, he wrote:

"It must be clear that there is no room for both peoples in this country... If the Arabs leave the country, it will be wide open for us. And if the Arabs stay, the country will remain narrow and miserable."

It would be difficult to argue that displacing the Arabs was a deliberate policy of Zionists in the years between the end of World War II and the establishment of the Jewish state. The birth of the state came about as a result of an almost unimaginably complex, many-sided struggle and a full-scale war. But Weitz did speak with the voice of a Zionist consensus. Zionist effort in the middle 1940s focused on taking over territory and filling it with new inhabitants. In the process the Palestinian Arabs were of marginal concern.

Breaking Through

There has to be a realization that the Palestinian is not going to disappear. He is there, asking questions that Jews cannot avoid: Why is it right for a

Jew born in Toronto to immigrate to Israel, whereas a Palestinian born in Jaffa or Jerusalem is a refugee? Are you going to eradicate me to make way for someone else, and if so what right do you have to do it? Can you deny that the land you love is an Arab homeland too?

We cannot pretend any more that there are no ethical problems to face. Ethics and justice—that is what being a Jew is all about. Not only justice for ourselves—the history of oppression has taught us to cry out for that and we do it splendidly—but justice for those who for too long have been treated as if they weren't there.

Two things are certain: The Jews of Israel will remain; the Palestinian Arabs will also remain. It is perhaps as difficult for Jews to believe they will remain as that the Palestinians will.

Most Jews feel that Israel's security at any cost is a genuine guarantee against future genocidal attempts on the Jewish people. But there can be no satisfactory life based on a central concern to keep the past from recurring.

What we have done is to make the Palestinians the equivalent of a past experience reincarnated in the form of a present threat. The result is that the Palestinians' future as a people is mortgaged to Jewish fear, which is a disaster both for them and for us.

What we have to do is to begin to talk rationally about the Palestinians. It is a hopeful sign that some Jews have made such a beginning. Amnon Kapeliuk, who covers the West Bank for *Al Hamishmar*, an Israeli daily, and writes impressively for *Le Monde* in Paris, is a non-radical Jew who sees the Palestinians as they are and Israel's strong hand over them as "immoral, ineffective and dangerous."

Another voice clarifying the Palestinian position is that of Dov Ronen, an Israeli who was a fellow at Harvard's Centre for International Affairs. Kibbutznik and officer in the Israeli Air Force, trained at Hebrew University, he believes that the principle of self-determination which brought statehood to the Jews also applies to the Palestinians.

Shulamit Aloni, member of the Knesset and leader in civil rights for Israeli citizens of whatever origin, gives a justification for two states, Israeli and Palestinian:

"I understand and sense in every fibre of my being the desire to possess Gaza, to hold on to Beth El and Anatot, to Givon and Samaria. But then this is precisely why I should understand the strong desire of the Palestinian for Jaffa and Ashkelon, for Gaza and Ramle. And since for the Arab there is no return to Jaffa, Acre, Ramle and Ashkelon, we should forego ownership to Beth El and Anatot."

Diaspora Voices

Outside Israel there is the vigorous voice of Nahum Goldmann, former President of both the World Zionist Organization and the World Jewish Congress. At 85, speaking with cogency and force, he is the one Jew in all the world who literally makes a practice of coming face to face with Palestinians, even with members of the PLO.

Goldmann, like most Jews, cannot be sure the Palestinians will be satisfied with a mini-Palestine and will not want all of the land of Israel. "But," he asks, "what is the meaning of certainty in politics? Politics are a permanent risk. There is never anything more than a possibility in politics. And I believe there is a possibility that the Palestinians will be satisfied with a mini-Palestine."

Another Diaspora Jew, noteworthy for his attitude toward Palestinians, is I.F. Stone, the American newspaperman, perhaps the first to recognize that the Palestinians are now playing the role of the Jews. "To be a Jew," he wrote half a dozen years ago, "is not quite to belong. Israel's Jews are its Arabs."

It is possible for Jews and Palestinians to see each other in the flesh. Once, Jerusalem-born Edward Said, professor of comparative literature at Columbia University, said to Abba Eban, former Israeli foreign minister: "I know we must be open to each other's reality. Our representatives, yours and ours, must be made to respond to what, as human beings sick of war and exile, we feel, you Jews and we Palestinians. Together we must make... equality for Arab and Jew in Palestine, no war, no persecution for anyone."

And Eban replied: "Surely it is time for the peaceful, lucid voices of Palestine Arabs to be heard... History has decreed that you and we give our love and devotion to the same skies, hills and earth. For all others this region is an object of interest or controversy. For you and us it is home. It is only as sovereign nations within a regional harmony that we can make the abode of peace and sanctity."

That is how a breakthrough begins, when the solitudes are broken down, not when land is conquered and its inhabitants held in servitude, or driven into exile.

June 1983

The Shalom Committee

JOHN MATE

The Shalom Committee was formed on an ad-hoc basis to organize formal Jewish representation in the April 23 End the Arms Race March in Vancouver. The initial move to organize a Jewish representation came from Sol Jackson (Vancouver Peretz School) and Hank Rosenthal (*Canadian Jewish Outlook*). Last year, while many civic groups (churches of all denominations, labor unions, professional associations, public schools, political parties, cultural organizations and so forth) were clearly identified with banners and placards, the absence of any formal Jewish presence or Jewish banners was quite evident.

The Shalom Committee comprised representatives from the Peretz School, Ichud Habonim, the United Jewish People's Order, the Forum for Peace in the Middle East, and Chavurat Shalom.

An initial concept of the committee was to approach the End the Arms Race steering committee with the proposal of having Israeli Member of Knesset Yosi Sarid as a guest speaker at the mammoth rally of sixty to eighty thousand people. Yosi Sarid has distinguished himself as a spokesperson for peace, justice and good reason by opposing the war in Lebanon right from the start, and by constantly promoting understanding and negotiations between Israel and the Palestinians.

With the Middle East being one of the most volatile areas of the world—the powder keg of superpower relations—the Shalom Committee thought that Sarid's presence and talk would have been most appropriate. Unfortunately, the proposal was turned down on the grounds that no politician was to be given a platform at the rally. As it turned out, the most recent developments in the Middle East would have made Sarid's visit untenable, and his tour of North America has been postponed until September (Middle Eastern political climate permitting).

The Shalom Committee's second step was to invite the entire Vancouver Jewish community to attend the march under the banner: "Shalom + Salaam = Peace." This simple formula was to convey the message that no matter in what language or in what part of the world it may be written, the prerequisites of peace are mutual respect, negotiations, understanding and compromise. In our case this truth was expressed through Hebrew, Arabic and English words, but the same would apply to all the languages of humanity. This invitation was printed in the form of an article in the *Jewish Western Bulletin*.

On the day of the March, up to one hundred Jews marched under the banner. Though we carried a specific identity with a specific message, we shared the universal concern of the other tens of thousands—that of SURVIVAL.

December 1983

Grenada
October 25th, 1983

DIONNE BRAND

The planes are circling,
the american paratroopers dropping,
later Radio Free Grenada stops for the last time
In the end they sang—
"ain't giving up no way,
no I ain't giving up no way"

the OECS riding like birds on a cow
led america to the green fields of St. George's
and wait at Point Salines
while it fed on the young of the land,
eating their flesh with bombs,
breaking their bellies with grenade launchers

america came to restore democracy,
what was restored was faith
In the fact that you cannot fight bombers

battleships, aircraft carriers, helicopter gunships,
surveillance planes, five thousand american soldiers,
six caribbean stooges and the big american war machine,
you cannot fight this with a machete
you cannot fight it with a handful of dirt
you cannot fight it with a hectare of land free from bosses
you cannot fight it with farmers
you cannot fight it with 30 miles of feeder roads
you cannot fight it with free health care
you cannot fight it with free education
you cannot fight it with women's cooperatives
you cannot fight it with a pound of bananas and a handful of fish
which belongs to you

certainly you cannot fight it with dignity

because you must run into the street
you must crawl into the ditch
and you must wait there and watch
your family,
your mother, your sister, your little brother,
your husband, your wife,
you must watch them
because they will become hungry,
and they will give you in to the americans,
and they will say you belong to the militia,
or the health brigade,
or the civil service,
or the people's revolutionary army,
or the community work brigade,
or the New Jewel Movement—
they will say that you lived in the country,
they will say that you are Cuban,
they will say that you served cakes
at the Point Salines airport fundraising,
they will say that you are human,

they will say
that one day last month
you said that for four and a half years
you have been happy,
they will say all this because they want to eat.

And finally you can only fight it with the silence of your dead body.

December 1984
Mission to Nicaragua
An Interview with Ruth Herman

In British Columbia there is a group which calls itself Central American Legal Workers Support Group. Prior to the elections in Nicaragua, fifteen lawyers, five journalists and one biologist, all of whom are in one way or another affiliated with this group, organized themselves for a trip to Nicaragua. Paying their own expenses and in co-operation with the B.C. Law Union and the organization B.C.-Nicaragua, this group left for a two-week visit to Nicaragua. There they were hosted by the Association of Democratic Jurists of Nicaragua. One of the people in this group was Ruth Herman, a practising lawyer in the city of Vancouver.

CJO: Could you please tell us why your group decided to go to Nicaragua?
RH: Our primary purpose was to observe the election and the process of the election. There was no official Canadian observer group but we did know that others from across the country were going and in addition we wanted very much to see what the revolution had done for Nicaragua.
CJO: What were your general observations about the country?
RH: Very clearly, the FSLN [Sandinista Liberation Front of

Nicaragua] are truly the legitimate representatives of the people. They fought from 1962 to 1979 for the overthrow of Somoza and achieved success in July of '79. It is clear that even in this short five-year period the FSLN has brought about tremendous social change in the country. One of the truly great achievements was their Literacy Crusade. When the Sandinistas came to power 52 per cent of the population was illiterate. Today the figure stands at 13 per cent. During this period they also engaged in a health campaign. For the first time in the history of that nation health care is available to all, and diseases which were rampant not so very long ago (e.g., polio) are now coming under control. It is no wonder that a nun in a barrio said to us, "What the revolution has brought for us is hope." What she was saying is that while the material gains have, as yet, not been significant, the people nevertheless have a great deal of hope for the future. It is clear that the people are dedicated to their country and will fight to the death to preserve their revolution. There is no doubt that the major issue in the country, and it supersedes even the elections, is the war being waged by the United States against the people of Nicaragua. All the people we met spoke to us about their yearning for peace. We who were there heard that call and hopefully we can pass it on to the Canadian people. Everywhere in that country you can feel the enormous effects of the war being waged by the U.S. For example, the United States has been instrumental in cutting the import of food and other supplies. International lending institutions have, under U.S. pressure, cut loans to Nicaragua. Other countries have been pressured to isolate Nicaragua, both economically and politically. We were told that because of the war 40 per cent of the economy of the country is geared to defence and tens of thousands of young people are conscripted into the army.

CJO: Did you move about the country? Did you meet with ordinary people?

RH: Our group was housed in a privately owned hotel in Granada, a city 40 kilometres from Managua, Nicaragua. We visited a collective farm, a barrio, and on election day we were in the southern part of Nicaragua in the city of Rivas. Five members of our group could speak Spanish and we had two guides and interpreters, so we had no problems speaking to people and being understood at all.

CJO: By now, most of our readers will have heard about the elections and the outcome, but it would be interesting to hear from someone who was there.

RH: The election was very efficiently organized. It was orderly throughout. There was no sense of intimidation about it. In point of fact, the thing that stood out was the pride the people had in the process. You should know that 40,000 people were trained to be election officials prior to the elections and they took their work very seriously. On election day, at 7 a.m., when we arrived at the polls, people had already lined up for more than an hour. For the people, the entire process was educational. After all, it was the first time in 50 years that these people had a chance to vote in a free and democratic election.

Your readers may be interested in some figures. There were, during the elections, many international observers. Canada did not have any official observers, but the Interchurch Council sent a delegation of six people who have since reported back to External Affairs Minister Joe Clark and the media here at home about the absolutely democratic nature of those elections.

Ninety-three per cent of the people of Nicaragua registered to vote. Eighty per cent actually voted. Of these, 68 per cent voted for the FSLN. Seven parties were on the ballot. Two of these parties each received 12 per cent of the vote. There were 90 deputies to be elected and for each of 15,000 votes received by a given party a seat was allocated in the Assembly. So that, for example, a party which received 45,000 votes would be allocated three seats according to the list provided by each party.

Our whole group came away with a real sense of having witnessed a truly democratic election.

CJO: Naturally, the readers of our magazine are interested in learning something about the Jewish people in Nicaragua. After all, there have been news stories about anti-Semitism there.

RH: I can tell you that our delegation met with the head of the Human Rights Commission in Nicaragua. The person who heads this commission is Sister Mary Hartman, a nun in the Catholic Church who is an American, but has been in Nicaragua since 1962. Her answer to this question is as follows: First, prior to the earthquake in Nicaragua in 1972, there were approximately 150 Jewish families there. As a result of the earthquake many families left. Then, too, there were some who left after the Somoza government was overthrown. The situation today is that there are ten Jewish families in Nicaragua. Ever since the stories of anti-Semitism in Nicaragua surfaced she tells of dozens of rabbis who have come to investigate the situation and none could find any reason for these stories.

It is true that the synagogue is no longer being used as a place of worship, she said, but this was because the members of the ten families were themselves not religious, or they did not feel that they could financially support that institution. In fact, they had sent a cable to Rabbi Rosenthal of the B'nai B'rith in the United States asking whether any aid could be forthcoming in order to reopen the synagogue and they received a reply stating that he would inquire from members of the Nicaraguan community now living in the States about this possibility. No word has been heard from him since.

The whole issue of anti-Semitism in Nicaragua originated with a man by the name of Abraham Gorn. Mr. Gorn, who was implicated as an importer of armaments from Israel for Somoza, was jailed for one week by the Sandinistas. He left the country upon his release, taking the synagogue artifacts. He now resides in Costa Rica. This incident was used by Jeane Kirkpatrick, U.S. representative at the United Nations, to attack the Sandinistas for their so-called anti- Semitism. Sister Mary Hartman offered to put us in touch with members of these ten families if we so desired. Unfortunately we didn't have the time to do that.

CJO: Some final thoughts?

RH: Yes, Nicaragua is a small nation of three million people, half of whom are children. Today it is confronted by the largest and most powerful nation in the world. Its borders are being attacked and its harbor threatened by the American fleet. There are frequent overflights into the territory of Nicaragua. All that the people of that country want is an opportunity to live in a sovereign and free country and create a better life for themselves. I believe that we here in Canada should support them in these endeavors.

CJO: Thank you.

April 1985

Forty Years Later...
An Editorial

Nineteen forty-five was a fateful year in the history of humankind. It was the year of defeat for Hitler's fascism and its Japanese militaristic variant. It was the year of victory for a coalition of Western capitalist democracies and the world's only socialist state—the USSR. It was a coalition which had the support of the great majority of mankind. Hundreds of millions of people supported the combined struggle against fascism with dedication, courage and sacrifice, and rejoiced in the final victory. But the cost of that struggle was ominous, not only to the Jewish people who lost six million souls victimized by the Nazi murder machine, but some 30 million people who lost their lives as a result of Nazi aggression.

The Yalta Agreement, signed on February 11, 1945, by Churchill, Roosevelt and Stalin, was the first step in ensuring "that Germany will never again be able to disturb the peace of the world." This was followed by the momentous collapse of Nazi resistance and the occupation of Berlin by the victorious Red Army on May 8, 1945. The final consolidation of post-war peace plans came with the Potsdam Conference, July 17-August 2 1945, which defined conditions for the destruction of Nazism and the democratic transformation of Germany. It also agreed on revised border lines now in effect in Europe, and on the division of control of occupied Germany between the United States, the Soviet Union, Great Britain and France.

It did not take long for war-time amity and concord to turn into mistrust, suspicion and hostility, whipped up into a state of paranoia by a venal press. The opening gun in the Cold War was Churchill's "Iron Curtain" speech in Fulton, Missouri, some thirteen months after Yalta. But a more important event signalling the onset of the Cold War was the dropping of the atom bomb on Hiroshima and Nagasaki in August 1945, shortly after the Soviet Union's entry into the war against Japan. This awesome display of technology and destructive power was designed, in the opinion of objective analysts, to announce the beginning of "The American Century."

That Cold War, with brief periods of relaxation, has persisted to this day. In fact, under the Reagan government it has reached heights of unprecedented fury and paranoia. It has produced an arms race which is the world's single most important obstacle to human progress and which shows no convincing signs of abating in the foreseeable future. Celebrations of the victory over fascism have been bypassed by both the British and French governments for fear that there might have to be some acknowledgment of the role of the Soviet people in that victory. The West German chancellor saw fit to lend support to the demand for a return of Silesia to Germany by Germans who were expelled from Poland. The Austrian minister of defence personally greeted the return of a notorious war criminal from his imprisonment in Italy. And so it goes...

One must hope that the growing peace movement in Europe and North America can bring about a return of sanity and detente in world relations. They deserve every ounce of support from all people of good will. The victory of the peace movement can provide the key to a world attack on the true enemies of mankind—starvation, drought, disease, illiteracy and poverty. Let us hope that the 50th anniversary of Yalta will see a Europe of independent states, with no foreign troops posted on their soil, and the elimination of nuclear arsenals.

V
Israel and the Middle East

October 1969

Voices of Reason
A Symposium in Israel of Great Significance

GEORGE LEWIS

Some 25 months ago, the ceasefire lines between the Middle East states of Egypt, Syria, Jordan and Israel were arranged through the good offices of the United Nations. It was the hope of all peace-lovers that this was to be the first step towards accommodation and eventual peace in this important and much-troubled area of the world.

Alas, in these 25 months *the fire has never really ceased*. The chain of violence has been so continuous that it is most difficult to discern which action is a retaliation for what incursion that preceded it.

The unceasing guerrilla and terrorist activities, both those originating in the Arab lands beyond the so-called ceasefire lines and those arising inside the present Israeli lines; the artillery duels across the Suez Canal; the air battles and the large-scale military penetrations by the Israeli army (now referred to by General Dayan not as "retaliations" but as "attacks of anticipation"), all make the ceasefire agreement a thing which, in reality, has practically ceased to exist.

Is peace feasible in the Middle East? Will the Arab states directly concerned depart from the infamous Khartoum doctrine of "No recognition, no negotiations"? Will those states earnestly consider the crying needs of their own people for peace and for alleviation of their stark poverty? Will Israel reject the suicidal voice of the "Greater Israel" champions, the Dayans, the Begins and their ilk who, in pursuit of the mirage of "greatness" through annexation, sacrifice the very hope of a future of constructive co-existence and eventual friendly partnership? Will Israel depart from the unbending, sterile and unproductive formula of "face-to-face negotiations with the Arab states or an indefinite situation of neither peace nor war," and embark upon an all-sided, flexible search for peace which, while fully mindful of Israel's security needs, would welcome the work of any intermediaries who might bring the day of peace nearer?

The New Outlook *Symposium*

The growing consciousness among thinking Israelis, especially intellectuals, that the above-posed questions cry for some answers, undoubtedly motivated the editors of the *New Outlook* of Tel Aviv to arrange the symposium under the terse title "To Make War or Make Peace." For some years this journal has dedicated itself to the promotion of Arab-Israeli understanding and the recently held symposium will certainly go far to enhance its prestige and point up its constructive effort.

This symposium was held in March [1969]. However, it is only now that the proceedings have reached us in the form of a combined June-July-August issue of some 300 pages. Some 50 individuals from Israel, Italy, England, France, Belgium and Czechoslovakia participated in the three days of discussion.

The spirit in which this assembly was convened is well indicated by the following statement from the introduction to the report on the symposium. The *New Outlook* editors write:

> The Jewish-Arab conflict is one of the most absurd, tragic, complicated and at the same time most resolvable conflicts. Absurd because it concerns two peoples who have an unequalled record of friendship, co-operation and symbiosis; tragic because it involves suffering and destruction without bringing either of the two sides nearer to the realization of their essential aims—the national and social emancipation of the Arabs and the renewal of Jewish statehood in conditions of peace and security; complicated because in addition to the real conflicts, passions and emotions intervene to prevent rational attitudes. *It is resolvable because under conditions of peace, in a Middle East free from war and an armaments race, the problems in question could be solved equitably and to the benefit of all* [my emphasis—G.L.].

Inevitable War or Initiatives for Peace?

The above was the subject of the first day's discussion at the symposium. Some fifteen speakers took part.

It seems that it was Gideon Hausner, the liberal member of the Knesset, who enunciated the prevailing mood in the ruling circles of Israel when he declared:

> I think that in order to remove the danger of war and to enforce our security, we have to put Jewish settlements in those areas of the occupied territories that we shall have to continue to hold. We have the right, once and for all, after three wars, to secure borders that won't invite aggression or make it easier. That is why we have to

settle in the Golan Heights, in the Jordan Valley, and in other strategic points, even if, when peace comes, we shall be prepared to make agreements that will return part of the occupied territories to the Arab countries in return for true peace.

It must be stated that the overwhelming majority of the participants in the particular panel disagreed with the above contention. It was the feeling expressed by most that the kind of security Hausner's policy envisages is unreal and can only lead to the perpetuation of the present state of affairs.

Avigdor Levontin, professor of law at the University of Jerusalem, discussed security and what it implies for the people of the Middle East. He declared:

> A secure border, to the extent that such a thing exists in our world, isn't a "natural boundary" like a mountain range or a river. This is an anachronistic conception. Nor is it a border mentioned in signed documents. *A border is secure when those living on the other side do not have sufficient motivation to infringe on it* [my emphasis—G.L.].

Answering the annexationists in Israel, Yehoshua Arieli, professor of history at the Hebrew University in Jerusalem, declared:

> The problems facing Israel as a result of the war have increased out of all proportion to the achievements of this war. The areas Israel is holding have become the centre of a total crisis. The struggle between the two sides has gone into a new stage; more extreme, more comprehensive and more fanatical. All the agreements and other balances differentiating between disguised and open war have disappeared. *The region has become the focus of a global struggle.*
>
> While control of the territories created a "security zone," it also created a state of actual war and made the state responsible for the fate of a million Palestinian Arabs subject against their will to the Israeli authorities. Though the deterrent force of the Israeli Defence Army has been increased, the status of the national leadership of the Palestinian terrorist organizations, wearing the garb of a national liberation movement, has also become stronger. The stability of the Arab countries has been shaken. *Israel is paying the price of human sacrifices and is becoming a state living in a state of siege* [my emphasis—G.L.].

The Israeli-Arab member of the Knesset, Abdul Azis Z'ubi, raised the banner of reason for the Arab people when he declared in addressing the symposium:

> At every opportunity I have called on the Arab leaders to give up their political blindness and see that Israel is an independent and sovereign state with the same rights to exist in the Middle East that all other nations have. That is what I have demanded of the Arabs. But I tell the Jews no less, that there will be no peace nor conditions for peace that will be good only for the Jews or just for the Jews.
> *It has to be just and good for both. Settlements, annexations of any kind, don't have anything in common with the striving for a true peace* [my emphasis—G.L.].

Social Implications of the Israeli-Arab Conflict

The second day of this very important symposium was devoted to a consideration of the social implications of the conflict. Many of the speakers discussed the effects upon the moral fibre and the very essence of the existence of the peoples embroiled in the Middle East impasse. In warning those assembled, and Israel, against adopting the policies advocated by the so-called "Greater Israel" movement, Professor Arieli declared that if the policies of such movements were adopted they would bring the State of Israel to the very abyss and "threaten its very existence." He went on to say:

> They would destroy our democracy, damage our souls and create a fanatic and retrogressive society in Israel, culturally and morally... The partisans of annexation, and of including the territories within the State of Israel as an aim and goal of our policy, bar the way to any other solution and are prepared to endanger both peace and security...

A Tel Aviv teacher speaking in this part of the symposium devoted great attention to the effects of the Dayan policies and speeches on the young people. Dani Peter pointed out that more and more Israelis begin to view problems only from their own immediate considerations of what is good for them alone. There is less and less of serious consideration of the problems facing the Arab people and their needs.

Friends of Israel are very conscious of the need to replace the implacable spirit of confrontation with one which aims to make it possible for those in the Arab world who seek peace to place their view before their people without seeming to be traitors to their national interests. It is clear, as was repeatedly pointed out in the symposium, that annexations, the establishment of settlements in the occupied territories, "punitive expeditions" on a mass scale, only help those who seek to impress the Arab people with the idea that Israel is a land of usurpers, expansionists and people who are guilty of total disregard of the rights of their Arab neighbors.

The Refugee Problem

The third day of the symposium was dedicated to the discussion of the thorny refugee problem. With the addition of the Arab population of the occupied territories, especially the Gaza Strip and the territory on the West Bank of the Jordan, Israel's Arab population has grown to a full third of its total population. Hundreds of thousands of Arab people still live in the refugee camps that have existed in Gaza and in West Jordan for more than twenty years. The refugee problem is now more acute than ever.

A great deal hinges on the entire matter of the Palestinians. These are the Arabs who were displaced in the original partition of Old Palestine. These are the Arabs who are not Egyptians or Jordanians. The question that requires a solution hinges on the *full recognition of the right for national self-determination of the Palestinians including the possible formation of a Palestinian state.*

It was the consensus of opinion that such a state cannot be a satellite of Israel and cannot be "created by Israel" as a pseudo-solution to the refugee problem and the Arab-Israeli conflict.

Enlightened opinion, as expressed at the symposium, visualizes the settlement of the refugee problem over a long period of time and as the responsibility of the Arab lands, Israel and the United Nations. Professor J. Khouri of Villanova University in Pennsylvania summed up the problem well when he declared:

> There is little hope that a final solution of the refugee issue could be arrived at until the emotional climate in the Middle East has substantially improved and the Arabs and the Israelis have decided to seek some kind of a political solution to all their major differences. Moreover, any future solution of the refugee problem would entail considerable time, patience and money, perseverance and sacrifices on the part of the U.N. and all the states directly and indirectly involved. *Nevertheless, the Israelis, as well as the Arabs, would probably find that, in the long run, they would have*

to pay a far higher price if the deadlock on the refugee dispute is not broken—for, until it is fully and equitably resolved, the Arab-Israeli dilemma will persist; peace and stability in the Middle East will remain gravely endangered, and Israel will find neither lasting security nor acceptance by her neighbors and will continue to live an isolated and garrison existence in a sea of hate and distrust [my emphasis—G.L.].

The *New Outlook* symposium was of great significance. Although some months have passed since it was held, the problems it has raised *all remain as acutely real today as they were in March.*

Naturally, in a review of proceedings reported on 300 pages of the special issue of *New Outlook*, one could not do justice to all shades of opinions expressed. Those who are actively studying the Middle East situation should read not only the recent encouraging statements of such men as the Egyptian foreign minister, or the proceedings at the U.N.; a reading of the proceedings of the *New Outlook* symposium *is a must*. Here indeed from the three days of broad discussion there emanated the warming and elevating voice of reason.

July-August 1975

An Israeli Coup?

REUBEN SLONIM

Could a military coup occur in Israel? It has happened in Portugal and in Cyprus, but why not Israel?

The question may sound like over-imaginative journalism. This "bastion of democracy in the Middle East," the boast and pride of a generation of liberal Zionists—how can it happen? The very coupling of the State of Israel with military dictatorship appears like something out of fantastic fiction.

Israelis have raised the question themselves, and it is not altogether theoretical.

Months ago, the historic Zionist experiment seemed to be turning sour. Relations with the Arabs were at their lowest in twenty years. Egypt had not yet signed an agreement on the separation of forces at the Suez Canal. The Yom Kippur War had revealed fallacies in sole reliance on the policy of military power. Inflation was—and is—rampant. The government was in a state of near collapse, with religious political parties insisting on their definition of "Who Is A Jew?" before they would enter a coalition, an issue which most Israelis consider marginal if not trivial.

The general elections in December had resulted in a sharp swing to the right. A palpable demoralization had set in.

It was in the depths of this depression—spiritual as well as political and military—with the breakdown of authority seemingly imminent, that the editor of a leading newspaper suggested "a democratic dictatorship" for a limited period.

A strong hand was needed for a time, he said, to galvanize the debilitating will of the people.

The idea was rooted in a recommendation to the late David Ben-Gurion, ten years ago, by his "young Turks" as a way to transform Israel's party-list voting system into the constituency parliamentary pattern (similar to Canada's) in order to introduce greater responsibility into government and the behavior of cabinet ministers.

During the October war there was again talk of a military takeover in Israel. The press, reflecting the general mood, gave the idea extensive coverage.

Now the concept is being revived with the elevation of a former military chief of staff to the premiership and the formation of a government based on a narrow majority that could easily collapse by the defection of several supporters in the Knesset. The country could again be thrown into political confusion.

Israel has had several generals enter politics—Yigal Allon, Moshe Dayan, Hayim Barlev, Ariel Sharon—but this is the first time a general, Yitzhak Rabin, has become the chief politician.

For the next few months, as Rabin reveals the calibre of his leadership, Israel will continue to run the risk of a strong-arm takeover because of the lack of stability in the civilian system.

That is the view of several political scientists and sociologists at Tel Aviv and Jerusalem universities.

Dr. Erik Cohen, sociologist at the Hebrew University, has written the most authoritative article on the possibility of a coup d'etat in Israel as "an exercise in futuristics." He believes that open discussion of the subject is a sign of the nation's strength and a means of helping to prevent such an eventuality.

The Lebanese press has noted Israel's agonizing on "the possibility of a Latin American military coup," but if it ever took place it would be scant comfort to the Arabs. A Jerusalem dictatorship would mean inflexibility of a kind that intensified and provoked animosity and violence.

The mention of a possible coup in Israel triggers the name of Menahem Begin, leader of the right-wing opposition Likud Party and former commander of the Irgun Z'vaei L'umi, the terrorist group that fought the British mandate government and blew up the King David Hotel in the period before the establishment of the state.

Ben-Gurion once called him a fascist, as many Arabs do today. Surprisingly, nobody in Israel has suggested him as an organizer of a coup, and for good reason.

The Likud, which is a combination of Begin's Herut Party and former liberals, is an integral part of the establishment. During the emergency of the Six-Day War in 1967, he served in Golda Meir's wall-to-wall coalition.

In the last 25 years Begin has become not only a skillful parliamentarian but a fervent believer in the democratic method. Some years ago, he visited London and made his peace with his erstwhile British enemies. Israelis see Begin as "a gentleman," who has abandoned the rabble-rousing populist stance.

In Dr. Cohen's view, the person closest to the coup d'etatist image is General Ariel Sharon, who, like Dayan in the Six-Day War, became the national hero in the October war and subsequently joined the right-wing Likud. Since the war, he has attracted considerable support by his criticism of the conduct of the war, the establishment and negotiations with the Arabs.

Much of Likud's increased strength in the general elections may be attributed to Sharon's popularity. Yet even he has immersed himself in the business of parliament and the army and is less noticeable these days.

Nevertheless, Dr. Cohen envisions a scenario in which a right-wing group, oriented mainly to military goals and acting in the spirit of military ethics, could decide that the civilian government is too soft for the hard decisions that must be made vis-a-vis the Arabs and would take over. He calls this the Coup of the Extremists.

The takeover could come once the necessity of returning the occupied territories became an issue of immediate concern, as it will this summer and fall. Sharon, Likud, the religious political parties and the Greater Israel movement are vigorously opposed to any restoration to the Arabs of what they consider sacred soil, promised to the Jews in the Bible.

This stand has considerable support and is bound up with "the Masada spirit," the willingness to die rather than surrender honor, tradition and scriptural faith. It is a powerful weapon in the hands of an ambitious strongman.

Against this is the incipient sentiment in Israel opposed to the saving of border settlements. Dr. Cohen considers these settlements a "sacred cow." The whole idea of settlement and security is a carryover from the 1930s when lightly armed infiltrators constituted the security problem.

In this period of mobile warfare and missiles, fixed border villages are a liability, "unnecessary ballast," in Dr. Cohen's phrase. Contrary to the romantic Zionist literature, he doesn't believe the Masada spirit is strong in Israel. The Israelis are more practical and realistic than people abroad believe. Gradually the sacred cow's importance will diminish, especially when its demise will be crucial to a permanent peace agreement.

So the prospects of a takeover to prevent territorial concessions are small, though they are not to be dismissed.

Of even lower priority is Dr. Cohen's second scenario, which he calls the Coup of the Disenchanted. It envisions a takeover by middle-high officers of the army, disillusioned by the Yom Kippur War.

"In terms of purely military consideration," says Dr. Cohen, "the army did prove itself in the field. But in terms of the myth of Zahal [Israel's Defence Force], of the expectation of the populace, which romanticizes its soldiers, the army fell short."

The encouraging feature of the army is that it is a citizen force, with no military traditions as once existed in Prussia. In possession of such a tradition, Israeli officers, caught between the conviction that they acquitted themselves more than adequately in the field and the popular impression that they did not, might feel themselves "stabbed in the back." But without the appropriate military tradition the theory doesn't have much of a chance of materializing.

Yet, the frustration of the officers could lend support to a government takeover by extremists, although the officers themselves might not initiate the coup.

Dr. Cohen's third scenario is the most plausible. He calls it the Coup of the Responsible, a situation in which politicians become irresponsible and haggle over irrelevant matters, like Who Is A Jew? (Ben-Gurion had the best answer for this—"anybody who thinks he is.")

According to this script, "some military officers, of the type of the present chief of staff (General Mordechai Hod) could decide that the politicians were putting us in an impossible position if somebody does not take hold of the reins of government—not so much in the name of national glory or military tradition but in the name of saving the bloody country."

The sense of responsibility has motivated coups in other countries, most recently in Portugal. It is not impossible in Israel, especially if assisted by the realities of the other two scenarios.

Such a military coup may not occur in the near future, but it is always on the horizon. Israelis may be too sophisticated to succumb to the stupidity of extremist government; their historic experience and the sorrow it engendered argue against such an occurrence.

But a responsible general could walk in some day and simply sit in the prime minister's chair.

July-August 1982

Shadows of Lebanon

PHILIP RESNICK

(On seeing the film Circle of Deceit
by Volker Schlondorff)

Poems begin from inside out
just like films hatched from the story of a sordid war,
Syrians, Christians, PLO
midst the debris of West Beirut's shell-torn streets.
The photography—
staccato shots snuffing out match vendors, rival bands,
walls of flame, burning tires,
hill-top countryside haunting as Galilee or Crete—
holds film-goers riveted
as do the love scenes,
sweets licked off fingers,
lovers crawling in the candle-light
while bombs burst overhead.
Who is deceived, however,

by this cruel hoax of war,
journalists as fickle for a fix
as gamblers at the wheel,
nativists deserting tribe for an orient
where neither Arabist nor Westerner
is quite at home?
In the end Falangists come out as thugs (which they are)
Palestinians as martyred innocents (another verity)
with journalists the hungry Roman crowd,
egging gladitorial combatants on to fraticide.
Our hero, washing blood from his shirt and suit and limbs
edges toward some metaphysical truth
too difficult for the readers of *Der Stern*.
And viewers wandering home
wonder whether Sharon's ring of steel around Beirut today
snuffs out such sights
or sets the stage for pyres so high
Judean hills are scorched by the cedars of Tyre.

July-August 1982

The Lebanese Tragedy

HENRY M. ROSENTHAL

At time of writing, the Lebanese situation is still confused. Israeli troops remain ringed around West Beirut, and artillery and aerial bombardments continue to rain death on helpless civilians trapped within the city. Periodic ceasefires are arranged, only to break down in artillery exchanges which each side blames on the other.

From the beginning, Israel has claimed that it was engaged in a "defensive" action to stop unending raids and attacks on Israeli civilians by the PLO. Israeli spokesmen talk invariably of "mopping up" actions—all very sanitary and reasonable. Begin has repeatedly asserted that Israel covets not one inch of Lebanese soil. The only objective was said to be the setting up of a 25-mile buffer zone. But, in the meantime, Israeli forces overran the UN peacekeeping force, destroyed Tyre, Sidon, Nabatea and other centres of population, invaded areas under Syrian control, and have surrounded Beirut, cutting off all roads leading to this important city.

If the situation is still confused, there seems to be no doubt about Israel's objectives. They demand nothing less than the complete elimination of the PLO as a military and political force in Lebanon. Whether this comes about through the mass deportation of PLO supporters from Beirut or through their annihilation by means of block by block assault on Palestinian neighborhoods seems to make no difference to Begin. His minister of defence, it would appear, favors the military option.

The second objective is the elimination of Syrian forces from Lebanon. According to Israeli spokesmen, this would produce an independent, sovereign government able to act without pressure from Palestinians and Syrians. In fact, it is clear that the Israelis would install a Christian Falangist government in Lebanon which would be nothing more than a puppet administration, acting on behalf of its Israeli/U.S. masters. As a minority faction within Lebanon, the fascist Falange could only maintain power with the direct assistance of Israeli armed forces.

Up to this point, the military scenario, reputedly authored by Ariel Sharon, seems fairly clear. It is also obvious that invasion plans were developed many months, or years, ago, to be held in abeyance until a suitable pretext could be found. What is now becoming clearer is the extent of U.S. complicity in this plan. Of course, the appearance of the U.S. Sixth Fleet off the coast of Lebanon at the beginning of the invasion indicated that the U.S. had prior knowledge of Israeli plans. But it may be that the Israeli policy-makers have gone beyond the limits of jointly planned strategy in their assault on Beirut, and that the U.S. now sees the need for some restraint to avoid massive reactions within Arab countries which could produce serious destabilization in the Middle East. What is still not clear is the extent of complicity on the part of other Arab states in the U.S./Israeli plans.

Will these plans work? One can be sure that these plans will not work in the long run. The Lebanese invasion will simply shore up the tide of rising resentment against Israel by all Arabs, and may produce the kind of Arab unity feared by many Israelis. It will trigger escalating pressure from below on the governments of conservative and "moderate" states, including Saudi Arabia and Egypt, which will endanger existing U.S. alliances in the Middle East. When all is said and done, Israel's current adventure in militarism is an attempt to impose a simplistic military solution on a set of complex problems which require *political*, not military solutions.

What of the short run? Israeli forces are still tightening their ring of steel around beleaguered West Beirut, and periodically cut off access to food, water, medicine and electricity. On top of this, shelling and bombing with fragmentation and phosphorus bombs continue to exact fearful civilian casualties.

The plight of Palestinians becomes more analogous with each passing day to that of Jews before the establishment of the State of Israel. Deserted and betrayed by their friends, driven from their homeland, from Jordan and now from Lebanon, the Palestinians seem slated to be the "Jews" of our time—homeless, stateless and surviving at the whim of foreign governments and hostile occupation forces.

In the meantime, a worldwide wave of revulsion at Israeli actions is steadily mounting, and with it, some increasing questioning of the U.S. role in this ghoulish scenario. The scale of the Israeli invasion is so obviously out of all proportion to the alleged threats to its security that one is almost required by the demands of simple logic to examine the larger blueprint. It can be found in U.S. overall strategy for the Middle East, which casts Israel in the role of *gendarme* enforcing "stability" on the area and its oil supplies.

What of the future? Israel claims it has only two options—full-scale assault on West Beirut or a war of attrition. Either course spells disaster to Israel's survival as a member of the family of nations, and to the future viability of the Jewish state. It can only produce increased Arab hostility, increased isolation in the world, and increasing polarization from within. The only viable option is Israel's complete withdrawal from Lebanon, combined with the recognition of the legitimate national aspirations of the Palestinian people. This is the time for Jews of conscience to make their voices heard.

Ushering in a New Year (papercut) by Joshua Grossbard (August-September 1979)

From the album The Song of Solomon (The Song of Songs); drawing by Shraga Weil (January-February 1987)

September-October 1982

'Peace Now' is Needed Now!

ELIEZER FEILER

On July 3, about 100,000 people demonstrated in Tel Aviv against the war waged by Israeli forces in Lebanon. An anti-war demonstration of such size (in a country with 3.6 million inhabitants), while the fighting is continuing, is quite a feat; it is, by comparison, not less impressive or sizeable than similar demonstrations against wars or war dangers in other countries. "Peace Now," which organized the rally, again proved its grassroots nature, expressing real emotions of wide sections of the Israeli people (unlike the counter-demonstration of war supporters on July 17, organized by the government in support of itself). As such, it came into being instaneously in 1978, and as any such pragmatic movement it has had its ups and downs, and has its strong sides and its weaknesses. It might thus be of interest to dwell in some greater detail on the development of Peace Now.

On March 7, 1978, some 350 reserve officers and combat soldiers of the Israeli army sent to Mr. Begin an open letter wherein they stated: "We write you out of deepest concern. A government that will prefer the existence of Israel within the expanded borders of greater Israel to its existence in peace in the context of good neighborly relations will arouse in us grave misgivings.... A government policy that will lead to the continued rule over one million Arabs is liable to damage the Jewish democratic character of the state, and would make it difficult for us to identify with the basic direction of the State of Israel...." It turned out that the letter expressed genuine feelings of masses of mainly young people and also of intellectuals; over 100,000 signed petitions to the prime minister in the spirit of the letter, and mass demonstrations and vigils for peace began to be frequent events in our country. Since Peace Now was a non-party pragmatic movement, different shades of opinion naturally made themselves manifest; but there were two main slogans which united all of them: "Better a Land of Peace, Than a Piece of Land," and "Peace is Greater Than Greater Israel."

It was only natural that whenever there was a basic change in the Israeli (or Israeli-Arab) political scene, discussions and hesitations appeared within Peace Now. Politically mature circles, both within the movement and around it, always aired their opinions strongly but always tried to avoid endangering the unity and very existence of the first authentic mass peace movement in Israel. In the days of the Camp David euphoria, most of the Peace Now leaders had illusions with regard to Begin, and did not assess correctly the so-called Autonomy Plan. Nor did they pay attention to the global-strategical implications of the Camp David Accords. Later on, during the elections, some thought that an extraparliamentary organization should remain aloof, while others concluded that they should dive into the sea of party politics. Of course, the best political teacher is reality, and thus, after some bitter experiences Peace Now had to reappear in public. Life and political developments in 1981 have shown that an extraparliamentary peace movement is a vital necessity; that Begin's signature at Camp David was meant to facilitate the annexation of the West Bank and Golan—while the so-called Autonomy Plan would annul forever the rights of the Palestinian people. Moreover, within Peace Now, questions were asked why the movement stressed the Zionist basis of its platform, thus preventing the formation of a united Jewish-Arab peacefront. Yoela Har-Shefi, journalist and authoress, expressed this in the MAPAM weekly, *Khotam*, on May 14, 1982: "*This rubber-stamp* [Zionist—E.F.] prevents the affiliation and mass activity of Arab-Israeli citizens in the framework of Peace Now; and it makes doubtful the honesty and seriousness of our claim to fight for the preservation of the democratic character of Israel and for equality of rights of its citizens...."

The "strategic understandings" reached between the Israeli and the U.S. governments served a further item for controversy within Peace Now. Many young peace-fighters didn't grasp what all this was about. But, again, reality made things clear: The Begin-Sharon War in Lebanon with quite open U.S. consent, the Orwellian name of "Peace for Galilee Action" given to the aggressive war against the Palestinians forced Peace Now supporters to make up their minds. After a ceasefire of eleven months, observed fully by the PLO, the Israeli government started a war, but Peace Now hedged. It became incomprehensible that a movement, which expressed courageous and consistent views against the government's policy of oppression in the occupied areas should remain silent at the outbreak of war. But the credibility of Peace Now was at stake. Certainly it was not easy to defy the "national consensus" which had existed during most of Israel's previous wars. Hesitations made themselves felt within the leadership, and all kinds of arguments were introduced for refraining from action: "Israel's war was not necessary, but it is a just war, because the PLO doesn't recognize Israel"; "To push the PLO back 50 km is okay, because they shelled settlements in Galilee"; "Our soldiers are fighting, we should not weaken them by discussion and doubts; the time for criticism will come later...." But the rank and file in Peace Now, the young soldiers themselves, the kibbutzniks, the students and professors demanded action, and criticized those leaders who tried to hold back. A flood of readers' letters swept the MAPAM press to denounce Imri Ron, MAPAM Member of Knesset, who advocated the war. Benyamin Yassur, MAPAM secretary, also came under fire when he tried to prevent kibbutzniks from joining an anti-war demonstration which "The Committee Against the War in Lebanon" had called a week prior to the Peace Now rally. Sporadic anti-war actions took place in towns, campuses, in front of government offices, and soldiers held press conferences. In short, pressure for action mounted, and finally achieved the breakthrough also within Peace Now.

What happened was a classic example, proving the role played by the most conscious political forces in giving expression to the emotions of the masses and initiating a struggle against the war.

1. The relatively narrow Committee for Solidarity with Bir Zeit University called a march in Tel Aviv on June 5 before the invasion into Lebanon which turned into a militant anti-war march of about 2,000 people; the organizers were surprised at the relatively large turnout.

2. This Committee later took the initiative to form together with other left-wing forces, including HAVASH and SHELI, the Committee Against the War in Lebanon. They launched a signature campaign of wide scope, and called for a mass rally to protest against the war on June 26. By that date Peace Now was still hesitating on whether to go into the streets. The success of the rally was spectacular. Between 25-30,000 people followed the call, including many young people, soldiers and kibbutzniks who usually identified with Peace Now.

3. One of the results of this demonstration was that the Peace Now leaders became convinced that it was not only possible, but also vital for their own movement, not to stand aside, but to initiate the widest peace demonstration ever held in Israel. On July 3, the Peace Now rally drew about 100,000 people and found a worldwide echo.

We could give more examples of how the interaction between avantgarde actions of small groups and the emotions of masses makes itself manifest. In 1978 there were groups of gymnasts who told the Ministry of Defence that they doubted the defensive intentions of the government. Later, groups turned up who refused to serve in the occupied territories. In 1981-82 soldiers came out against governmental oppression in the territories. Finally, Peace Now also came to life again and became prominent in such activities. During the present war soldiers have come from the front determined not to keep silent. They publish ads in the press, organize protests in Tel Aviv and Jerusalem (in front of the GHC offices and the PM's Office) and have now started to campaign against serving in Lebanon. The most consistent peace forces in Israel, HAVASH and SHELI, courageously fulfil their political vanguard role, but are wise enough not to attempt domination of the wide, popular anti-war movement. They now stress the necessity to recognize and deal with the Palestinians/the PLO and warn of the evermore dangerous signs of McCarthyism and fascization on the part of the Israeli ruling establishment. But in day-to-day struggles, all opposition forces in Israel try to unite in the widest possible manner around slogans which express the "lowest common denominator": Not to enter (attack) West Beirut and to start talking to the Palestinians.

Were I asked to suggest what progressive Jews the world over should do, my reply would be to try winning over ever greater parts of their Jewish communities and organizations, presenting the Israeli government with these very same demands: REFRAIN FROM ATTACKING (WEST) BEIRUT and START TALKS WITH THE PALESTINIANS.

In urging this, supporters of Peace Now everywhere would also be acting for peace...NOW!

December 1982

Nahum Goldmann: Israel's Government Has Cheated the People

MIKE CASS

CJO European Correspondent

In the holiday resort of Bad Reichenhall where he died, just a few days before his death Nahum Goldmann granted an interview to two reporters from the West German magazine *Der Spiegel*.

Goldmann stated that the aggression against Lebanon was the peak of a false development that Israel took from its inception, since the foundation of the Jewish state. It even goes back to the misconception of Herzl, who failed to recognize that Palestine was populated by Arabs, and not "a land without a people" (for a people without a land). The second mistake Herzl made was to believe that the Jewish problem could be solved by the conception of a modern West European state. Achad Ha'am, opposing Herzl, was of the opinion that what was necessary was a spiritual centre. Since religion, whose power kept the Jewish people in existence for 2,000 years, had lost its hold over most of the people, a new spiritual power, an idea, became necessary to take its place.

Based on his intimate knowledge of the situation, Goldmann maintained that all the wars between the Jewish state and the Arabs could have been prevented. In his opinion, the Six-Day War of 1967 was a misfortune for Israel. From then on began the megalomaniacal expansion with its aggressiveness. Nasser did not want the war, but Israel saw a good chance for a big victory. The misfortune with the wars of the Israelis is that they are "victorious unto death." (Goldmann uses the German term *Totsiegen* and points out that only in the German language does such a word exist.) As a result, the major effect of Israeli politics is the preoccupation with "security," on which most of the money is spent.

Major blame for the wrong political development of Israel, Goldmann put on the USA, who determined Israel's policy. Goldmann recalled that after World War II he convinced the Americans that the only solution was the division of Palestine (into a Jewish and Arab state). After the UN decision the U.S. State Department and the Pentagon wanted to reverse the decision, but the Russians prevented this and helped the young Jewish state in its war of 1948. Goldmann recalled that Ben Gurion twice stated to him: "Without Russia, Israel would not have been created." The Russians expected the new state to remain neutral, as Goldmann had always stressed in negotiations with the Russians. But then, in the developing East-West conflict, Israel totally sided with the Americans and the U.S. became pro-Israeli.

In the course of time it came to the point that the U.S. looked upon Israel as a bulwark against Russian influence in the Near East. "*De facto*, Israel today is a satellite of the United States, what in my opinion is a travesty of Jewish history. We did not have the prophets and the bible and our whole culture to become, after 2,000 years, a satellite of the United States in the Near East," said Goldmann, and he continued: "You cannot have peace in the Near East without the Soviet Union."

Goldmann stood for a neutral Israel, guaranteed by the big powers. The idea of a neutral Israel Goldmann discussed with United Nations General Secretary Dag Hammarskjold, who then presented it to Egyptian President Nasser. Nasser's response to Hammarskjold was: "Tell Mr. Goldmann his idea is a basis [for peace]." Goldmann continually maintained there is no alternative to constant war except a neutral Israel.

Goldmann recalled that in 1947, before the proclamation of the Jewish state, he got a hint from the Egyptian embassy in Washington that Egypt wanted a secret discussion with Goldmann and Sharett on how to prevent a war with the Jews. Goldmann telephoned to Ben Gurion and asked him to delay the proclamation of the State of Israel by three or four weeks. Ben Gurion later told Goldmann that, due to the existing enthusiasm amongst the people, a delay was not possible.

Camp David, Goldmann said, only brought a partial peace, and this was not enough. Camp David rests on a misunderstanding, if not an outright deceit. Goldmann referred to three long talks he had with Sadat. Sadat believed that the return of Sinai would be a precedent for the withdrawal from the West Bank.

"Israel," Goldmann said, "has not become a state of intellectuals, not a state that lives by the spirit, not a state of social renewal, but a little America in the Near East, with a strong army and a large armaments industry, with friends like Nicaragua under Somoza's rule, and South Africa. All Zionist leaders, from Herzl to Weizmann, would turn in their graves, if they could see what has become of Israel... The Jewish people has stayed alive thanks to the prophets, thanks to Moses and the bible, thanks to Einstein and Heine, but not because of the generals or Begin demagogues. If Israel remains as it is today, it is a caricature of Jewish history, a total disfiguration. If Israel remains as it is today, it will very quickly throw all Jews in the world into conflict."

To expect that a majority of Jews would go to Israel is an illusion, Goldmann said, a naive belief of Herzl's. Begin's aggressive policies and the solidarity of most Jews with him will strengthen anti-Semitism in the world. In history, Jews have been bearers of unrest. The world accepted it, as long as the unrest-bearers were such men as Yeshaya and Einstein. But bearers of unrest like Begin and Sharon, or generals who have gone wild, the non-Jewish world will not suffer for long.

Goldmann then said he was for the Palestinians to have their own state, in a confederation with Jordan. But they themselves would have to decide this—it cannot be forced on them.

The bombardments of Beirut, Goldmann said, was a criminal action. The Israeli government has cheated the people. Sharon has cheated the government and the government has cheated the people.

Two positive factors have arisen, said Goldmann:

1. The PLO has become convinced to give up fighting by war-like actions and terrorism and Arafat's position has been strengthened against the radicals. Goldmann hoped Arafat would form an exile government that will be recognized by a UN majority.

2. The relationship between Israel and the U.S. has become strained; if

it comes to a confrontation between the U.S. and Israel, the Israelis will overthrow Begin.

The most difficult problem concerns the issue of Jerusalem. The Arabs will never accept Old Jerusalem as the capital of Israel. So Jerusalem will have to be divided—not physically by a wall. The new city of Jerusalem, where the parliament and the government of Israel is, where the Arabs have no holy places, can remain the capital of Israel. The old city must be neutralized. The Arabs must be able to go there without an Israeli visa. There could be a mixed Jewish-Arab police force.

Nahum Goldmann, in conclusion, spoke of his great dream, a kind of Near East federation between Palestine, Israel and Jordania. If the three states co-operated economically, Goldmann visualized that they could become, in one or two generations, one of the great centres of the world.

October 1983

Chomsky, Israel and Nuclear War

NORMAN EPSTEIN

Since the fateful Six-Day War of 1967, which resulted in Israel's occupation of more than double its UN-sanctioned territory, Noam Chomsky has issued a veritable torrent of passionately written, carefully annotated letters, articles and polemics on the subject of Israel and the Palestinians.

These articles culminated first in the book *Peace in the Middle East?* (Vintage Books, 1974) and now in *The Fateful Triangle: The United States, Israel and the Palestinians* (South End Press). An excerpt from the latter, still unpublished book recently appeared as "The Middle East and the Probability of Nuclear War" in the July 1983 issue of *Socialist Review*.

Noam Chomsky's international reputation as a linguist is almost matched by his reputation as a combative political writer uncompromisingly committed to the causes of peace with justice. He espouses first, second and third world liberation; civil and human rights the world over, not just in myopically selected areas which depend on one's loyalties to one or other of the two great imperial powers; and libertarian socialism. This brand of socialism is derived from the traditions of both anarcho-syndicalism and council communism (a left Marxist theory of self-government via workers' councils in industry—attacked by Lenin as "infantile leftism"). It is poles apart both from the social-democratic brand of parliamentary "socialism" which attempts to put a human face on avaricious corporate capitalism, and from the Leninist brand of vanguard "socialism" which does away with private corporate entities only to vest all power over the producing classes in a privileged monolithic state bureaucracy.

Chomsky has cited as one of the models for libertarian socalism the earlier "Israeli kibbutzim, which for a long period really were constructed on anarchist principles: that is, self-management, direct worker control, integration of agriculture, industry, management" (N. Chomsky, *Radical Priorities*, Black Rose Books, 1981, p. 246). After the establishment of the state in 1948, adds Chomsky, the kibbutz ". . . became integrated into the State and in my view lost a fair amount of its libertarian socialist character through this process and through other processes which are unique to the history of that region," though a few years later he himself ". . . spent several very happy months working in a kibbutz and for several years thought very seriously about returning permanently" (*Peace in the Middle East?*, p. 51). No doubt it is the superimposition of the subsequent tragic political and military events in the Middle East on this happy personal experience which accounts for much of the force and passion of Chomsky's writings on Israel and the Palestinians.

In the aforementioned excerpt from his forthcoming book, Chomsky attempts to broadly summarize his own basic assumptions and those of a large international consensus with respect to the territory of the former Palestine and its claimants. He also analyses the assumptions of three important protagonists in the Middle East crisis—Israel as represented or misrepresented by successive Israeli governments, the Palestinians as represented or misrepresented by the PLO and the government of the USA. Chomsky himself asserts ". . . the principle that Israeli Jews and Palestinian Arabs are human beings with human rights, equal rights; more specifically, they have essentially equal rights within the territory of the former Palestine. Each group has a valid right to national self-determination in this territory. Furthermore, I will assume that the State of Israel within its pre-June 1967 borders had, and retains, what everyone regards as the valid rights of any state within the existing international system."

By artfully defining "rejectionism" as ". . . the denial of the right of self-determination to one or the other of these two groups," he is able to show that *both* sides have been guilty of rejectionism. However, he maintains that, given the power relations between Israel, the world's fourth greatest military power, and the Palestinians, anti-Palestinian rejectionism is at present much more significant a problem for the Palestinians than anti-Israel rejectionism is for the Israelis. A broad international consensus, which includes most of the Arab governments and the dominant wing of the PLO, is now prepared to recognize Israel's right to exist in return for a Palestinian state in the West Bank and the Gaza Strip. But this consensus excludes both Israel and the USA.

The Reagan peace plan, which called for a freezing of Israeli settlements on the West Bank and a "domestic authority" transfer from Israel to the Palestinian inhabitants of the West Bank and Gaza, nevertheless opposed "the establishment of an independent Palestinian state in the West Bank and Gaza." Even this rejectionist plan was angrily denounced by the Likud government of Israel, which is not about to give up the West Bank's water supply, nor the West Bank "guest workers" who do much of the "dirty work" in Israel. The West Bank also provides a controlled monopoly market for Israeli goods and it now houses an unconscionable number of Jewish settlements.

It is when Chomsky attempts to answer the question as to what might happen if in the future ". . . the United States comes to join the international consensus which recognizes the right of Israel and the Palestinians to self-determination within secure and recognized boundaries" that we are suddenly confronted with a nightmarish possibility. Drawing liberally from an article by Yoram Peri in the Israeli Mapai (Labor Party) Journal, *Davar*, of October 1, 1983, he argues that the earlier Israeli government policy of maintaining the political status quo in the Middle East has now been supplanted. Israel now seeks the progressive de-stabilization of surrounding countries, starting with Lebanon, with the aim of creating a new reality, i.e., a Greater Israel. This new strategy could conceivably lead Israel to undertake adventures without American military support. Some American military analysts have in fact begun ". . . to fear that Israel's military power had reached such a high level, thanks to United States assistance programs, that the state could no longer be controlled and might pose a major national security problem for the United States by carrying out aggressive actions on its own contrary to American interests." Should the U.S. attempt in the future to force a non-rejectionist settlement on Israel, both Chomsky and several Israeli observers fear that Israel could quite conceivably behave like a "crazy state," to use the language of the international affairs literature. They could unleash their whole military arsenal, including the nuclear weaponry which most military analysts attribute to them, against surrounding targets (they will even have the capability in the near future of striking the southern USSR with Cruise missiles). This could force the USA and the USSR into an inevitable Armageddon, with Israel wreaking on these "Philistines" a collective "Samson's revenge."

This terrifying picture of Israel, as potentially a blindly destructive *golem* created by the USA, is the sharpest inversion yet imagined of the utopia conceived by the original socialist-Zionist *chalutzim* and *chalutzot* (pioneers). The evidence for this picture adduced by Chomsky in the present excerpt from his book is too skimpy to be entirely convincing, and one must await publication of the entire book before appraising it more definitively. Even without this extrapolation of present reality, however, the situation in the Middle East today is horrifying and untenable, and one does not have to be a "Jew Against Zionism" to support Israelis such as those in Peace Now who are making concerted efforts to change the ultimately self-destructive military and political course being taken by the State of Israel.

January-February 1984

On the Threshold of 1984
Some Afterthoughts

J. LIPSKI

It is not an easy task to share with the readers some afterthoughts on problems of Israel that are extremely complicated and have been seriously aggravated. It is hard for a progressive tribune to reflect the life of the Jewish state that was born after so many years of torment, as the realization of so many hopeful dreams. The vision of the state, that was meant to be a light to the nations, has led to disappointments because the reality has proved to be entirely different. It has become hard, therefore, to describe the real life, because people wanted to "hear good news from Israel," or a balanced account of "the good and the negative things" in the State of

Israel, preferring to hear the myths about Israel rather than its reality. We have not only pictured the daily life and reality, but have pointed day after day, week after week, to alternatives that will lead the country to a safe harbor of peace and security. We have identified the forces, moves and actions that are detrimental to the achievement of peace while pointing at the same time to the Jewish-Arab forces in Israel, in the region and in the world, where actions can lead toward a safe peace, by dragging the state out of the swamp of costly wars. We did not hesitate to emphasize that there is a choice of preventing wars and putting the country on a safe road toward peace and co-operation with the neighboring Arab world, based on Soviet-American co-operation.

In the course of many years a myth has been created, that all wars between Israel and the Arab countries have been defensive operations on the part of Israel, because the neighboring Arab states have never accepted Israel's existence. Therefore, there was no choice but to concentrate upon building a strong army for the defence of Israel. In this context, accusations are raised by the peace-loving circles that the Israeli leaders (of the Alignment and still moreso of the Likud government) are half-hearted about seeking peace, and pile up roadblocks to a peaceful settlement. People simply would not believe the accusations that Israeli leaders are sometimes opposed to peace initiatives or even initiate wars.

The costly, bloody war in Lebanon has shed light, like a projector, on this myth and destroyed it. Not only the Jewish-Arab Communists and the Peace groups, but many other segments of the Israeli public understand that this war could have been prevented. It was initiated by the Likud, in response to U.S. global strategy, not to the interests of Israel. A deeper analysis of the developments since the establishment of the State of Israel, in the light of the war in Lebanon, helps to understand that an entirely different development would have been possible if another conception was adopted, seeking co-operation with the neighboring Arab countries instead of confrontation. This would not have been an easy, but a possible alternative, saving casualties and economic ruin.

It is a historic fact that after the foundation of the State of Israel after the war of independence was over, an armistice was concluded in 1949 between the young Jewish state and all neighboring Arab countries. An appropriate, clever policy could have turned the armistice into a stable peace. This does not mean that it would have been an easy task, but the very fact of signing the armistice proves that there were partners for negotiations. Even in the Israeli government of those days there were differences of opinion between those supporting Ben-Gurion's militaristic conception, who proclaimed that we are not ready to "yield an inch, nor to accept a single refugee," and the conception of agreement advocated by Moshe Sharett. Maybe, if the policy of understanding would have prevailed, Israel's history might have taken another course and we would have peace now. How many sacrifices, tears and pain could have been saved.

It is also an almost indisputable fact that the Sinai-Suez campaign of 1956 had been prepared by Ben-Gurion in partnership with the Anglo-French imperialistic forces against the Arab peoples. That war, initiated by Israel, had nothing in common with Israel's true, fundamental interests. How many tears and how much blood has been shed for the interests of the Anglo-French oil magnates of the Suez Canal? That war surely has not brought nearer the understanding with the Arab peoples.

Eventually it turned out that even the Six-Day War was no defensive war, launched because Israel's existence was in danger. The former chief of the general staff, "Raful," declared in an interview, published in *Yediot Aharonot*, in reply to a question by a journalist, asking whether there was no other choice, since a knife was pointed at our throat: "Now you say that one has started the war because a knife was pointed at our throat. What knife has been pointed at our throat in 1956 [in the Sinai-Suez war]? What knife has been pointed in 1967? Egyptian divisions in Sinai? This is a knife? *Maybe if we had not started shooting in 1967, the war had not broken out...*"

Haaretz (January 12, 1982) has reported that "Robert McNamara has *approved the outbreak of the war in 1967.*" This was also confirmed by A. Sharon (in *Kol Israel*, June 4, 1982) and M. Begin (in *Yediot Aharonot*, August 20, 1982). M. Begin pointed out that "we could have waited. We could have sent the army home. Who knows if they would have attacked us at all. There is no proof of that. There are some proofs to the opposite." This means that notwithstanding hysterical outcries in some extremist Arab circles about throwing the Jews into the sea, an astute policy might have prevented the war. How many casualties could have been avoided? How many young soldiers might still be with us?

Peace-supporting circles are convinced that the Yom Kippur War could have been prevented, if the Israeli government had accepted in 1971 the Jarring proposals involving a withdrawal from Sinai. However, we remember Moshe Dayan's declaration that "better Sharm-e-Sheikh without peace than peace without Sharm-e-Sheikh." At the same time, the developments among the neighboring Arab peoples have been underestimated and people were confident of Israel's military superiority.

The main reason for the defeat of the Alignment (Labor Party-Mapam) in the 1977 elections and the rise to power of the Likud was the disappointment at the policy of the Alignment that failed to achieve peace while the masses were tired of wars. After its rise to power, the Begin government concluded a peace agreement with the biggest Arab state. For a minute there was a flash of hope that it was the Begin government who, contradictory to all predictions, had led the country toward the much-desired peace. However, this was but an illusion, because the Begin government believed that after giving the Sinai Peninsula back under the pressure of the American rulers (who, in return for that prize—Sinai—wanted to include Egypt in their strategic global plan), they would be able to hold the other territories that were occupied in 1967. The Likud rulers have intensified the oppression of the Palestinian population and, at the same time, achieved a closer stratigical co-operation with the American rulers, directed against the Soviet Union.

Just as the victory in the Six-Day War and the addition of territories, the annexations of East Jerusalem and the Golan Heights have not strengthened Israel's security, neither has the peace with Egypt and the co-operation with the U.S. rulers consolidated peace in the region. On the contrary, it led to the war in Lebanon which was aimed at liquidating the Palestinian movement and establishing a "new order" in Lebanon, as part of American global strategy that has nothing in common with Israel's interests. How many lives were sacrificed on that altar—for what purpose?

"A year and a half we are stuck in that cursed war, that isn't a war any more, but a death-post, mobilizing against us new enemies, nagging at the motivation of our youth to defend Israel... the Lebanese adventure is but harmful to Israel and we don't know how to end it." So writes Chana Zemer, chief editor of *Davar* (November 11, 1983). However, the peace forces in Israel are growing. "Bring home the soldiers from Lebanon!" is the loud call voiced by increasing numbers of Israelis.

The war in Lebanon has crushed the whole conception that there is nobody to negotiate with, that there is no Palestinian people and that all Arab countries only want to destroy Israel. True, there are extremist tendencies in the Arab countries and among the Palestinians. But in recent years the dominant tendencies call for solving the tragic conflict by way of negotiations. All neighboring Arab countries, as well as the Palestinians, agreed in Fez, Morocco, to a peaceful solution, thereby accepting L. Brezhnev's peace plan for the Middle East that guarantees Israel's right to exist. No need to say that one has to show readiness to give up the areas occupied in 1967.

These occupied territories plus the southern occupied part of Lebanon are a heavy burden for Israel, causing casualties and at the same time devouring colossal resources that are needed for the development of the country. That is what virtually ruins the country economically. This is the main reason for the galloping inflation. It also sharpens the conflict with the Palestinian population which resents the Israeli occupation. Let us point out that among the Palestinians, among the Arab population in Israel and in the occupied territories, those circles which are opposed to the occupation but are prepared for a peaceful co-operation are growing in influence.

In previous years, only the Communist Party and peace-loving circles emphasized the need to change the present policy in Israel's best interests. As a result of the war in Lebanon, various other groups have started raising their voices and warn against the expanding danger of war. For the first time in Israel's history, scores of soldiers have preferred to go to jail rather than serve in Lebanon. For the first time, a high-ranking army officer has refused to lead his military unit in the battles in Beirut, because his conscience did not allow him to join the fighting in the densely populated city. "Women Against Silence," mothers, wives, sisters of soldiers call for an end to the silence, and raise the alarm against sacrificing young lives in the Lebanese bloodshed as being against Israel's best interests. This opposition against the war in Lebanon shows that people understand that every "victory" weakens the country, and instead of building schools, hospitals, homes, factories and farms, money is wasted on keeping an army in Lebanon, on guarding the settlements in the areas occupied in 1967, thereby enriching the well-to-do while lowering the living standard of the poor.

That is why the struggle against this policy is in Israel's vital interest. Broad circles have adopted the slogan that "Peace Now" is possible, that "there is a limit," that the attempt to silence, to justify, to smooth this policy clearly contradicts Israel's interests. The opposition against the war in Lebanon, against the attitude that was dominant so far, is a sign of honor for Israel. It serves Israel's best interests.

That is why I wish you success in the courageous struggle, not only against the war, occupation and policy of discrimination, but also in your efforts to enlighten and to mobilize the Jewish public, to support the fight for "Peace Now" that can be turned into a reality. The solidarity with these efforts, with the Jewish-Arab struggle for "Peace Now," is the best support in the fight for preventing another dangerous war, for pulling the bandwagon of the State of Israel out of the political swamp in Lebanon and out of the economical blind alley. For these endeavors you must be strengthened and encouraged in your struggle for progress, for democracy, for an Israeli-Arab peace and for an Israeli-Palestinian peace. Only the victory of peace can guarantee the existence and peaceful development and upbuilding of the State of Israel.

November 1984

Report on the Geneva Conference

ASHER NEUDORFER

We stood in the cavernous halls of the UN Palais de Nations in Geneva, Switzerland, where royalty, presidents and dictators had walked before us. Four of us, two Israeli Jews, two Palestinians, enjoying a moment's break in the UN-sponsored conference of non-governmental organizations (NGOs) on the question of Palestine. To the untrained eye we were but small actors against the backdrop of Middle Eastern tragedy and passion. Yet as we all shook hands and resumed our seats as the next meeting was called to order we felt part of an historic movement—one which must end in peace because the alternative is too horrendous to contemplate. The thoughts running through all our minds asked whether the bonds of solidarity we were building would be strong enough to face the violence and prejudices that others will surely throw against us.

Over a hundred NGOs and 26 experts from the legal community and governmental sector attended, drawn from over 30 countries, including delegations from both Western and Eastern Europe, Africa, Asia, North America, and most significantly, from both Israel and the occupied territories of Palestine. Included among the long list of notable speakers were Zehdi Labib Terzi, permanent observer of the Palestine Liberation Organization (PLO) to the UN, Neil MacDermott, secretary-general of the International Commission of Jurists, Rabbi Elmer Berger from the American Jewish Alternatives to Zionism, and Bishop Kapuchi from Jerusalem.

Israeli Peace Groups

Israeli society is not a monolithic community blindly supporting its government's policies of expansionism and repression, contrary to the impression often given in the Canadian press or by the self-proclaimed leaders of the North American Jewish communities. In 1982, for example, over 400,000 Jews marched in the streets of Tel Aviv (out of a total Israeli population of 3.5 million), condemning their government's invasion of Lebanon and complicity in the horrible massacres at Sabra and Chatilla.

In Geneva I met with a wide variety of these Israeli peace activists, from such organizations as Israeli Council For Israeli-Palestinian Peace (which includes two Knesset members), Democratic Front For Peace and Equality (four members of Knesset), Israeli League for Human Rights, New Direction (Sephardic Jewish community), Democratic Women's Organization, etc. All of them recognized that the key to a just and lasting peace in the Middle East is the recognition of the right of self-determination for the Palestinian people, including the creation of an independent Palestinian state on the now-occupied West Bank, Gaza and Jerusalem. Dr. Joseph Algazy (League for Human Rights), in his moving address to the conference, said:

> The Israeli-Palestinian conflict has cost till today a very high price of blood and resources, has left behind widows and orphans and brought pain and torment to a lot of people... Till all parties will be convinced that there is no choice but peace I shall continue, together with my colleagues in Israel, to fight for human rights, collective and individual, to fight against the camp of war and hatred, to consolidate the camp of peace inside Israel.

Maxim Ghilan (International Jewish Peace Union) added:

> The first and foremost struggle just now is that leading to the creation of a Palestinian national state in the West Bank and Gaza. And it is up to us, democratic and progressive Jews and Israelis, to mobilize our efforts in this direction. For whoever controls the destiny of another people cannot remain free.

This brave struggle did not go unnoticed by the Palestinians present. Shafik el Houte (executive council, PLO) extended his solidarity to them by telling the delegates:

> These courageous men and women in Israel who are campaigning for peace represent a pioneering generation of Israeli people. These people need your support as much as the PLO needs your support. They face harassment and threats which we understand... It is ironic that those who strive for war are deemed heroes while those who strive for peace are not so considered.

Palestinian Situation Deteriorates

Palestinian delegates travelled to the conference at considerable personal risk. Raja Shehadeh, from the occupied West Bank city of Ramallah and a founding member of Law in the Service of Man (a West Bank legal aid organization) described the ruthless policies of land annexations which continue unabated. Although only 4 per cent of the West Bank population are Israeli settlers, some 40 per cent of the land has been annexed by them. A variety of measures are used to discourage the Palestinian population from remaining—from violent repression (including the universally condemned practice of "collective punishment") to more subtle but no less effective measures. Bus routes are rerouted from Palestinian population centres, scarce water resources diverted, century-old olive orchards are bulldozed for Israeli settlements or military highways.

Yet despite the understandable bitterness towards Israel, many Palestinians are willing to live in peace with Israel if only they were given the freedom to their own land. Anwar Nusseibeh (chairman of the Jerusalem Electric Co.) remarked: "The alternative to debate is violence and by all evidence violence compounds the problem. We need peace to eliminate the nightmare of occupations and the indignity of refugee camps."

And in a special panel discussion concerning the role of religious institutions, Bishop Kapuchi of Jerusalem (now in forced exile) said:

> To applaud the progress towards peace needs two hands. Palestinians have on numerous occasions expressed willingness to negotiate and recognize Israel. Have the Israeli government done anything to join in this process towards peace... Peace is a capital, a treasure, without which we are condemned to violence, but with which all is possible.

International Peace Petition Adopted

At the closing session, delegates strongly supported the convening of a UN International Peace Conference on the Middle East. It was seen as essential that the conference be inclusive and be attended by the representatives of Israel and the PLO, those Arab states party to the conflict and both the U.S. and USSR. Just as the UN General Assembly resolutions recognize the right of both Israelis and Palestinians to self-determination and statehood, these principles were seen as the basis for any negotiated peace.

To support this proposed conference and to bring it to the attention of peoples throughout the world, a decision to launch a campaign to collect millions of signatures (proposed by the International Jewish Peace Union) through an international petition was adopted. Montreal's Le Regroupement Pour Un Dialogue Israel-Palestine then proposed that the petition would be launched simultaneously throughout the world on November 29, 1984—the UN Day of International Solidarity with the Palestinian People.

Some Personal Reflections After Geneva

When I left for Geneva I was apprehensive. On the one hand the fanatic Kahane had just been elected to the Israeli Knesset. On the other hand I, as an Israeli-born Jew, worried how the legitimate aspirations of my people were going to be seen against the history of the persecutions committed against the Palestinian people. I left Geneva reassured on two levels—one, that the fanatics in Israel represent just one side of the coin, the progressive forces for peace the other; and two, the international community which has been active in promoting Palestinian rights, including the PLO, recognize this fact and do not deny Israel's right to exist. This, however, cannot be affirmed at the expense of another people.

The tragedy of the Middle East is that two peoples, each with its own history of oppression and persecution, find themselves today thrown together, for better or for worse, on a small sliver of land, rich in history and tradition. Each can claim with some justice a need for a homeland, yet the past 35 years have witnessed the realization of a centuries-old dream for one people at the expense of denying another people that same historic right.

The Middle East has for too long stood on a powder keg. The violence of the continued oppression of the Palestinian people, or the denial of Israel's right to exist, is being rejected by peace forces on both sides. In short, the dangers to both peoples of the region, and with it the ever present nuclear threat to the whole world, must rule out violence as a solution to the Middle East question. Only a peaceful solution, based on justice to the Palestinian people and mutual recognition of both peoples—a two-state solution—can bring about a resolution to the fighting. The tragedy is that till men like Dr. Algazy and Raja Shehadeh are given a chance to sit down and negotiate their futures, many more mothers and fathers will bury sons and daughters before their time. As a father of two boys myself, I can understand no greater senseless waste than that.

January-February 1985

Mattiyahu Peled
Peace Advocate

ASHER NEUDORFER

The Palestinian problem cannot be eliminated. It can only be resolved.

Question: When does a major-general fight for peace?
Answer: When he has witnessed the sufferings and injustices that war brings with it. Such a man is Matti Peled.

In November Mattiyahu Peled, Jewish member of the Israeli Knesset and an outspoken advocate of peace with the Palestinian people, spoke to receptive audiences in Montreal, Toronto and to an inter-parliamentary senate committee in Ottawa. "There is a need for a dramatic political reappraisal of Israeli policies," Peled cautioned. "Peace in the Middle East cannot be achieved without involving the Palestinians and their representatives, the PLO, in that process." Who is this man that some, like Meir Kahane, the racist champion of the Israeli fanatic right-wing, have labelled a traitor; whose successful candidature in the last elections was blocked till the last minute by the minister of defence and the Likud; who is considered a personal friend of PLO chairman Yassir Arafat and the late Palestinian martyr Issam Sartaoui?

Peled, born in Haifa in 1923, joined the Jewish Palmach in 1940, remained in the army for 21 years, from 1947-68, reaching the rank of major-general, and became a member of the general staff during the Six-Day War. In 1968 he left the army convinced that its policies in the occupied territories were unjust to the Palestinians and suicidal for Israel. He became head of the Arab Literature Department in Tel Aviv University and in 1975 helped found and became chairman of the Israeli Committee for Israeli-Palestinian Peace (ICIPP). In that capacity he has had many dialogues with representatives of the PLO, cementing friendships which have endured the bitterness of the region. In 1984, just months before the election, he helped found the Jewish-Palestinian Progressive List for

Peace (PLP) and today with Palestinian lawyer Mohammed Miary represents the fledgling PLP in the Knesset. He was elected on a platform which includes (1) immediate Israeli withdrawal from southern Lebanon, (2) direct face-to-face negotiations with the Palestinians and the PLO towards a peaceful solution of the Middle East conflict, and (3) the creation of a Palestinian state in the now-occupied territories of the West Bank, Gaza and East Jerusalem.

In the course of his talks Peled covered many areas:

Discrimination

A vital plank in the PLP's platform is the struggle for full equality of Palestinian citizens of Israel and against government discrimination and racism:

"Arab discrimination is based *in* the law (unlike the discriminations that other groups like the Sephardim must also face). Social services are denied Arab citizens of Israel. Vital governmental funding to Arab population centres are denied because, for example, they are simply never given the status of cities or towns and the consequent increase in development monies. Arab centres of 20-25,000 are still considered villages."

(In a recent development, and due in part to the initiative of the PLP, the new Israeli coalition government has decided to grant city status to one of the largest Arab centres in Israel, Um-El-Fahm—the same city where Kahane tried to march a few dozen of his brownshirts to force the evacuation of all Arabs, only to be met with a human chain of tens of thousands of Jews and Palestinians.) "All forms of discrimination must be eliminated," Peled said, "because firstly it is unjust and secondly if there is no equality within Israel how can Israel live in equality with the Arab states in the region?" To that end the PLP is calling for the rights of all Israeli citizens to be guaranteed by a democratic constitution.

Economic Crisis

The economic crisis of unprecedented dimensions has brought the Israeli economy to the brink of total collapse. Peled attributes this to three main causes:

1. A military defence budget which today occupies 30 per cent of the GNP (comparable figures for the U.S. are 6 per cent, the USSR 12 per cent, Western Europe 4-5 per cent, Eastern Europe 2-3 per cent). "Economically this represents a waste. Israeli industry can no longer compete on the international market because much needed capital goes, not to the renewal of machinery, but to the war effort. In turn this has resulted in

massive social cutbacks—the only return from the defence budget has been increasing insecurity."

2. Government subsidies to Israeli settlements in the occupied West Bank ate up an additional $600 million in 1983 alone. These settlements (started under the Labor government, intensified by Begin and now continued by Labor's Peres), opposed throughout the world, have attracted less than 40,000 settlers (less than 1 per cent of Israel's population) despite attractive government encouragement.

3. The disastrous Lebanese mire which adds $500 million in occupation costs with each passing year.

The result is an inflation rate of 1200 per cent, unemployment, emigration, complete bankruptcy of all reserves, and an annual pilgrimage to Washington by Israeli leaders begging for money. "Economically Israel cannot continue supporting a policy based on war with its Arab neighbors. The treasury is empty and even American aid is insufficient."

Lebanon

"The Lebanon invasion has been an acknowledged failure," said Peled, "from a military, political, economic and moral point of view. After failing to destroy the PLO, Israel now finds itself trying to figure ways to withdraw from Lebanon!" The solution is no mystery, according to Peled—immediate and unconditional withdrawal, a demand supported by hundreds of thousands within Israel. "The Lebanese fiasco," Peled warns, "should teach us one lesson. The Palestinian problem cannot be eliminated. It can only be resolved and that through political negotiations."

A number of questions from the audience allowed Peled to further elaborate:

PLO—'Terrorist'?

How can Israel negotiate with a "terrorist" organization like the PLO, one person asked, one which doesn't even have an elected leadership? "First of all," Peled explained, "I am not disturbed by your use of the term 'terrorist' in relation to the PLO because I used to belong to an organization—the Haganah—that the British called 'terrorist,' but we thought we were concerned with fighting for a noble cause. We did not let the term overly distract us. Secondly, it is not unusual that the PLO is not an elected body and has within its ranks various tendencies. Certainly that was the situation in the Zionist movement before the establishment of Israel. In fact, before 1948 the majority of Jews did not support the self-proclaimed Zionist leadership. It is in the nature of any national liberation movement not to have the luxury of conducting elections, precisely because they do not yet have a state. But today Israel is not talking to the PLO, not because it is terrorist or not an elected body, but because it would then be forced to recognize that they would have to return the occupied territories.

"It is a tragedy when Arab leaders like Arafat offer to negotiate peace and Israel turns a deaf ear... Why is Arafat in so much trouble with the dissidents of the PLO—precisely because of his moderate line and his support for an international peace conference. This is why the Israeli government fears Arafat!" (An excellent example of this occurred when the current government refused to allow Palestinian delegates from the West Bank to travel to Amman to attend the recent Palestinian National Council. These delegates were acknowledged moderates and supporters of Arafat. When Peled rose in the Knesset to petition for exit permits for them he was turned down immediately by the government. "Here the Israeli government," continues Peled, "was helping the pro-Syrian dissidents—a co-operation between extremists on both sides to undermine the moderate PLO leadership. But whereas the extremists among the Palestinians are a small force, in Israel they sit in the government.")

Peace Forces Within Israel

How did Peled evaluate the forces for peace inside Israel? "After the last election we are able to carry between 15-18 votes on certain questions in the Knesset [total 120 deputies]. A considerable percentage of the population is willing to engage in a peace process with the Palestinians, but sentiment is not enough. Few of the peace forces have a political platform to offer. Peace to many remains an abstract idea, but in order to be effective it must be made specific. The major problem with most of the peace forces today is that they are still hesitant in calling for open negotiations with the PLO and a two-state solution."

Secure Borders

Peled was questioned on how he, as a high-ranking military man, understood the problem of secure borders for Israel. "The notion of secure borders is an invention to take someone else's territories. In order for borders to be secure we need peace!" No, he didn't think that Israel must return to the 1947 UN partition lines. "The one thing that borders need is that they be acceptable. The Arab states and the PLO (Fez Conference, 1982) and the United Nations have recognized the 1967 borders (pre-war), and they should serve as Israel's borders." To the extent that there are continued security problems, Peled recognized that every state (Israel or a Palestinian state) has the right to organize whatever contingency programs they deem necessary within their borders, but he categorically rejected that Israel needs occupied territories for its protection. On the contrary, "nearly twenty years of occupation and increased military spending have made Israelis more insecure than ever before."

Law of Return

Finally, with respect to the controversial Law of Return, Peled said that insofar as it expressed the will of the majority of citizens of Israel to allow for Jewish immigration he was not as such opposed (despite the fact that certain "unsavory elements were also allowed into the country"). However, "the main fault of this law is that it does not apply to Arabs and this is discriminatory. Thus I would prefer not to have it as a law. It is an unnecessary law, it creates a sense of discrimination and this should be eliminated."

Peled concluded on a note of guarded optimism. "I hope as a nation we are intelligent enough to make the right decisions. The Israeli people are today faced, more than ever before, with a clear choice. Extremism of the right or the forces for peace. We must make a choice soon."

January-February 1986

Israel and the Rise of Zionism
The South African Connection

ZAYED GAMIET

South African Jews, like those in most Western countries, participated in the Zionist movement and campaigned for the creation of a Jewish state, to the extent of their individual conviction of the correctness of the Zionist ideal. This was to be expected.

But what is probably not widely known is the extent of the support for the Zionist cause historically, and later for the State of Israel, of non-Jewish South Africans, particularly that of Afrikaner leaders.

Both Jews and Afrikaners have drawn attention to the parallels in the struggle of each group to achieve "nationhood" for their peoples; the belief that each was in some way fulfilling a biblical prophecy or destiny; that each was colonizing an inhospitable and even hostile land; that each had to contend with British Imperialism or at least a "hostile" British government; and that each was seeking to impose a Western and therefore more "civilized" culture in a backward land. For, just as the Afrikaners were the descendants of a European nation, Holland, so Zionism was a concept of European Jewry (Ashkenazis), with which Herzl, Jabotinsky, Weizmann, et al., intended to solve the problems of European Jews.

It was an Afrikaner, former South African Prime Minister Jan Christian Smuts, a Boer general in the Anglo-Boer War of 1899-1902, who early in the century perceived the similarity between the struggle of international Jewry to create a Jewish state and that of the Europeans in colonizing Southern Africa.

In his historical work *The Balfour Declaration*, Leonard Stein points out that while it is difficult to detail the part played by Smuts in having the Balfour Declaration approved, "mainly because he exerted his influence in the background," Smuts "must rank among the architects of the Declaration," even though his contribution "was not of the same order as [Lord] Balfour, [Lord] Milner and Lloyd George." Indeed, as a leading representative of the British government at the turn of the century, and sometime prime minister of the Cape Colony, Lord Milner must have been well known to Smuts in South Africa after the Anglo-Boer War, when Smuts became "converted" to the British cause in Southern Africa.

As the representative of the South African government in the British "War Cabinet" during World War I, General Smuts often visited London. It was there that he met Chaim Weizmann, then president of the English Zionist Federation and active campaigner to convince the British government to implement the Balfour Declaration, adopted the year previous. In his book *Trial and Error*, Weizmann later declared that he was received by Smuts

> in the friendliest fashion, and given a most sympathetic hearing.... He assured me heartily that something would be done in connection with Palestine and the Jewish people. He put many searching questions to me . . . and treated the problem with eager interest, one might say with affection.

From that first meeting in London in 1917, a strange, yet close, friendship developed between the two men over the 33-year period until the death of Smuts in September 1950. They exchanged extensive correspondence and Weizmann was to call on Smuts many times to use his influence with British prime ministers such as Lloyd George, Ramsay MacDonald (Labour) and Winston Churchill, in dealing with problems and difficulties in implementing the Balfour Declaration, and problems in the administration of the Palestinian Mandate. In an article such as this it is not possible to deal at any length with the details of this correspondence, but it is abundantly clear that Smuts played an important role in helping Weizmann and the Zionist cause, as a member of the United Party government in South Africa from 1933 on, and as prime minister from September 1939 until his defeat at the hands of the Afrikaner Nationalist Party in May 1948.

During this correspondence, Weizmann never questioned the racial basis of the South African state, even during the Nazi period and the persecution of the Jews, or Smuts' role in maintaining white supremacy in South Africa. Smuts in turn assumed without question "the right" of Jewish settlers to occupy Palestine without regard to the rights of indigenous Palestinian Arabs.

The writings of early Zionists abound with evidence that, philosophically, they were convinced that they would impose a Western and therefore "superior" social and political system in Palestine. In fact, Theodor Herzl spoke of the proposed Jewish state as being "an outpost of civilization against barbarism." Vladimir Jabotinsky described Jews as Europeans having nothing in common with the Orient, "where everything was doomed." David Ben-Gurion saw many similarities between Zionists and other colonists. In an essay in 1917, "Judea and Galilee," in his book *Rebirth and Destiny*, he described Jewish settlers as "conquering a land," and as "a company of conquistadores."

Abba Eban, a South African Jew and sometime Israeli foreign minister, spoke decades later of "the great apprehensions which affect Western-born Israelis." He feared that "a predominance of immigrants of Oriental origin" would "force Israel to equalize its culture with that of the neighbouring world," i.e., Asia and Africa. These immigrants should not be regarded as being "a bridge towards our integration with the Arab-speaking world," he warned, maintaining that "our objective should be to infuse them with the Occidental spirit, rather than to allow them to draw us into an unnatural orientalism." Speaking in a similar vein, Moshe Dayan, Israeli minister of defence, told the annual convention of the South African Zionist Federation in 1974 that the fact that Oriental Jewish immigrants outnumbered immigrants of European origin was

"Israel's biggest problem," and appealed to South African Jews to help solve it "by immigrating there."

In the first political party, founded with his ex-Boer War colleague General Louis Botha, Smuts declared the party to be open "to all white men, Boer, Jew or Briton." According to the South African Jewish author Dan Jacobson, 80 per cent of South African Jews came from Lithuania. Jews, like all white immigrants to South Africa, were given great scope for upward mobility, to such an extent that, according to Jacobson, South African Jews had after World War I become "the wealthiest Jewish community in the world on a per capita basis." At a reception held by the South African Zionist Federation on November 3, 1919, General Smuts spoke of the Jews as a "little people" having "a civilizing mission in the world," and declared that the language of the Old Testament was the basis of "our white culture" and "your Jewish culture."

There is no doubt that politically the majority of South African Jews supported Smuts' United Party. Some, like Morris Kentridge and Bernard Friedman, held cabinet rank when the party was in power, while Harry Schwartz, a Johannesburg lawyer, was leader of the United Party opposition in the Transvaal Provincial legislature in the 1950s. It made good political sense to support Jewish causes, and Smuts appreciated the value of broadening the basis of white support for his policies.

In the extensive correspondence between Weizmann and Smuts already referred to, Smuts used his full influence with successive British governments to promote the interests of the Zionist movement, in response to requests for assistance from Chaim Weizmann. Indeed, in 1931, Weizmann and his wife Vera visited South Africa on a fundraising tour and the trip was described by Mrs. Weizmann in her book *The Impossible Takes Longer*, and by Weizmann in his autobiography, *Trial and Error*.

Mrs. Weizmann wrote that "the condition of the African population appalled us," especially "the distended bellies of African children" they saw at many stops at railway stations during train journeys in South Africa.

Many South African Jews struggled to change these conditions. But the experiences of the Weizmanns on their tour did not affect their close relationship with Smuts, and in consequence his support for their cause remained undiminished till the end. At the United Nations during 1947 and 1948, the South African representative lent valuable support in promoting the acceptance of the State of Israel as a national entity. Shortly before his defeat on May 26, 1948, Smuts extended de facto recognition to the State of Israel, and on that very day Weizmann sent Smuts a cable of thanks. Immediately after his election on May 26, 1948,

Afrikaner Nationalist Prime Minister Daniel Malan extended de jure recognition to the new state. As early as 1950, the first Israeli prime minister, Moshe Sharett, visited South Africa, and in 1951 the Nationalist Party, then in power, opened its Transvaal Provincial branch to Jewish membership for the first time. This warm relationship was carried a step further when Prime Minister Malan became the first foreign prime minister to visit Israel, in June 1953. He was, however, not the last South African Prime Minister to do so.

After his defeat as prime minister in May 1948, General Smuts continued to be honored by the State of Israel and South African Jewry.

At a banquet to celebrate Israel's first anniversary, sponsored by the South African Zionist Federation in the Johannesburg city hall, Smuts, who was the guest of honor, declared that South Africa's recognition of the State of Israel "had put both countries on the map." At Chaim Weizmann's invitation, Smuts attended a dinner in London in late 1949 to honor Weizmann's 75th birthday, at which Smuts stated that without Weizmann, then Israel's first president, "there would have been no Balfour Declaration." On December 4, 1949, Smuts presented a bust of himself by the well-known South African sculptor Moses Kottler to Supreme Court Judge Mr. Justice Greenberg, expressing his happiness that South Africa had played a part "in the return of the Jews to their ancient homeland," describing this as "an historic act of justice."

After his death on September 11, 1950, fervent tributes were paid to Smuts by Jewish leaders both in and outside South Africa, where he was eulogized as "a lifelong Zionist," as well as an "architect of the South African Union." Acting Israeli Prime Minister Joseph Sprinzak said that "General Smuts is written on the map of Israel and in the heart of our nation."

Two years later, on March 18, 1952, with South African and Israeli flags flying side by side, and in the presence of representatives of South African Jewry, the Smuts Forest, overlooking the Weizmann Forest, was formally dedicated on the southern slopes of the Judean Hills in Israel.

With the passing of General Smuts, a chapter in the South African-Zionist-Israeli relationship was brought to a close. But the importance of South Africa for the Jewish state would remain. A new and more intriguing, even if at times stormy, relationship lay ahead.

VI
Yiddish Literature

February 1964

The Negro in Yiddish Fiction

ISAAC E. RONCH

> Isaac E. Ronch is a prominent New York poet and novelist. He has published a number of books of poetry, including the trilogy *Motek and Saltcha*. The first volume of the trilogy, *The Awakening of Motek*, appeared in an English translation. A book of his selected poems, translated into English, has also been published recently. The following article was specially written for this issue of *Canadian Jewish Outlook*.

The comparatively young American Yiddish literature is part and parcel of American native cultural life and aspirations, and as such it is reflected in the works of its *belles lettres*.

The Yiddish novelist and poet doesn't fail to depict his non-Jewish neighbor and his environment. The Italian, the Irish, the Pole, the Ukrainian, the Chinese and even the Gypsies mingle freely and harmoniously in the realm of American Yiddish literature.

But of all the peoples with whom the Yiddish writer comes in contact, none fulfills such a prominent position as the American Negro. There is hardly a volume of Yiddish short stories or poetry which does not include a theme on the lot of the Negroes. And for a good reason. The Negro is the most discriminated against of all racial groups in our country; therefore the sympathies of the Yiddish writer are on his side. It is the "brotherhood in misery" bond, the consciousness of the persecutions and sufferings endured by us Jews for centuries that brings closer the Negro to the heart of the Yiddish creative writers.

And not only is it so in the USA. While in Warsaw in 1935 I attended an outstanding performance of L. Malach's play, *Mississippi*, which was a dramatization of the Scottsboro case. Its author was a resident of Argentina.

A Yiddish anthology entitled *Songs of the Negro People* appeared in 1936, compiled by Zisha Bagish of Romania. The book was printed in Romania and published in Chicago (Ceshinsky Publishing House). Mr. Bagish wrote in his foreword that the Yiddish translation of Langston Hughes' poems was made with the special permission of the author.

As early as the end of the eighteenth century, one of the pioneers of Yiddish poetry in the USA, David Edelshtadt, wrote a short story entitled "The Ungrateful Negress." Like all of his stories, this one was very sentimental. The author sought to reveal the struggle that was going on in the heart of a free Negress after the Civil War, who was attached to her master's child with motherly love but who could not at the same time accept the status of a slave any longer.

Of all the modern Yiddish novelists, Joseph Opatashu has given us the most poignant picture of the mistreatment of the Negro in our country. The fifth volume of his collected stories bears the title *Lynchings*. His story "A Lynching" is considered one of the best in Yiddish literature. An American-born son of immigrant Jews joins a posse of lynchers. His father begs him not to. The plain, unsophisticated Jew realizes the effects of the legal murder. He warns his son: today they lynch a Negro, tomorrow it will be the Jew's turn.

Lynchings first appeared in 1915 and has been translated into French, German, English, Russian, Polish, Ukrainian, Spanish, Danish and Hebrew.

In the same volume of Opatashu's works is the story "The Four Negroes," written in a similar vein. It is full of horrible, grim suspense. The Negroes, thrown into jail, hear a lynch mob calling for one of them by name.

The twelfth volume of Opatashu's collected works contains two short stories with Negroes as the main characters.

Baruch Glassman, a prolific writer on the American scene, has a collection of short stories entitled *On the Fields of Georgia*. The two stories with Negro themes are considered the best in the volume. The third volume of Glassman's works (*Across the Ocean*, published in 1928) has a story describing Negro life in the South. "The Dance of the Negroes" draws the contrast between the hard-working Negro and the decadent whites.

Glassman's *On the Fields of Georgia* reminds one of Peretz's folk tales. A Jewish peddler in the South is stranded in an open field at twilight. He knocks at the door and an elderly Negro woman confronts him. She's alone. It is Christmas eve. She had expected her husband, who disappeared some time ago. She befriends the Jewish stranger; she serves him her best food and she prepares for him a place to sleep in the other room.

Her guest is a pious Jew. He will not touch her food. He is tired. He goes into his dark room to get some sleep. But there is no sleep. He departs quietly and when the hostess enters his room in the morning, she finds the bed empty. Her sobbing fills the room. Glassman evokes the reader's sympathy for both, the Negress and the Jew.

Sholem Asch in his novel *Judge Not*, published in 1920 and included in the English edition of *Three Cities*, depicts the Negro boy Rapp, one of the book's most memorable characters. The Jewish businessman, Stone, who is in Sing Sing prison awaiting execution, asks the governor for a pardon, not for himself, but for the lonely Negro boy who has not yet lived, and who he believes to be innocent.

Lamed Shapiro, the fine, subtle Jewish storyteller, wrote an unfinished novel, *The American Devil*, which had appeared in his magazine, *Studio*. There the figure of Luke, a Negro, appears quite often. Luke, a coal miner from Pennsylvania, becomes a radical and participates actively in the protests against the death sentences of Sacco and Vanzetti.

Of the younger generations of Jewish novelists and storytellers, Pesach Markus has a collection of stories entitled *A Bridge Across the Atlantic*, published in 1932, where themes on Negro life predominate. Pessie Bach's first volume of stories, *A Girl's Diary*, published in 1941, is rich in material on Negro life. One-third of her book consists of character portraits of poor, unhappy Negro children. The writers Moshe Shifris, Aaron Rappaport, L. Forem, A. Maisel, Chaver-Paver, J. Krepliak, have included in their works sympathetic stories on Negro life.

It seems to me that the Negro is portrayed more humanly, more understandingly in Yiddish literature than in American literature. He is neither excessively praised, nor sentimentalized. The Yiddish writer in his portrayal of the Negro generally attempts to study the social causes for the situation in which the Negro finds himself. The writer, himself a child of an oppressed people, which struggled for centuries against persecution and discrimination, is forever on the alert to hear and sense the ever-present protest of the Negro against his white discriminator.

In the writings of the younger American-Jewish authors, especially of those who are concerned with present-day life, we find that the trials and tribulations of his Negro neighbor are an integral part of his writing.

A Poet of the Sweatshop Era

ITCHE GOLDBERG

The Jewish labor movement was born in relentless struggle. It gave the dignity of struggle to the emerging Jewish life in our country. At that time it was the most electrifying force in our national regeneration in the United States. From this background of tenements and sweatshops, the sounds of new voices were heard—young, naive, heartwarming, and often heartbreaking, consoling, often tearful, and yet full of militancy, dignity, and promise. These were the voices of the new labor poets—Morris Winchevsky, David Edelshtadt, Joseph Bovshover and Morris Rosenfeld.

Theirs was not an appeal for pity for the poor working people, but a dignified outcry against oppression and evil. These were voices never heard before in Jewish creativity for there were never similar conditions mature enough to produce them. This poetry did not only reflect the times, it often anticipated them.

When Rosenfeld Sang

When Morris Winchevsky, first in England and then in the United States, and Morris Rosenfeld addressed themselves to the Jewish "proletarians," they spoke to a class which had not yet come to life. These were only poor immigrants, Sholem Aleichem's *Kasrilifkeits*, lost in the jungle of the sweatshop, suffering without understanding or reason, exposed to conditions which were dehumanizing.

When Morris Rosenfeld sang out *Zei shtoltz oif dein arbet* (Be proud of your labor), he was speaking in the idiom of the future. Labor, under conditions of the sweatshop, was undignified and could not be a source of pride.

There was give-and-take between Yiddish literature in the United States and Eastern Europe; they influenced and complemented each other; many writers, like Sholem Aleichem, Sholem Asch, Joseph Opatashu and others, wrote about Jewish life in both major Jewish communities. Yet, what was created in the United States was a Yiddish literature indigenous to our country. It could only have come to life in the

Die Kappellia by Maurice Kish (March 1975)

Kindling the Chanukah Candles (woodcut) by Jacob Steinhardt (November-December 1981)

1859-1916

May 13th marked the 48th Yohrzeit of the immortal Jewish humorist writer Sholom Aleichem. It is well to remember the stirring words of his will.

"No matter where I die, I am to be buried not among aristocrats, men of high lineage, or men of great wealth, but among common Jewish workingmen, with just ordinary folk; so that the tombstone to be put on my grave will honor the ordinary graves around mine, and the ordinary graves will honor my tombstone, in the way in which the plain, honest people honored their folk writer in his lifetime."

SHOLOM ALEICHEM

Sholom Aleichem (June 1964)

My Baba (wood carvings) by Sidney Sarkin (March 1980)

United States, although it influenced Jewish life in Eastern Europe. A poem written by David Edelshtadt in New York was recited and sung in Warsaw or Vilna within months.

It created new forms, new expressions, new language elements, in order to portray a people in the state of transition and becoming. This period of becoming has created an unevenness in the development of American Yiddish literature; poetry developed at a much faster pace and reached artistic perfection much sooner than did prose. The labor writers at the turn of the century were practically all versifiers. The prose literary form common at the end of the century was primarily the so-called *skitze* (sketch), depicting a single instance in the life of the hero, and was written for the daily or weekly newspaper.

It Was a Process of Discovering America

This literature adds a high sense of social consciousness, seeking to help an uprooted immigrant mass become integrated in America. It often wavered between acceptance and rejection of the new life, between alienation and *heimishkeit*, between shedding tears for the Haymarket martyrs and the self-deception of eventually returning "home," i.e., to Europe. In its totality, however, although strongly critical of the new life, it tried to find sense in the bewilderment of the new environment. It was, in the first period especially, a process of discovering America for themselves without any romantic veil. All the shortcomings and blemishes of the new land were seen under a spotlight of social realism, at times with tears, at others with a sense of social castigation or with good-humored self-ridicule. It spoke out in defence of the "greenhorn" seeing America through unaccustomed, bewildered eyes.

The literature gave a true reflection of American Jewish life and helped the immigrant mass tame and conquer the early chaos of the new and strange life, helping them reach a degree of self-awareness in an alien environment which held them in a vise of terror and loneliness during the first years in America.

It was a variegated literature. At times naive, simple, even primitive, but always vital and human, reaching artistic heights as it developed. It was an affirmative literature, depicting a people under strain and stress, but always advancing.

It essentially helped the immigrant mass of the day step over the abyss of forlorn self-negation, caused by the new life, into a state of dignity. Or, as one of its leading creators, Leon Kobrin, expressed it as early as 1910: "We were faced with the need to create a substance out of nothing... And only the One above was given the prerogative to create something out of nothing..."

Yiddish Literature Taught the 'Little Man'

It was no easy task that Yiddish literature took upon itself—a proud affirmation of life and justification of the "little man," often not for what he is, but for what he might or will be.

Among the voices of the Yiddish poets in the United States at the turn of the century, the voice of Morris Rosenfeld possessed a lucid and lyrical quality of enduring value. He reflected and responded to the social and national currents of his day with a great measure of sensitivity and understanding. He was not the singer of the sweatshop alone, but a true poet of his people.

October 1972

Two Soviet Yiddish Poems

Translated from the Yiddish by Ben Chud

For Whom I Write

MOTL TALALAYEVSKY

For whom do you write? enquires a neighbor
Who has forgotten what his mother tongue is all about.
The little wick which once upon a time did burn
He long ago himself put out,
As one extinguishes, in one fell swoop, both lights and
    shadows on the wall.

For whom do you write? Wretched and poor
Is your word. Of what earthly use to you?
Like Latin, once alive and now no more.
Why even your child of these words has no clue.

For whom I write? If truly you do answer seek,
Then in response, my conscience I give leave to speak.
Does one ask of the tree, for whom its leaves profuse,
Or of the sun why its golden rays infuse
Each tiny crevice and every mountain peak?
I write for those with whom I'm destined in this
    tongue to speak.
Of no account the size—be they many or few—
In the chorus of humanity my voice is ringing too!

Beyond the Dream

SHEEKE DREEZE

Skipper, I beg you,
Though I have not the fee
Row me across to
Beyond the dream.

Certain I am that
What I'll find there
Will not likely increase
The grey in my hair.

Gather will I from
Human shadows oppressed
The drippings of tallow,
Of candles unblessed.

And from this I'll fashion
A candle, straight as a pine.
I, Sheeke of Krosne
That birthtown of mine.

The pine I will carry
Though my body's in pain
To the Eiffel candelabra
By the shores of the Seine.

The name I will kindle
In mourning and awe
For the martyred of Vilna
Kiev and Warsaw.

From the top of the tower
Will a steady drip stream
Off the candle I carry
From way beyond the dream.

December 1972

A Vibrant Poet
of the Sweatshop Period

SID RESNICK

The radical Jewish labor movement in America in the 1880s and the 1890s introduced the ideas of militant trade unionism, social protest and socialism to the many thousands of newly arrived, Yiddish-speaking immigrant workers. This was the period of the sweatshop and the beginnings of the garment workers' unions. Anarchist and socialist newspapers and organizations became an important influence in the Jewish immigrant communities in many American cities and the radical Yiddish-speaking workers provided the audience for a vibrant, socially alert Yiddish literature and poetry.

An American scholar, Professor Sol Liptzin, writes of this period: "This [social] struggle was sparked by the kindling verses of young Yiddish poets, verses of poverty's heavy affliction, the dignity of labor and the joy of self-sacrifice, verses that were sung and recited in sweatshops, at cellar assemblies, on the picket lines and in the prison cells into which strikers were herded. Many of these poets were merely pamphleteers in verse, but the most gifted among them, David Edelstadt (1866-1892), Joseph Bovshover (1872-1915), Morris Rosenfeld (1862-1923), and Morris Winchevsky (1856-1933), left as their heritage a few lyrics of enduring value."

We believe the gifted Yiddish radical poets named by Professor Liptzin left more than only "a few lyrics of enduring value." At any rate, they were idolized by the early Jewish left and their poems were recited or sung at gatherings of Jewish workers in the first decades of the century in this country, England and Russia. Today the Jewish establishment's literary men disdain and ignore them and they are unknown to the new generation of radicals. With the exception of Morris Rosenfeld's, most of their work has not been translated.

Of these four major Yiddish radical poets of that period, Joseph Bovshover, who was born in the rigidly orthodox town of Lubavich, was the only one who turned to writing English poetry. After having been in the United States less than five years Bovshover's first English poem, "To the Toilers," was published in the New York magazine *Liberty*, an intellectual anarchist bi-weekly publication. The magazine's editor was ecstatic in his praise for Bovshover and hailed him as "a new star, perhaps of the first magnitude."

Benjamin Tucker, the editor of *Liberty*, described his first meeting with the young 24-year-old Bovshover in the comment, "A Remarkable Young Poet," which appeared in the March 7, 1896, issue of the magazine. Tucker wrote: "A few weeks ago a young man called at this office in search of literary employment. He was a Russian, of not more than 25 years, I should think... with delicate, refined features, a dreamy expression and a soft voice, in fact, a typical Slav of the finer sort. He was profoundly convinced that he had literary talents of a high order and his chief desire was to develop them... The young man's sincerity impressed me, but his willingness to appeal to strangers for aid in getting employment rather than take the (to him) somewhat unpleasant work that lay within his grasp made me a little impatient with him. . . .

"For some weeks I heard nothing of him, but the other day he called at this office in my absence and left for my examination several specimens of his verse. After reading them I was filled with astonishment and joy, for I was convinced that a new and great poet had discovered himself to me. Though some of his work was inferior to the rest and much of it bore marks of crudity, all of it was indicative of genius; and now it seems to me that the poem which I print in another column, if we remember that its author is a youth who two years ago knew not a word of the English language, is nothing less than a wonderful performance.

"I feel chagrined that I did not perceive the young man's power at my first interview with him. And now I am inclined to say to him, as Emerson said to Whitman: 'I greet you at the beginning of a great career'. . . Am I too enthusiastic over this young man? Is not this poem, 'To the Toilers,' a really majestic utterance? Does it not constitute a really noble debut in the history of American letters?. . . ."

Bovshover signed his English poems with the pen name Basil Dahl. Perhaps at his request, we cannot know, Tucker corrected his statement that Bovshover was a Slav. Tucker wrote in the following issue of *Liberty*: "I was in error in describing Basil Dahl as a Slav. Though born and bred in Russia, he is one of the Jewish race."

The radical poets who were associated with *Liberty* magazine confirmed Tucker's high opinion of Bovshover's poetry. Among the first to respond was John Beverley Robinson, who wrote:

"You have not in the least overestimated Basil Dahl. I do not think he could be overestimated. The fellow talks poetry as if he really meant it, and with the dignity and solemnity of a chanting priest. . . The poem is singularly affecting in its simplicity."

Another poet, William Walstein Gordak, wrote:

"I share your enthusiasm in regard to Basil Dahl. The case is a marvellous one; here is a mere boy. . . with a poetic gift surprisingly brilliant. . .

"The thoughts contained in 'To the Toilers' may be common among the highly intellectual (I know not), but never since the earth was made or made itself have they before been put into such magnificent shape. The lines are as loaded with thought as a vine with fruit; but so clear, so simple, so direct and strong are they that they bear the burden lightly" (*Liberty*, March 21, 1896).

Bovshover became something of a cause for Benjamin Tucker. Week after week he published Bovshover's other English poems, as well as further letters praising him, and he replied to the letter of a lone detractor. In the issue of May 2, 1896, another poet, J. William Lloyd, wrote in praise of Bovshover but added a perceptive remark directed at Bovshover's own spiritual condition. Lloyd wrote:

"Basil Dahl is a poet, and 'To the Toilers' is 'a really majestic utterance.' I lift my hat and give him my hand.

"If I might venture on a word of unasked advice, I would warn him at the outset against the melancholy and pessimism which are the peculiar vices and perils of the poet..."

Unfortunately, the acclaim lavished on Bovshover by *Liberty*, a magazine of small circulation and limited influence, aroused no response in other circles. Whatever anticipations Benjamin Tucker's high regard evoked in Bovshover were to be disappointed. Bovshover also suffered from the fact that his own merits as a Yiddish poet were not fully appreciated by the Yiddish cultural world of his time; his greatest fame came after he ceased to write. He was never able to keep a job and he often lived off his friends. His creative life lasted only ten years.

In the late 1890s he became subject to increasing depression and melancholy and his irrational behavior finally caused him to be confined in an insane asylum in Poughkeepsie, N.Y. There Bovshover remained the last fifteen years of his life and he died on December 20 or December 25, 1915.

To the Toilers
(An Excerpt)

JOSEPH BOVSHOVER (1872-1915)

I hate your superstition, workingmen,
I loathe your blindness and stupidity.
Your pointed quips have never made me laugh;
Your senseless chat is wearisome to me;
Your shallow joy is not the joy I like.
But when I contemplate your ceaseless toil,
Your quiet activity and sunless life,
Your works of splendor, and gigantic strength,
I bow my head in reverence to you.
The cliffs are mighty in the wilderness;
The woods are terrible when shook by storm;

The streams are awful in their nasty course;
But cliffs, and woods, and streams, all disappear,
When touched by your unconquerable hands.
Were you as wise as you are powerful,
You would be happy, great, and revered.

You live, and know not what existence is;
You die, and know not what the grave entombs;
You trust, and know not what your faith implies;
You hope, and know not what it is to hope.
If you would know the mysteries of life,
And know the secrets of the dismal grave;
If you would know the meaning of your faith,
And also know the sequel of your hope—
You would not then abide in wretchedness,
And not be dead not having lived before;
You would not then believe in wind and dust,
Or ever hope for that which cannot be!
Your wrinkled faces would be fresh with health,
And bright with joy your nigh extinguished eyes;
Your weary hands would be as strong as steel,
And swifter than a stag's your strengthless feet.
Your hearts would feel, but never sigh with grief;
Your heads would think, but never ache with care;
Your lips would speak, but never reek with fume.
Each word of yours would be a pleasant sound,
And you—a spring upon the beauteous earth.

Let birds awake you with a joyous air,
And fragrant breezes lull you into sleep.
And let your streets resound with joy and mirth,
With sounds of cymbals, mandolins, and flutes.
Expand your life, and make it free and full;
Create yourselves anew in health and strength.
The aged people vigorous, like oaks;
The children lusty, beautiful, and good;

The blooming youths as stately cedars hale,
Endowed with beauty as the god of light,
And full of glee and life as life itself;
The maidens' faces sweet and roseate,
The eyes effulgent with desire and love,
The breath voluptuous and redolent,
The laughter trilling, loud, and musical:
What joy it were to see you thus transformed!

March 1975

Crazy Levi

ROCHL KORN

And no one knows what became of him, Crazy Levi,
who tied the roads
from Yaverev to Moshtsisk
to Samber to Greyding in a bow,
carrying always in his bosom pocket
his letters to Rivtshe,
his uncle's youngest daughter.

All the houses in the villages knew him,
the road accepted his long shadow
like a horse that knows its rider,
and the dogs lay quiet in their doghouses
when the familiar smell of Levi's flaring black coat tails
spoke to their doggy hearts.

Women broken in the middle like sheaves
were in the field when Levi came by.
They toyed with him
and with a laugh that smelled of goodness, like dark bread,
they would say,
"Levi, you have no father or mother.
Why don't you take a wife
like the rest of your people?
She would wash your shirt for you
and cook you a spoonful of something warm for supper."

And Levi would look at their raw, swollen feet
and plow the brown field of his forehead
with the painful thought that was always present to him:
"Because my uncle wouldn't give me his daughter for a wife.
I carry my heart around
like a cat in a sack,
and I want to leave it somewhere
so that it won't be able to find its way back to me."

And he would take a filthy piece of paper
out of his bosom pocket
and read aloud from a letter in German,
"An Liebchen!"
and a red berry would blossom
in the dark moss around his lips:
Levi's crazy, melancholy smile.

But after one long hard winter,
worse than any the old people could remember,
the small eyes of the windowpanes
looked for Levi without finding him
and the dogs put their heads to the ground
and sniffed at all the tracks on the road,
thinking he might have come by.

And to this day, no one knows what became of him.
Maybe the hungry wolves in the woods tore him to pieces
or maybe his mother who hung herself in her youth
missed her son, and a small, white hand
reached out to him from the dark attic of the old house.

—*Translated from the Yiddish by Seymour Levitan*

July-August 1976

Poet Radiates Compassion for His Fellow Man

THE WHITE HOUSE by Sholem Shtern. Translated from the Yiddish by Max Rosenfeld. Montreal: Warbrooke Publishers, 1974.

REVIEWED BY SOL LIPTZIN

> The Canadian Yiddish poet Sholem Shtern has become more and more prominent in recent years among the English reading public. Our reviewer, Prof. Sol Liptzin, is an eminent scholar who now resides in Israel.

In this volume, Sholem Shtern, the Canadian-Yiddish poet, attempts in verse what Thomas Mann attempted in prose in *The Magic Mountain*. Both narrators let a cross-section of humanity pass before the eyes of an impressionable young person in a sanitarium for tubercular patients and both describe these patients with their philosophies, past pains, and present foibles. There is, however, a tremendous difference in outlook and social consciousness between the German novelist and the Yiddish poet.

Thomas Mann is a reserved intellectual with an ironic attitude toward life. He has no real sympathy for his characters, assembled from all parts of Europe, in various stages of dissolution, hovering between life and death. He remains the objective outsider and channels his observations of the passing scene through the mind of the mediocre Hans Castorp, who comes to visit a no less mediocre cousin, a patient in the sanitarium high up in the Alps. Castorp lingers on, when he is himself infected by the disease, and is exposed during his enforced stay of seven years to an overdose of scepticism as he listens to the various patients airing their views on the decaying society in the murky lands below. In the end, he leaves the Magic Mountain to hurl himself into the maelstrom of war, preferring patriotic group frenzy to the solitary, critical questioning of life's meaning in the rarified atmosphere of Davos.

In Shtern's poetic novel of a Canadian-Jewish sanitarium, the narrator is not an objective outsider with an ironic smile and the ear of a psychoanalyst but the sick poet himself, who is in need of convalescence and does indeed convalesce. However, his sickness is purely physical and not spiritual, and when he is healed, he returns to creative life and not to a senseless war.

Velvel Greenblatt, Shtern's autobiographic hero, is an immigrant lad who was typical of the Jewish youth that, by the thousands, left the Old Country after the First World War with romantic visions of fabled cities beyond the Atlantic. On arriving, he was immediately set to work in a clothing factory. From the grinding toil at the sewing machine, illness brought him surcease. As a sensitive poet, he listens with a believing heart and a sympathetic mind to his fellow patients, who tell him of the wonders and woes of their life in the Old Country and the New.

There is the artist Gorin, who paints not only mountain landscapes, gold corn and blossoming apple trees, but also hunger marches and the struggle of exploited workers for a more dignified existence. There is the more militant, rancorous communist, Itzik, whose faith in a glorious future for the proletarian masses comforts him throughout his own illness. There is the aged, devout Reb Shmuel, who is always ready to help a fellow Jew. There is the dying tailor, Joe Perlman, who was saved from Europe's revolutionary horrors after his body had already suffered irreparable damage.

There is the repentant smuggler, Mickey Goldberg, who is torn apart by guilt and does not want to fight the ravages of his disease. There is Izzy the Barber, who long hesitated to give his loving wife a conditional divorce so that she might remarry without the difficulties and humiliations of Halitza, but who finally does so before dying. There is the one-lunged supervisor of the commissary, who writes a novel about the suffering of the French-Canadian farmers. Each of these Jewish characters knew poverty and pain in their childhood in Eastern Europe and toil and travail in their immigrant years in Canada. As a result of their personal experiences, they are full of kindness, sympathy and understanding for each other.

The central theme of the poetic novel, however, is the love of Velvel Greenblatt for his nurse, Miss Alman. This love is portrayed from its budding on the first day of the poet's arrival, through various stages of tender maturing, until the wedding climax and the happy return of the couple to responsible, normal life in the big city. In the delicate delineation of ripening, untainted passion this work remains in the finest tradition of Yiddish literature, perhaps the purest of all contemporary literatures in depicting sex experiences, and far removed from the aberrations of Bashevis Singer. In the emphasis on the happiness that accrues to people in social involvement, in mutual help, and in living beyond self, the epic continues in the path followed by most Yiddish writers throughout the past century, ranging from the mystic followers of Hassidic Brotherhoods and Musar Yeshivot to rational and irrational apostles of Communist utopias.

The poetic narrative is irradiated by Sholem Shtern's tolerance of all honestly held views and his compassion with all his characters, French-Canadian farmers no less than Jews in various walks of life. But his special affection is reserved for human beings who have been hurt in the cruel struggle for survival and who yet remain morally immaculate.

September-October 1976

Melech Ravitch
Dean of Yiddish Poetry

DAVID ROME

Melech Ravitch, dean of Yiddish poetry and a cultural leader in the Canadian Jewish community, passed away on August 21, 1976, at the age of 83.

Mr. Ravitch was the author of some twenty volumes of verse, memoirs and studies in cultural history issued since 1912. He edited a number of important journals and contributed to scores of serious Jewish periodicals all over the world. His books were published in Vilna, Brno, Jerusalem, Buenos Aires, Lemberg, Vienna, Warsaw and Mexico City, as well as Montreal.

He was born Zechariah Chona Bergner in 1893, in Redem, Eastern Galicia. He entered banking service as a clerk and had served in the Austrian army during World War I. He early discovered the values of the Yiddish language and decided to devote himself to its culture and literature.

He settled in Warsaw in 1921 where he became, simultaneously, the energetic director of the establishment Union of Litterateurs and leader of "The Gang," off-beat experimentalists in Yiddish poetry. He founded and edited the most respected critical journals of Yiddish literature, even as he was issuing volume after volume of lyrical poems in the expressionist tradition.

The surrealism of his personal nightmare of the years between the wars coincided with the realism of his vision of the coming conflict and the violent fate closing in on mankind and upon the heartland Polish Jewish community. He warned of the urgency of flight from the certain scene of battle.

His travels through Africa and Asia and his removal successively to Australia, Mexico and eventually Canada were a loud warning of the Holocaust that was so near and that was to cost millions of Jewish lives. He became prophet, rescuer, memorializer, rescue agency—Cassandra, Jeremiah and International Red Cross—for Jewish life and letters before, during and after the Second World War. Montreal became his home and the Jewish Public Library was his widely known address.

Since his arrival in Canada in 1938, he was the outstanding figure in Yiddish literature in this country, together with the late J.I. Segal and later with Rachel Korn and Mordecai Husid. He had been editor of the literary pages of the Montreal *Jewish Daily Eagle* and was closely connected with the Jewish Library where he founded and led the People's University and was instrumental in building its home, then on Mount Royal and Esplanade avenues.

Ravitch's literary work here has been largely that of a stupefied elegiast. Even his very personal recollections, such as his three-volume *The Story Book of My Life* and his *My Lexicon*, are both autobiography and literary history. His continuous and systematic efforts to maintain Yiddish culture in Canada against odds, to build the Jewish Library as a unique temple which could perpetuate the Yiddish literary and artistic traditions, were a development of Galician consecration to the Jewish civilization of Eastern Europe. His considerable literary archive constitutes a treasury of this phase of Jewish culture.

In the same sense of striving for survival after cataclysm was his recurrent plea for the canonization of a "New Bible" which would perpetuate and convey the essence of two thousand years of Jewish spiritual creativity, as the Old Testament and the Talmud were the culling of centuries of Jewish experiences and thought of their centuries.

He reached out to the younger generation of students and was popular among the participants in the multiplying Jewish studies programs in Canadian and American universities.

He was among the most highly regarded cultural personalities of world Jewry. His work was included in anthologies in many languages, including German, Polish and French. Among his translators in English was his friend Irving Layton. A local committee of friends found little difficulty in arranging for the publication of his volumes. All levels of the Canadian community appreciated the honor of hosting Ravitch as a Canadian citizen and the Canadian Jewish Congress awarded him several citations. The Ministry of Cultural Affairs, then headed by the Hon. Jean-Noel Tremblay, sponsored a dinner in his honor at the Quebec Pavilion at Expo.

Despite ill health, Ravitch continued his intellectual activity well into his eighties. He had issued an auto-anthology, "Songs of My Songs," in 1954, which included selections from each of his thirteen earlier volumes of verse. But he continued writing poetry and his collection *Post Scripture* of unweakened vigor appeared fifteen years later. He was active in the preparation of his later volumes of his *Story Book of My Life* during his last days.

August-September 1978

Kol Nidre

PERETZ MARKISH

Panic broke so suddenly upon the town that no one understood. The whirlwind churned its evil; homes lay broken, doors hung open and askew, Old Levi heard the lowering tread, the cries of people one despairing step ahead of slaughter. Uncompleted thoughts of 80 years paraded through his brain. For 80 years The One Above had given him his bread, a long, full life. What more was left for him? Here he'd stay, and here, if it were fated, he would Sanctify the Name. Here, beside the holy place where 50 years his carver's hands had won a share of honest fame.

The rumble of the beast's approach was foul and loathsome in his ears. The blood-gorged German had a special reckoning with him. His nephew—and his son—both Bolsheviks. And then... he was a Jew. The world was curiously grey outside his windows: Night fell earlier, he mused... the Holy Days... And with the evening of *Kol Nidre* came the Germans, two of them, who mockingly broke down his door, as silently he stood in *talis* and in *kitl* awaiting them. He studied them. Before he died he had to understand: Where had Creation erred? What had these two to do with Man?

He stared, and fixed each one into his brain. The color of their skin was like a snake's: each one's face a *golem*. Black revolvers pushed him to the door, and through the town, and past the streets and houses to the mill. Here, carting lumber from the woods, he'd often stopped for a convivial *l'hayim*. Now there was no sound except the crow's: a proper welcoming. The windmill shook and groaned. Jews lay with their faces to the ground as they had often done *Yom Kippur* at their prayers. But now there were no tears, nor any fist that beat upon a penitent breast.

He recognized his neighbors, meeting here in death: smiths and woodsmen, carpenters and coopers, as if all the barrel-staves on earth had split apart, and craftsmen here had come to study out the cause. The hangmen brought him to the mill and stuck a spade into the hands which once had carved the Torah's Ark and later, cartidge cases for Red Army men. The wind crept weirdly through the mill and played *Kol Nidre*, as a jackal led a devil's-choir chant. The windmill's wings, like twisted hands, wrung heavenward. But Levi could not comprehend this evil thing. He thought: A *dybbuk* has been breathed into the world.

"Dig yourself a grave!" the German barked, and Levi took a step toward his executioner. He tried to fathom out this Nazi brain and saw, not one, but all the enemy personified. And suddenly the autumn cold no longer chilled, and fear no longer froze his heart. He saw the end of life depicted in the Nazi's face. The world would not be worth the living in. And pushing back his spectacles upon his head, as was the habit of his life when starting on a piece of work, his fingers gripped around the handle of the spade.

But this was consecrated time, *Kol Nidre* eve, and digging earth *Yom Kippur* was a sin... The hangman laughed and ordered Levi to begin. But breaking Holy Law was three times worse then death! He took his *talis* from his shoulders with a prayer and laid it tenderly upon the bloodstained earth. He lifted the foreboding spade into the air and eyeing steadily the Nazi's gleaming head, roared lion-like the wonted introductive words of the *Kol Nidre* chant: "My witness be Almighty God!" and brought the spade down like an axe, as often in his life he'd done upon a screaming, splintering log.

—Translated from the Yiddish by Max Rosenfeld

January 1982

In the Quiet of the Morning

SHOLEM SHTERN

To my grandson Jeremy

Laugh, laugh, little boy,
The sun is dancing
In the road with joy.

Little boy, the sky
Is awash with blue.

Agile and happy,
Leap into the valley-dew.

Gaily your dog is barking,
Lapping up the gleaming rays
That glide in golden ribbons
In the peace of morning.

From the forest, little boy,
Where the silence rests
Your white-specked cow
Is calling you—
M-O-O-

Full of water in the belly of the lake,
Go, fill your pail at its brink,
Your cow is calling for a drink.

Your cow, your little cow
Is goring the sun-gold with its tiny horns
and nibbling the grass among thistles and thorns.

Near the well—so full and deep—
Chimney-smoke is rising steep.
And a squirrel comes and drinks its fill,
In golden spray the droplets spill.

Silent mountains look in wonder
How swallows pierce the air,
How the smoke curls way up high
From the farmer's house near by.

Little boy, in forest and field
Your happiness tenfold is my yield!
Your laughter is ringing in me, too.
It's true! It's true!
Never will I take leave of you!
Young and joyous, without fears,
I will face the rush of years.

In the forest's sparkling dew,
Little boy, your barking dog is calling you.
Tie your shoe-lace, there, you see.
Now run swiftly here, to me.

Yes, little boy, tenfold true—
I will never take leave of you!
Our secret—
Bright and gay
It flutters with the wind away.

Tie your shoe-lace,
Don't delay.
See the morning golden spray
Disappear from hill and dale—
And the lake, now
                mirror-faced,
casts bluish lights out into space.

Let's hurry home now, little boy,
A motor-boat, a greedy toy
Cuts through the waves, the bluish air—
As if it had full time to spare.

Run, little boy, laugh out loud.
The farmer's truck is on the road.
The sun is also riding high,
Weaving her web far in the sky.

Run to your mother,
Run fast, little boy!
See there, she's waiting
And glowing with joy.
                    —*Translated from the Yiddish by Martin Birnbaum.*

December 1984

Ber Green in Canada

AN INTERVIEW BY AARON KRAMER

In June of 1982 I embarked on a project focusing on social poetry in Yiddish, and emphasizing the work of several dozen proletarian poets, many of whom later became my friends. They were widely popular in the thirties as members of the Proletpen. Rather than limit my research to scholarly works such as Alexander Pomerantz' volume, published in the Soviet Union in 1934, I decided to conduct a series of recorded interviews with my dear old friend Ber Green, a primary leader of that group, whose body had long since failed him, including his sight, but whose mind has remained extraordinarily keen and creative. Whenever our conversation reminded him of a particular episode in his own life, I encouraged him to expand on it. The following excerpt from our first transcribed meeting, held at the Home of the Sages in Lower Manhattan on June 17, may be of more than passing interest to Canadian readers.

GREEN: I wrote at one time under the name of Alef Toronter, because I spent fourteen months in Toronto, Canada, I was the underground editor of *Der Kamf*.

KRAMER: Why were you the *underground* editor?

BG: Because we had a fascist regime there. A hundred and ten writers of progressive magazines and newspapers were in jail. I had to be there incognito. I starved mostly [chuckling]—that was my main profession.

AK: Starving.

BG: There was no money, and the persecution was terrible. They would come and attack the office—I never saw it. I was in a room all by myself. The manager would bring me manuscripts, and I published a weekly *Der Kamf*, for fourteen months under the most terrible working conditions. One day I nearly fainted from hunger.

AK: Hunger! So—you had no support from the readers? They didn't know who you were or where you were?

BG: Well, they supported the paper, but they themselves were terribly poor. Conditions were dreadful...the year was 1933.

AK: Have you ever written about that?

BG: It was dangerous to write about it then. But Yud Gershman who later on was the editor of *Canader Yiddisher Vochnblatt*, did mention a few times my contribution to Canada, to Canadian literature.

AK: I think you should write your reminiscences of those fourteen months. It would be fascinating...and valuable.

BG: At that time I discovered a number of poets whom I encouraged to write. One of them was Sholem Shtern.

AK: Yes. He's 75 years old now.

BG: A very important, very good poet. At that time he wrote his early poetry.

AK: There was a woman—she lived in Montreal and wrote some beautiful children's poems. I know that she saved a lot of lives during the Holocaust.

BG: At the moment I can't recall... [This turned out to be Ida Maze].

AK: What about Nepom?

BG: Oh! Good you mentioned him. Shien Nepom. Him I met. He was a trolley driver. A very good proletarian poet.

AK: I feel that. He wrote two poems about Sacco and Vanzetti. One of them, "Martyretum," is very powerful.

BG: Exactly. There was also Shien Perel, a very fine young poet. Then there was Itzik Fraiman...In the house where I lived, where I had my room—my room was very, very secluded...it was like a cell of a jail. The owner of the house didn't know who I was, because he wasn't supposed to know. We just told him I'm representing a publishing firm from New

York—because he would always come in and see manuscripts... books... After some months he found out; it turned out that he himself was a Yiddish poet... I have to remind myself of his name... He was a manufacturer himself—that's how he made a living. But when I rented the room he didn't know who I was.

AK: If you can, I urge you to create an essay about those fourteen months.

BG: Yes. Those were extremely interesting months. One [weeps] —one thing that I remember... I was not supposed to go into restaurants where I could meet people who might know me. I would go to the cheapest cafeterias in the city to have my lunch or supper. Then I tried to avoid being on the street altogether. One Friday night I was very [breaks down quietly] very hungry. [Long pause. Kramer puts hand on his wrist.]

AK: It's not easy to remember such things, I'm sure... [The silent weeping continues].

BG [sobs and turns it into a chuckle]: I... I decided to go to the market and buy pork because it was cheaper, and because it could keep me alive. [Sobbing] For the first time in my life I tried to eat pork and... I couldn't eat it. [Still crying] I couldn't digest it. I had to throw it away.

AK: With that precious little money you had.

BG [half-sobbing, half-chuckling]: I had to throw it away. [Recovers] And then there was a raid on my house. The police raided the house when I was in Montreal. Very often I would go to Montreal for lectures. Saturdays and Sundays. Each time they represented me under different names. "A gast [guest] fun [from] New York—Chaver Gold." So each time some other name. And there would be a group of people around me, in case there should be a personal attack.

AK: I'm sure there were plenty of government spies everywhere.

BG: Everywhere. So one morning, when I came back from Montreal, the children in the house told me: "Mister, the police, the secret police were last night here."

AK: They searched your room?

BG: "They [chuckling] searched your room... they searched all over... and they said you should report to them immediately." So I went across the street, and got the help of a friend, Glassman—an excellent teacher and school organizer, a real idealist. He died a couple of years ago. He and his wife helped me to pack up my two valises and I went to stay overnight in the home of Yud Beis Salzberg. J.B. Salzberg, a leader of the movement at that time. Later he left, but he's still a very influential Jewish leader. He was more or less well-to-do. He's a brother-in-law of Itche Goldberg.

AK: Is he still in Toronto?

BG: Yeah. So I went to him; we took a taxi and he kept me overnight in his place. It was dangerous for him too. And in the morning his wife showed me where to go to look for an apartment. I went into the Jewish market place, and got myself a room. I introduced myself [chuckling] as a businessman from New York. I had my best clothes on, and a woman who spoke a most wonderful Yiddish-Polish, which sounded [crying] like music to me, she said: *"Mitn grestn fargenign!"* (With the greatest pleasure). When she spoke, she was singing... and I enjoyed that singing. And she showed me a room... to me it was like a palace. And not only that [crying], "I will also supply you with breakfast." [Crying, next words unclear.] That moment I'm picturing to myself. So every morning [the crying becomes gentle laughter] her two little daughters, young kids, would bring up a tray with breakfast, as if I were a sort of prince.

AK: Which is what you were: A. Printz [one of the poet's earliest pseudonyms].

BG: Haha! And I stayed there a few months, and enjoyed myself immensely. I stayed—I didn't leave the rooms. Stayed all day long: editing manuscripts, preparing to print—

AK: But you didn't actually produce the newspaper?

BG: I would bring the manuscripts from time to time to the printing press where Katz, Benyomen Katz, also a poet, worked.

AK: I wanted to ask about him. He's in Israel now.

BG: Yes. With his wife, Broche Kopstein.

AK: Also a poet.

BG: Yes. A very fine poet who was underestimated.

AK: Did Benyomen Katz contribute poetry to your magazines in New York? Was he with the Proletpen?

BG: He was; in his spirit he was a proletarian poet, but he was eaten up by economic conditions; he always had to work hard to make a living, and his poetry was not properly accepted. He was underestimated.

AK: And so was Broche.

BG: Oh yes, she was underestimated completely, because she was a Zionist, and a very active Zionist.

AK: I don't feel that now, in her letters to me.

BG: When I was in Canada, as the editor of *Der Kamf*, some of our readers would tell me: "Be aware—she's against our movement."

AK: But she was *for* another movement. She was *for* something else.

BG: They told me she was against, at that time. So, I remember: once she invited me for supper at her house, and the three of us spent a nice afternoon; but it took me quite some time to begin to like her, because of [chuckling] those prejudices.

AK: I had the same kinds of experiences...

BG: *Mir hobn alle genung gezindikt* [We have all sinned enough] ...Yes. One of the writers, by the way, should be mentioned, who is now a leading writer in the other camp, Shien Apter.

AK: I met him recently at the CYCO.

BG: He writes historical novels.

AK: But he knows Canada...he spoke to me about Canada.

BG: Yes. Yes. He *was* in Canada. He brought me his very first story to print. Both of us were very young, and he wrote nicely; he knew the technique of writing, and his Yiddish was very fine. But I didn't like the content.

AK: Yes.

BG: I like his style, I like his serious approach to literature. At that time he was a shopworker, and in his story, he depicted the Jewish shopowner in a very bad light.

AK: But Rosenfeld did the same thing in his shop poems.

BG: Yes, yes—but in poetry it's different. This was a story, supposed to be built on episodes. Anyway, the Jew, the owner, came out like a very terrible person who made a fire in his shop—for insurance...

AK: I see.

BG: So I had arguments with him, with Apter.

AK: You felt that would add to anti-Semitism.

BG: Anti-Semitism. I told him these words: It sounds, it smells anti-Semitic. How can we print in a Yiddish paper such a story? Why emphasize the fact that he was Jewish? He could be anybody. You don't have to mention the nationality. So finally I printed—I took out the sharp edges, and printed it—that was the first story he printed...Now, to get back to Benyomen Katz. He was the printer. I would bring him the manuscripts, just give him the manuscripts. I would leave quickly, by a different route.

AK: It was brave of you to stay in Toronto.

BG: After a few months the police raided that place too.

AK: The printshop, or your apartment?

BG: The apartment. I wasn't in the house. I used to hide away things. I had mainly bourgeois magazines on the desk...the local newspapers, and so on. And my real manuscripts I would hide away where nobody could find them. So that here I had to use various [chuckling] inventions. Once more I had to move. On the same day I had to move to another place, which had a lot of exits. I felt this was a good place for me. The house was run by two elderly women—old maids, teachers. I paid them by the month, and I stayed there, in that place a few more months till I went back to New York...At that time the main leader, Tim Buck, was in jail, and the police shot through the window into his cell, a number of times. They nearly killed him. It was a terrible regime. And then the police would come to the office of *Der Kamf*. There would be Sam Lapedes, the manager, who also starved naturally. [Chuckling] They would ask him: "Where is the editor?" And he would say: "We don't know." "How come," they asked, "how does the paper appear on the stands?"

AK: A good question.

BG: They couldn't take it off the stands, according to law.

AK: Do copies still exist?

BG: Yes. On the wall there was the death mask of the former editor, Philip Halperin was his name. So they would say to him, to Lapedes, the manager: "You see the death mask of Philip Halperin on the wall? That will be *your* end!" [Too moved to continue.]

AK: Terrible intimidation. But he still didn't tell where you were.

BG: He would come and tell me this... And my official wages were [chuckling] fourteen bucks a week.

AK: But you didn't see that.

BG [chuckling]: No. I didn't see that... they had to pay for the printing... and for the paper. But we kept it up for fourteen months.

AK: Amazing. Really. It's a great story.

BG: And later on my friends and co-workers from Canada sent me over a volume, a book of the time of those fourteen months. I had a lot of articles and poems there. Very often I had to fill out the paper because I had no assistants.

AK: So, much of it was your own work.

BG: Yes. Altogether I was fourteen months there.

AK: In hiding. Like Neruda...

BG: Very memorable months.

June 1986

This Is Not the Road

RAJZEL ZYCHLINSKA

And where *is* the road?
Where *is* the city?
The sun is ready to go down,
and I have not yet found
the spot
the stone
on which to lean my head for a night's rest
and again see the ladder in my dreams
with the angels
who still deliver me
from the flames.

—Translated from the Yiddish by Aaron Kramer

VII
Culture

September-October 1965

'An Art of Anger...'

AVROM YANOVSKY

A painter can't leave people out. The artists who eliminate people are in trouble...That's why I think the abstractionists have reached the saturation point. Their work has become so clinical, so full of attempted purity. So devoid of people that it's killing them...

This quotation, depicting so accurately the major reason for the moribund state of contemporary Canadian (and not only Canadian) art and artists, was made only the other day by Toronto painter and art gallery owner Jack Pollock, when interviewed by an art critic of a local newspaper.

Clearly then, it seems that "Western" art needs saving—by artists who will not "eliminate people" from their paintings and sculptures, by artists who are humanists to start with. Last summer, during my visit to Mexico, I met the founder of just such a humanist art movement who said, "I could not eliminate man from my work, deny his existence, and content myself with painting only forms, textures, abstract excitement. To paint a universal theme in terms that could be understood in Tokyo and Tel Aviv, New Delhi and Birmingham, in universal language grown out of the grammar of Mexican realism, this was my goal."

This was 35-year-old Calgary-born Arnold Belkin, now a resident of Mexico for many years and one of that country's prominent muralists. Vancouver is graced by his *Warsaw Ghetto Uprising* mural which he presented last year to the Jewish Community Centre in memory of his late father.

Significantly enough, my personal acquaintance with Belkin began last summer at the first public demonstration welcoming back Mexico's leading muralist, David Alfero Siqueiros, a few days after his release from prison. It was in front of Siqueiros' as yet uncompleted mural in Mexico's National Museum. Artists and art students marched in with banners bearing greetings to the "Maestro," as he is called.

Why significantly? Because the presence there of Belkin and his colleagues symbolized the relationship of this young humanist art movement toward the "old" Siqueiros, the only one living of Mexico's

"Big Three" great revolutionary muralists, painters of Mexico's turbulent revolutionary history. (Diego Rivera and Jose Clemente Orozco were the other two.)

Thus, while Belkin and his group sharply disagreed with Siqueiros' continuing adherence to "Social Realism" in art (they believed that although it was an inevitable and necessary outgrowth of Mexico's revolutionary history, today it was outdated; something new and different was needed), they nevertheless looked up to Siqueiros as the Maestro, and living symbol of Mexico's greatness in the world of art.

This was most clearly demonstrated in the third issue of their magazine, *Nueva Presencia* (New Presence), edited by Belkin, which was devoted entirely to honoring the then incarcerated Siqueiros, on the occasion of his 65th birthday.

Sometime later, in his studio, where I spent a stimulating afternoon, Belkin explained for the readers of *Canadian Jewish Outlook* his humanist art philosophy and the painting movement that resulted from it.

Before anything else, it was driven home to me that they considered themselves disciples of Orozco, who in his murals often depicted, in a powerfully violent expressionistic manner, man's inhuman deeds against his fellow man. Injustice, bigotry, dictatorship, militarism and war filled his murals. He included revolution too. Lacking a class approach, his powerful art stressed the negative aspects of reality, with no one to change it.

But let Belkin explain: "When Jose Clemente Orozco died in 1949, there were no disciples to carry on in his direction. He left no school, no following. Instead, the influence of Rivera was more marked. His colorful stylizations of Mexican history and folklore were more accessible to a generation of painters who were just discovering their own national identity—at a time when nationalism elsewhere in art was disappearing."

Rivera, according to Belkin, led Mexican art up a blind alley. Reaction came violently: abstract expressionism made its appearance in the commercial galleries of Mexico City, establishing itself firmly as the art of the "vanguard."

Mexican gallery-goers began accepting "action painting" as the expression of our times, twenty years after the battle had been fought out in New York, Paris, Rome and Tokyo. (This reminded me of Canada.)

Two divisions formed, continued Belkin, "abstract" and "realist." The abstract deviated from the strictly descriptive indigenous trappings and customs to geometrized shapes and cubistic stylizations—or to violent "action" painting that the artists had learned from reproductions in the American *Art News Magazine*. Realism was equated with such terms as "the Mexican School" and "Revolutionary," although, according to Belkin, it was revolutionary neither in form nor in content.

Belkin could not be content with the depiction of local customs, nor painting only forms, textures, abstract excitement. MAN must always be the centre of his work, and expressionism the method of depicting him.

Belkin explained expressionism as the art of inner conflict, of the tension and nervousness of man engaged in a moral struggle with his own conscience. It is an art of soul searching in order to comprehend the exterior world. *It is an art of anger,* stressed Belkin, *an art that fights complacency and wants to reform the world, an art of content and of communication.*

Soon Belkin discovered that he was not alone. While developing as a figurative painter, working in an expressionist vein, he met other painters of his age who were also developing in the same Orozco direction, rejecting the Mexican school conditioned by Rivera. They had understood and assimilated the challenge of Orozco. They wished to create what Belkin termed a new image of the human condition, an image of inner vision, of powerfully felt and powerfully expressed emotion.

Rafael Coronel, then 27 (in 1959), held an exhibition in the Palace of Fine Arts of a series of portraits of "social types": clowns, whores, procurers, chorus girls, members of the bourgeoisie. (Again the negative features of reality.) And Francisco Icaza, who in his European travels became influenced by the Belgian expressionist Ensor's vision of a world of madness.

The ferment was there. What brought these artists into a cohesive group was Arnold Belkin's review in the publication *Mexico en La Cultura* of Seldon Rodman's book *The Insiders*, published in 1960. In this book, Rodman presented a group of figurative artists working in the expressionist tradition of Orozco against the current of formalism prevailing as the official school in the Western world. Belkin, in his review, proposed a re-evaluation of contemporary Mexican painting, saying that the spirit of Orozco was not dead and that artists of a younger generation, yet unknown, would come forth with a new humanism in painting.

Shortly afterwards, on July 20, 1961, these artists held their first joint exhibition of paintings in Mexico City, which included some works by the late Orozco. The exhibition was called *Los Interioristas* (The Insiders).

But, concluded Belkin, we are not united as a group. Some of us reject the term "Interioristas." Some of us rebel against labels or tendencies or even ideas of affinities, but all of us feel that if a new art is to arise in

Mexico, it will most likely come from our generation.

We need such a movement in Canada too, one of art that is *not* "devoid of people," in order to rescue Canadian art from the "non-objective" stranglehold, but minus the *flaw* in the Mexican humanist movement. Because they view man as being engaged *only* "in a moral struggle with his own conscience, an inner conflict," thus reflecting the theory of man in general being guilty for all the evils in this world, they depict in the main their human beings in contorted, abnormal and often hideous forms.

There are such people in our society who can only be *artistically depicted truthfully* in that manner—the *real* guilty ones. What of the others, who "fight complacency and want to reform the world"? They must be pictured differently; true, not prettified—done expressionistically, emotionally, but shown as positive human beings—it can be done.

Seldon Rodman, in an article in the *Mexico Quarterly Review* about this art movement, wrote that because of the "tragic realities" today, "The guilt must show. Pastorales are hardly appropriate to the walls of Buchenwald or a bomb shelter."

We heartily agree. But why not also depict the forces active in the elimination of future Buchenwalds and the need for bomb shelters?

September 1971

Marc Chagall Pavilion at 'Man And His World'

RUTH PRESSMAN

The prevailing mood, as we enter the little pavilion at Expo 67 exhibiting graphics, books and posters by Marc Chagall while listening to the voice of this great master on tape (an interview with him on his life and art), is one of being in a Chagall Sanctuary.

A recent photographic portrait of the master taken by Daniel Fresnay greets you from the centre of a wall in the first room, where many books are on display, and still more photographs of him, Mme. Valentina

Chagall and his family. The sensitive handsome face of the aged artist, a youthful gleam in his eyes coupled with a kind of sweet solicitude, establishes strong impact upon the visitor.

A thought strikes you at once: One can never see enough of the immensity of this great painter of extraordinary visions. And though there is always an existing gap in the taste and appreciation of the individual in the realm of aesthetics, here in this small Chagall Pavilion viewing the exhibit one simply experiences a miraculous transformation in self. A kind of spiritual power overtakes you in praise of human beauty and without any shock to our visual sensibilities. Looking on, one easily breaks away from the traditional forms in art, evoking a sense of humanity and loving empathy for the master's world. Such a pattern of reflections is set for us by the artist himself.

Marc Chagall was born in Vitebsk, Russia, July 7, 1887. Love and faith in mankind are the spiritual ingredients of his imagery. From childhood on he was caught up in colorful village life in Vitebsk, sharing with us the beauty and sadness, the poverty and joys never to be abandoned from his work. His art extends beyond the boundaries or the subject matter. Lovers, peasants, his Vitebsk and his later discovery of Paris, given a kind of marital aura uniting both cities in his blessings. His love for his people, the wandering Jews, all these dynamic forces Chagall binds harmoniously with noble spirit guarding over his fantasies and folk tales, depicting on canvas, generating artistic excitement in a multitude of ways.

In his autobiography, *My Life*, the master writes, "If my art played no part in the life of my parents, their life and their creations have strongly influenced my art. It might be said that while still in my mother's womb I had become aware of the purity of the colors of flowers and that when I first saw a young girl I was dazzled by her beauty. Since my childhood I have been wedded to purity of color and nothing which I was taught ever satisfied me."

Hence, no modern work of art has penetrated so deeply into the world of fantasy-reality as has Chagall's. Thus he paints in his unique manner with a most profound love for the universe.

To be in his world is probably comparable to being in the imaginary Garden of Eden and yet more mystified, perplexed by his floating lovers amid lilac blossoms, fiancees with bouquets, birds, landscapes, expressing a way of life and beyond it all the hovering spirit of infinity, a longing for brotherhood amongst people and nations.

Such if you wish are the ringings of this great painter's brush, poured out on canvas in bold and magical colors.

The little Chagall Pavilion given to us in 1971 is a remarkable contribution to our artistic involvement at Man and His World. It is primarily an exhibit of graphics; there are no paintings. Last year we had a rare opportunity to view in the French Pavilion stage sets by Chagall for the ballet *The Firebird* by Igor Stravinsky, performed by the Metropolitan Opera. Now, at this Pavilion, we see some of the exquisite etchings as illustrations for the poetic novel by Gogol, *Dead Souls*. Altogether there were 96 etchings. Also several etchings for La Fontaine's "Fables," a great work which took Chagall three years to complete. And the six unusual illustrations for the "Letter to Marc Chagall," the title of a poem by the Polish poet Jerzy Ficowski. (This poem was printed in the May-June 1971 issue of the *Canadian Jewish Outlook* and it evoked great interest in the reader.) The opening bars of the poem pull the reader in with such poignancy: "What a pity that you don't know Rosa Gold/The saddest golden rose."

"Letter to Marc Chagall" is the poet's anguish against the Nazi crimes committed against Polish Jews during the Nazi Holocaust. Chagall, deeply moved by Ficowski's poem, illustrated the French translation, published in 1970, printed by Adrien Maeght, Paris.

The lament of the Jew, plea for the innocent children who perished from Nazi brutality, the Jew fiddler crying from the rooftops in soulful mourning, a human soul crucified, time is eternal, such are the delicate, sensitive tracings in these illustrations. And looking on we begin to feel and penetrate under the master's creative spell, captivated by his rendition in the fusion of man-animal, fish, rooster and in all of the master's symbols that are part of his world. And here also are forever present his *shtetl*, Vitebsk, the gentle woman, his betrothed Bella with the many caressing images which appear in these poetic illustrations. It is the master's echo from his very depths to a soulful poem.

Chagall does not simply romanticize. He is also a great storyteller. He stirs a hidden, mystic force within our own sensibilities and thus we glide along in his and what temporarily becomes our world in blended dream and reality—soaring up on his wings, reaching out towards a universal love.

In the Pavilion we also find unusual and unfamiliar posters. Many of them bear Chagall's personal signature. Such are two from an exhibit in Kyoto, Japan, held there in 1963. One from the National Occidental Museum of Art, the other from the Municipal Museum in Kyoto.

One depicts the bride in some strange reverie. The face is virtually drowned in mystic, Chagallesque blues, with only a violin resting in mid-air in colors of yellow melancholy. And as if suddenly, a striking face above again in blue with haste to place flowers upon the bride's veil. I experienced an agonizing moment while looking at this poster, sensing the prophecy of his beloved Bella's premature death.

And the poster from the Municipal Museum. What do the two juxtaposed profiles of green cow and woman whisper to us on this silent moonlit night?

The eyes of both cry out in innocence. Both soft, maternal, gentle images. A bouquet of red roses carried by a hand from the mystic unknown distance. Might it not be the cry for Peace on Earth against evil that lurks in such a dense moonlit night, so green, so blue, so terrifying.

The Geneve monotypes are represented in this exhibition through a whimsical, smiling self-portrait with pigeon upon his head. A masterly drawing.

Another famous poster arrests your attention, from the painting "The Russian Revolution," telling us in his colorful manner of the complexities a revolution brings with it in its radical social changes, and above all the perplexity and uncertainty of its new order by the masses.

We see the Russian people swept by the Red Banner with hammer and sickle. A forlorn Jew sits in the middle of the street clinging to his Red Torah, while still another Jew leaves his home with sack upon his shoulders in readiness to join the march. And in some far distance we recognize the painter's easel with fingers touching canvas.

Here is master, creator, eternal recorder of events, prophet who comes to us through his art to immortalize an epoch for generations to come.

So many posters in homage to Marc Chagall's 80th birthday from France, Israel, Switzerland, etc. Honors flow upon him from all corners of the world, in marking this great occasion. And rightly so, for Chagall has become the lighthouse for the contemporary painter. Chagall's imaginative mind has united beautifully our past Jewish traditions with today's secular ways, inspiring young and old. He helps break the shackles of all conventional thinking in liberating the path to new realities and thus ennobling our psyche in the search of creative acceptance.

This great master being a mystic in essence, a believer in prophets and their dreams, paints memories, reminiscences, lovers descending from exalted heights in laudation of the woman, mother of earth and man, projecting the splendors in the Kingdom of Love.

The bible themes as seen on display in his book are of his greatest creations, deeply stirring. Universal in concept, they reach out into the sublime. This Pavilion also brings into view in book form Chagall's famous stained glass windows, dedicated to the Twelve Tribes and placed

Adoration of the Moon (oil on canvas, 1944) by Max Weber (November 1987)

Joshua at Jericho (drawing) by Avrom Yanovsky (February 1964)

Land of Plenty (woodcut, 1936) by Lucienne Block (July-August 1983)

Poster by Marc Chagall (September 1971)

in a specially built chapel in the Hadassah Hospital in Jerusalem. Since the Jewish religion does not permit the portrayal of the human figure in synagogues, the master solved the problem by taking advantage of the use of sacred bestiary, thus providing an excellent outlet for his great masterpieces in stained glass, bequeathing yet more strength and feeling for humanity.

Perhaps to some visitors the little Chagall Pavilion brought another discovery of that being: that Chagall not only paints lyrically, he actually writes lyrics himself. Here we have a glimpse into some of Chagall's poems in the French book printed in 1968 in Geneva with the original engravings.

Mysterious is the engraving for the poem *"Je ne sais pas"* (I do not know). And exciting the one for *"Ma Fiancee Blanc"* (My White Bride). We also see on display the one for "The Road." All these engravings are his reverence for Birth and Eternity, surrendering his dream-like realism, these subtle and sensuous utterings of his. In a deeper sense it is poetry of the scriptures, a "Song of Songs," a return to faith and love for Mankind.

March-April 1974

In Siqueiros' Studio

SAMUEL L. KAGAN

David Alfaro Siqueiros died on January 6, 1974, at the age of 77 in Cuernavaca, an hour's ride from Mexico City. He was one of the most controversial figures in the world, especially in his native Mexico, loved by many but hated by the establishment; admired and ridiculed, feared and revered.

His revolutionary career started early and at the age of seventeen he was made a staff officer of the "Baby's Brigade" in the Carranza army. Later, in 1938, his military experience was again used, as an officer in the Spanish Republican Army.

In 1919-21, as military attache at the Mexican Legation in Paris, he came into contact with stimulating contemporary artistic movements. On his return to Mexico he became a leader of the Syndicate of Technical Workers, Artists and Sculptors and a founder of the magazine *Machete* which expounded the principles of a new national "people's art." In subsequent years he travelled extensively to Moscow, New York, Los Angeles, Havana and several South American cities, making his influence felt as an artist and revolutionary.

He, together with Diego Rivera, Jose Clemente Orozco and others, were responsible for the revival of painting frescoes and murals. They created hundreds of murals of social significance where the struggle for life and national independence were the main themes. Siqueiros' style was a dynamic contrast of light and dark, depicting violent social protest. His works can be seen in many public buildings and large hotels in Mexico City, Cuernavaca and other centres in Mexico. One of his murals is in the Mexican School in Chillan, Chile. Two murals which he painted in Los Angeles, at the Chouinard Art Institute and the Plaza Art Centre, were both destroyed.

For many years he was active in the Communist Party of Mexico, serving as its National Secretary for a period. He was persecuted, jailed and deported. For the four years 1960-64 that he was imprisoned in Mexico, he carried on his work, making sketches and painting without breaking stride. Two years after his release from jail he was granted the highest national honor for art by the same government that had sent him to jail for his politics—perhaps trying to separate these two aspects in a way that Siqueiros himself never could. Just as the government, which he hated and which hated him, was nevertheless overwhelmed by his artistic creativity, so it was that one of his most devoted and admiring patrons was a member of the wealthy class. In 1967 he received the Lenin Peace Prize from the Soviet Union for his activities on behalf of peace.

I had a personal encounter with Siqueiros early in 1966, while spending some months in Mexico. He was working on one of his large projects, planned for the Casino de la Selva in Cuernavaca. A tremendously large studio had been specially equipped for this work and he employed about twenty young artists of many countries to work with him. I went with Malca Rabal, the cultural leader of the Centro Deportivo Israelita, who knew Siqueiros personally. She warned me that should I find him at work on the scaffold, I was to run as fast as I could for he was quite likely to throw a can of paint at any intruder.

I carefully planned to come after the lunch hour, hoping that the staff of apprentices would be on the scaffold and Siqueiros in his studio on the ground floor. It turned out differently, when I opened the door (leaving Malca outside), Siqueiros was standing on the scaffold working with his brush. He noticed me as soon as the door closed and there was no retreat for me. I introduced myself as a sculptor from Canada and how surprised I was at his warm, cordial reception. When I told him that Malca was with me he himself went out to invite her into the studio.

Siqueiros explained the whole project to us. There was a large maquette built proportionately to the size of the building which was to house the murals, and hundreds of panels were to be individually painted, transported and set up in the site. With the little English and Russian that he knew, with my few words of Spanish, but particularly with the help of Malca, we spent a most enjoyable hour. He posed with us for photographs and was genial and courteous throughout. I remember one of his most emphatic comments: "If I cannot serve the people, I feel my art is worthless." It was an unforgettable experience for me.

In my discussions with young painters and sculptors in Mexico, many objected violently to Siqueiros' style and theme of work, calling him "old hat" and "propagandist." However, people generally, and the working people in particular, were his greatest and faithful admirers.

When he died, his body rested for 24 hours in the Palazzo des Bellas Artes in Mexico City (where one of his murals was executed) and he was interred in the Rotunda of Famous People in the Dolores Cemetery. After his death, President Alvarez declared that "Siqueiros in his creations pulled together the dynamic forces of revolutionary thought, nurtured by the progressive social movement of our revolution, which has contributed to a better understanding of the process of independence for the Mexican people."

January 1980

Enriching Introduction to Cree Culture

JACKSON BEARDY—LIFE AND ART by Kenneth James Hughes.
Winnipeg: Canadian Dimension.

REVIEWED BY HENRY M. ROSENTHAL

Congratulations are in order to *Canadian Dimension* for this handsomely produced introduction to the life and work of Jackson Beardy, Ojibway Indian artist. Containing some 28 illustrations of Beardy's art, including nine in full color, this book combines attractive layout and design to produce maximum visual impact. At the same time, one must appreciate the efforts at economy on the part of the publishers to keep this fascinating book within the reach of Mr. Average Man.

Kenneth James Hughes, the author, is dean of studies and a teacher of Canadian literature at St. John's College, University of Manitoba. His critiques on Ojibway-Cree art and artists have appeared in *Canadian Dimension* and have done much to enlarge our understanding of this new burgeoning art among our native peoples.

Hughes' portrait of Beardy's evolution as an artist describes eloquently the dilemma of marginalized man, alienated from his own cultural background, yet not accepted by the majority culture. This tragic brew of conflict and alienation, so familiar to many of our native people, has produced widespread social pathology, despair, alcoholism and suicide. It is a tribute to the enduring spirit of human beings that such conditions may also produce an expressive art form or powerful social movements for survival.

Jackson Beardy, like his compatriots, absorbed the oral traditions of his Woodland Cree ancestors at his grandmother's knee. Removed from his Cree environment to a distant boarding school, Beardy underwent the familiar educational process of church-run residential schools. The main effect of such schools was to alienate youngsters from their culture and language and above all to implant a different way of looking at the world. Beardy's school experience produced confusion and deep self-hatred which would remain as a malevolent influence in his make-up.

But his exposure to white man's culture also sparked and encouraged his interest in visual art. Since that time, Beardy's life has been a dialectic of struggle between contending forces. His art represents a triumphant synthesis of this struggle between the white conscious mind and the dreams and visions of his Indian subconscious. It goes without saying that Beardy's synthesis of the warring elements was not achieved without much travail and pain. In providing visual symbols and forms for the myths and legends of his people, he enriches all of us. The richly annotated illustrations in Hughes' text provide not only explanation of Beardy's symbology, but also a useful introduction to the Cree culture.

Finally, a special note should be taken of Hughes' appendix on Art and Society. It represents one of the most cogent efforts yet made to explore the role of art and the artist in the Canadian context. It probes searchingly the problem of the native artist—his relationship to white society and to his own culture, and their differing concepts of individualism, esthetics and the nature of reality. For all of this, we are much indebted to the sensitivity and insight of Kenneth James Hughes. He deserves a wide readership.

May-June 1981

A Special Man, A Special Musician
A Tribute to Emil Gartner

EDWARD PARKER

Emil Gartner had much to say about the role of music in healing a people's wounds, in restoring its energies and pride, and in creating bridges between peoples. Not enough of what Emil had to say found its way into writing. It was through his melding of the Toronto Jewish Folk Choir into an eloquent instrument of communication that he was best able to place his thoughts, beliefs and convictions on record. But Emil did write, as the pages of the Souvenir Programs of the Toronto Jewish Folk Choir attest.

Emil Gartner came to the choir in 1939. In September of that year the world was at war. Choir members were in the armed services, but the choir continued to function under Emil Gartner's direction. In 1943 its concert was dedicated to the struggle of the people of the world to defeat fascism. A featured work, "Death to the Enemy," a dramatic presentation of Jewish folklore, was arranged by Emil Gartner. The program included the premieres of two works dealing with the main theme—"My Wheat Fields Shine Against the Beauty of the Sun," music by Max Helpfman, and "A Call to Arms by the Rabbis of Vilna," text and music by Herbert Haufrecht.

In the Souvenir Program Emil wrote: "It is our privilege to keep up the great traditions of Jewish culture and its folklore in song and melody as well as classical music. At the same time we do not lose sight of important works of contemporary composers who have something to say. We feel that understanding these messages will bring the vital unity needed of all people for the final crushing of Hitlerism... That unity we owe to the millions of our brothers and sisters chained and murdered by the Nazi beast. We owe it to all those, who, while there is still a spark of life left in them, are hoping and praying for the hour of deliverance."

In 1947, in an article entitled "Our Life Our Art," he asks himself, "What is Jewish music? Is there such a thing as Jewish music? Is there any real necessity for the existence of a Jewish choir? Is there a Jewish culture?" and further, "Is the existence of a Jewish culture possible in a country where Jews constitute a small minority and a widely scattered one at that?"

Emil Gartner had no difficulty with the answers. He wrote: "The culture of a people can best be described as the sum total of all its achievements as well as its mode of living. Suffice it to say that as long as Jews continue to be a people with their own history, religious, ethical and moral heritage, so long will its culture remain Jewish. No, we Jews need not fear being lesser Canadians by being better Jews: on the contrary, we shall be better Canadians by being conscious Jews. To those who doubt, let it be said that the coming of a distinctly Canadian culture will be moulded out of the cultural contributions of all peoples, who, in their entirety are called: the Canadian People. We contribute to Canadian culture something priceless and absolutely irreplaceable: originality of creation. A beautiful color in the rainbow of the world's cultural beauties. How could we in a better way show our love for Canada?

"It may be said that Jewish music, for instance, has been greatly influenced by the music of many countries whence the Jew has come. Of course that is true. But it is equally true of the music of all other nations and peoples. There is no single instance in the history of art where one people did not benefit by the influences of others. George Gershwin, for instance, was both a Jew and an American, and he, who created a distinctly American music practically by himself, drew heavily from the rich well of Negro folklore. In his music one most assuredly finds the musical language of the American Negro as well as certain Jewish inflections.

"There are in our country living Jewish composers who create living Jewish music, regardless of the many different influences they may have absorbed. They will as human beings feel the pain and joy our people experience and will give expression to these feelings."

He continues, "Therefore our Jewish folk choir endeavors to bring to life such Jewish music. We are simply singing our people's song and there are always thousands who come to hear us. By opening our minds and hearts, we can feel the pulse of another people. It usually proves to be closer to ours than we anticipated, thanks to the continuous interchange and thanks above all to the kinship of all humanity. We shall be able to sing the great song of Canada that is yet to be written and we shall have contributed to it, we may hope, a phrase or two."

We go to the year 1950—the 25th anniversary of the Toronto Jewish Folk Choir. In that Souvenir Program Emil sent a greeting to the choir which is his estimation and his tribute to the individuals who formed the choir. Emil wrote: "...Many critics and audiences have experienced and commended our choir for its spontaneous and spirited singing. This indeed is a very great compliment and we are forever thankful for it. How many weary hours and weeks have our singers spent to discover the heart of a new musical work? How earnest was the desire to know the secrets of what made it beat? Yet this is the only road to artistic worthiness in every age and moreso in this day of superficial art which only tries to please desires not worth pleasing, excite emotions unworthy of excitement."

In the same 25th anniversary Souvenir Program Emil also wrote: "To perform with truthfulness is the greatest achievement of a body of artist-singers... To penetrate into the spirit of a song is to have succeeded in getting to the deepest wells of the fountain of the overflowing wells of life itself."

Emil Gartner never tired of explaining that understanding the role of music in human society did not automatically equate with merely knowing music. "To sing of love, one must have known and experienced love; to sing of work, is to have worked oneself; to sing of suffering is to know suffering, to have experienced it well." Emil's credo and the heritage he left us was expressed by him in that same statement—"Music is the artistic truth of life itself, life in all its overflowing colors and richness. To communicate truth to an audience is the artist's supreme reward."

This is what Emil Gartner told us he believed. We then may believe that Emil Gartner experienced his artistic reward by bringing to his audiences music about the essential power and goodness of universal man.

Music and Humanity Flowed Through His Baton

The late Emil Gartner's memory is very much alive with me. He was a pupil, a warm friend and a professional colleague. He had a profound understanding of the role of the composer in our society, and the Jewish Folk Choir followed his compelling leadership through numerous performances of music by living composers. His interpretive and conducting talents made voices sing out with spontaneous fervor to unite music and meaning. He was the conductor as teacher. And his singers, too, were enriched by his instinctive musicality. But there was also another dimension to Emil Gartner's music-making: his concern for the human condition. Music and humanity were never separated in his mind and they flowed through his baton to inspire both singers and listeners. Under his direction the Jewish Folk Choir became the voice of the Toronto Jewish community. Emil Gartner left a tradition of choral conducting that has kept the Toronto Jewish Folk Choir alive today. His is a memory to cherish for all time.

—*John Weinzweig, O.C.*

Emil Gartner and Toronto's Composers

Emil Gartner was a very special man and an equally special musician who earned a place in the history of composition in Canada and the gratitude of many of its composers.

He was a musician with an extraordinary sense of service to his community, for whom it was important to live with challenges and the opportunities for growth. He was one of the very first in Canada to work consistently with the composers of his time, to seek them out and to pull them into the service of his choir, the Toronto Jewish Folk Choir. It is not easy for us today to realize and appreciate how unusual and risky that was.

Composers were rare beings in Canada in the forties. A few in Toronto had ventured into the dangerous waters of contemporary music, anxious to make a mark in a society that had no way of understanding or acknowledging their aspirations. The composers were mostly ignored except by a few sensitive citizens who reacted to the ferment of creative energy around them. Emil was one of the first to sense what was going on and moreover was able to respond in the way that counted most; he commissioned new works for performance by the Toronto Jewish Folk Choir.

Here was a man, a choral conductor with unique talents and highly individualized views about vocal production and choral techniques, who built this choir into one of the city's treasures. It was nevertheless an amateur choir, learning its repertoire not from an ability to sight-read easily and efficiently, but by rote. This was Emil's instrument.

If there are some in the choir today who go back to Gartner's days, they can appreciate the amount of *chutzpa* and hard work that accompanied the gesture of having new works commissioned for, and performed in such large numbers by, this choir.

The works premiered in concert after concert were not all successes. I know that the ones I wrote for the choir were far from good. Many of the new works were unnecessarily difficult, sometimes pretentious and, as often as not, suffering from the arrogance and ambition of youth. But the important thing is that Emil made them happen, gave them a chance to be heard and gave the composers a chance to assess the quality of their work in actual concert conditions.

It was Emil's sympathy, his real interest and concern for his composer friends and the encouragement that flowed so naturally from him, that was so immeasurably valuable. In the wisdom of retrospect we can appreciate and cherish those qualities today. They didn't rise to the surface, but were taken as normal during those intense conversations Emil and I used to have as we strolled Toronto's streets near the Christie Pits on a summer's night. Life was different then, Toronto was different and its musicians thin and undernourished artistically as well as financially. In that city Emil and the musicians of my generation shared their emerging maturity.

The progress and improvements these past 30 years have been really astounding. The intensity of Emil's life and his remarkable work during those earlier days are strands in the fabric of the musical life that has been woven since then. We owe much to Emil Gartner, that special man and that equally special musician.

—Louis Appelbaum

April 1984

A Legacy To Be Treasured

SOLOMON SHEK

On October 3, 1983, the Koffler Art Gallery at Toronto's Jewish Cultural Centre opened a month-long exhibit of the sculpture of the late Samuel L. Kagan. The festive launching of the exhibit attracted a large crowd of friends, relatives and art lovers, and throughout the period of the show many more viewers came to see the impressive and excellently arranged exhibit of this talented artist's work.

The Kagan exhibit was an important cultural event for Toronto in general, and particularly for the Jewish community. In this city, the late sculptor lived, worked and created his outstanding figures. At the same time, he was an active educator and worker on behalf of progressive Jewish cultural institutions. Not only did he leave behind him a most impressive array of works of high esthetic value which justly won him a reputation of being a leading Canadian sculptor, he is also recognized as having contributed a great deal to Jewish communal and cultural activity. Over a period of nearly six decades, he gave unstintingly of his time to develop the Morris Winchevsky Children's School, the Toronto Jewish Folk Choir and the YKUF (Yiddishe Kultur Farband). Thus he is doubly remembered—and doubly missed—thanks to these activities.

The attractive catalogue which accompanied the exhibition had on its cover Sam Kagan's exquisite interpretation of Peretz' *Der Nemerover* (the main character of his unforgettable story "If Not Even Higher"), with the folk sage weighed down by the bundle of wood on his shoulders. On the back cover, there is a reproduction of the artist's commemorative medal to David Bergelson, one of the series dedicated to the Soviet Jewish literary and cultural martyrs.

The catalogue has evaluations of the sculptor's work by a number of art critics and other commentators. Pat Fleisher, for example, refers to Kagan as a "man of the people and a people's artist" in her overview of his creativity during some 40 years. Aileen Hooper Cowan, president of the Sculptors' Society of Canada, speaks of Kagan as a man whose interests "centred around people, mainly working people, and ideas." She also points to the help that Sam Kagan offered freely to younger sculptors, his principles and convictions, his warmth and humaneness. Cowan also quotes Itche Goldberg's description of Kagan's character: "Ages of kindness flowed out of him."

Beatrice Magder reflects, on similar lines, on Sam Kagan's artistic credo: ". . . to reflect and emphasize human life, to influence the condition of life and to express it in a creative manner."

The retrospective exhibit displayed some 30 pieces, a representative sampling of the output of Sam Kagan over nearly four decades of artistic activity. Included was the panel of twelve medallions depicting the Soviet-Jewish artists and writers who perished in Moscow on August 12, 1952. Other works on specific Jewish themes that stand out in one's mind are the following: the head of Moishe Nadir; a *Hagba* (a Jew carrying high a *Sefer-Torah*); a silver-painted wood and plaster architechtonic sculpture, entitled *Lo amut ki echya* ("I will not die; instead I will live," a line from Psalm 118); and a number of portraits of Jewish writers, cultural workers and publicists like Moishe Dickstein, Leibl Basman, Morris Surdin, Joshua Gershman and Sam Urbas. (Let us recall that a large sculpture of the classical writer I.L. Peretz, created by Sam Kagan, has for many years adorned the Vancouver Peretz Institute.)

Other striking subjects of the exhibition which emerged from Sam Kagan's deep social sense were his *Coal Heaver*, a 40-centimetre full figure, and his 30-centimetre high plaster head of an unemployed worker of the Dirty Thirties. There are also portraits of the late Canadian progressive poet Joe Wallace and a memorable head of Mexican artist Xavier Guerrero, whom Sam and Anne Kagan became friends with in the 1960s. There are also fine pieces of members of the extended Kagan family.

Sam (Shmuel Lazar) Kagan was born in 1906 in Slovene, near Minsk, in czarist Russia. He arrived in Canada in 1922. Throughout his life he was one of the most active cultural workers in the progressive Jewish movement of Toronto. From our first days in Canada, my wife and I became fast friends with Sam and his first wife, Sarah, sister of Itche Goldberg. We worked closely together in many activities around the United Jewish People's Order, and our children, our son, Ben, and the Kagans' daughter, Gittl, grew up together, both becoming teachers in the Morris Winchevsky School, and counsellors at Camp Naivelt. (We remember fondly Gittl's wonderful rendition of Jewish and other folksongs, and recall with sadness her tragic death as a young adult.) Later we developed a friendship with Sam and his second wife, Anne Adler Kagan, as well as having warm relations with both sides of the Kagan-Goldberg families, and the Adler family. Thus, for the writer of these lines, many threads are linked to the creative artist Sam Kagan and those close to him. Our ties with him were not only to his artistic activities but to the many-sided humanity of the man. Characteristic of Sam Kagan was the unique way in which he combined his art with his humanity ...simplicity, with outstanding talent. He was a gentle, kind friend to many, Jews and non-Jews, people from nearby or far away. He was a total man, both within his family and within the community.

As far as evaluating the esthetic quality of Sam Kagan's work, this task has to fall on others. One thing I do know, though, is that he had a most talented pair of hands in every sense of the word, whether he was building a studio for himself in Camp Naivelt, repairing machinery or shaping a sculpture. Why do I mention these details? Because Sam Kagan was always willing to use his talents to help others.

Sam Kagan joined the revolutionary movement in his native Russia as a young man, barely an adolescent, and he remained a Jewish socialist until his last breath. He was a creative, dedicated and idealistic human being, with strongly humanist convictions. He was a man for all seasons, and thus we will remember him and mourn his passing. The legacy he left behind belongs to all of us, and is one we should treasure.

March 1985

The Artist Speaks

MARGARET ENNENBERG

That's my lost boy-time hanging on the wall.
    We had windmills in the Ukraine, too—
See—one for water, one for grinding grain.
    Look at the fields of yellow ripening wheat!
Such wealth was not for us, except to look,
    For Jews could not own land. My father was
The village blacksmith—you know, shoeing horses,
    Mending plows—a man of iron, his voice
Hoarse and loud over the hammering.

He wept that I was weak—but practical,
Apprenticed me to learn the cobbler's trade.
    I hated it. The thing that I liked best
Was studying machines and how they worked.
    To cut and glue and hammer all day long
    The endless broken shoes was hell for me.
But holidays I walked and walked and walked
    Until I saw this creek. The swimming boys
Yelled *Yid*, threw stones and would not let me play,
    But I stood on the bridge and soaked up peace.

My style, you say, is now called primitive.
    I wouldn't know. Until they fired me
For being sixty-five, the only paint
    I used was painting fences and the house.
But *paint by numbers*—have you seen that toy?
    My boys, they gave me one to please their mom
To keep me busy out of kitchen space.

    I found it was more fun to make my own
And cheaper too. And when you make mistakes
    You paint them over! Here, if things are big,
These are the things that I remember clear.
    The boys are small—I cannot make them real—
But geese and windmills, sky and golden grain,
They go so easy—and they bring me peace.

April 1986

The Precious Legacy

A REVIEW BY RIVA DOLGOY

"The Precious Legacy"—Judaic Treasures from the Czechoslovak State Collections, was lent by the State Jewish Museum in Prague under the sponsorship of the Ministry of Culture of the Czechoslovak Socialist Republic.

In no way does the above title prepare the viewer for the intensity of this display. Photographs of vistas of old Prague streets, exteriors and interiors of synagogues, as well as intimate views of scholars' libraries, all are enlarged so that one walks in Prague, while moving around cases filled with precious items, gigantic candelabra and humble wooden cooking utensils.

Enormous tapestries that covered the entrance to the tabernacle hang in rows; the words of prayers and exaltation, and the decorative borders embroidered with the finest of colored and metallic threads reveal a skill rarely mentioned in our history books. Whole artisan communities flourished in the eighteenth and nineteenth centuries dedicated to and dependent on the enhancement of religious activities.

So we see silver ornaments, from small pointing fingers on hands to pitchers and bowls for ritual handwashing and much more.

Blown glass pitchers with delicate enamel paintings tell us of a burial society's activities, and on the wall nearby hang a series of commissioned portraits, as well as a set of narrative paintings describing all the responsibilities of their society, from visiting the sick, to death, mourning, preparing the body, the walk to the cemetery, burial and the final drink!

But before death comes the beginning of life, and chairs for a *bris* are arranged, the godfather's chair for holding the infant, and nearby the instruments used. In between one must eat, so we have metal and wooden kitchen utensils. Bits of clothing, samples of finery, ceramics, *tallis* and *t'fillin*, portraits of wealthy individuals. Parents and children speak of comfort and ease and a culture, although separated by religion, very much a part of a whole society. And while there are many biblical references in decoration, there are also strong echoes of the prevailing styles and tastes in architecture, painting and the decorative arts. It is the latter which is so highly developed while the paintings range from the naive art of itinerant painters to the sophistication and elegance of the salon portraitist.

Scholarly texts and commentaries by famous rabbis, written in their own hand, exquisite lettering flowing between leather covers are placed next to their portraits in miniature and breathe life and thought even though encased in glass. Nearby appear large photographs of the Nazi program to collect as much as possible of the heritage for their planned museum of a vanished race. Dozens to hundreds of artifacts, tagged and stacked, sit on shelves—the rapidity of the "collection" accelerating into a madness, revealing a parody of scientific and social accumulation of knowledge. The curators of the original Jewish museum are seen organizing the material under the glare of metal shaded lights.

The physical artifacts diminish. Echoes of faded color, textures of fabric, metal and glass, texts describing a middle European life of unbroken tradition disappear as black, white and grey granular enlargements of photographs taken by the Germans appear on the walls. We see Jews rounded up and we are presented with an environment of fear and doom as suitcases are piled up, and finally, a few actual suitcases —methodically numbered. The exhibit is at an end.

Other than stressing the great skill of the manufacturers and embroiderers of the religious tapestries, none of the notes on the walls of the exhibit indicates whether or not the painters/decorators/potters/glass blowers/ furniture makers were or were not Jewish. If they were, we have a deeper tradition and greater links with European life than has ever been explored or explained. If not, there is an important group of patrons who elicited specific responses from non-Jewish artists and craftspeople. This again demands more research and discussion.

July-August 1986

Is Huckleberry Finn Racist?
How Burlesque Operates

PAUL SCHMIDT

Huckleberry Finn has been attacked as racist. Huck, it is claimed, is a white chauvinist and Jim is a stereotyped, chuckleheaded Black. These charges arise in the main from failure to understand the burlesque humor which is the main literary strategy of the novel. The critics without exception misread the deadpan on Huck and Jim as the mark of their idiocy. As in most vernacular American humor, Huck and Jim *pose* as simple-minded backwoods hayseeds in order to take in the presumably refined and superior genteel. It is these Protestant slave-holders who are the ultimate target of Huck's burlesque. An analysis of Clemens' humor in the novel reinforces Bernard DeVoto's claim that this is the great novel to come out of the Civil War. It is great because it strikes a powerful blow for Black and white fraternity and equality, great because of the intensely real drama of Jim's escape from slavery, great because it mounts a profound criticism of upper-class slave-holding culture.

At thirteen Huckleberry is more man than boy, and his humor engages issues of significance. It is neither the bright sayings of children, nor Don Quixote tilting at windmills. He takes on the racism and religious hypocrisy of WASP—White, Anglo-Saxon Protestant—culture, and the demagoguery of bourgeois republican pretensions, the hollow claims of democracy and plenty in a class-divided society. Certainly he uses the boy pose to carry it off and to protect himself, but it is a mask behind which laughter demolishes the Mississippi Valley genteel.

Property is often Huckleberry's target. He and Jim are floating down the Mississippi on a raft, at night so they won't be caught. He says,

> Every night, now, I used to slip ashore, towards ten o'clock, at some little village, and buy ten or fifteen cents' worth of meal or bacon or other stuff to eat; and sometimes I lifted a chicken that warn't roosting comfortable, and took him along. Pap always said, take a chicken when you get a chance, because if you don't want him yourself you can easy find somebody that does, and a good

deed ain't ever forgot. I never see Pap when he didn't want the chicken himself, but that is what he used to say, anyway.

It is not surprising to find Huck a thief; thieving is a necessity if he and Jim are to eat. Nor is it out of character to hear Pap quoted as an authority for Huck's stealing, but Pap's pose as a boy scout authority—"a good deed ain't ever forgot"—is splendid. Huck continues,

> Mornings before daylight, I slipped into corn fields and borrowed a watermelon, or a mushmelon, or a punkin, or some new corn, or things of that kind. Pap always said it warn't no harm to borrow things, if you was meaning to pay them back, sometime; but the widow said it warn't anything but a soft name for stealing, and no decent boy would do it.

A collision of authorities: the widow, the genteel, the "quality," as Huck usually describes them, versus Pap, lumpen proletariat, lower if not working class, "white trash" in the vernacular. And now Jim and Huck enter the discussion.

> Jim said he reckoned the widow was partly right and Pap was partly right; so the best way would be for us to pick out two or three things from the list and say we wouldn't borrow them any more—then he reckoned it wouldn't be no harm to borrow the others. So we talked it over all one night, drifting along the river, trying to make up our minds whether to drop the watermelons, or the cantelopes, or the mushmelons, or what. But towards daylight we got it all settled satisfactory, and concluded to drop crabapples and p'simmons. We warn't feeling just right, before that, but it was all comfortable now. I was glad the way it come out, too, because crabapples ain't ever good, and the p'simmons wouldn't be ripe for two or three months yet.

On the face of it this discussion of how to decide the issue of Pap's versus the widow's moral judgment is so transparently idiotic that it marks not only Huck but Jim too as a mindless child. Exactly. It is the obvious idiocy of conscious clowns. Huck and Jim, idly drifting down the great Mississippi at night, while away the time playing out the burlesque roles of vaudeville comedy comic set-ups to the widow's straight. They play their roles with the unsmiling deadpan which is required to take in the widow—and us if we go along with her—and thereby laugh her off. We laugh with Huck and Jim, not *at* them; the comic butt we laugh at is the widow.

If we suppose, as Huck's critics do, that he and Jim are chuckleheaded idiots, then we are taken in by their humor just as the widow and the judge are: we become, with them, the butt of the humor. Huck and Jim exaggerate the idiocy of which the widow accuses them, make it taller and taller until finally the pose is so egregious it collapses into laughter. At the widow's expense. She is the comic butt for believing Huck and Jim are lower-class dolts, and we laugh off her and her genteel pretensions at superiority.

One may well ask where this leaves the moral issue. Is it good or bad to steal? Huck's morality is, as usual, bedrock, and as usual not expressed explicitly. There is a higher law than property—brotherhood. Huck's and Jim's morality put the widow's and Miss Watson's Christian piety to shame. And the triumph of the novel is its realism: we believe in Huck and Jim as ordinary working people, alive as you and me.

Huck burlesques and laughs off the heart and soul of American leisure-class culture. He turns his caustic wit on Christian conscience on page one and throughout the novel. He burlesques the American Republican Reform Movement, specifically temperance. He burlesques the literary romanticism of the graveyard poets descended from Gray's "Elegy." He burlesques the commodity fetishism which inspires bourgeois home decoration. Finally he gives a scorching account of what Marx called the "rural idiocy" of small towns along the banks of the Mississippi—their hysterical credulity at a Protestant revival meeting, the spineless ease with which they are swept up into a mob lynching, their meanness and their sadism. He demolishes the romantic ideal of back to nature, the primitivism which we take in with our mother's milk, and the idyl of the backwoods yeoman.

Swindling, thieving, murder. Whenever Huckleberry puts in to shore he finds nothing but ugly violence. Perhaps the ugliest is the murder in this little town of the town drunk, Boggs, a stupid and ranting but nevertheless harmless old fellow, by the town's Southern aristocrat, Colonel Sherburn. This searching rejection of the rural ideal, of a return to nature, is conscious in Huck. It is part and parcel of his adequacy to whatever bourgeois slave society confronts him with. He is the comic on top of every encounter with slave-hunting sheriffs, feuding slave-holders, and a father with the DT's—in the fullest sense, then, a hero. And as such the diametric opposite of the lonely, alienated wounded hero of romanticism. He is not the heir of Hamlet nor Melville's Ishmael; nor are Hemingway's Frederick Henry and Salinger's *Catcher in the Rye* his proper descendants. His great distinction is to be altogether outside the established tradition of romantic individualism and alienation.

If Huckleberry is not alienated, what is the source of his power? From what community does he draw this intrepid strength to stand up to the bourgeois quality? He belongs to the community of men who work the boats on the Mississippi, the sailors, raftsmen, keel-boatmen, roustabouts and pilots of what in Mark Twain's time was the main artery of shipping. Like Pablo Neruda, Huck is "fully empowered" by their strength. The raftsmen and Jim are the only ones along the Mississippi who speak his language, the only ones he can't lie to—they catch him up in a split second. In Huck's serene strength, his infinite capacity to take whatever this vicious, violent fake world of the Mississippi Valley dishes out to him and be on top of it, he is the diametric opposite of the castrated and suffering heroes of Hemingway, the infinitely introspective Ancient Mariners of the inner world, those Lost Generations. It is this sense of working-class strength and solidarity which gives Huckleberry and Jim's burlesques moral foundation/conviction.

Huck and Jim figure the universe as a warm barnyard, as some great brooding hen in a fertile spree of laying the millions of stars. The world is peaceful, contented, luxuriantly expansive. It reflects the inner calm and poise of these two. They have no illusions about the vicious world of the quality which exploits Jim as a slave and Huck as a potential slaveholder. Their serenity comes from accepting their place at the very bottom of society. They have, as Karl Marx said, "nothing to lose but their chains." The propertyless can afford, Thoreau points out, to live what is essential.

Unfortunately *Huckleberry Finn* is not all of a piece. Hemingway goes on, "If you read it you must stop where... Jim is stolen from the boys. That is the real end. The rest is just cheating." Both the opening and closing chapters of the novel are seriously marred by Tom Sawyer's taking over and directing the action. Tom *is* racist. He is conventional and respectable and what Huck calls "quality." His boyish games have, as Huck himself recognizes on occasions, "all the marks of a Sunday school."

Tom plays practical jokes on Jim, and through his conventional eyes we see Jim in chapter two as a superstitious fellow who is proud of having been, as he supposes, visited by witches. But once Jim makes a break for freedom he becomes heroic, a strong-hearted intelligent man. Huck's attempts after that to continue playing Tom Sawyer practical jokes on him backfire. If any education of Huck takes place in the course of the novel it is his learning that the man he instinctively allies himself with when he says "they're after *us*" is not going to tolerate childish games and that he, Huckleberry, can no longer be a boy. They are both men and have to face and outwit the violence and rapacity of bourgeois Christian law and order. Jim has dignity beyond any white man in the book. He is strong, capable, decisive. His decision to make a break for freedom is heroic. He is the heir of the freedom which the Black folk hero, Brer Rabbit, fights for. As a portrait of a Black he deserves comparison with the magnificent Frederick Douglass. Douglass was a personal friend of Clemens'.

Tom Sawyer takes on freeing Jim as a game, for he knows, as Huck and Jim do not know, that Jim has already been freed by Miss Watson. Tom's Alexander Dumas hijinks make the last chapters of the novel what Bernard DeVoto calls "the most chilling descent in all literature." Jim in captivity on the Phelps farm docilely follows Tom's Sunday school Boy Scout plots and his racist point of view. He couldn't, the novel tells us,

> see no sense in the most of it but he allowed we [Tom and Huck] was white folks and knowed better than him; so he was satisfied, and said he would do it all just as Tom said.

The ending makes hash of all the brilliant and profound satire on bourgeois culture and religion. Miss Watson is whitewashed. Huck falls into the same treachery. He observes about Jim, when he insists on calling the doctor to take care of Tom's gunshot wounds, that he knows Jim "was white inside." When Mrs. Phelps asks Huck if anyone was hurt in the steamboat accident, Huck makes the most abysmally racist reply, "no'm. Killed a nigger." One may argue that Huck's use of the term elsewhere is natural and inevitable in his speech, but here it denies the very humanity of Blacks.

The book is not, then, a consistent whole. What comic masterpiece is? Chaucer, Cervantes, Rabelais, all are flawed and fragmented in their greatness. Only in the twentieth century do geniuses like Chaplin and Brecht and Hasek sustain large comic designs. Perhaps the burlesque detonation of bourgeois presumption on the working class is too explosive for Mark Twain to carry through to conclusion: Tom Sawyer affords a way of weaseling out. Theodore Dreiser points out a strong dualism in what he calls "Mark, the Double Twain." There is, I think, a division between his solidarity with the working riverboatmen and his uneasy membership in the bourgeois genteel.

In the last analysis we cannot let Tom Sawyer destroy the achievement of this novel. It lies altogether outside the bourgeois literary traditions of individualism and romanticism. I rub my eyes at the notion that a nineteenth century humorist should be class conscious, that he should conduct such a profound satirical attack on the individualism which is the gospel of capitalism. Perhaps I am reading this into Huck's brilliant laughter? The offered alternatives make bright sayings of children out of this great folk hero, or twentieth century *weltschmerz*. Excuse me, I think I do him more justice.

Huckleberry Finn is flawed then, but it still richly deserves its place in the canon of world literature. Its accomplishment is nothing short of miraculous, a work of genius, and one which heartens and enlightens and empowers the struggle in our country for Black and white equality and for economic equality—a struggle led by working-class whites like Huck and working-class Blacks like Jim.

October 1986

The Rediscovery of East European Jewry

SKETCHES OF LATVIA, BYELORUSS AND KURLAND by Hermann Struck and Herbert Eulenberg. Berlin: Strike Verlag, 1916.
THE COUNTENANCE OF EAST EUROPEAN JEWRY by Hermann Struck and Arnold Zweig. Berlin: Welt Verlag, 1920.

REVIEWED BY MICHAL BODEMANN

The First World War brought immense turmoil to German middle-class youth and uprooted traditional ways of life and received ideas. The Nietzschean philosophy of an elite of *Übermenschen* and of the death of God, enthusiasm for the German nation and for the war, romanticized notions of nature, the traditional community and the uncomplicated earthy men and women who allegedly constituted it—all this was suffused with socialist and anarchist ideas and the profound awareness of a deep transformation of the old order and its traditional structures.

Of course, the highly assimilated German-Jewish youth were exposed to these contradictory sentiments no less than their non-Jewish counterparts. This is true at least up to the end of the war—a war in which German Jews participated with no less patriotic fervor than their non-Jewish friends. With the end of the war, however, German-Jewish harmony began to wane: the Treaty of Versailles humiliated Germany and its army, "undefeated in battle"; the monarchy was abolished, a fiercely reactionary opposition to a republican-democratic constitution notwithstanding; and finally, the profound economic crisis impoverished especially the petty bourgeoisie and other traditional segments of the German middle to upper-middle class. In the working class, these developments intensified the class struggle (and, regrettably, the fratricidal war between communists and social democrats). But in the middle and upper class, these experiences called for a scapegoat, in the form of the Jews—that element in German society which epitomized both capitalism and socialism. Jews were seen as denying the traditional order and promoting democracy. They were portrayed as anti-nationalist, anti-war, and as war profiteers all at the same time.

The form of anti-Semitism, then, which led to the rise of German fascism and the unspeakable catastrophe which followed, really began in great measure at least with the end of World War I and the increasing rift between Germans and German-Jews. Two works by Hermann Struck signal that rift. In 1916, Struck published together with Herbert Eulenberg, their *Skizzen aus Litauen, Weissrussland und Kurland*, a set of 60 lithographs accompanied by a commentary on the lands and the peoples under German occupation. The volume was dedicated to, of all people, General Ludendorff, a rabid Prussian reactionary and anti-Semite. The introduction praised the effort of the German High Command to bring the achievements of German administration and culture to these "neglected" areas. The authors of these sketches and commentaries on Lithuanians and Jews, Poles, Latvians and Russians, on Kovno and Vilna, Mitau and Karelia, Bialystok and Grodno, on monasteries, churches, synagogues, bridges and castles, conclude their introduction with greetings to the Germans back home: *"Alle Wege führen nach Deutschland"*—all roads lead to Germany.

Four years later, Hermann Struck published, with Arnold Zweig, his volume *Das Ostjüdische Antlitz* (The Eastern Jewish Countenance), a paradoxical formulation because it mixed what amounted to an epithet—Ostjuden—with the nobility of a "countenance," a noble facial expression. There is little left of his enthusiasm for Germany. In the face of rising anti-Semitism all over Europe, the mood had changed completely. *Das Ostjüdische Antlitz* was written with a sense of mourning for the victims of the pogroms and recent persecutions in the Ukraine, in Hungary and Poland. It was an affirmation of the beauty of the people and of their traditional way of life.

There was, then, a peculiar parallel development in the thought of many young Jews and many young Germans in the days of the Weimar

Republic. The German youth movement turned to what they saw as their German and Germanic roots—roots which ipso facto excluded the "oriental" Jew and which elevated the "Germanic" features, physically and culturally, of the romanticized German peasant. The German-Jews, on the other hand, were in the difficult position of being part of these general ideological currents, while being excluded from the particular substance of this ideology. They therefore had no choice but to return to their own Jewish roots.

But in Germany, with its assimilated Jewry, what specifically *Jewish* roots were there to identify with? As Arnold Zweig has put it in this volume, the Western Jew was on the path to self-isolation in an exclusive, rigidified religious denomination (hence, in the 1920s, the enthusiasm for Martin Buber's discovery of Hasidism!) which enticed Jewish youth onto a "rosy path to extinction in the mishmash of the modern metropolis." Zweig, under the influence of Thomas Mann's *Buddenbrooks*, had sketched this development autobiographically in his novella *Notes About the Klopfer Family* (1909). The *Ostjude*, previously despised in German Jewry as backward, uncultured and filthy, was now being reinterpreted as the backbone of Jewish nationhood: the Eastern Jew "preserved his face" in a traditional, "childlike" and "serene" way of life.

The contact of German-Jewish soldiers with Polish, Russian and Lithuanian Jews in the World War I years on the Eastern front was therefore an inspiring discovery. Last but not least, German-Jews at the time were brought into contact with Bundists, Labor Zionists and Jewish socialists in the East who—most welcome especially for Arnold Zweig—showed a way of combining Jewish nationalism and culture with socialism. As Zweig puts it, Zionism may have begun as a bourgeois movement; only the strength of the young Zionist-socialist groupings, however, could guarantee the construction of a Jewish homeland in Palestine, and therefore, a truly "religious" renewal of Judaism.

The two collaborators on *Das Ostjüdische Antlitz*, who became lifelong friends, nevertheless had quite different outlooks and strengths. Hermann Struck (1876-1944) was born into an orthodox Berlin family, and remained a Zionist, religiously orthodox and a member of the Mizrahi movement all his life. Shortly after the second edition of this volume had appeared, in 1923, Struck moved to Palestine, where he died. He was one of the most outstanding lithographers of his time and taught graphic techniques, especially etching in stone, to fellow artists Chagall, Liebermann, Israels and Clovis Corinth. He excelled as a portraitist, of Ibsen, Nietzsche, Freud and Einstein, and gained fame, especially for his widely known portrait of Herzl.

Arnold Zweig (1887-1968) probably had the more eventful career. He was born in Silesia to a family which had turned early to Zionism, especially as a reaction to local anti-Semitism. Early on, he was greatly influenced by the religious socialism of Martin Buber and by the German-Jewish anarchist Gustav Landauer. For a time in the 1920s, he was the editor of the *Jüdische Rundschau*, and after 1933, by way of France, Czechoslovakia and Switzerland, went to Palestine. Disenchanted with Israel and increasingly isolated, he had slowly moved away from the anarchist and idiosyncratic socialist ideas of his early years and embraced Marxism, then left Israel for East Germany in 1948. After the death of Heinrich Mann, he assumed the presidency of the Academy of Arts. Arnold Zweig is well known especially for his correspondence with Sigmund Freud and his novel, based on experiences at the Eastern front in World War II, *The Case of Sergeant Grischa*.

VIII
Women

March 1982

Equality of Kibbutz Women: Myth or Reality?

An Interview With Pnina Feiler

S. CATHY BERSON

In our preliminary discussions, Pnina Feiler stated that in talking with people from abroad she has come to believe that a mythology exists about the equality of women in Israel. Further, that the kibbutz is the "embodiment" of this equality. This is a myth; while it is believed by some, in reality equality does not exist. There is a disparity between the ideal and real. Israel has proved to be one of the countries where the stereotyping of women is decidedly pronounced. The following is an excerpt from an evening's conversation with Pnina.

S. CATHY BERSON: How do you see yourself, as a woman, functioning on a kibbutz?

PNINA FEILER: Quite a lot has been written about kibbutzim and women on kibbutz, so I would like to tell you about my personal experience and not dwell on theories and things like that.

SCB: What did the kibbutz movement think about the role of women on kibbutz in the beginning?

PF: In short, that it should be an egalitarian society and women should be equal to men—not, however, in the sense that we understand it today as equality, but it meant that women should do men's jobs. It was quite a task then; it was the beginning of the century, 1910-12. In the first kibbutzim and even before in *g'dood ha'avodah* (work troups), women did work similar to that of men, and there were no machines. You had to do some hacking of stones, you had to do some building, you had to work outdoors in all kinds of weather, you had to tend the hens, sheep, cows, etc.—everything. At that time, it was mostly young people so there were almost no families, no children, so the problem of who is going to take care of the children didn't exist. Who is going to do the cooking? Now the laundry was a huge problem because people perspire in this climate and

271

you have to wash clothes often. Already there was the beginning of the division of labor; some men and women went out to work in the fields and construction and some of the women remained and did the washing and cooking and tending to the tents. What happened later was that in spite of the basic theory, or ideology of equality, slowly—or not so slowly—the division of labor along sexual lines evolved.

SCB: How was it explained?

PF: Of course, women can do all kinds of work but not everything. So, there is, for example, the carrying of some very heavy sacks which men said would be very hard for women. But there are jobs where both men and women can function similarly, like with children, teaching, dining room, etc.

I think it would have been possible had the men wanted—had they been prepared to let women continue doing all kinds of jobs and taking part in the administration. But I believe the men were used to being bosses. But not only this. It is possible that all this was too, too shallow. They [the men] began with this equality but it wasn't so deeply ingrained and so at the first opportunity or the first difficulty the true feelings came out.

SCB: What happened during the years of development of the kibbutz?

PF: The kibbutz has had very few women in the top positions. A small percentage of women had worked in production. Most women have worked in the services, that is, cooking, serving in the dining room, looking after children, laundry and clothes, gardening, looking after the sick, etc.

SCB: You wanted to say something about the kibbutz ideology and its attitude towards women.

PF: I think it is a kind of paradox. In the kibbutz movement there is a kind of looking up to somebody who works hard; who comes dirty into the dining room. These are the good people. These are the kibbutzniks. The man who does things with his hands (or today the technician)—he is the symbol. In most kibbutzim there is difficulty finding people to do jobs in services. So, no matter how much it is stressed that service is important, it is all words. In this society people who do services are not respected as those who do manual work, and so the women, if they do only services, do not belong to this high class, this respected class. So here lies the paradox.

SCB: Now what happens here on your kibbutz, on Yad Hanna?

PF: I would like to give you a few examples. First of all on the kibbutz we don't have unemployment. We are always short of hands, of people to do this, to do that. We have never enough. There were a few young women who insisted on not working in the services, without being feminists.

They just didn't like to work in it. One of them really was not good with the children. It wasn't her cup of tea. A second one said she would prefer to work in the orange groves or avocados or in the bananas. There is one who is working in the cotton fields and doing very, very hard work.

These women had to fight hard against the public opinion on the kibbutz which was very, very much against them: How can you? On the kibbutz you have to be prepared to do all kinds of jobs and you dare to take yourself out of doing work with children, even your own children? How is it possible? (My personal feeling is that to work with children you have to find the right person, with the right attitude, who likes children, who knows and is ready to give his utmost and if you are a man or a woman it doesn't matter. You have to have something in you. Like with many kinds of jobs.)

Anyway, we had discussions and meetings about these women and at one meeting a leading member stood up and said: "Yes, there are men who can do work in the children's house or in the kitchen, but show me one woman who can carry a banana stalk weighing 30-odd kilograms or doing some work in the garage. This work has to be done and since somebody has to do it, it has to be men!" *This* is the typical argument.

So you see, nobody is against giving women the opportunity—God forbid, no, no, no! They can do everything.

SCB: I have been told that the opportunity for a woman to be in the leadership is available if she wants it.

PF: There is a legal possibility for women to do some leading here. A possibility, I said, because in reviewing the situation in the secretariat [executive committee], we see that some years ago there was one woman amongst five, then there was none, then again one. But not one woman secretary—that is an important position.

Of course, not one woman looked after money problems either. Now we have a young woman who is responsible for the work committee. I don't want to say we should elect a woman because she is a woman. We have women who are not good in their jobs. I find that although, theoretically, in the kibbutz, all the opportunities are available and equal for everybody, the fact is that women are in a different class than men. Who is to be held responsible? The kibbutz is not an island. It is influenced by the way of life all around. Men and women still don't understand that their lives could be much more meaningful and fuller if their aim was to help each other to accomplish their potential. What is needed is to open a dialogue without anger, without prejudice.

SCB: When you speak of administrative officers, like in the secretariat, are these elected positions?

PF: Yes.

SCB: So women themselves are not doing anything for themselves?

PF: You see, it is so. I don't want to make too much of it. It is not only the men's fault that it is like that. (Or maybe yes, because it is a man's society; they are ruling and so on and the society as such is their doing.) In kibbutz we have an arrangement about working hours. The young people, men and women, work eight hours. The women who have children work seven hours. Why? Because it is expected that a woman take care of the home: to clean, bring home the products, take care of the child, and so on. So she works one hour less, so that it is easier for her to perform these home tasks in addition to her work. I think this speaks for itself far more than all the other things we have talked about.

There is still another point that I want to make. After the heroic period of doing men's jobs and wearing trousers and simple clothes and working shoes and all that, funnily (or not so funnily), women started to take care of the way they looked: their skin, cosmetics, hairdo and manicure, all this. And I know, some girls feel that they are not going to do all these dirty jobs that make their skin look wrinkled because of the sun and the wind and the influence of the climate. We want to be beautiful—we want to be womanly! I personally have nothing against it. I like to dress up myself and I don't find anything wrong with it. Of course, it is not the only way in which I am going to respect myself or find satisfaction in what I am. I think it is normal. Everybody likes to look his or her best in different ways. So this is another aspect.

You ask how I see the status of women in general and on the kibbutz. Speaking about women in general, not just for myself, I have a lot of respect for them. In many ways women can take things much better than men. I'm a nurse and I see people when they are ill or when something is wrong with them or their families. Most of the men, the big ones, the big strong he-men type, are invariably very childish when there is something little wrong with them. Most women generally are much stronger. I, myself, think I'm physically quite strong and I feel I can take very many things better than quite a lot of men.

It is important to mention that doing service on the kibbutz is different from being a housewife and a working woman. At least here it is your work and you are working in a team which makes it completely different from an individual household.

As far as my personal experiences go, it was difficult at first when I had to do service in the kitchen and laundry. It was a kind of disillusionment. I didn't expect it. I preferred to work in the bananas or garden. Later on I became the nurse on the kibbutz.

SCB: You are a nurse because you are one by profession. Being able to work on kibbutz in your chosen profession must be a luxury for a woman.

PF: Oh yes, it is! I was lucky. But as I mentioned before, not all women on kibbutz can choose. And then a pattern evolves as follows: The woman is not happy, dissatisfied. She becomes bitter, angry, sad, everything. Maybe she doesn't say it. Consequently the husband suffers too. Of course, if they think and talk about it, it then comes out that she is not fulfilled. Here you have one of the reasons why families leave the kibbutz and try to find something else.

Another pattern which evolves: when the woman is not being fulfilled socially and professionally, the role of wife, mother or grandmother becomes her focal thrust. As such she is important, necessary and not exchangeable. And she wants her children to sleep at home. Not in the children's houses as was customary in the kibbutz of the past.

SCB: You have some interesting cases on kibbutz in regard to the question of separation and divorce. Could you talk about how women function in these situations, given that you are a small community?

PF: I understand what you mean. I know the cases and they are each one different and individual. I think it goes along the same lines as everywhere else. These are, in most cases, people who think logically, who know how to control their feelings about each other. Still it is difficult to separate and to separate amicably so that you retain friendly relations with yourselves, your children and others in the small community. This happens in town as well as in kibbutz.

SCB: In town a person can separate oneself and is not forced to be on display 24 hours a day as in kibbutz.

PF: Oh yes, it is more difficult on the kibbutz, you are right. We have cases where one of the partners leaves for another, making it awkward for the former spouse to remain on the kibbutz. There are cases when both have left. On the other hand, there are couples who have separated and decided to stay on kibbutz. I think that this is a good thing, especially from the point of view of women's rights and possibilities. In this respect, the woman is much better off on the kibbutz than outside because there is no problem of who will take the child, or who will provide for the wife and children. And we don't have long drawn out proceedings in court regarding settlements and how to divide the property, etc. It is much simpler in this respect. One partner gets one flat and the other gets a different flat. The children are in the children's houses and if they are little they usually live with the mother. The divorced woman with a child or children whose former husband is not in the kibbutz has much fewer problems than her counterpart in town.

SCB: Would the kibbutz not be far more supportive than the outside in such cases? A woman would not have to worry about daycare for the children, looking for a job, coming home after a days work to cooking, washing, etc. Not having all these worries would leave her free to be a person and she would have more time and energy for her children and herself. Yes?

PF: Of course! But in the kibbutz... let's take a simple thing like putting a child to bed. If the children who sleep in the children's houses are of different ages the mother has to go from one house to the next house because all the children don't sleep in the same house, and if she has a baby at home it becomes even more difficult and she has less time to participate in social situations on the kibbutz. This leaves her very much alone. As to feeling deserted, to blame, a failure, lonesome—well, this is another pair of shoes.

SCB: In questions of marriage and divorce I understand that the woman has very few rights in the State of Israel. For example, if the husband does not give the wife a divorce, she is not considered divorced according to Jewish Law.

PF: There is no other law! The religious law is one and the same as the legal one. There is no such thing as a civil divorce. Now our kibbutz is not a very religious kibbutz. We are almost all of us not religious. If a couple wants to separate they can do it without doing it officially. A woman cannot give a divorce. In Israel the rights of women remain as a very, very big problem.

SCB: Change. Do you see changes coming, Pnina?

PF: Let us see. We spoke mostly about the kibbutz, so let us begin with the kibbutz. Lately there are some men who work with little children, even babies, and don't find it degrading. They even like it. It is being discussed and it could be a new beginning.

In general, the new type of women's movement is becoming more established in Israel. At the same time this "new woman" is becoming more involved in existing organizations. And it is growing. How? Well, not so much in numbers but in their awareness and consciousness. This is exhibited in the press, the radio (less on TV) and it is more widely spoken about. There is a greater amount of research about women done by women. There are women reporters, newspaperwomen and there are shelters for battered women, organized and managed by women, etc.

What seems to me most important is that this myth of the women in Israel enjoying equal rights is being smashed (slowly, too slowly) and perhaps this is a good beginning for achieving these rights, not only on paper but in real life.

SCB: Thank you, Pnina. Living on kibbutz has been an enjoyable education for me. I would like to sincerely thank the members of kibbutz Yad Hanna for providing me with the opportunity to work beside you and learn from all of you. Shalom.

Sculpture by Eve Turley (October 1980)

Right: Mother and Child (lithograph) by Walter Womacka, East Germany (June 1986).

Below: Rosa Luxemburg (1871-1919) (March 1983)

Special issue honouring International Women's Day

July-August 1982

Being a Working-Class Jew
An Autobiographical Story

LILITH

It sometimes appeared during my childhood that we were the only ones; that we were the only poor Jewish family in the whole world. We were the only kids whose parents couldn't work. What a shame, especially in a *goyishe* neighborhood!

My parents were victims of the Holocaust, unable to hold gainful employment for any prolonged period of time. My mother suffered from numerous physical ailments. My father was one of the unfortunate many who survived in body, but not in mind. Whenever he was given orders at work, his memory would jar his senses and he would call his boss "a dirty Nazi."

Repeated incidents of this nature made it easier for the rest of us to live on the "pension," as Germany's monetary apology was referred to, rather than suffer my father's tirades time and time again.

So where did that leave my family?

Certainly not in the village of Forest Hill! With an income barely above the poverty line, we could afford to live in a working-class, primarily Black/ethnic neighborhood.

My sister and I were the only Jewish kids. At the local school we were "Jew beggars" and "Christ killers."

Some rowdies, looking for entertainment, would throw pennies at me and challenge me to pick them up. How hard it was not do so when I thought of all the candies they could buy at the corner store!

I remember being confused. My surroundings, the Jewish and mainstream media, and my Gentile classmates stated clearly that all Jews were rich.

They had fancy houses, many cars, a maid, swimming pools in their backyards and, of course, they donated lots and lots of money to Israel! That's a Jew!

But we were Jewish and had nothing of the sort. So what were we and how come we weren't like all the rest?

I did not understand.

As I got older, my alienation increased. My parents thought it important that I be familiar with my religious background, so they sent me to a small synagogue Hebrew school.

This time, instead of being the only Jew in the class, I was the only poor one. I remember taking the school bus and seeing everyone else's home. They were mansions, large villas with wide, carefully manicured front lawns. Often, a Black woman would be waiting near the curb to pick the kid up because it was a few minutes walk to the main entrance.

At first, I didn't understand why these children's houses were so much grander than mine, and why all these kids had Black mothers. It took me a few months to realize that these were the rich Jews everyone talked about and that the Negro women were the maids. Normally, because I lived further away, I was the last one off the bus. None of my classmates had ever seen where I lived and I certainly never volunteered the information.

One night, my mother requested that I be brought home early, so Phil, the bus driver, dropped me off first.

There was an uncharacteristic silence on the bus as the other kids gazed out the windows.

I was afraid of what insulting remarks they would make about the small decrepit looking house I lived in. No front lawn, no well-trimmed hedges, no swimming pool, no Black woman—just my mother. As I hurriedly descended, one girl asked: "You being let off at your nanny's today?"

I gulped, glanced at Phil, at my mother greeting me from across the street and answered: "Yeah, my mom is sick." And ran off.

And so, during my childhood, while I felt apart from the anti-Semitic *goyim*, I did not fulfill the traditional requirements of a Jewish "princess."

It wasn't that my parents didn't try. My father took me to ballet, guitar and even speech lessons. However, as I complained about each one in turn, he complied by not taking me back.

I used to wonder why my dad, so forceful on other issues, never pressured me to attend these classes. I realized only later that it was because he really didn't want me to go.

He felt obligated to offer me the choice in spite of his total lack of funds. Education was the most important thing in the world. He wanted to be able to proclaim proudly, "My daughter does ballet, too." He simply couldn't afford it.

Other kids would complain about having to practise on their pianos, but I jealously guarded my "instrument," made of wooden clothes pins on a window sill.

If my parents hadn't been Jewish, with their traditional high regard for education and intelligence, it is doubtful that I would be nearly as articulate or well read as I am today. As I entered adolescence, I became more consciously aware of the widening gap between me and other Jewish kids.

My parents informed me of their humiliation in begging for a free Jewish education. They could not afford the tuition and so I was being admitted on "special consideration." It was therefore my duty to be the best behaved and come home with the highest marks. And I did, much to the dismay of my classmates, who saw me as a "browner" and a "goody-goody." They could not fathom my studious habits, my diligence, my determined will to get top marks. They didn't realize what was at stake for me.

Then there were dances, expensive weekend conferences and summer camp, all of which I was unable to attend.

My money went for basics like food and clothes. There was never a sliding scale, an acknowledgment that one did not have to pay to get in. It was assumed that all Jews had money or that only the Jews that did wanted to go, anyway.

As an observant Jew, living in a non-Jewish neighborhood, my only opportunity to interact socially was through these activities that were beyond my economic means.

I'll never forget the trauma to the monthly budget when my mother bought me a long skirt for a girlfriend's formal party. I felt so guilty asking for the money, I couldn't enjoy myself.

For a time, during a period of frustration and questioning, I sought a deeper communion with God. I practised an extremely orthodox form of Judaism, constantly berating my parents for not being Jewish enough, and desperately trying to figure out why the world was as it was.

I discovered no great *answer*, no illuminating response to my intense search, only more of the same class oppression.

I recall going to a large synagogue for *Yizkor* on one of the major festivals.

Only members who paid the $2,000 annual fee could enter the main sanctuary. My friends went in there with their parents. My father and I went into a small room in the basement for the "poor people." At fifteen, I still couldn't understand why God saw rich and poor differently.

All these experiences, in synagogue, in Hebrew school, at Jewish youth activities impressed upon me the fact that I was "different" because I had less access to money. The economic gap between my co-religionists and I created a chasm, just as spiritual faith had succeeded in alienating me from my neighbors. I was a misfit in every sense of the word.

Having been raised in an environment fraught with financial tensions, it is difficult for me to relate to other Jews whose life experiences have been so different. The working-class mentality remains long after the economic hardship. My values are not the same as someone who grew up in the "village."

I see nothing wrong with going through the pickings on garbage night or buying a sweater at a local Goodwill store. It is simply a way to save money. And I who did not have it for so long, want to hang on to what I have now.

I tend to be gregarious and loud at parties, less respectful than is required by social etiquette. To me, being myself is the most important thing in the world. For so long as a child, I tried desperately to fit into a different social stratum, and realized only after great pain that the only person I could comfortably be was me. This attitude, however, is not generally understood by others who were taught to respect the rules. The "rules" just never worked for me. Being Jewish, people often assume that I enjoyed a wealthy background. My father must have been a doctor or a lawyer and if not, surely I am moving in that direction...

Till recently, I too held this myth dear to my heart. It made it easier to deal with the grim realities of my day-to-day existence. It is only now that I am able to acknowledge that I will never be a professional, nor a millionaire and that even if I as an individual were to make it, so many others of the working class would not. Tokenism is not enough.

Now I look for support and understanding from other working-class Jews, although I have in the past tried to communicate with everyone. Some individuals reacted by saying that I made them feel guilty for being middle- or upper-middle class. Others justified their material status by describing how hard their parents had struggled for it.

Both these comments show a clear lack of consciousness. The purpose of this essay and my openness around class oppression is so that others can become more aware of it and work towards changing the current situation.

Make facilities in the Jewish community more accessible to everyone, regardless of social status. Don't assume, as Gentiles do, that "all Jews are rich."

Put less emphasis at gatherings, in the papers, at services, on those who have donated millions. Those of us who have little to give are embarrassed. And is not the highest level of *Tzedakah* (charity) to give but not to say so?

Work for the redistribution of wealth in our community, not just by giving to social services, which is certainly a good thing, but by creating non-exploitative jobs at which we all can work.

Institute working collectives so that those of us at the bottom of the power rung can feel like we have some control over our own lives.

To me, this is just the beginning. Many will say it is impossible. But surely a good Jew, one who can offer thousands or even millions to the State of Israel, would be willing to lend a hand to some of his fellow Jews right next door?

March 1984

Two Outstanding Women of Our Time

I: Fania Fenelon

Music in the Death Camp

MIRIAM SILVER

This incredible story is of a French woman who survived Hitler's Auschwitz crematorium because she had a beautiful voice and knew music. Her name was Fanny Goldstein.

She was born in Paris, France, to an affluent family. Her father was Jewish, her mother Catholic. When she was ten years old, she entered the Paris Conservatory of Music. At seventeen she was an accomplished singer and pianist. She did not identify with either her father's or mother's religion until she became aware of the creeping anti-Semitism pervading France in the late 1930s. When Hitler came to power and subsequently invaded Paris, she swore that she would devote the rest of her life to eradicating anti-Semitism and to doing whatever she could to help destroy Nazism.

As Fania Fenelon, she became a very famous entertainer. To carry out her promise, Fania engaged in espionage.

In 1940 she joined the French Resistance. She entertained in cabarets where German officers went to enjoy themselves, and when the officers were drunk, Fania would photograph the contents of their briefcases and pass the films to French authorities. For three years Fania carried out the espionage work. She was finally discovered in 1943, arrested and tortured and sent to Drancey, a detention house outside Paris.

Nine months later, on January 20, 1944, Fania was deported to Auschwitz. When they arrived, the victims were stripped, tattooed and completely shaved. This, Fania recalled, was the worst humiliation—having no hair. Then she spent two days in the quarantine block, where 1,000 women slept on shelves awaiting extermination.

There were five crematoria at Auschwitz, with a capacity of 24,000 people a day. On many days they were full around the clock. One morning a Polish guard appeared with an unbelievable request for someone who could sing the opera *Madame Butterfly*.

Fania Fenelon volunteered, and soon found herself in a warm, well-lighted room with musical instruments, including a grand piano, and neatly dressed woman. From then on Fania sang, played and transcribed music for the all-female orchestra at Birkenau Extermination Camp, where women sang in spite of empty stomachs, hoping to survive.

For the commandant of Auschwitz, just murdering and torturing Jews and other victims was not enough, so he invented the humiliating idea of playing marching music for the groups leaving the camp to dig ditches for the murdered Jews. Later, when they were not able to work any more, the orchestra played when they were marching to be burned in the crematoria.

The orchestra members received certain privileges, the chief one being exemption from being burned in the crematoria. Fania Fenelon declared, "It was now that I began to grasp the insanity of the place, and the farcical nature of this orchestra, conducted by this elegant woman, and these comfortably dressed girls, sitting on chairs, playing to virtual skeletons, shadows, showing us faces which were faces no longer."

The orchestra also played indoors for the SS and their wives. Fania pointed out again: "We were not saints. We did what we were forced to do to stay alive... We would have done anything to please our murderers, to live *one more month, even one more day*."

One day the orchestra girls were transferred to Bergen-Belsen. The women lived practically one on top of the other, with little food or water, dirty, ragged, covered with vermin, many of them sick with dysentery and typhus.

At last the moment they had been hoping for arrived. When the British Army arrived on April 15, 1945, Fania was on the brink of death with typhus. A British soldier carried her outside and she was free at last. Someone gave her a microphone and, weak as she was, she sang the French "La Marseillaise" and "God Save the King."

Fania arrived in Paris on May 17, 1945. All she could think of was that she wanted to see Germany destroyed. When she recovered, she joined a troupe of entertainers that played for the American soldiers.

Fania soon resumed her career, which took her all over Europe. For many years she lived in East Germany, and eventually became a professor of music at the conservatories in Dresden, Leipzig and East Berlin. She wrote a book, *Playing for Time*, which depicts her life in the Nazi camps. The book was published in many countries, including the Soviet Union, but she never allowed it to be published in West Germany where, she said, neo-Nazism and anti-Semitism did not end with the war. This was her greatest disappointment.

Fania Fenelon was the heroine of the controversial television movie *Playing for Time*, based on her book. The television movie sparked protests from Jewish groups when Vanessa Redgrave was chosen to portray Fania Fenelon. The protesters objected to Redgrave's financial support of the PLO and her personal friendship with Yasir Arafat. Fania Fenelon came to the United States to criticize CBS TV for what she said was its insensitivity in broadcasting the movie with Vanessa Redgrave as its star.

Fania Fenelon's life came to an end recently. She died of cancer in Paris on December 20, 1983. She was 74 years old. At the time of her death, Fania was at work on a new book recounting her experiences after the liberation.

There was no funeral. Fania had donated her body to medical research.

—*Morning Freiheit*

Two Outstanding Women of Our Time

II: Bess Horowitz

'Like Water in the Desert'

HILLEL SCHENKER

"If Israel would be living in a state of peace, it would liberate the Jewish people and give them a chance to cultivate their wonderful abilities in the fields of science, technology, arts and music. After all, the three great leaders who have changed the face of the world have been Jews: Einstein, Marx and Freud." These are the words of Bess Horowitz, a committed, passionate woman who has been involved with *New Outlook* since its inception, and is currently serving as its honorary U.S. president. In addition, Bess Horowitz is a member of the executive of three American peace groups—*Promoting Enduring Peace, Women Concerned* and the *Political Action Committee*. She is an NGO (non-governmental organization) delegate to the UN and is active in the *Women's International League for Peace and Freedom*. Her husband, Harry, is a director of *Sane Nuclear Policy*. During a recent visit to Israel, Bess Horowitz talked with *New Outlook* about her remarkable life.

"My father," she says, "was a socialist back in Russia. He came to America in the 1890s to get away from the czar's police who wanted to arrest him and send him to Siberia. My mother came to America from Poland, where her family used to hide in the cellars to escape from the pogroms. It was from her that I first learned about anti-Semitism and the struggle for Jewish rights. In America my father became a union organizer for the carpenters' union. As a little child, I remember that he would come home sometimes all black and blue from his struggles out in the street. Mother would cry, but he said he had to do this. I became convinced of socialism not because of my father's ideas, but because of my mother's difficult life. I saw how she worked as a seamstress, twenty hours a day, and then came home to raise the family.

"I was born in Brooklyn, but I grew up in the Bronx, in a Jewish-Italian neighborhood. I remember that when I was five years old, a little Italian boy said to me,'You killed Christ, and when I grow up, I'm going to beat you up!' And I said to him, 'Why would I do a thing like that to Jesus, I have nothing against him, I wasn't even alive then. And I won't let you beat me up!' He ran away.

"You know, back in the thirties, I gave my children a progressive education. They went to the Ethical Culture School, and when they needed it, they got orthodontia to straighten out their teeth. But I used to say to myself, 'What are we doing to keep them alive, what are we doing for peace?'

"My only son, Bill, was killed in the war. He was accepted to medical school, but refused to go. He said, 'Mother, this is my war. You always taught me to hate Nazism and fascism, and now what should I do, hire somebody to take my place? I'll go to school when I come back.' But he never did come back.

"My first husband had a heart attack and died as a result of the loss of our son. I myself was in an oxygen tent for twelve weeks. But when I saw how skinny our thirteen-year-old daughter was, and how sad she looked, I told myself that I had to live for her sake. Not a day goes by without me thinking about Bill."

In the wake of these tragedies, Bess Horowitz began working for world peace. She joined the American Association for the United Nations, which eventually merged with the United Nations Association, and worked with Eleanor Roosevelt. "I had an office next to her," she recalls. "We always used to get a lot of flowers. Mrs. Roosevelt used to put a little vase on my desk, and take a few flowers from her collection, and put them in mine. She really was a remarkable woman. Whenever I brought a new idea to her, she would say: 'Bess, that's a wonderful idea. Go ahead and do it.' When we made films on the United Nations, I suggested that we also show them in the UN itself. This had never been done before, and it was a tremendous success. I also began an information newsletter for all the NGOs. Once, I came to Mrs. Roosevelt and suggested that we start a United Nations University. 'That's a wonderful idea, Bess,' she said, 'go ahead and do it.' So I took a friend and went off to Africa. We met with Jomo Kenyatta in Kenya, with Julius Nyerere in Tanganyika [Tanzania today—ed.] and with the leaders of Uganda. They were all enthusiastic and excited by the prospect of hosting such a university. Unfortunately, when we brought the idea back to America, the administration in Washington killed it.

"I made my first trip to Israel in 1948, right after the state was created. It took 30 hours on the plane, and now it takes only eleven hours. I remember how wonderful it was at the time. People kissed the soil when they got off the plane. The pioneering spirit was everywhere. Today, there's too much materialism and alienation. Too much imitation of America. The only thing that keeps me coming back is the kibbutzim and the peace movement. I have wonderful friends on the kibbutzim, some of them are like family for me.

"On my first trip to Nazareth, I met the late Abdul Aziz Zuabi, who was deputy minister of health [and one of the founders of *New Outlook*—ed.]. I remember that we used to meet and talk. We used to eat in the dining room. The women, including his mother, who was a remarkable woman, used to serve, but they wouldn't sit down to eat with us. So once I said to Aziz, 'Would it be so terrible, would you mind if your mother sat with us?' He said, 'Why not?' He was a very open guy, open to suggestions. At first, she demurred, but then she too said, 'Why not?' Once that was done, whenever I would come, even if there were others around, she sat with us. In a way, I think I started a very, very minor revolution.

"We set up a Jewish-Arab kindergarten in Nazareth in memory of Bill, but we decided not to name it after him, because my family doesn't believe in that. We named it after two children, one Jewish and one Arab, who were killed because they wanted peace."

Bess Horowitz believes that working with children is the key to the future. She believes that there should be more meetings between Jewish and Arab youth, and between Ashkenazi and Sepharadi youth. One of her proposals is that all school children in the more prosperous neighborhoods should give up their hot lunches once a week, and know that the lunches were being transferred to disadvantaged children in poorer neighborhoods.

Concerning Diaspora Jewry, Bess says: "I think that many people, particularly Jews in America, are not ready to give sufficient trust to the Arabs. People say that there is no one to talk to, but Sadat came over, and he lost his life. And I say, did you ever risk your life to talk to someone for peace? American Jews, and Americans in general, haven't suffered the direct effects of war on their own soil for many years. Even the Russians are more aware of the price of war, since they lost twenty million lives in World War II, and had one third of their country ravaged.

"When *New Outlook* was formed, I was asked by Simha Flapan to take a role in it. I knew of no Middle Eastern magazine emanating from Israel that had such a positive view towards the Arabs, inside and outside of Israel. *New Outlook* believed in a dialogue that would eventually lead to a national state for the Palestinians. Since we had already achieved a Jewish state, I felt that we should also achieve a national state for Palestinians. Having already been to Israel, I had noticed that there was great discrimination against the Arabs. They had separate schools, lived in separate neighborhoods, weren't represented in the army, and they were underrepresented in Israeli political life. I felt that *New Outlook* was needed like water in the desert."

Bess continues, "We need people to work for peace. I think that people who work for peace—whether it be to increase subscriptions or to take out ads for *New Outlook*, or to go to conferences and demonstrations—are really doing a service to their children. People must have some commitment to peace; verbalizing it is not enough.

"I was very happy when *New Outlook* was born, and I'm still working for its continuance. I think that Jewish people in Israel and in the Diaspora should realize its importance, even if they don't always agree with it. It's like supporting the right to have another voice, the right to democracy. And of course, those who do agree with it should realize that agreeing isn't enough. An active role must be taken.

"We who believe in peace are the minority, and *New Outlook* has to try to reach the Diaspora majority, who are sceptical. They are harder to convince than the Israelis, who are aware of their proximity and kinship with the Arabs, and are aware of their need for peace."

This is Bess Horowitz' twentieth visit to Israel. At the age of 78 she still has plenty of youthful spirit and energy left to continue the struggle. As she says: "We all must put our hearts and heads together to find ways to convince people of the need and possibility for peace in the Middle East."

—*New Outlook*

July-August 1985

So That Another Generation Will Not Deny

LILITH

Dear Mother,

It is so rare to address you as a "dear" one, our lives so often forces of hostility directly aimed at one another; our time apart nine years of cultivated ice. Nonetheless, in discovering my dark otherness, I am forced to look back to you. I welcome your straight jet black hair, your penetrating black eyes and your olive-brown skin. They are as if my own. Before, when I glanced in the mirror, I would see societal reflections of my white acceptability; my right of passage into the "greater" Jewish world. I attempted to maintain this guise by denying my bloodline that lay beyond the pale of Eastern European tolerance.

When I wrote my autobiography in eighth grade, I disguised your maiden name. "Habib" echoed Habib Bourguiba, and I feared the association, feared an Arab (terrorist, sheik, harem-owner, primitive, savage, rapist) in my family, so you became Nira Haviv—acceptable, Hebrew, Jew.

Yes, I denied you, Mother, but how you too denied yourself. How many times your intestines must have twisted as you swallowed the lies, the poisoned policies of the Ashkenazis. I remember my second grade teacher, Mrs. Mateus. She told me not to play with Nina and Alegria because they were "schvartzes" from Morocco. I was angry, not wanting to spend time away from my friends. Imagine my relief when you insisted that the teacher was wrong. I watched in stunned silence as you screamed at the school principal about Jews hating other Jews. I realize now why I was so wide-eyed with surprise. Mother, that was one of the few times in my life when you protected me, validated the aching inside of me. It was so out of character. I did not know then that you were a "schvartze" too.

I also recall that once while listening to the "Jewish Hour" on the radio, you became very agitated and upset. The program described the situation of Soviet Jewry. You called up the radio station, crying, "Why always Soviet Jewry? Soviet Jewry? What about Syrian Jewry? Egyptian Jewry? Lebanese Jewry?" But, Mother, did you not share the agony of your own Libyan Jewry? You did not tell them of your relatives in Tripoli murdered a few months before in a pogrom. Why was it so hard to acknowledge that the pain was personal? That when you demanded the visibility of Arab Jews, you were finally speaking up for yourself?

Mother, I can no longer hide your birthplace, the origin of your family. Libya is not a country to be ashamed of. Each memory of the uttered lie ("My Mom was born in Rome") is etched firmly upon my conscience. You may continue to flaunt the Italian accent and letters from Roma, Napoli, Milano, but I will no longer lie, grit my teeth and smile. Acrobatics of such a nature are merely another form of self-denial. Today, I do not hide. I tell everyone: I am a Jew. My father is from Poland. My mother is from Libya. They are both Holocaust survivors. Yes, the Holocaust happened in Libya. It was an Italian colony. Hitler and Mussolini were allies. There were anti-Semitic laws. My grand-aunt was sent to Treblinka. My mother survived by hiding in the countryside. The Arabs saved her life. Not Christians, but Muslim Arabs.

I tell everyone of how you arrived in Israel and waited endlessly in a city of tents; that all the European Jews were at the top of the hill and all the Arab Jews were at the bottom. When the spring rains flooded the area, firemen came to rescue Grani, who was short and would have drowned. I speak bitterly of European Jews who took donations from around the world and rode in fancy cars through the *maabarot*. Is it any wonder that the youngsters threw stones at them?

I want to tell everyone everything you have ever taught me about always being different; a Jew in Libya, an Arab Jew in Israel, and a brown woman in a very white North American Jewish community. But, Mother, you've shared so little. What aches and pains have you left unspoken? How many times has your throat constricted in fear? And who am I to even dare to ask the question? This evil daughter, the lesbian one, who fits in even less than you? Why should I, of all your children, demand an honest account of your life?

Perhaps because I, too, had locked away my soul, hidden my identity. Before a staff party recently, held at my house, I disposed of all my lesbian posters, books and records. I was simply afraid to lose my job. And I, too, have lied. In the past, when I spoke of a lover, I would often change "her" to "him" and offer a masculine name. I did not want to be harassed or viewed with derision. So, far be it from me to stand in judgment of yet another. I reach out to you in empathy and in recognition of our common struggle.

With hope,
your daughter,
Lilith

March 1986

International Women's Day
An Editorial

March 8 marks the celebration of International Women's Day around the world. It is a time for looking at the balance sheet of human rights on our planet, for recording successes and celebrating victories, for analysing the unfinished agenda for shortcomings and failures, and for mapping out strategies for future struggles to achieve equal rights for women.

The past decade has seen the accession of women to positions of top leadership in several countries. True democrats have been heartened by the examples of Golda Meir, Indira Gandhi and even of Margaret Thatcher. The heroic examples of Chana Senesh, Winnie Mandela and Coretta Scott King will not be forgotten.

But the individual, personal triumphs of outstanding women must not be allowed to obscure the fact that the women's fight for equality and social justice still must be won. There is much evidence to show that in North America, despite the emergence of a small, managerial elite of women, the gap in status and earning power between men and women is widening. The facts of increasing computerization, decline in the industrial work force and corresponding increase of women workers in the service trades will tend to increase and aggravate that gap. There is an urgent need for trade unions to pay more attention to the organization of women in the work force. This is, in fact, a question of survival for the trade union movement!

On the social front, we are witnessing an onslaught against women's rights—campaigns against abortion rights, campaigns against the Equal Rights Amendment in the USA, even campaigns of terror against Family Planning. These well-funded campaigns are being carried out by fundamentalist Christian churches, TV evangelists, segments of the Catholic church and right-wing Republicans. It is our shame that they have been aided and abetted by some small segments of our own ultra-Orthodox Jews.

From our point of view, it is obvious that the crucial struggle for equal rights in a democratic society cannot be won by women alone. They must be aided in this struggle by all democratically minded individuals and organizations. All of us are the victims of a social arrangement which allows half of our population to be exploited and abused!

May 1986

Piece Work

MONA ELAINE ADILMAN

The knot of women,
heat-shrivelled,
hunch over their machines
—piece work puppets
manipulating bits
of fabric, the whir
and hum of technology
stinging the air
like a giant wasp.

Steam iron in hand,
the girl from Barbados,
soaked in sweat,
dreams of the sea.
The hissing iron distorts
her crested vision
with a vaporous
river of sound.

Dialects in Greek,
Portuguese and Italian
are savory fruits
in the sweltering
factory heat.
Conversation rises
like yeast
in the industrious
oven of humanity.

Pockets, collars, sleeves,
in rainbow streams,
flow from each
punctuating needle.
Buffeting
buttonhole machines
bite sharply
into polyester tissue.
Precision speaks
with geologic force.

The factory is canopied with
plastic-swathed garments,
candy-cane copies
of haute-couture originals.
Operators, cutters,
pressers, shippers

scurry across
the room, hunchbacked,
ducking under 4 foot high
metal pipes
supporting parades
of dresses and slack suits,
labelled, tagged,
inspected,
ready to be shipped.

In the show room,
air conditioners
articulate
a comforting chill.
Buyers
finger the goods,
and eye the models.
The designer
is all smiles.
The boss has
order forms
at the ready.
The season looks
promising.

In the factory,
the odor of sweat
mingles with the smell
of steaming garments
and dry-cleaning fluid,
but the women
are lucky to be working,
and live in fear
of seasonal
layoffs.

The needle trade
marches on,
populated by
its human machines.
Immigrant women,
shapeless
in sleeveless smocks,
are mechanical tools,
overexposed film
        hemming, pressing, basting,
        threading, cutting, stitching.
The fashion treadmill
goes round and round
on the laws of
supply and demand.

Production
is an adrenalin flow,
a cover-up for
yesterday's cop-out,
today's emptiness,
the lost look of tomorrow.

Piece work is the
name of the game.
    Pieces of soul.
      Pieces of bone.
        Pieces of sinew.
          Pieces of gut.
            Pieces of pride.
          Pieces of pain.
        Pieces of flesh.
      Pieces of people.
    Pieces of profit...
            PIECE WORK.

November 1986

Miriam Waddington
A Warm, Rich Collection

MIRIAM WADDINGTON: COLLECTED POEMS. Toronto: Oxford University Press, 1986, 422 pages.

REVIEWED BY HELENE ROSENTHAL

Spanning a half-century of richly lived and observed life, the *Collected Poems* comprises Waddington's eleven previously published books plus a large group of uncollected poems. The range of subject matter reflects her self-awareness as a Jew born and raised in Winnipeg, her careers in social and academic work and her lifelong feeling for people, place, nature and language. The sensibility is a woman's, the personal life being shared with the reader. For each birth and renewal of self in her seasons from childhood to beginning old age there is a naming, a celebration and a mourning for the inevitable betrayals and losses that occur with change and time.

The lyrical gift is evident from her first book, *Green World* (1945), onwards; the craft sings. She had married the previous year. Twenty-one years later, coinciding with the dissolution of the marriage, she began writing the short-line poems that have remained her most characteristic form. This was at least partly a response, she says in her autobiographical afterword, to the *Zeitgeist*. New hopes and new ways of understanding the world had been undercut by the atom bomb: "new anxieties were everywhere." It wasn't the time, she felt, to spin out "long literary lines." Literary *influences*, however, were always important and resulted at this time in a purely formal omission of commas for the sake of spatial design, a choice she soon had second thoughts about, returning to a sparse use of punctuation in her later books as her "original passion for meaning reasserted itself."

The Glass Trumpet (1966) marks the new short-line style. Though her most eloquent poems, here and elsewhere, are those about love and its loss, let us look at some lines from "Canadians," a poem in which she expresses some of the ambivalence of those years in which a sense of nationalism was struggling to be born:

> We look
> like a geography
> but just scratch us
> and we bleed like
> history are full
> of modest misery
> sensitive
> to double-talk, double-take
> (and double-cross)
> in a country
> too wide
> to be single in.

Though this touches on a complexity of issues—the French-Anglo split being perhaps the most obvious—her allusion to Shakespeare's Shylock in "just scratch us/and we bleed like/history" broadens the theme, deepens the meaning and suggests the need for working out our national/racial oppressions in a one-world context informed by lessons from the past. The play on the three hyphenated words with their repetition of the word "double" emphasizes the need for a marriage of viewpoints to end divisions "in a country/too wide/to be single in." This is the kind of concise statement that shows what Waddington can do in making available a certain terrain of associations with an economy of means. Such organic relationship of craft to purpose serves her equally well for her most typical poems of private revelation. Where, for instance, has the erotic been so powerfully evoked in so few words as in these lines from "Dream Telescope" (*Say Yes*, 1969)?

> I am singing
> with the rosy
> softness of
> only
>   the inside
> of your mouth

In other poems from *Say Yes* she talks about words (what poet doesn't?) and about the silence that is a failure of words; about the power of nature to speak through the human tongue and the desolation of the human landscape in the silence of departed love. Always her images and metaphors passionately bespeak the natural environment, whether the mood be rejoicing or lamenting. Her involvement with the world of human lives comes across, in all the books, as a sorrowing acceptance of it as a given. She is a witness to the world rather than protester of wrongs. We find no poems that demonstrate the "personal is political" outlook of the new feminists, with its revolutionary implications, nor does she seem to believe that people can improve their lot by organized resistance, when driven to do so by intolerable conditions.

In "The Nineteen Thirties are Over" (*Driving Home*, 1972) she talks from the vantage point of the affluent seventies of surviving the Depression, the "Sacco-Vanzetti of childhood" tragedies, the Winnipeg strikes and winter storms,

> but in my mind
> summer never ended on the
> shores of Gimli where we
> looked across to an Icelandic
> paradise we could never see
> the other side of

This nostalgia for the dreaming innocence of childhood, equated with happiness, seems stronger than the cold realities she grew up with, though further on in the poem she passes the

> rich houses and double
> garages and I am not really
> this middle-aged professor
> but someone from
> Winnipeg whose bones ache
> with the broken revolutions
> of Europe

The ache is genuine, but "broken revolutions"—does she not see any triumph of spirit or improvement in the lot of the people who made them?

Her chosen profession of social work up to the mid-sixties was, like teaching—the second career she followed up to her retirement—an attractive field for a nurturing woman. But because so much of the person is involved with the care or instruction of others in these extensions of the mothering role, the prospect of old age, with its loss of that function can seem frighteningly empty and lonely, especially when one is without a love partner. A great many poems dwell gloomily on this theme in the later books. One poem treats an aging women as an object of disgust; one senses a certain amount of self-hatred.

In "How Old Women Should Live" (*Mister Never*, 1975), there is disillusionment with the times, also; childhood, no longer a state of wondering innocence, has assumed sinister dimensions, as in

> The children
> of Ireland are
> also in the news,
> they have become
> hardened street
> fighters some of
> them murderers.
> I ask myself
> where will it
> all end?

from "How I spent the Year Listening to the Ten O'Clock News" (*The Price of Gold*, 1976).

The poems of the last decade reflect her travels as well as this growing concern with aging and death. But, as throughout the entire collection, there remains an undefeatable interest in things, in thought, and the lives of ordinary people. I recommend this as a warmly rich addition to anyone's library.

IX
Canadian Political Issues

July-August 1968

Our Enduring Dilemma—
1867 And All That

STANLEY B. RYERSON

How the birth of an industrial, business society, i.e., capitalism, influenced and interacted with the relations between French- and English-speaking Canada: this is the theme of Stanley Ryerson's *Unequal Union: Confederation and the Roots of Conflict in the Canadas, 1815-1873*. In the concluding chapter of this book—excerpts of which we reproduce here with kind permission from the publishers, Progress Books, Toronto—the author draws together some of the threads, in terms of class and nation, that he has explored in the preceeding 400 pages.

Throughout the story of our peoples, patterns of class interest and social structure intersect with the national problem. The fact that the colonial-Victorian constitution of 1867 ignored in large part the bi-national reality of the Canadas has not a little to do with our present tensions and unresolved dilemma. *Unequal Union* sheds a fresh light on the roots and present nature of a crisis that is social and economic as well as constitutional and political; and in so doing, points toward possible solutions.

The vision of "a new nationality," the project of creating a new country, was present in the minds of the business-politicians. Their grand design transcended their class limitations. As for the working people on the land and in the towns and cities, the sense of a new identity merged with the pride in accomplishment of builders, producers, craftsmen. At the same time, for some of those who were hired "hands," the status of labor in the business society, its exploitation at the hands of the masters, its hardships and conditions of existence, gave rise to questioning.

For French Canadians, the new political state had mixed connotations. Having regained, with the Province of Quebec, an area of limited but distinct autonomy, some sensed a new beginning. Yet having had to accept a British-colonialist state structure as the larger framework for a provincial existence, they experienced foreboding.

The nineteenth century Anglo-Canadian bourgeoisie was not able to create an effective consciousness of Canadian political nationhood. For one thing, the new ruling class clung to a British-colonialist mentality; British investment in the new dominion was, it could be said, political as well as financial. The attitude derived in part from inherent weakness and dependency; more particularly, from the need for a buttressing counterweight to United States expansionist pressures. Equally operative was the role of the idea of "British ascendancy" as an instrument of rule over French Canada. The Anglo-Canadian nation, then still in process of formation, was not so solidly or consciously constituted as to impose its will unaided; the link of empire was required to lend authority for a posture of superiority. The British Crown weighed helpfully on the side of English-Canadian dominance.

At the same time, the relationship of political and economic inequality, as between French and English, impaired the prospect of a common emerging sense of Canadianness, of any strong feeling of dual national identity. The ruling social forces in Quebec, while collaborating for their own private reasons with Anglo-Canadian capital and imperial authority, were not averse to the growth of a narrow clerical-traditionalist variety of nationalism that crusaded against the Rouges, and shunned democracy.

What made it an unequal union was not so much a plot by English-speaking Canadians to repress the French—although impulses in that direction were not unknown. Nor was it a stubborn refusal of French Canadians to compete on equal terms with Anglo-Canadian business. (The latter argument has been advanced by Fernand Ouellet, the former by Gerard Filteau and others.) The sources of inequality were multiple and complex; the chief ones were:

● Uneven capitalist development: the priority in time of the English bourgeois revolution of the seventeenth century and of the Industrial Revolution in England in the eighteenth meant that when England defeated France in the Seven Years War, and annexed Canada, a certain imbalance was built into the colony's development, economic as well as political.

● When to the structure (emanating from the conquest) of British-colonial political rule over a population of Canadian French there was added a mass influx of English-speaking settlers, there resulted a dualism of national communities; one of which, quite apart from its own volition, was from the outset closely and advantageously associated with the imperial power and English investment capital; while the other not only suffered the direct consequences and side effects of the defeat of the French metropolis, but labored under the handicap of that semi-feudal underdevelopment which was the heritage of the French *ancien regime*.

● Against this background, the unfolding of early capitalist industrialization and of the related class-political struggles for self-government, against colonialism, followed a tortuous and contradictory course: one marked both by joint efforts of national and class groupings to win colonial autonomy (1837, 1848, and more narrowly, 1867) and by deep cleavage between the national communities resulting from inequality and oppression. As against Downing Street (much later, it would be United States domination) it was possible to achieve a measure of unity. As between the two nations within Canada, only an uneasy compromise was ever reached, charged with the tension of persisting inequality.

● The centralized, unitary federalism of 1867 bore the imprint of this inequality in several respects: the British-monarchical configuration of the colonial dominion proclaimed a British (and Anglo-Canadian) ascendancy; the demographic pattern (since 1850) of an English-speaking majority and a permanent minority position for the French Canadians was reflected in limited linguistic-religious concessions to the latter as a "cultural minority" and denial of political recognition as a national entity; while the economic thrust of expansion through railway-building and manufactures, which the unitary state structure was to subserve, tied the society in its growth to the English and United States capital markets—with both of which English Canadians possessed the kindred connections that French-Canadian business lacked. The "business democracy" of 1867 was weighted in favor of the Anglo-Canadian capitalist class that was its architect.

The ruling bloc of social forces of the Canada of 1867, the inheritor and continuator of that of 1774, while capable of promoting capitalist enterprise, proved inadequate as a creator of national values or of democratic solidarity. The positive, creative forces in the two Canadas were to be found elsewhere, in the mass of those who toiled and built, from whose work sprang the roads and farms, canals and factories, the mines and lumber camps and homes and schools, the substance and material underpinnings of a modern community.

Just at the time when Canada First and the Parti national were seeking ways to express a sense of identity in each of the Canadas, a movement of quite a different kind was getting under way. Not national but social, class consciousness was taking form in the Nine Hours Movement for the shorter working day. The working men who in 1871 established the Toronto Trades Assembly and nine-hour leagues in Hamilton and other industrial centres; who in 1872 conducted the Toronto printers' strike and the mass demonstrations in support of it, and founded the *Ontario Work-*

man—they were asserting, in the face of the masters, the class identity and solidarity of "the men," of the wage-earning working class.

The concept of the nation held by the men of property who had founded the new dominion was colored by their preoccupation with the "cash nexus." Nation-building was a huge transaction in real estate and railway company shares, an investors' challenge. Such an approach might unite the business classes of the two national communities; it would with difficulty inspire the great mass of working men and women who did the work of production, who by their labor built the new country. Still less could it offer an answer to the deep-seated inequality between the two national communities. It would take an approach that transcended the exploitive individualism of a private-business society to encompass the radical democratization on which alone national equality would be achieved. The motto at the masthead of the *Ontario Workman*, for all its note of utopian-socialist simplicity, pointed towards the answer of a new order, recalling now at a new stage the dream of Toon O'Maxwell. It read: "The Equalization of All the Elements of Society in the Social Scale Should be the True Aim of Civilization."

Such a social equality, realistically understood, could only mean the overcoming of class rule: ending the class cleavage based on private, minority ownership of the modern large-scale tools of labor. The processes now working for such a social transformation in contemporary Canada are interwoven and interact with the struggle for national equality and self-determination. The dictum "No people that oppresses another people can itself be free" has social as well as national implications. *"Maitres chez nous!"* means mastering alien monopolies as well as achieving sovereignty. While distinct, the political and social-economic struggles are convergent. The peoples of the Canadas, facing the need to rectify the "unequal union" of a colonialist confederation, begin to sense the need to call in question something else as well: the social system of corporate-business rule, the unequal society of "masters and men."

June 1970

Observations on a Centenary

JOSEPH ZUKEN

But to those who fight for freedom Louis Riel lives again.
—Louis Riel song

A hundred years after Manitoba was born, its founder and chief architect, Louis Riel, continues to be the centre of controversy. WASPs and other bigots are maligning Riel as did their counterparts in his day. Manitoba has its full quota of such bigots and they have reacted with anti-Riel epithets of "traitor and half-breed" to the provincial government's decision to erect a statue in Riel's honor on the grounds of the legislature. The historic figure of Riel looms ever larger as Manitobans celebrate the first hundred years of their province.

Three great events have shaped and moulded the radical-democratic traditions of Manitoba: the Red River Rebellion, the great 1919 Winnipeg strike, and the contributions made by the immigrants from many lands.

Our province was born in conflict and revolution. Ignored and spurned by the establishment of Eastern Canada, which served the interests of Anglo-Canadian financial groups, the settlers on the Red River and the Assiniboine fought for their rights and responsible government with mass protest movements and a resort to armed struggle.

Led by Riel, a people's uprising proclaimed a republic on the banks of the Red River and led to the establishment of Manitoba as the fifth province in confederation. Although the Metis Provisional Government was suppressed by the armed intervention ordered by John A. Macdonald and the class interests he served, and Riel was hanged after the Saskatchewan armed uprising, it is he who is the founder of Manitoba and under his leadership the people of the Red River Valley fought for the right to be equal and for their rights as a people.

Riel and his work are an inseparable part of the democratic and revolutionary traditions of Manitoba and an inspiration to generations. Speaking at the unveiling of a monument to Louis Riel in Regina in 1968, Prime Minister Trudeau conceded that *"Louis Riel's battle is not yet won."*

As Manitoba enters upon its second century, the descendants of the people of Riel—the Metis and the Indian people—continue to live in poverty, unemployment and a climate of racial discrimination. The struggles begun by Riel are unfinished.

Some 50 years after a Provisional Government was proclaimed and established, there took place the second great event which helped to shape the history of our province—the great 1919 Winnipeg General Strike. Out of this powerful demonstration of the working man's militancy and unity came the victory—although the strike was suppressed by armed forces and repressive laws—of the right to collective bargaining and the moving of labor into political action. Today a plaque on the wall of city hall honors the 1919 strikers in almost the very place where the Riot Act was read to the strikers from the steps of the former city hall.

And last year in a decisive act of protest against the old-line parties, the people of Manitoba made political history by electing an NDP government—a government which has a great opportunity but still has to prove that it has the will and courage to challenge the monopolies, many of them foreign-controlled, which dominate the Manitoba economy. Labor's tasks are also unfinished. So many unorganized workers! And where is the full participation of the trade unions in the urgent protest movement against the carnage in Vietnam and Cambodia? And where is the trade union movement and the labor movement as a whole in the celebrations of 100 years of Manitoba? After all, it has been the workers and farmers who have built Manitoba. They broke the land, worked in factories, helped to build the labor movement, participated in many struggles for social justice, and it is due to Riel, and to these workers and farmers and the immigrants from many lands that Manitoba has achieved the reputation of having strong progressive and democratic traditions.

We need a people's history of Manitoba. In that history the immigrants who brought to Manitoba a passion for social justice will deserve an honored place. They are the third force which helped to mould the development and promise of Manitoba. The Ukrainian progressive movement, through its publications and magnificent Centennial Concert, has performed a valuable service in paying tribute to the Ukrainian pioneers and the contribution of radicals of Ukrainian origin to the building of Manitoba.

The story of the contribution of the Jewish radical movement has yet to be written—and it is a proud and honorable story. It includes the participation of Jewish workers in the 1919 strike; the fight against sweatshops and the battle to organize the garment industry; the needle-trades strikes in the late twenties and early thirties; the mass movement against fascism in the 1930s when Jewish radicals organized the Jewish Anti-Fascist

League and together with *folksmenchen* of the Landsmanshaften helped to drive Whittaker's Brown Shirts from Winnipeg's streets; the tremendous Aid to Russia campaigns during the war years when a great united front of Jewish organizations was built; the participation of Jewish workers and middle-class sympathizers in helping to establish "the North End" as a labor and radical stronghold which has won a reputation across the land; the colorful, extensive and dedicated cultural activity in the Liberty Temple (later the Sholom Aleichem School for secular Jewish education) and a secular, humanistic ideology; the sowing of the seeds of Jewish activism for peace and socialism. These and other activities come to mind. They are an integral part of the history of our province and their roots are deep and strong.

The fusion of these three streams—the revolutionary heritage of Riel, the militant traditions of the labor movement and the contribution of the progressive section of the waves of immigration—has written some of the most stirring chapters in our history and has enriched the history of Canada. In wishing the people of Manitoba—and those who at one time lived and worked in that province—"Happy birthday and great advances in the 1970s for peace and social progress," we are confident that the greatest victories for the province of Riel and its multinational people still lie ahead, and it is the people who will make that history.

January-February 1984

Will Hunger Stalk the Land?

HENRY M. ROSENTHAL

No matter where one turns, there is talk of "recovery." This past year, the retail sales giants gleefully reported increased sales. Shopping malls in all the major cities have had record Christmas sales. The Dow Jones average keeps going up, as do other stock market indices. Bank profits have shown dramatic increases all across the country. To all intents and purposes, inflation has been brought under some kind of control.

On closer examination, one suspects that much of this vaunted "recovery" is pure media hype. The message coming out of corporation boardrooms is "restore consumer confidence." If only people can be persuaded to liquidate their savings to buy all the things that make America great —cars, fridges, TVs, houses, etc.—then the economy can be brought on track again. It is as though our whole experience of recession/depression has been nothing but an exercise in perverse psychology, and the only real weakness of our economic system has been its failure to "communicate." There are undoubtedly some persons in the media/advertising industry who believe in this self-serving argument. In order to hype others, they have to hype themselves first.

What are the facts? First, despite the increased profits of the banking fraternity, and increased productivity and profits in certain select sectors of the economy, unemployment continues at record levels. Slight decreases in the rate of unemployment have not been sufficient to affect the hundreds of thousands of new entrants into the labor force graduating from high schools. The new technologies coming on stream, by definition, can create very few jobs. In the meantime, unemployment insurance benefits have been running out for hundreds of thousands of unemployed workers. Many have no recourse but to swell the growing ranks of those reduced to living on meager welfare benefits. One can already see the effects of steady pauperization of increasing numbers of families and individuals throughout the land. For those prepared to see, the evidence is at hand—in the form of soup lines, food banks, homelessness, begging, scavenging, stealing, prostitution and all the other means used by desperate people to survive.

A recent article by Stephen Nordlinger for IPS, printed in the Vancouver *Sun*, documents some of these effects in the USA. He reports that there are now thousands of soup kitchens and food distribution centres all over the USA, even in the farm belt where wheat elevators and corn bins are overflowing. All indicators point to increased need in the months to come. Food corporations and grocery chains are now delivering three million pounds of damaged food products each week to 150 food banks around the country.

There seems to be some difference among academics and government officials about the extent and nature of the problem, but for those on the firing line dispensing food to needy persons, there seems to be a consensus. A study by the Centre on Budget and Policy Priorities shows an increase of 50 per cent in the number of persons served between February 1982 and February 1983. The U.S. Conference of Mayors stated that "hunger is probably the most prevalent and the most insidious" problem they are facing. According to U.S. government statistics, there are only about eight million unemployed now as compared to ten million a year ago. But only a third of these are still receiving unemployment benefits, the remainder having exhausted their entitlements. Statistics for poverty for 1982 show over 34 million Americans living below the poverty line, or about 15 per cent of the population. But government calculations do not include the increased costs of heating, rent and transportation, since they are based on an economy food budget.

Another factor in the growing soup lines is the removal of 850,000 persons from eligibility for food stamps, as a part of Reagan's cuts of social services to help pay for the tremendous escalation of military expenditures.

What of the effects? As might be expected, the prime victims are children, and most particularly, Black and Hispanic children. Stark evidence is now appearing of what is officially termed "silent undernutrition." Its symptoms are not always apparent to the untrained eye, but medical tests show an alarming increase in the incidence of iron deficiency anemia in pre-school children. Medical experts point out children under five are particularly vulnerable, since this age group experiences the most rapid brain growth. It is well known that nutritional deprivation can cause irreversible brain damage.

How are Jews in North America being affected by these trends? A recent study by the American Jewish Committee, entitled "Jews on the Edge," was presented to the 52nd General Assembly of the Council of Jewish Federations. It presented a "grim litany on the growing problem of Jewish unemployment and the plight of the Jewish poor" (*Sentinel*, December 1, 1983). It concludes that *the economic structure of Jewish communities is changing due to significant downward mobility*. An estimated 15 per cent of the total Jewish population in North American is considered to be "economically disadvantaged and vulnerable." Those most vulnerable are workers over the age of 40, working women in *all* age brackets, and young people entering the labor force.

Like the general community, the elderly in Jewish communities are the ones most affected by poverty. Reports from Miami, St. Louis and Seattle show 17 per cent of people over 65 with household incomes of less than $5,000, and another 43 per cent with incomes between $5,000 and $15,000. Studies in New York, Chicago and Philadelphia show similar results. There is also a consensus that large numbers of middle- to lower-class families are being drastically affected by unemployment and under employment, and the class of the "new poor" is increasing. The report indicates that Jews in the serving professions—teaching, social work, health—and small business have been specially vulnerable to budget cuts by the Reagan administration. But Jews are being also affected by the downturn in manufacturing jobs, including decreases in the number of engineers, sales and marketing personnel, accountants, etc., as well as those on the production lines. One can safely assume that Canadian Jewish communities are also carrying the impact of the same trends. (See "Jewish Communal Responsibility in Light of Government Cutbacks" by James Torczyner in Part I.)

Given the swamping effect of "recovery" propaganda, information like the above tends to be ignored or buried by most of the media. In fact, releasing such facts is even seen by some as hindering the effort at restoring "consumer confidence," or as an attempt to undermine Reagan policies. In addition, the propensity of the comfortable middle class for avoiding knowledge about how the other half lives is well established. Friedrich Engels commented on how mill owners managed to route their daily trip to their factories so as to avoid seeing the slums inhabited by their workers. Given our elaborate systems of freeways, the avoidance of any contact with poverty is even easier today. Whatever the reasons, most middle-class people are remarkably well-insulated from the facts of human misery—both physically and psychologically.

Nevertheless, it is obvious that the number of persons in distress in our society has increased to the point where it is difficult to hide or explain away. This is well illustrated in a recent poll conducted by the Los Angeles *Times*, which found that only 30 per cent believed that the economy had entered a period of long-term growth. Some 42 per cent saw the recovery as being short-lived, while 25 per cent said that there was no recovery taking place or that the economy may even be getting worse. The latter view was strongest among poor people, and Blacks. Most people polled felt that unemployment remains the number one problem. It appears that no amount of hype can convince people of assessments of the real world which run counter to their own direct experience and knowledge.

However, given the growing escalation of human misery, one must ask why there are not more repercussions on the political level. Why are the forces of the left and centre unable to mobilize public opinion to reverse these trends? Why has no widespread movement arisen among the poor and dispossessed to demand jobs and a proper share of their rightful inheritance? Why has the growing peace movement not emphasized the organic link between increased U.S. military expenditure and increased pauperization?

The Hands of Workers in Iron and Steel; photo: Robert Doisneau (February-March 1978)

Pickets—Glace Bay Coal Strike (lithograph) by Avrom Yanovsky (January 1980)

Child labour in Canada, early 1900s; photo: Public Archives of Canada (June 1983)

Portage Avenue, Winnipeg, Manitoba, circa 1920; photo: Public Archives of Canada (October 1983)

April 1984

Lotusland
The Wages of Restraint

STAN PERSKY

Hugh Curtis was hemmed in by a scrum of reporters in the legislative corridor. It was February 20, 1984, just moments after British Columbia's Social Credit finance minister had brought down the first provincial budget in the country within living memory that actually *reduced* year-to-year government spending. Instead of the $8.3 billion Curtis had spent in 1983, Premier Bill Bennett's chief number cruncher proposed to expend only $7.9 billion in 1984, a reduction of nearly 6 per cent.

To do it, he would have to: cut welfare payments by $25; fire several thousand government workers; chop back by 5 per cent on an already beleaguered education system; make the elderly pay more for prescription drugs; shred the legal aid system and raise taxes by 8 per cent. And although the jobless rate in the Great Rain Forest stood at 15.2 per cent, the word "unemployment" did not appear once in Curtis' 15,000 word speech.

The reporters in the Victoria legislative hallway wanted to know just what kind of heartless brute they were interviewing. Having delivered the sacrificial lamb to the altar of "restraint," the buzzword of these neo-conservative times, Minister Curtis assured all and sundry that he was neither "callous" nor "cruel." In fact, the budget author, a practising Roman Catholic, had gone with heavy heart to his confessor just the day before, he told the media.

Presumably, the priest to whom Curtis unburdened himself of his sins was not a member of the government chaplain service. You see, the province's 60 or so chaplains, who minister to B.C. prisoners, had recently been informed that as part of the government's heroic efforts to "downsize" the government, they would be "privatized." (Translations of West Coast Newspeak will be provided in due course.) That is, the chaplains would now have to form a company, say ABC Prayer Service Ltd., and bid for the job of praying. The cost of praying wouldn't change, but the government, humming "Nearer My Privatized God To Thee," could claim that the size of the government payroll had been significantly reduced. Neat, eh? The same fate was in store for dozens of other government services. Gallows humor aside, the reason that these fiscal finaglings from Lotusland ought to be of interest to the rest of the country is because B.C. is in the midst of the most extreme conservative financial experiment attempted in Canada since World War II. Its outcome will affect Canadians from Galiano Island to Gander.

The day after Curtis delivered his soak-the-poor document, Michael Walker, director of the Fraser Institute, a right-wing free enterprise think-tank, gleefully explained that Curtis had simply dropped "the other shoe." Whether it was merely the other shoe or a jackboot in the face, the unprecedented process had begun more than a year earlier.

Premier Bill Bennett, heir to a political dynasty that had ruled B.C. for some three decades with scant interruption, was seeking a third term in office. The election was set for May 1983. The province was, like the rest of the country, reeling under the capitalist recession. But moreso, because B.C. has a banana republic economy dependent upon forestry exports. Unemployment was at near-Depression levels. The Socred government had been plagued by a series of mini-scandals ranging from vote-juggling to cabinet ministers guzzling expensive French wine on the taxpayers' tab. Pundits, nestled in various of the province's mountain hideouts, unanimously conceded that Bennett's chief political opponent, former premier and NDP leader Dave Barrett, stood a better than fair chance of unseating the Socreds.

It was at this point in the proceedings that the boys in Bennett's backroom (mostly imports from Bill Davis' Big Blue Machine and the ubiquitous Michael Walker) came up with "restraint," the cure-all for capitalist economies in recession. It was one of the new Three R's: recession, restraint and recovery, a steady progression from the doldrums to prosperity. The government had already flirted with a murky incomes policy to restrain public sector wages for the last year. But it had not really sold well. Nor was it selling on the campaign trail. Barrett was drawing the crowds, and Bennett was on his political deathbed, according to those in the know.

But then a reporter asked NDP leader Barrett, who was in the midst of a triumphal procession through the Kootenay mountains in eastern B.C., what he would do with the Bennett restraint program. Scrap it, said the would-be future premier, in a moment of fatal candor. That was enough to get Bennett and the province's editorialists out of their deathbeds.

Soon the son of W.A.C. Bennett was standing before crowds brandishing a headline that said, "B.C. will lead the country into recovery." You know what will happen if the dangerous socialists get into office? Bennett asked. He then eloquently shredded the headline. That's what.

On May 5, 1983, when the dust cleared, Bill Bennett was still premier of Lotusland. What's more, he had an increased majority in the legislature (36-22, up by four seats). Emboldened by this vote of public confidence, Bennett and company retired to a sleepy lakeshore in the interior of the province to listen to the sweet nothings of the free enterprise lunatic fringe.

Two months later, in July 1983, finance minister Curtis delivered his first restraint budget. At least, it was called a restraint budget, even though government spending would increase by 12 per cent. But, in a series of twenty or more accompanying bills, the government proposed to restrain the people.

Among the proposals: firing a quarter of the public sector. To facilitate this, the Socreds would eliminate traditional seniority provisions and normal collective bargaining procedures. As well: elimination of the Human Rights Commission, the end of rent controls and the Rentalsman mediation process, educational cutbacks, a new health care scheme that looked suspiciously like the infamous "double-bilking" arrangements being tried elsewhere, and centralization of power in the hands of the government of every local institution possible. On top of this: a wide range of social service cutbacks to the downtrodden. It was, by everyone's admission, an unprecedented program.

Within days, the demonstrations began. The trade unions in the country's most highly organized province announced the founding of Operation Solidarity, and sponsored an even broader coalition of community groups and unionized workers dubbed the Solidarity Coalition. Though pooh-poohed at the outset, the coalition gained momentum. On October 15, 1983, as the Socreds met in annual convention, more than 50,000 coalition marchers took to the streets of Vancouver. Never before had a social movement of such proportions appeared in the province. As for the NDP legislative rump, it dutifully attempted to filibuster the legislative package, but had only limited success as Bennett held all-night sessions and invoked closure an unprecedented twenty times to ram his plan through. As a social force, the NDP was on the sidelines, its parliamentary devotions rendered almost irrelevant by the people in the streets.

However, the important point in all this was now grasped by most everyone. It was this: "restraint" was an ideological slogan, not an economic remedy. It was a way of attacking all the institutions of the welfare state that make private enterprisers sleep uneasily. For workers, educators, ethnic minorities and other defenders of civilization it appeared as a clear and present danger to the fabric of democracy.

Three weeks later, in early November, Solidarity began shutting down the province. Government workers, teachers, civic employees—some 80,000 people altogether—with thousands more waiting in the wings, were on the picket lines in a political protest designed to bring an intransigent government to its senses. B.C. was on the brink of the first general strike in the country in 60 years.

On the way to the barricades, something happened. The trade union movement lost its nerve. Or perhaps it merely remembered that it was fighting to retain labor rights, and not a broad-scale social battle. Late Sunday evening, November 13, Premier Bennett and labor leader Jack Munro appeared on the front porch of the premier's home in Kelowna and announced a settlement. Go back to work, said labor boss Munro. In return, the government would drop its demand to eliminate seniority and negotiating rights, and would even be prepared for a bit of "consultation" on human rights and tenant issues. When Solidarity Coalition supporters sought in vain for the fine print of this verbal agreement, they called it, justifiably enough, a sell-out.

What they didn't foresee was the aftermath. They had revved up hundreds of thousands of people across the province with the cry, "An injury to one is an injury to all." When it became obvious that the "all" meant only trade unionists, and thousands of the poor would indeed be injured, the coalition collapsed more rapidly than it had risen. Worse, it left community groups, teachers, members of the women's movement, ethnic minorities, and others demobilized, disappointed and cynical.

Three months later, when Curtis brought down the real restraint budget, there was barely a peep. The most outrageous of statements instantly became tomorrow's fish wrapper. Asked why the government was reducing the already measly $375 welfare rate for young singles, Human Resources Minister Grace McCarthy blithely explained that the young didn't need as much money as others and were easily able to move to where the jobs were. "Where were the jobs?" asked startled reporters. McCarthy named one or two of the government's current money-losing megaprojects. The reporters rushed to the phone and called distant Tumbler Ridge where a billion public dollars were being poured into coal development. "How many jobs are available?" asked the fourth estate. "Forget it," said the Tumbler Ridge foreman, "we've got a waiting list of 45,000 applicants."

Meekly, the media returned to McCarthy for further instructions. Well, said the unperturbed protector of the impoverished, if B.C. welfare recipients didn't like it in Lotusland they could always move to Brandon, Manitoba. Brandon, Manitoba? Yes, Brandon, Manitoba. Never mind that the headlines that had once proclaimed B.C. would lead the country to recovery had now been changed to an admission that B.C. was still in the recession and that the vaunted restraint program had merely added to the misery. If you see any caravans, wagon trains or mule teams wending their way across the Rockies, rest assured they're bound for Brandon.

May 1984

What Happened to the 'Just Society'?

ED SCHAFFER

Earlier this year an era had come to an end. Prime Minister Trudeau, after sixteen years in office, announced that he was retiring. His announcement brought forth the eulogies normally accorded to those who have passed away from either political or physical life.

As is customary in eulogies, the unseemly aspects of the departed one's life are either glossed over or forgotten. Rabbis and priests are, after all, permitted to lie at funerals. In keeping with this hallowed tradition, no one in parliament raised the question of what happened to the nation's economy during his reign.

Conveniently forgotten was his promise of the "Just Society." This "Just Society" was supposed to reduce poverty, alleviate social ills and open new opportunities for young people. The millenium, he implied, lay in the not-too-distant future. Trudeau thus became prime minister in an era of hope, in a time when people were looking forward to an increasingly better future.

When Trudeau announced his retirement, gloom had displaced hope. The Cruel Society had replaced the "Just Society." Fresh on everyone's mind was the budget message delivered two weeks earlier by Finance Minister Lalonde. In that message Lalonde could offer no hope for the 1.5 million unemployed. Calling unemployment, which stood at more than 11 per cent of the labor force, "a national tragedy," he predicted that it would remain above 10 per cent in 1985. He took pains to remind the nation that "there are limits to what Government alone can do." The government, which was to bring Canada the "Just Society," could now only promise a continuing "national tragedy."

A glance at the unemployment figures when Trudeau came to power shows just how far Canada has moved away from a "Just Society." In contrast to the 1.5 million officially admitted unemployed in February, there were only 358,000 in 1968. During the same period both the population and the labor force increased at a much slower pace, approximately 50 per cent. As in the thirties, unemployment is beginning to affect wide segments of the population.

Why has Trudeau ended his reign in a period of despair rather than one of prosperity? The answer to this question requires more than a mere assessment of the prime minister's competence or an evaluation of his policies. One must look at the developments of the world economy in the post-World War II years. These years witnessed, first of all, the abandonment of the ideology of laissez-faire capitalism. The leaders of the major market economies realized that it would be politically impossible to return to the conditions of the pre-war years, characterized by high unemployment and an inadequate system of social benefits. They adopted policies whose stated aims were to guarantee full employment, stable prices and economic growth.

The ideological mentor of these policies was the English economist John Maynard Keynes. The main point in Keynes' thesis was that the private economy would not automatically generate full employment. A modern capitalist economy, he argued, would always be plagued by an insufficiency of demand. This insufficiency arises because people will save a fixed proportion of any increases in income. This demand insufficiency leads to an "under-employment equilibrum," i.e., to a condition in which unemployment becomes permanent.

Keynes' thinking represented a sharp break with perceived wisdom. Most bourgeois economists at that time accepted uncritically Say's Law, named after the French economist, Jean Baptiste Say. According to Say, a free market economy would automatically generate full employment because "supply creates demand." No supplier, according to Say, would offer anything to the market unless he or she received something in return. Therefore the products supplied by one individual automatically constituted the demand for the products of other individuals. Overproduction, in the sense that more goods are supplied than are demanded, could therefore not exist. To the extent that it did exist, it was but a temporary phenomenon which the free market forces would quickly cure.

Though Marx and some bourgeois economists, like Malthus, rejected Say's Law, it became the sacred cow of conventional economics. It was the intellectual "proof" that capitalism was not a system of contradictions but one of harmonies. Left to itself, the free market system was to make everyone better off from "here to eternity."

The Great Depression rendered a severe blow to Say's Law. Most bourgeois economists then adopted Keynes' analysis, not only because it corresponded more closely to reality, but, more important, it offered an alternative to Marxism. Though Keynes, like Marx, recognized there were contradictions in capitalism, he did not believe these contradictions were irreconcilable. The government, according to Keynes, could overcome the deficiency in private demand by increasing its expenditures. Through the creation of a deficit the increased demand by government would fill the gap caused by the insufficiency of private demand. By proper "demand management" the economy could be kept on an even keel. There was, thus, no need to change basic property relationships to recover from a crisis.

Governments, in varying degrees, accepted this analysis. Attempts were made to create a welfare state. These policies appeared to work in the fifties and during most of the sixties. In this period we witnessed rising living standards, expanded social services and high profits in most of the advanced capitalist economies. To the extent that recessions did occur, they were relatively quickly overcome through government expenditures.

During this same period another important change was taking place in the structure of world capitalism. The war had shattered the pre-existing power relationships. German and Japanese capitalisms were defeated. The economies of Britain, France, Italy and the other Western European countries were severely weakened. The United States, which had escaped the ravages of war, became, by far, the most powerful capitalist nation. The United States used its power to penetrate the economies of these other countries through the expansion of its corporations. In those years the major American corporations exported capital to these economies. Corporations which had been essentially national in character became international. The age of the multinational corporation (MNC) had arrived. Capital had become "internationalized."

This internationalization had important implications. First, it made the market economies more interdependent than ever. A disturbance in one country would be quickly transmitted to another through the mechanism of the MNC. Second, the expansion of capital added to the "industrial reserve army." If labor in the United States, for example, made "excessive" demands, production could now be moved to countries where labor was more "reasonable." Third, it forced the United States to adopt policies protecting the foreign investments of its corporations. These measures, as the recent history of Canada-U.S. relations clearly shows, often infringed on sovereignty.

These infringements were resisted by the bourgeoisie of the other countries. As they recovered from the ravages of the war, they began to challenge the dominance of the United States. The European and Japanese corporations began taking larger shares of the world market and posed a serious threat to the dominant position of the United States. Starting in the late fifties, the U.S. position began to erode. An important reason for this erosion was its heavy armaments expenditures. So many of its scientists and engineers were gobbled up by the military that its corporations were not able to retain their technological leads. Countries like Germany and Japan, which had relatively low arms budgets, were able to make serious inroads in markets previously dominated by the U.S. An era of "economic warfare" began to develop among the MNCs.

A third important change was in the relationship between the industrialized and the non-industrialized countries. During the fifties and the sixties, the prosperity of the industrialized nations was accompanied by the impoverishment of the non-industrialized ones. The ability of the major capitalist countries simultaneously to raise living standards and to increase profits arose from a decline in raw material prices. The crisis of the Western World was exported to the third world.

This situation changed when OPEC succeeded in raising oil prices dramatically in the early 1970s. The profits that would have gone to the capitalists of the industrialized countries were now flowing to the newly created capitalists of the oil countries. This new bourgeoisie was threatening to displace the old, established bourgeoisie. In the United States there was fear that OPEC had the resources to buy out the major American corporations. Bogged down in Vietnam, the U.S. could not act militarily against OPEC. Its only defence was to wage "economic warfare" against it.

Ironically, the success of OPEC resulted from the expansion of the market economies, an expansion, as was pointed out earlier, that was due to "demand management." The growth of the Western economies created a "shortage" of oil, thereby enhancing the bargaining power of OPEC. The only way to reduce this power was to recreate a "surplus." With a "surplus," the oil countries would fight among themselves for markets, causing prices to fall. But to create a "surplus," the West had to reduce demand. The most effective way to reduce demand is to have a recession. Kissinger summed up the situation by stating that the West must attain "strength through misery."

The crisis, which the West had previously exported to the third world, had become internalized. In the advanced capitalist countries, inflation became rampant, debt piled up and unemployment grew. The Keynesian remedy no longer worked. New solutions were called for.

It was at this time that the analyses of monetarists, like Friedman, and "supply side" economists, like Laffer, became fashionable. While there are some differences in their approaches (the monetarists place their main stress on expanding the money supply at a constant rate while the "supply siders" focus on tax reforms and other such measures to encourage business), they both advocate the dismantling of the social welfare programs built up in the post-war years. The crisis, they argue, has flowed from the heavy burden these programs have placed on business and from excess government regulations. "Free business," they argue, "and prosperity will return. Let the market do its job!" Say's Law has again come into vogue. Forgotten are the post-war promises of full employment, stable prices and economic growth.

The capitalist world is now in an era of "economic warfare." In any war there are casualties. In an economic war the casualties are the unemployed, the bankrupted businesses and the impoverished farmers. But this warfare is necessary for the continued existence of the system in its present form. Not only is the policy of "strength through misery" necessary to fight against OPEC but also to finance the unprecedented arms build-up against the socialist countries. It is also necessary for the restructuring of the capitalist economies in their struggles with each other to develop the new technologies, and especially the new forms of energy, so necessary for achieving dominance. This restructuring can be accomplished only through a shift of national income from consumption to investment. In more mundane terms it means keeping wages low and profits high. Large-scale unemployment is necessary to achieve this end. The unemployed do not receive any wages and those working are, as we see in the news almost every day, willing to take wage cuts to retain their jobs. What we are now witnessing is a Stalinist policy of rapid industrialization within a capitalist setting.

The Lalonde budget is consistent with this policy. Through such measures as giving increased tax breaks to buyers of RRSPs, it is encouraging savings at the expense of consumption. By relying on the private sector to revive the economy, it is resurrecting Say's Law. It is an open admission that the Trudeau government cannot make good on its promises of earlier years.

The end of the Trudeau era thus coincides with the admission that capitalism cannot solve its contradictions. Under capitalism, the "Just Society" will always remain what it is today, an unattainable dream.

March 1985

The Generic Drug Controversy

JOEL LEXCHIN

Brian Mulroney has been telling anyone willing to listen that Canada "is open for business again." In order to attract foreign capital the Foreign Investment Review Agency is to have its few remaining teeth pulled. However, Mulroney's enthusiasm for foreign investment could end up making health care more expensive for Canadians by driving up the cost of prescription drugs.

By the late 1960s, a succession of three government reports had all concluded that prescription drug costs in Canada were among the highest, if not *the highest*, in the world. After the publication of the last of this trio of studies in 1967 the government finally recognized that something had to be done. The result was a 1969 amendment to the Patent Act setting up a system of compulsory licensing.

Traditionally, once a drug was on the Canadian market, the patent taken out on it prevented any other company from importing the same drug into Canada for up to seventeen years until the patent expired. This monopoly on the product for such a long period of time was one of the major factors keeping drug prices so high. The foreign-controlled multinational drug companies that dominate the Canadian market were quite content with the pre-1969 system since they were the ones with the monopoly. A monopoly made for high prices and high prices made for high profits; almost double those of all other manufacturing industries.

When compulsory licensing came along, the situation changed drastically. Now a company did not have to wait until the patent expired before marketing its own brand of a drug. The company could go to the federal commissioner of patents and request a compulsory licence to allow it to import and sell the drug in Canada. Compulsory licences are granted routinely and in return for receiving the licence the original patent holder is paid a royalty of 4 per cent of the licensee's sales.

Since 1969 about 300 compulsory licences have been issued. The major beneficiaries of these licences have been the small generic companies, a significant number of them Canadian owned. Together with various provincial drug programs, these licences are estimated to be reducing Canadian prescription drug costs by up to $270 million a year.

Not surprisingly, the multinational drug companies, led by their association, the Pharmaceutical Manufacturers Association of Canada (PMAC), have not been happy with compulsory licensing. For the past fifteen years they have been fighting for the repeal of the 1969 amendment to the Patent Act. The degree of hostility that the PMAC has displayed towards compulsory licensing may seem unwarranted because, in fact, the profits of the multinationals have not been affected. Their profit levels are the same today as they were back in the 1960s. Furthermore, the Canadian market represents less than 2 per cent of the world pharmaceutical market. Losing a share of the Canadian market to generic competitors does not mean very much financially to the large multinationals. What these companies really fear is that countries with much larger markets will follow the Canadian example. That would hurt them in the pocketbook.

In the campaign to get rid of compulsory licensing one of the main rallying points has always been that the existence of compulsory licensing makes Canada an unattractive place for pharmaceutical companies to invest in. The claim is constantly being made that companies are closing their manufacturing plants here and that they won't build research facilities in Canada. Of course, even before 1969 there wasn't much manufacturing done in Canada and the little research that was done was necessary to satisfy the pre-marketing requirements of Health and Welfare Canada. Manufacturing may have declined in Canada since 1969, but only because companies are moving their plants to tax havens such as Puerto Rico and Ireland. The companies don't do research here because that is the nature of a branch-plant economy. Research operations tend to be concentrated in the home country of the company and Canada is not home to any large pharmaceutical company.

Back in 1980, the PMAC and the multinationals were promising that if favorable changes were made to the Patent Act, then the industry would be prepared to increase its manufacturing and research activity in Canada. However, when the industry's package was analysed by the federal Departments of Industry, Trade and Commerce and Consumer and Corporate Affairs, it became apparent that most of the new research and development and manufacturing promised by the industry was either already planned or was to be financed through government incentive programs. More recent promises from the multinationals have not had any more substance than those offered in 1980.

However, if you repeat yourself over and over and over again as the PMAC has done, aided by groups such as the Canadian Medical Association, the deans of all eight schools of pharmacy in Canada and the Chemical Institute of Canada, then eventually someone listens. One senior official at Consumer and Corporate Affairs in Ottawa called the PMAC's efforts "the most superbly orchestrated lobby campaign I've ever seen... They've hired consultants, gone to the provinces, universities, anyone they could possibly use to make it look like the sky is falling in."

In the spring of 1983 the Consumer and Corporate Affairs Minister Andre Ouellet appeared to be ready to give in to the drug companies. His department announced three possible alternatives to compulsory licensing, all of which were basically sell-outs to the multinationals; legislation was promised by that fall. However, over the summer there was a storm of protest against the proposals, led by groups such as the Canadian Drug Manufacturers Association (a group of Canadian-owned generic companies), the Consumers' Association of Canada, the National Anti-Poverty Organization and the Medical Reform Group of Ontario (a group of progressive physicians). This opposition, coupled with a cabinet shuffle that brought Judy Erola in as the new minister, delayed the entire process until the spring of 1984. At that time, in the true tradition of Canadian governments, a special commission was set up to study the matter. The commission, headed by University of Toronto economist Harry Eastman, received briefs over the summer and held hearings in Ottawa in the fall. A report is expected sometime in early 1985.

What the Eastman Commission recommends and how those recommendations are received in Ottawa will be crucial for the future of the Canadian generic drug industry and for the prices of prescription drugs. The Ontario drug plan currently saves about $40 million annually because of the availability of generic products, and by substituting just one generic for a brand name drug, the British Columbia plan saves about $700,000 yearly. The generic drug industry is currently undergoing rapid expansion, with sales rising by about 20 per cent annually and employment climbing by 5 per cent per year.

Unfortunately, in light of the current mood in Ottawa, the government may be willing to scrap compulsory licensing and sacrifice substantial consumer savings and a fledgling Canadian industry in return for vague promises of increased foreign investment.

April 1985

The Shamrock Shambles
An Editorial

Historians are still debating as to whether Montcalm or Wolfe was the winner on the Plains of Abraham. No such debate will ensue about the so-called Shamrock Summit. Winner was the U.S. president. Loser was the Canadian people and the movement towards peace. Responsible for the loss was Prime Minister Mulroney.

Reagan is opposed to action on the acid rain issue: he effectively blocked any action for another period of time. The Pacific Coast Salmon Treaty was signed, but the fishermen on the Canadian coast got the raw end of the deal. Trade barriers are to be discussed but even in advance of any decisions the only outcome can be dumping on our market and the extraction of raw materials, water and water-power for the United States.

But even worse than all of that is the affrontery of the secretary of defence, Mr. Weinberger, who takes it upon himself to tell us what kind of weapons should be placed on Canadian soil, while the presidential press secretary doesn't even know the name of the Canadian minister of defence.

All of this is crowned by a presidential speech which, to this day, goes unchallenged by our "leader" Mr. Mulroney. On Canada's soil the president of the USA chooses to do a repeat performance of his "evil empire" sermon. Mulroney had only just returned from Moscow where he had met Mr. Gorbachev, and had apparently come away on an up-beat note about future possibilities of settling outstanding issues with the USSR, only to be slapped down by the "great father" for harboring such thoughts, let alone saying them out loud. And all of that while the president's men are sitting in Geneva, presumably negotiating in good faith with the Soviets. Imagine what would have happened had a Soviet leader made a similar speech at this time!

Canadians must tell our prime minister that we will not put up with that kind of summit on our soil. We refuse to be turned into losers!

July-August 1985

Human Rights and Civil Liberties

ABRAHAM J. ARNOLD

People often ask: "What is the difference between human rights and civil liberties?" or "What is the difference between civil liberties and civil rights?" To understand these differences it helps to examine the historical background in the development of human rights concepts. This should be of particular interest to the readers of a Jewish publication.

The high-minded goals, contrasted with the devastating depths of harsh reality in the struggle for human rights in the twentieth century, may be traced back to the struggles of the Jews in Europe for political emancipation and equal rights in the nineteenth century. In this connection it is important to recall the contribution of Ludwig Börne (1786-1837), a Jewish contemporary of Heinrich Heine, who also converted to Christianity. Börne, who was born Loeb (Louis) Baruch, came to the defence of the Jews in the 1820s and criticized the Germans for their Jew-hatred. This was the time when attacks on the Jews were preceded with the cry "hep, hep," an anti-Jewish slogan dating back to the Crusades and formed from the initials of "Heirosolyma est Perdita"—Jerusalem is Lost.

Börne could not accept the folly of "hep, hep" in silence, and writing "for the Jews" he declared in response to a Jew-hating propagandist:

> What you call human rights, which it must be conceded you grant Jews, are only animal rights. The right to seek food, to devour it, to sleep and to multiply are enjoyed also by the beasts of the field—until they are slain, and to the Jews you grant no more. But civil rights alone are human rights: for man becomes man only in a civil society.

Börne's message was addressed to the "Men of Frankfurt" in particular when he asked:

> Why should the practice of medicine be restricted to four Jews, and that of the law be allowed to none?

He also recalled that in the same way they were then storming against the

Jews, they had twenty years earlier been storming against the Catholics. Börne added: "I love neither Jew as Jew, nor Christian as Christian; I love them because they are human beings and born to be free. Liberty shall be the soul of my pen. . . ." Börne clearly pleaded for Jewish rights as part of the struggle for civil rights and liberties for all people. Perhaps he was the first civil libertarian.

It was not only Jewish converts to Christianity such as Ludwig Börne and Heinrich Heine who pursued the civil libertarian cause in the nineteenth century. In the 1840s, Rabbi Dov Berush Meisels from Polish Galicia took part in the political movement that led to the 1848 revolution and was elected a member of the first Austrian parliament. When Rabbi Meisels took his seat in the assembly, a member of the autocracy asked why he chose to sit where he did. Rabbi Meisels replied: "I seat myself on the left because we Jews have no right."

Ever since the cry of "Liberty, Equality, Fraternity" began with the first French Revolution, Jews have been in the forefront of the struggle for human rights coupled with civil liberties. This is surely due in large measure to the casting of Jews as a group in the role of victim and scapegoat by reactionary forces marshalled against the principles of equality and against human rights and civil liberties.

In the 1980s some Jews are still victims and others see themselves as potential victims. Some Jews are still active in the struggle for human rights and civil liberties but others are disillusioned with liberalism and civil libertarian principles. Unfortunately, Jews who move away from basic liberalism, the adherence to social and political views and policies which seek progress and reform by non-revolutionary means, tend to move in the direction of reactionary conservatism. And Jews who would give up on civil liberties principles apparently tend to the view that only Jewish rights matter.

Can Jews really afford to give up on the civil liberties principle of the right to free speech, thought and action limited only to the extent that the exercise of these rights does not interfere with the rights of others? And are we prepared to deny the extension of human rights as civil rights, as urged by Ludwig Börne, to guarantee equality to all people by virtue of their status as citizens of a country and members of a society which proclaims itself a civilized democracy?

Let us consider the views of one of the towering figures of the twentieth century—Albert Einstein. In 1954, on the occasion of receiving a human rights award from the Chicago Decalogue Society, he said he was depressed that a more suitable candidate for the award could not be found because he felt that he himself had never made a "systematic effort" to ameliorate the human condition, "to fight injustice and suppression, and to improve the traditional forms of human relations." He did admit that he had spoken out on public issues at long intervals whenever they appeared so bad "that silence would have made me feel guilty of complicity." And then he set out his views:

> The existence and validity of human rights are not written in the stars. The ideas concerning the conduct of men toward each other and the desirable structure of the community have been conceived and taught by enlightened individuals in the course of history. Those ideals and convictions which resulted from historical experience, from the craving for beauty and harmony, have been readily accepted in theory by man—and at all times, have been trampled upon by the same people under the pressure of their animal instincts. A large part of history is therefore replete with the struggle for those human rights, an eternal struggle in which a final victory can never be won. But to tire in that struggle would mean the ruin of society.

Hopefully Albert Einstein's views will help to revive the weary and restore the cynics to a more healthy view of the need to continue the campaign for human rights in the context of today's needs. To consider the reality of today's needs we turn back once again to the words of Einstein, who also said:

> In talking about human rights today, we are referring primarily to the following demands: protection of the individual against arbitrary infringement by other individuals or by the government; the right to work and to adequate earnings from work; freedom of discussion and teaching; adequate participation of the individual in the formation of his government.

Canada now has a Charter of Rights in the constitution with a newly proclaimed Equality Rights section. The charter protects individuals against arbitrary infringements of rights by government. It does not protect individuals against infringements by other individuals and we must work for the extension of rights protection to apply to direct relationships between one person and another and between one group of people and another, e.g., employers and workers.

Guaranteeing the right to work equally to men and women, to racial and ethnic minorities, and to the disabled today requires a policy of affirmative action in employment, or as Judge Rosalie Abella put it in her recent report to the government—we need employment equity and equal pay for work of equal value.

Freedom of discussion and teaching surely means freedom from censorship, and understanding of the civil liberties approach. And adequate participation of people in government means working for all of the foregoing and much more.

In his 1954 address Einstein also said there is "one other human right ...infrequently mentioned...which seems destined to become very important...

> this is the right, or the duty, of the individual to abstain from cooperating in activities which he considers wrong or pernicious. The first place in this respect must be given to the refusal of military service. I have known instances where individuals of unusual moral strength and integrity have, for that reason, come into conflict with the organs of the state. The Nuremberg Trial of the German war criminals was tacitly based on the recognition of the principle: criminal actions cannot be excused if committed on government orders; conscience supersedes the authority of the law of the state.

Einstein's view of the supremacy of the conscience of the individual should be taken to mean that all people who follow their democratic conscience will strive to make certain that the law works for the equal benefit of men and women as now proclaimed in the new Charter of Rights. And to reject militarism means, of course, to work for world peace and to realize that the ultimate protection of human rights depends on the achievement of world peace.

Finally it is important to know that the Universal Declaration of Human Rights states in its preamble that "human rights should be protected by the rule of law" so that people "will not be compelled to have recourse, as a last resort, to rebellion against tyranny and oppression."

December 1985

The Macdonald Flim-Flam

DANIEL DRACHE

The Macdonald Commission Report is a shallow and meanspirited document. It tells the government that Canadians want free trade, that many of Canada's social welfare programs should be scrapped and that markets rather than governments are best able to allocate our resources and adapt to change. At a cost of $45, few are likely to buy the final report. The three densely written volumes read as though they were written by a team of high-priced consultants on loan from the C.D. Howe Research Institute or the Fraser Institute of B.C. It is easy to surmise that they supplied the commission not only with its chosen framework but the ideology of neo-conservatism that Canadians must learn to live within a market-driven economy, and those who fail to lower their expectations and accept market justice will be society's losers.

With a price tag of more than $20 million, how is it that a royal commission specially created to propose a new social consensus on economic policy has come up with solutions that are so crudely biased in favor of corporate Canada? And how, amidst the worst economic conditions since the 1930s, did the Macdonald Commission dare to recommend "business as usual" policies to deal with Canada's economic problems?

In theory, royal commissions are supposed to be an important fact-finding device used by governments to tackle potentially divisive and explosive issues. They are intended to undertake an impartial weighing and sifting of the views of all Canadians on major social and economic questions. By listening only to the business community, the Macdonald Commission's final report is nothing but a grotesque parody of what a royal commission should be.

Given its pro-business orientation, the final report hardly makes for enlightened reading. As a major policy document, its view of the way Canada needs to adjust to the next industrial era is, to say the very least, deeply disturbing. Largely, it is blindly ideological, tailored simply to meet the needs of capital. Macdonald proposes that the only way to achieve sustained economic growth is to return to a model of competitive capitalism. This means allowing market forces to operate with as few restraints as possible. In policy terms, the principle of universality will have to be gradually abandoned and social welfare spending curtailed. It is a philosophy that says, in effect, that Canada's problems won't go away until market discipline is restored and the size of the public sector is reduced. It is not surprising that much of the report reads like a Chamber of Commerce brief, replete with all the standard cliches about perfectly competitive markets and economic "man" as a maximizer of self-interest.

The most flagrant example of the commission's crudely deterministic views is its analysis of the problem of unemployment. It blames high levels of unemployment in Canada on UIC benefits, which the report says creates "a disincentive for the unemployed" to look for work. Another area which the report dispenses with is the future of the family farm and rural Canada. Basically, the Macdonald Commission comes to the conclusion that the family farm isn't worth saving because it costs too much in subsidies. Instead it favors agribusiness and large-scale agricultural exploitation. However the commission is at its most scandalous when it argues against equal pay legislation to end the gender gap, reasoning that mandatory legislation requiring employers to end wage discrimination would create further rigidities in the market. The most blatant example of its anti-human, neo-conservative philosophy is its concept of the guaranteed annual income. Presented as a badly needed "deep reform," designed to end the waste and duplication to Canada's social programs, this proposal does little to upgrade Canada's income support programs for the five and a half million Canadians who live in poverty. Macdonald recommends a guaranteed annual income of $14,000 for a family—a figure which is actually below the existing poverty line set by government agencies. This isn't a program designed to give people the means to overcome poverty but is, in fact, a one-way ticket to keeping them poor and at the mercy of employers who need cheap part-time casual labour.

It is macabre to realize that the Macdonald Commission attacks the principle of universality by invoking Marx's famous axiom in defence of the principle of equality, namely, from each according to his ability, to each according to his needs. The object of the exercise is not to chastise the rich for being rich. Simple arithmetic shows that substantial savings don't come from denying the 5 or 6 per cent of wealthy Canadians their baby bonus checks or their family tax deduction. Macdonald's real concern is about "cost-efficiency" (read cutbacks) in order to develop programs that are easy to administer and are designed for fewer people. Seizing on the idea that universal programs don't do enough for those who really need income protection, the Macdonald Commission comes to the conclusion that it would be better to design safety nets only for the deserving, which won't cost the government anything more than they are already paying. In the words of the report, programs like the guaranteed annual income can be accomplished with "little increase in the net cost of Canada's social programs."

The empirical evidence and supporting material which the MacDonald Commission relies on to justify dismantling Canada's welfare state are largely a rehash of information already published in academic journals by a small group of neo-conservative academics whose views dominate macro-economics, labor markets and public policy. Compared to the Gordon Commission of twenty years ago, the commissioned research is thin and disappointing. There isn't a single study prepared for Macdonald which in any way asks any searching questions about the adequacy of Canada's social programs. For instance, given the commission's mandate, it should have explained why we have two social welfare systems, one based on direct expenditures to individuals and the other based on tax subsidies for corporations and for the rich. For every $1 that the government spends on social welfare expenditures, it is estimated that they spend $3 on tax subsidies for corporations. For a country that supposedly doesn't have money to spend on the war against poverty, the Mulroney government has given the multinational oil companies more than $5 billion in tax subsidies in the last six months. The question that ought to have been posed is why do tax subsidies exceed direct expenditures on income maintenance programs? Publishing 72 volumes of research studies can't hide the fact that the Macdonald Commission opted for quantity rather than quality and preferred the comfort of ideological purity in place of bold and original thinking.

The most overtly ideological section of the report—and the poorest documented—is where Macdonald tells us that free trade will be an economic miracle for Canada because trade liberalization will give Canadian business greater access to the American market. Creating a free trade area with the U.S. is the key proposal of this commission, reflecting the influential views of Canada's neo-classical economists who dominate the debate on Canadian public policy. Canadian economists fixated on free trade may have persuaded themselves that Canada will come out a winner in any trade deal with the United States. The obvious question to ask is which firms and industries are going to benefit. But the report is so slapdash in its research that it can't answer with any clarity where the new jobs are going to come from. Nor does it present any hard evidence about which industries are going to make a massive breakthrough in the American market. Even if those economists could show that there are real economic benefits to be gained—and they can't—this is scarcely sufficient reason to go ahead and negotiate our subservience to Reagan. Negotiating anything with the Americans at this time is a mistake. With a $150 billion trade deficit, the United States isn't in any mood to agree to anything which is going to increase import competition from Canada or for that matter elsewhere. The hard truth is that the U.S. is looking for a new relationship with Canada which involves a great deal more than a new trade deal. It wants everything on the table, including not only our economic programs but Canadian social policy as well.

Nowhere in the final report does Macdonald have the political courage and the intellectual honesty to spell out all that is involved in negotiating a new trade arrangement with the Americans. For instance, he refuses to acknowledge that the most important cost is not strictly economic, but that it poses a direct and irreversible threat to Canadian sovereignty. Bit by bit it requires surrendering control of Canadian social and economic space. Faced with this prospect, Canadians are right to be alarmed by any sort of free trade negotiations with the United States. The fact that Mulroney regards the final report as an invaluable instrument in support of his larger economic goal, a new trade relationship with the U.S., is cause for real alarm.

It is now evident that free trade entails a dramatic turnaround in the way social and economic policy are determined. It would negatively affect not only employment but social services. In practical terms, a free trade agreement requires redesigning Canada's social programs to bring them into line with their lower American counterparts. It isn't too Machiavellian to point out that Ottawa is acutely aware of the enormous savings that come from downsizing Canadian entitlements to American levels. In effect, this entails creating a new social framework from top to bottom. The fact that these changes will save the government a good deal of money serves as an additional incentive for them to take seriously Macdonald's recommendations. With 85 per cent of goods now coming into Canada free of tariffs, the reorganization of Canada's distinctive national programs will become a top priority both for the government and business. This is not simply a question of fine tuning; it requires major changes to every piece of significant social legislation of the last 40 years.

Few people realize the extent of the difference between Canada and the U.S. in terms of social policy. For instance, a New York *Times* study found that less than 50 per cent of jobless Americans had any unemployment benefits to speak of and another 20 per cent were eligible for only 26 weeks of coverage. While Canadian benefits are not generous, at least a majority of Canada's unemployed are covered and, particularly, special provision is made for regions with high levels of unemployment such as the Maritimes. What is true in the case of UIC benefits also applies in a number of other key areas such as industrial health and safety, collective bargaining rights and affirmative action programs. Canadian programs reflect Canadian needs, and because we have a much stronger collective tradition, Canadian entitlements are much better than those available in the United States.

Recently American authorities have objected to Canadian fishermen receiving UIC payments on the grounds that these benefits constitute an unfair subsidy. Clearly, the Americans are anxious to get everything on the table that looks to them like an "unfair" subsidy. From their vantage point, many Canadian programs give Canadian business a competitive edge in cross border trade.

A free trade area is usually defined as one with no barriers to the movement of goods but each country can have its own tariff structure with the rest of the world. With tariffs declining, the biggest sticking point is what the "experts" call non-tariff barriers and which, in the eyes of most Canadians, are the institutional support programs vital to maintaining a distinctive way of life. This is why the Macdonald Report is so insidious. It provides not only a roadmap for the government's economic strategy but also a detailed policy rationale to bring Canada's social programs down to the levels of their American counterparts.

This is scarcely the way in which to plan Canada's future. If Canadians have the choice they aren't going to accept any of Macdonald's recommendations. But Canada's biggest corporations are pressuring the government to go ahead as quickly as possible and begin negotiating with Washington. Because they have convinced themselves that continentalism is inevitable, they have largely given up on Canada. For them, the Macdonald Commission's Report may be the new conventional wisdom of the 1980s, but it is not the view of a majority of Canadians. *The Other Macdonald Report* presents the alternative perspective on Canada's future which the commission chose to ignore.

In the public hearings, Macdonald heard from a broad cross-section of Canadians speaking through women's organizations, the churches, trade unions, farmer organizations, native people's organizations and social agencies. These groups were most articulate in their opposition not only to free trade but also, as they told the commission, to corporate Canada's policy agenda of letting the market decide the next industrial divide. They are also the most eloquent exponents to date of what can be called popular sector politics.

The most interesting thing about them is not their differing views. Rather, it's the fact that the popular sector has emerged as a serious force, is able to mobilize Canadians on a range of issues and perceives of an entirely different world not predicated on a traditionally conceived set of demands, especially defined by electoral politics.

The popular sector model of alternative politics is based on a loose-knit coalition of groups drawn from different corners of the social strata, having a diversity of interests, concerns and identities. Proof of its existence are the coalitions that have been built in the Solidarity effort in British Columbia, the court challenge to the cruise missile testing, the defence of abortion rights, the Eaton's boycott and the recently formed Social Policy Reform Group to monitor federal cutbacks of social services. Those who suggested an alternative consensus on Canada's future during the Macdonald Commission hearings—including such diverse groups as Women Against the Budget, CUPE, the National Farmers Union and the National Action Committee, to name only a few—are representative of the kinds of groups active in these coalitions. They are Canada's counter-institutions and they draw on a counter-discourse of political economy.

The ultimate failure of the Macdonald Commission was its inability to grasp this consensus. That failure has larger ramifications above and beyond the actual mandate of the commission. It makes Canadians justifiably sceptical of royal commissions as a useful forum within which to foster public debate. It also raises the most basic questions about how a royal commission is used to give the appearance of having produced a consensus by asking for public participation, holding public hearings and receiving briefs. The appearance is of genuine consultation but the reality is otherwise. Groups are co-opted into a process where their views are sought but not heeded. The fact is that the Macdonald Commission wasn't in the least bit interested in what they heard. It made no difference that the popular sector presented a fundamental alternative not only to corporate Canada's agenda but also to social democratic and even socialist thought, both of which, in one way or another, have fallen victim to the economic crisis.

In its candid confrontation with tomorrow, the popular sector presented a profoundly innovative vision of what could become of this country. The exciting and innovative dimension of its perspective is that it looks at society from the standpoint of the marginalized, giving the needs of the poor priority over the wants of the rich, and promoting the view that the bias of modern economics ethically violates the principle of the "priority of labor over capital." In rejecting the narrow conventional view of economic growth, the popular sector advocates that Canada should be pursuing alternative economic strategies.

In a fast-changing world, the popular sector believes that the standard concept of the economy working in response to market forces of supply and demand has little to do with economic reality and is unacceptable as social policy. Instead, the popular sector proposes a radically different economic order in which democratic control of the economy is strengthened by creating new forms of participation. These different groups call for an industrial strategy combining Canadianization with local control to deal with the immediate problems of economic restructuring. They insist that the economy must serve human beings rather than corporate balance sheets, and insist that a fundamental break with conventional policy-making is the only means available. Theirs is a bold vision on which to plan the next economic era. This is also the beginning of a consensus on Canada's future. Unlike the Macdonald Commission, Canadians are not likely to ignore it.

September 1986

Canada's Penal System Indicted

STILL BARRED FROM PRISON: SOCIAL INJUSTICE IN CANADA by Claire Culhane. Montreal: Black Rose Books, 1985, 196 pages.

REVIEWED BY R.S. RATNER

I am no disinterested reviewer of *Still Barred From Prison*. The author is one of my favorite persons. Hers is a divine transgression—going where she is not wanted, in order to help those who are least wanted. For that, she has been barred from most British Columbia penitentiaries and provincial jails. But Culhane is not only ministering to the pleas of a minority of tattooed reprobates. Setting aside humanitarian impulses, her efforts to expose the injustice and barbarity of the Canadian penal system should concern us all, if only because prisons are often the staging areas for more insidious and extensive forms of social control.

Even without Culhane's book, the alarm is sounding for all to hear. The unvarnished facts are that in 1986 there are an average of 27,099 adults imprisoned in Canada on any given day (a rate second only to the violence-prone United States amongst the western industrialized nations), approximately 78,000 persons are the average daily number on probation, parole or mandatory supervision, and 12,343 persons are presently incarcerated in federal correctional institutions, 4,018 of those in maximum security. These numbers hardly befit the image of a "good and peaceable kingdom." Explanations are not readily apparent; indeed, the sources of confusion are rife: more arrests and longer sentences produce swollen prison populations which defy government recommendations and fiscal cutbacks, but which provide the "merchandise" for moves toward privatization (i.e., the commodification of social control). Talk of early release programs and community corrections is buried by discourses on "dangerousness" and by new legislation to retain custody over prisoners who would otherwise be released on mandatory supervision. Public concerns about violent offenders are mocked even by the proprietors of prison institutions who authorize showing of films featuring graphic scenes of dismemberment to prisoners in maximum security institutions.

Claire Culhane, after more than a decade of experience as a valiant advocate of prisoners' rights, understands these contradictions and tells us why their elimination depends upon nothing less than the abolition of prisons. Picking up where she left off at the end of her first book about Canada's prisons—*Barred From Prison* (1979)—which recounted her controversial stint as a member of the citizens' advisory committee during the 1976 B.C. Penitentiary hostage-taking incident, Culhane documents the more recent string of prison atrocities (from British Columbia to New Brunswick), the lists of unanswered prisoner grievances, and the unheeded recommendations put forth by various government and unofficial inquiries. It is a pattern of massive neglect. Taken as a foregone conclusion are the high inmate suicide rate, the ubiquitous violence, the malicious abuse of segregated inmates and "voluntary" experimental subjects in large-scale medical research, and the cynicism of prison staff. The situation has deteriorated to the point where Amnesty International has now listed Canada among the number of nations requiring investigation for alleged torture of prisoners.

Efforts to contain internal violence through architectural modification and technical gadgetry have so far failed to reduce tensions. Riots, escapes and hostage takings continue. Indeed, it is now presumed that prisoners released back into society are likely to be more dangerous for having been in a "correctional" institution. Why is this madness occurring?

Culhane offers a rudimentary analysis of the criminal justice system as an arm of a state geared to the suppression of dissent at home and abroad. Through prisons and the military, the state accomplishes domestic and international pacification, justifying coercion in the name of "national security." If this portrait seems overdrawn in contrast to the standard brutalities of countries from which inhabitants are fleeing in order to get to Canada, it is nevertheless true that the explanation of prisons in Canada must be located at that structural level and be made coherent in terms of economic trajectories and the disposal of the surplus labor population, a problem endemic to capitalist societies.

Given the scope of the problem and the imperviousness of the prison system to piecemeal reform, Culhane calls for its dismantling. Abolition is the long-term goal, while the expedient strategy is one of conceding the need for "short-term prisons as a last resort for the smallest number of people for the shortest period of time" (p. 146). This latter objective is to be achieved by increased monitoring and heightened accountability, brought about by such local initiatives as a community prison board, prisoner liaisons accountable to the board, and local review panels replacing the bureaucratic and remote National Parole Board. Should such innovations fail to materialize, then civil disobedience is urged as a powerful last resort. These suggestions are not unrealistic, though it remains unclear how such pointed interventions mesh with developments at the legislative level and how they "link the prison abolition movement with other political struggles for fundamental change" (p. 180). Culhane's anecdotal style of argument does not lend itself to the systematic analysis that might forge such links. Even so, her account is valuable for the awareness that it forces upon us and the deepening realization that it imparts of the dire consequences of ignoring what we have learned. More important than any horrific fact or ironic insight, Culhane has given us an example of courage that we can elect to follow. "All ye who enter, renounce hope" doesn't loom over prison gates pried open by Claire Culhane. She writes to secure that access or win it back, and to acquire it for others. If I may be permitted the impudence of advising the readership, I urge you to read her book and join the struggle. There are more global and ostensibly dignified causes, but this is the best real fight in town.

X
Jews on the Left

May 1965

Experiences of a Scientist

LEOPOLD INFELD

Leopold Infeld, who has been described as one of the world's outstanding mathematicians, worked with Albert Einstein for three years at Princeton University. He came to Toronto in 1939 and for eleven years was a professor of mathematics at the University of Toronto. He returned to his native Poland in 1950.

My own scientific work of some consequence began at the age at which the best work of other scientists finishes. In my 35th year (just before Hitler came to power), I went for a few weeks to Leipzig and saw a flourishing scientific centre for the first time in my life. Owing to my meeting Professor van der Waerden, I brought home to Lvov some inspiration for research. Later in Cambridge, I worked successfully with Max Born, whom I regard as my teacher and friend.

My dream (after my return from Cambridge) was to become a professor in Vilnyus (a university town on the northeastern frontier now belonging to Lithuania), where the chair of theoretical physics was vacant. By a complicated intrigue, I, who was known as a progressive and a Jew, was prevented from getting it.

I was then 38 years old, definitely on the downgrade. I wrote to Einstein, the noble defender of all persecuted, asking him for help. He offered me a very small stipend in the Institute for Advanced Study in Princeton. I thought then that my goodbye to Europe was forever. I hoped to find a living on the new continent which welcomed the needy and the tired.

I went to Princeton by way of London in the summer of 1936. There, by sheer chance, I met Professor C. from Princeton. I knew him from my high school days in Cracow. I asked him generally about the United States, about its universities, and about the probability of getting a job in one of them. He gave me fatherly advice. If I were hunting for a job in the United States, I had better not work with Einstein.

Yet it was Einstein who had invited me and I thought therefore that I should work with him for at least a while. Einstein was then under 60—a comparatively young man. I was about twenty years younger.

When I accompanied Einstein home the first day we met, he told me something that I heard from him many times later: "In Princeton they regard me as an old fool."

Before he was 35, Einstein had made the four great discoveries of his life. In order of increasing importance they are: the theory of Brownian motion; the theory of the photoelectric effect; the special theory of relativity; the general theory of relativity. Very few people in the history of science have done half as much.

Einstein was usually very enthusiastic about his current work and dissatisfied with it some time after it was printed. For years he looked for a theory which would embrace gravitational, electromagnetic and quantum phenomena. I doubted then, and I still doubt whether such a unifying theory can be formulated at all. Yet Einstein pursued it relentlessly through ideas which he changed repeatedly and down avenues that led nowhere.

The very distinguished professors in Princeton did not understand that Einstein's mistakes were more important than their correct results. Einstein, during my stay in Princeton, was regarded by most of the professors there more like a historic relic than as an active scientist.

Einstein suggested that I work on the equations of motion. The professors in Princeton (remember this was 1936!) were convinced that the work would come to nothing. At the beginning I was as sceptical as the others and wanted to convince Einstein that the method suggested by him would lead nowhere.

But this turned out to be impossible. To all my arguments, Einstein replied quietly with deeper counter-arguments. In order to convince him, I had to make more and more calculations. Suddenly I saw the light. Einstein was right. From then on our collaboration proceeded extremely smoothly.

Yet Professor C. had told me the truth. When Einstein proposed me for a fellowship in Princeton for the year 1937-38, his proposition was rejected, because no one believed that our work would bring results. No invitation for a job or lecture came from anywhere. Princeton was then full of younger and better scholars working on more attractive subjects. I still—so they thought and said—could return to Poland. Then Einstein and I decided to write the "Evolution of Physics."

After we wrote our big paper on the equations of motion (Einstein, Infeld and Hoffman), and after the "Evolution of Physics" appeared in 1938, my situation changed completely. The offer that I received and accepted was from Professor J.L. Synge for a lectureship at the University of Toronto.

In 1939, Poland's tragedy started the Second World War. For the second time in their lives my generation experienced the horrors of war—I mostly through fear of what was happening to all those whom I loved and who remained in Poland. Like many scientists, I did what I could to help the war effort. I worked with my colleagues in Toronto—first on ballistics, then on radar. Since I was a theoretician and not an atomic scientist, my field was rather restricted.

In 1945, the war ended and the Government of the People's Republic of Poland was recognized by almost all nations. By then, I was a Canadian citizen. I wanted to see Poland, but I was afraid of seeing it. I was afraid that the country would seem to me a great cemetery where the members of my family, among 3,000,000 Jews, were buried. Yet at the same time, I felt a strong attraction to my native country, which had abandoned its half-feudal past and was building a new socialistic order. Thus, when an invitation came from the Ministry of Higher Education in Warsaw to come to Poland for a short visit, I accepted it gladly. This happened in late April 1949.

If I were asked what are the two most characteristic features of Canada I would say "decency and dullness." At least so it was up to 1950. The weekdays were bad enough but the Toronto Sundays, with closed restaurants and movies, but with open churches, were depressing in the extreme. I prayed to God that if I died in Toronto He would be good enough to take care that this last event of my life should happen on a Saturday to save me from one Toronto Sunday.

In 1945, during an afternoon visit to the great Polish poet Julian Tuwim (who also was in Toronto at that time), I learned from him about the atomic bomb and Hiroshima. He had just heard the news on the radio. I was astonished by the news, and shaken.

Billions of words were then written about this terrible event. They can be summarized in a few wrong sentences: "We Americans are the only ones in the world who have the know-how of the bomb. As long as we keep the great secret we are safe. Let's beware of spies—and this century will become an American century."

From 1945 to 1949 I gave some hundred popular lectures on the elementary physics of the atomic bomb and the importance of preserving peace. My message was very simple: in three years the Soviets would also know how to construct the A-bomb. Its so-called secret did not exist. This short time should be used to work for mutual understanding.

Poland in 1949 seemed poor in the extreme if compared to Canada. Yet this poverty was not repulsive to me; on the contrary I felt annoyed by the memory of the smugness and richness of the West. To this country, whose difficulties I saw more clearly every day, I became progressively more attached. I was convinced that if I stayed here longer I could be of some service to Poland. What contrasted most with my experiences in Poland was the frustration I felt in Toronto, much heightened after Synge's departure. All my efforts to help build a reasonably good department of theoretical physics had turned to nil.

The good young people left Toronto after receiving much better offers from the United States. Because of the stinginess of the administration I could not get anyone worthwhile. How different life in Poland seemed to me! It was full of a dynamism which seemed to be its most essential feature.

The Polish minister of higher education suggested that I come to Warsaw and work there permanently. After some discussion we agreed on the academic year 1950-51, providing that my wife agreed to it. I was sure that after an academic year in Poland and, in general, in Europe, I would be cured of my attachment to Poland and be glad to return to Canada.

I came back from Poland to Canada to face the academic year 1949-50. The year in Toronto promised to be especially unpleasant.

I told the head of my department (who was also the dean) that I intended to ask for a leave of absence for the next year.

One of my many friends in Toronto was Professor R. One day he told me that a journalist wanted an interview with me. This was not very unusual. Because of my writings and lectures, I was fairly well known in Canada (to some, as a dangerous progressive) and such a request was not isolated.

This newspaperman came to my home and introduced himself as the new editor of *Ensign*. I did not know anything about this weekly. Later I learned that it was issued in Montreal and sold almost exclusively in Catholic churches.

I did not like the man. When he asked me about my future plans I answered him briefly that I intended to spend some time in Poland and then return to Canada.

A few days later, a news agency (I don't remember which) rang me up from Montreal. I was asked: "Do you know what is appearing about you in the next issue of *Ensign*?" I answered: "No. Would you like to read it to me?" A monotonous voice began to read the long article. As I found out later, almost the entire issue was taken up by my story. The arguments were simple enough and could be summarized in these points: 1. I was a collaborator of Einstein, and as such I possessed the secret of the atomic bomb; 2. Additional proof: I had predicted correctly when the Russians would have the bomb; 3. I wished to go with my secrets behind the Iron Curtain.

I did not know at that time that the *Ensign* article would be quoted in all the Canadian dailies. An insignificant periodical became nationally known through this publicity. My denials were also printed, but to the majority of simple Canadians the accusation probably seemed just. Only a traitor could wish to cross the Iron Curtain. The only satisfactory denial would be that I never intended to go to Poland.

At that time, of the two parties that ruled Canada—the Liberals and the Progressive Conservatives—the first was in power. The leader of the opposition was George Drew, a handsome, middle-aged man generally called "Gorgeous George."

On an evening in early March 1950, I was called by a newspaperman who told me that half an hour ago Drew had brought up my going to Poland in parliament as a matter of extreme urgency. He quoted *Ensign* liberally, called me an atomic scientist who had too many secrets and would peddle them behind the Iron Curtain. I do not think that Drew was so stupid as to believe all this rubbish, but he thought that anything that would embarrass the government was good enough.

Then all hell broke loose. The next day in Toronto's only morning paper, the *Globe and Mail*, a long article with my picture appeared on the first page. I felt I was being called a traitor by the country of my adoption. I waited for a reply from the government. None came. I remember well the awful day at the university. On my way, I saw newspapers lying on the wet pavement, people treading on my picture, looking at me, recognizing me as the "traitor" to Canada. That day, the bank clerk gave me my money without any conversation about the weather. The students were especially quiet, pretending that nothing had happened.

Yet I found out a little later, through editorials, that at least a great part of the Canadian press had more sense than to believe in the accusation. But all the press and the majority of my friends were convinced that I should not go to Poland. The president of the university offered to double my salary if I didn't go. All these pressures had just the opposite effect on me.

My wife thought and decided exactly as I did. We chose Poland.

While in Poland I received via London a letter from my dean in Toronto. I was told that I must either come back to Toronto for the beginning of the academic year or cease to be a professor at Toronto University.

I answered the dean with a letter of resignation in which the entire story was once more formulated, of course from my own point of view. For a few days I became famous. In Canada, headlines and long articles were written about the case of a scientist vanishing behind the Iron Curtain.

After a few days the entire fuss died down. While in Poland, I was asked by the representative of Canada (only later was the post raised to that of an ambassadorship) to give back my Canadian passport. This I did, returning to my original Polish citizenship. Some years later, my children unexpectedly received letters from the Canadian embassy notifying them that by special order in council their native Canadian citizenship had been revoked—I believe legally.

There is one more interesting occurrence in connection with Canada. Not long ago (in 1962) one of my friends was invited to dinner at the Canadian embassy in honor of George Drew. The once Gorgeous George had grown old, and lost his political ambition. He must have mellowed in the meantime. He asked with great solicitude after my health and begged my friend to give me his best wishes.

Most important to me, late in my life, I have been allowed for the first time to create a reasonably good department of theoretical physics completely free of all external pressure. No other country allowed me to do it before, when I was younger and, therefore, more capable of doing it. Thus Poland has become for me a pleasant country to live in.

HONORING ALBERT EINSTEIN:
Prophetic Words Recalled on the Tenth Anniversary of His Death

The discovery of nuclear chain reactions need not bring about the destruction of mankind, any more than did the discovery of matches. We only must do everything in our power to safeguard against its abuse. In the present stage of technical development, only a supranational organization, equipped with a sufficiently strong executive power, can protect us. Once we have understood that, we shall find the strength for the sacrifices necessary to ensure the future of mankind. Each one of us would be at fault if the goal were not reached in time. There is the danger that everyone waits idly for others to act in his stead.

The progress of science in our century will be highly appreciated by every knowledgeable person, even by the casual observer who only encounters the technical applications of science. Nevertheless, its recent achievements will not be overrated if the fundamental problems of science are kept in mind. If we ride in a train, we seem to move with incredible speed as long as we watch only nearby objects. But if we direct our attention to prominent features of the landscape, like high mountains, the scenery seems to change very slowly. It is just the same with the fundamental problems in science.

In my opinion, it is not reasonable even to talk of "our way of life" or that of the Russians. In both cases we are dealing with a collection of traditions and customs which do not form an organic whole. It certainly makes more sense to ask which institutions and traditions are harmful, and which are useful, to human beings; which make life happier, or more painful. We then must endeavor to adopt whatever appears best, irrespective of whether, at present, we find it realized at home or somewhere else.

—*Albert Einstein*

August-September 1973

'Never Let Them Change the Truth of Our Innocence'

D.K. and R.K.

A few minutes after eight o'clock on the evening of June 19, 1953, Julius and Ethel Rosenberg were put to death in the electric chair in Sing Sing Prison, Ossining, New York. Twenty years have passed since that day. The cry that went up throughout the world to "Save the Rosenbergs" came from millions. This was the political trial of a generation that could also remember the frame-up of Sacco and Vanzetti.

The campaign to "Save the Rosenbergs" was unequalled. From all corners of the globe, pleas were made to President Eisenhower for mercy or clemency. Surely a pinnacle in man's inhumanity to man was reached when this president refused clemency, according to record, "one-half hour after the case was laid on his desk," declaring that he had given the appeal "long and careful consideration"!

In Canada huge rallies and week-long vigils in front of U.S. Consulates and the American Embassy took place. The U.S. government was flooded with letters and wires from Canadians from every part of the country asking for clemency. Addressing a "Save the Rosenbergs" rally of 2,500 people in Toronto's Massey Hall (January 4, 1953), the national chairman of the League for Democratic Rights dealt with the legal aspects of the case. He warned that the proposed Canadian Criminal Code amendments contained in Bill 93 included treason and espionage sections providing the death penalty in peacetime. The sections, he stated, were written so broadly and could be interpreted so widely as to result in Canadian Rosenberg cases unless the Canadian people compelled the defeat of the proposed amendments then before parliament.

On July 17, 1950, Julius Rosenberg, a young East Side engineer, father of two small children, was arrested by the FBI and charged in a statement jointly issued by J. Edgar Hoover and Attorney General J. Howard McGrath with having recruited his brother-in-law David Greenglass into a Soviet spy ring early in 1945. Ethel Rosenberg, Julius' wife, was arrested August 11 on a similar charge. When arrested, Julius and Ethel were 32 and 34 years old respectively. Their son Michael was seven years old and son Robert was three.

Julius Rosenberg had held a government job, but in 1945 he was charged with being a Communist and was fired. During the trial husband and wife denied being members of the Communist Party, but did not deny their support of progressive left causes.

For months prior to their arrest newspapers carried headlines, day in and day out, about the break-up of an international spy ring and the arrest of Klaus Fuchs and one Harry Gold. The political climate in the USA when the Rosenbergs were arrested and during their subsequent trial made a fair trial impossible. The incessant publicity about "atom spies" reached astronomical proportions. It was the height of the Cold War and the era of McCarthyism.

The indictment, from the start, showed clearly that the government did not intend to prosecute either of the Greenglasses. Emmanuel Bloch, lawyer for the Rosenbergs, charged that Saypol, the prosecutor, had made a deal to let the Greenglasses go free if they would finger the Rosenbergs.

Saypol denied this, of course, but a second indictment dated October 10 did name Greenglass as a defendant. The same indictment, for the first time, charged Morton Sobel with being a member of a conspiracy.

The very heart of the government's case against the Rosenbergs lay in David Greenglass' claims that he delivered sketches of atomic secrets to Julius Rosenberg and Harry Gold. This testimony remained uncorroborated by any witness. The prosecution had Greenglass duplicate

If We Die
ETHEL ROSENBERG

You shall know, my sons, shall know
why we leave the song unsung,
the book unread, the work undone
to rest beneath the sod.

Mourn no more, my sons, no more—
why the lies and smears were framed,
the tears we shed, the hurt we bore
to all shall be proclaimed.

Earth shall smile, my sons,
shall smile and green above our resting place
the killing end, the world rejoice
in brotherhood and peace.

Work and build, my sons, and build
a monument to love and joy,
to human worth, to faith we kept
for you, my sons, for you.

These lines were written by Ethel Rosenberg in the Death House at Sing Sing Prison on January 24, 1953, six months before the executions.

copies of these alleged sketches, later introduced as the government's most important exhibit. Greenglass swore that he had prepared these copies from memory and with no assistance of any kind. But Greenglass and Harry Gold lodged together for many months on the 11th floor of the Tombs Prison in New York, where they had complete freedom to confer because they were not placed in cells. There seems good reason to believe that means were provided for Greenglass to copy sketches from books and drawings and to receive instruction. For Greenglass was only an ordinary machinist, who had failed every science course in high school and had never been to college. How could he have prepared those sketches? In the opinion of the Court of Appeals (record page 1648) the point was made that "doubtless if that testimony were disregarded the conviction could not stand."

It was simply the word of two people, themselves confessed spies, declaring that Julius and Ethel Rosenberg were spies. O. John Rogge, Greenglass' counsel, requested that Judge Kaufman give David Greenglass "a pat on the back" by limiting his sentence to three years which, with parole, would be only one year. He repeated the perjured claims of his clients that they had "almost from the outset" stated to the government: "I'll tell you what happened." It was on the basis of this perjury that the widespread misconception arose that David Greenglass had indeed accused his sister truthfully and voluntarily—while the records were to prove that his agreement to involve Ethel Rosenberg was obtained by a step-by-step process of threats, promises and rewards—if he delivered the goods.

Professor Einstein, the American scientist Urey, and others pointed out that Ruth Greenglass, who admitted her guilt, was never brought to trial, just as the record proves that at first the government did not intend to prosecute David Greenglass. There was not one bit of documentary evidence brought forth by the prosecution which in any way linked the Rosenbergs to a conspiracy. Harry Gold at no time linked the Rosenbergs to espionage. He admitted that he had never seen or heard of them before in his entire life. Every attempt was made to compel Morton Sobel to testify against the Rosenbergs. He refused. The only specific charges against him were that he had five conversations with Julius Rosenberg. These charges were required to be proved in court. They were never even mentioned during the course of the trial. Sobel was sentenced to 30 years.

No proof was advanced for allegations that the Rosenbergs had received sketches from Greenglass, no proof that they knew Russian agents, no proof that they spent money freely in night clubs to entertain recruited spies. The Rosenbergs were not charged with treason, nor with espionage. They were charged with "conspiracy," and the testimony of three confessed conspirators which the prosecution could not corroborate with any other evidence was allowed to sustain the charges against the Rosenbergs.

Saypol wanted a conviction and the death sentence for "communism." The Cold War against communism was shortly to become a hot war. Two weeks before the Rosenbergs were arrested, U.S. troops were ordered to Korea. "The evidence will show," stated Saypol, "that the loyalty and the allegiance of the Rosenbergs and Sobel were not to our country but that they were to communism, communism in this country and communism throughout the world."

"The conspiracy to commit espionage" charge, many believed, was not proved. The Rosenbergs denied all charges that they had influenced or directed David Greenglass to commit espionage, or that Julius Rosenberg had paid Greenglass to steal secrets. The opinions of world renowned scientists that there were no "secrets" of the atom bomb were disregarded.

Judge Kaufman has been called the "hanging judge." He especially was a product of the McCarthy period. His statement when sentencing the Rosenbergs to death will long be remembered: "...I believe your conduct in putting into the hands of the Russians the A-bomb years before our best scientists predicted Russia would perfect the bomb has already caused, in my opinion, the communist aggression in Korea, with the resultant casualties exceeding 50,000 and who knows that millions more innocent people may pay the price of your treason." Judge Kaufman's actions and conduct throughout the trial proceedings prejudiced the case and created hostility against the Rosenbergs. Six years before Kaufman passed this sentence, Harold C. Urey, famed U.S. scientist, stated that there were no secrets to the A-bomb and that any spy who wanted to pass on secret atomic information would do better to stay home and work in his own laboratory.

The day following Kaufman's sentencing of the Rosenbergs, the New York *Times* published a small item which suggested that the government was prepared to bargain their lives for information. "Name names" was the price.

The Rosenbergs, to the very last moment of their lives, were pressed to confess, to save themselves for their children. They refused. If they confessed falsely, others would be harmed. They proclaimed their innocence—therefore they could not confess truly. It is a canard to say that the Rosenbergs received a full measure of justice. The historic fact is that the Supreme Court of the USA never reviewed the case.

Twenty years later the USA is in the era of Watergate. The American people and indeed the world are witness to the filthy bilge pouring out of the Senate inquiry—the torrents of deceit, corruption, abuse of power, usurpation of power, destruction of records, creation of false records. Henry Steele Commager, distinguished U.S. historian, refers to "the atmosphere of secrecy, *even of conspiracy*," that permeates the White House and indeed all executive and administrative offices. The seeds of Watergate seem to have been well and truly planted in the McCarthy era; after all, did not the then Attorney General McGrath hide from the White House, with who knows what kinds of conspiracy and collusion, the fact of the plea from Pope Pius XII to save the Rosenbergs. Shades of Erlichman, shades of Kaufman and the whole cabal.

The struggle that was conducted throughout the world to save the Rosenbergs was not only a struggle to save the lives of two human beings; it was their principled resistance that aroused so many to act. But the struggle took on deeper meaning and significance in the continuing efforts for world peace against the war policy of the U.S. government. For after Korea came the undeclared war in Vietnam. As this is being written, the U.S. has congressional sanction to continue "legally" to bomb the life out of Cambodia until August 15.

In their petition to President Eisenhower for executive clemency, Julius and Ethel Rosenberg declared: "We are conscious that were we to accept the verdict, express guilt, penitence and remorse, we might more readily obtain a mitigation of our sentences. But this course is not open to us. We are innocent as we have proclaimed and maintained from the time of our arrests. This is the whole truth. To forsake the truth is to pay too high a price even for the priceless gift of life—for life thus purchased we would not live out in dignity and self-respect. We are not martyrs or heroes, nor do we wish to die. We long to see our two young sons, Michael and Robert, grown to full manhood..."

The day before execution, Julius Rosenberg wrote to Emmanuel Bloch: "Never let them change the truth of our innocence."

May-June 1976

The Death Kit of Irving Howe

WORLD OF OUR FATHERS by Irving Howe. New York: Harcourt Brace Jovanovich, 1976.

REVIEWED BY M.J. GRANITE

With the assistance of Kenneth Libo, Irving Howe claims to have recreated "the world of our fathers," or, as his subtitle proclaims: "The Journey of the East European Jews to America and the Life They Found and Made." So he says.

But his "story" not only falls short, but fails for various reasons. Reasons that have to do with patronage, condescension, personal bias and an overall attitude of evasion.

The result is a banal soap opera world of high speed nostalgia, meandering in a fluctuating disarray of movement without logic or sense; it consists of hapless episode-lifting that is somewhat in between fantasy and reality; a chronicle that is neither entirely true nor entirely false.

What he, in fact, says throughout the 700 pages of his story is that our fathers lived out their precarious lives on a, so to speak, short-term lease, without knowing or understanding the, to them, unknowable extent of their estate, or the extent of the world beyond their estate, in a ghettoized parochial world that is now "all but forgotten," except, of course, by himself.

He concludes rather smugly:

> Like all stories of human striving, it [the story of our fathers] ought to be complete, with its beginning and end, *at rest, in fulfillment and at ease with failure* [my emphasis—M.G.]. Here in these pages is the story of the Jews, bedraggled and inspired, who came from Eastern Europe.

A tangential statement, considering his countless foreclosures, evasions, briefings and the source of his briefings.

The source? (Those who guessed raise your right hand.) Almost exclusively the *Jewish Forward*.

Considering the Jewish immigrant world of America, from the eighties of the past century, through the forties of ours, with its maze of bewildering barriers, its Horatio Alger fables, its hot and cold wars, its frustrations, loneliness, alienations and struggles that have not yet ceased or stopped—considering it from today's vantage point, as Howe is considering it, we might ask:

Who is, or was, or ever will be competent enough to delineate historically (even with 20/20 vision of hindsight) the precise beginning and end, as he says, of specific human aspirations and/or striving?

If we consider them as Howe does, in terms of projects, cultural projects in terms of language (Yiddish), economic, educational and welfare, protests, etc., where (does Howe know?) is the beginning, the middle and the end? Isn't it true that one project derives from another, in terms of situations, threat, terror, backlash and change, so that there is never a precise beginning or a precise end?

I am quite certain that Howe knows that the Dark Ages, for example, were not altogether dark, nor was the Age of Enlightenment all sunshine, nor did the Russian Revolution, to pose another example, begin in 1917 or end with the recent Congress of the Communist Parties in Moscow. There were, to be sure (as in all historical developments), setbacks, reaction, counter-reaction, falsifications, even terror, and no one in their right mind can say, precisely, when they began nor when it will all end. All we know for certain is that just as it didn't start at once it will not end at once.

There are, as we all know for certain, in our present world a number of socialist states, but there does not exist, not anywhere, a single communist state; not in the real sense of the Marxist meaning of that term. We also know for certain that man's will to aspire and strive is indestructible. It will never cease or stop.

William Faulkner, the great American novelist, proclaimed in his Nobel Prize acceptance speech that "man will not just survive but prevail." May I add, on my own, that having prevailed, man will go on striving and aspiring ad infinitum, forever.

So that when Howe states pompously that the world of our fathers, their culture, language, moral and ethical aspirations have come to an end, he therewith cancels his *voluminous effort of describing and recreating that world.*

One more trouble with Howe's story is that it consists of a great deal of roller-skating from the pushcart oblivion of New York's East Side (with its cafes, theatres, clubs, unions, comedians and what he calls half-baked-self-educated lecturers, poets, artists, playwrights, novelists, etc.) towards the eschatological wall-to-wall vulgarity of nostalgia-tinted assimilation. He seems to ask, why disturb the "half-forgotten" ghosts of Mendele, Peretz (a small talent), Sholem Aleichem, Sholem Asch, H. Leivick, Moishe Leib Halpern, Moishe Nadir, Mani Leib, Avrom Reisen? Why indeed? Isn't it best to drop the curtain on that world and forget? Now that we have Irving Howe, Podhoretz, Meyer Levin and company, these so-called Jewish "mentors," we are at long last out of the woods. Aren't we?

Yet one more trouble with Howe is conversion—converts. Howe, who was once drastically (to his everlasting regret) on the left is now on the right. On the right with the "angels," who were always and forever *right* for all the *wrong* reasons, but "right."

Our converts played, to be sure, a big role in the history of our people. The Catholic Church used them, Joe McCarthy used them, our plastic establishment is using them. If you, for example, want to know the truth about Jewish communists, the Russian Revolution, the Spanish Civil War, the Rosenbergs, Hiss, Vietnam, Israel, Angola, don't ask the presidents of our streamlined synagogues, or the Jewish Congress, ask the ex-Jewish communists. They hold a monopoly on the truth. Never mind Marx, socialism, dialectics, historical materialism: the-gods-who-were-and-failed-us. No?

They, the ex-communists in their toxicity, with their digestive disorders, venom, breast-beating, penance and clogged colons know the "truth." They, in fact, saw the light in the nick of time... and found new gods. They saw the light late, but not too late to sound the rage-impacted toxin: *Right is beautiful!* And right means Ronald Reagan, Jimmy Carter and the portfolioed three-star generals of the Pentagon.

Howe is extremely knowledgeable. He knows, for example, that it's much more difficult to unravel half-truths than to spot an outright falsehood. He knows that only fools tell outright lies. He, moreover, knows that if things don't fit, they must be made to fit. How? There are a thousand ways and one of them is the Madison Avenue statutory of negative values: *How to sell is more important than what you sell*—a lesson he absorbed in the marrow of his bones.

In Chapter Sixteen, for example, under the heading of *The Jewish Press*, Howe devotes some 35 pages to the *Jewish Forward* and then proceeds to dismiss all other dailies, weeklies, periodicals and ad hoc Jewish publications in a few very peripheral paragraphs. The *Morgen Freiheit* is, of course, left out altogether. Why? (The *Freiheit* is given cursory mention by Howe in other places in the book, but only to take a jab at such fine journalists as M. Olgin, P. Novick, K. Marmor.

Completely ignored are writers like Moishe Katz, N. Buchwald, I. Bailin; poets like Z. Weinper, I.E. Ronch, Ber Green, Yuri Suhl, Martin Birenbaum and scores of others.) Why? Is it perhaps because of who fathered the *Freiheit* and for what purpose? It seems strange. There was hardly an issue of the *Jewish Forward* that didn't vent its venom against the *Freiheit*'s robust influence upon the Jewish immigrant masses. Even Chaim Nachmen Bialik is conspicuously absent, as though he and the aforementioned had never existed.

Abe Cahan, however, receives throughout the pages royal treatment. He is "a convinced socialist," a "gifted writer," "a major novelist" and a man of great intuitive perception. Reason? He proves, time and again, amply and authoritatively, Howe's thesis of total dissolution.

> Balancing himself from his involvement he [Abe Cahan] sensed and sometimes stated the overarching paradox of Yiddish culture in America: That the sooner it [Yiddish culture] began to realize its visions, the sooner it would destroy them.

To presume that Abe Cahan "sensed" the meaning or the "paradox" of Yiddish culture is an exercise of stretching the truth beyond its point of elasticity. Cahan's views of Jewish culture were not only puerile, but to say the very least, Philistine. He was, in fact, diligently engaged throughout his career, till the very end, in fashioning the pages of his newspaper in the image of the Hearst yellow press. He was the *guide*, *promoter* and *advocate* for the American melting pot. His task was, says Howe, "to educate them in Jewish culture and then tear them away from it *in behalf of American fulfillment*" (my italics—M.G.). In other words, to hell and back. I am very glad that Howe can see the justice and humor of it. I can't. What Cahan advocated and Howe supports is the conversion of Yiddish culture into *lampshades, decorative memorabilia*.

If Cahan, the editor of the *Jewish Forward*, came back to us here, today, and saw the fully Americanized members of the Jewish establishment, he would rub his dry hands together and crow with glee: That's just it, that's precisely what I meant. Of course. That was his goal, what he worked for, tirelessly; why he humiliated and persecuted and destroyed more Jewish writers than I can count or name. He was in a rage to transform the Jewish immigrants into Americans, with spats, immaculate handkerchiefs, good manners, capable of using the right fork for the right edibles; indistinguishable from his already *melted* fellow Americans, *sans* identity, *sans* tradition, *sans* language, *sans* historical memory. Look at any head table of any Jewish establishment banquet and you will recognize them. *Not much joy in them, not much future*, not much of anything.

"In 1917," Howe writes, "Cahan published *The Rise of David Levinsky*, a minor masterpiece of genre realism." (Whatever that may mean.) The book was written in English and its prose was even more stilted, mummified and dry than his unwieldy, hapless Yiddish. A novel already dead and buried in 1917, when it was written.

But let me present Howe's own definition of Yiddish, in his own words, presented in one tediously impossible sentence that makes as much sense as some of Nixon's (expurgated and censored) tapes:

> Yiddish was the language that sprang first to a Jew's lips, a language crackling with cleverness and turmoil, ironic to its bones; yet decades of struggle were required before the learned, somewhat modernized Jews could be convinced—some never would be—that his mere *zhargon*, this street tongue, this disheveled creature wearing the apron of the Jewish week, this harum scarum of a language recklessly mixing up bits of German, Russian, Polish, Provencal, English and God alone knows what, could become the vehicle of a literature through which Jewish life would regain its bearing.

Whew!

But, according to Howe, not much of a literature! Winchevsky, Edelstadt, Rosenfeld are classified as "sweatshop poets." He indicates that their naivete, lack of polish, lack of sophistication and lack of worldliness was symptomatic of the indices of taste and behavior of the Jewish immigrant readers of their times. Perhaps. I don't know. Besides how much does Howe know about the tastes and behavior of our fathers in the New York sweatshops? All I know is that these poets, who wrote about their times at the turn of this century, are just as valid today as they were then, just as Langston Hughes, for example, is as valid today as he was in the thirties. All I know is that without our so-called "sweatshop poets," Leivick (the poet of doom), Mani Leib (half-educated and totally ignorant of world literature), Moishe Leib Halpern (trying to become a Baudelaire), Glatstein, Grade, I.I. Shwartz, Avrom Reisen, Opatashu, Raboy, Bialistovsky, J.I. Segal, Nadir and so on and so forth, American Yiddish literature would have been barren.

But Irving Howe, with his holier-than-thou attitude and his worldly elegance, peers down his nose at the whole "raggedy" lot. They do not measure up to the Baudelaires, the Villons, the Cranes, the Eliots, the Pounds. Of course not. They didn't mean to. They had no such ambitions. They had their ears down, listening to the grassroots of their people. Their people's wants, needs and strivings were the entire extent and meaning of their creativity.

True, they disagreed with one another, sometimes violently, on literary, political and moral issues of the times. They took sides on literary and political issues and participated, more often than not, in the rampant struggles between all shades of left and right, but they were never niggardly towards those whose views they opposed and never wary in their writing of being *pushed towards the precarious edge of terror and apprehension.*

No, Mr. Howe, Leivick was not a poet of doom. If he were he couldn't have written such lines (no matter how depressed a situation he depicted) as: *Ikh hoyb zikh of un gey vayter* (I pick myself up and go forward). His kindness and loyalty cut through all shades of isms. He even believed in friendship (which is very rare in literature). And his loyalty did not merely extend to his people in general, but to the single individual whom he raised and enriched through his presence, with his enormous ethical and moral strength.

Nor was Moishe Leib Halpern a Baudelaire. He was Moishe Leib Halpern and that's enough. He did not try to be provocative or original, he *was* provocative and original. And I don't know, maybe Mani Leib didn't know any languages other than Yiddish. It may also be true that he knew very little of our world's literatures, but then, need I remind Howe that Maxim Gorky had no formal education whatsoever, neither did Jack London or Jim Tully or Theodore Dreiser, but they became what they were, on their own, and so did Mani Leib.

Those early "sweatshop poets" were the carriers of the virus of uprootedness and cannot be compared to any other writers of any other literature. Not because, as Howe says, they wrote in a harum scarum language that was not a language but a "*zhargon*" but because of the unique (unheard of in any other literature) intimacy and oneness with their people. It often rendered them impatient, angry and cantankerous, which amounted, more often than not (as Howe is so quick to point out) to quirkiness and one-sidedness, but never without empathy, never without concern and never without love for their people and their language which enabled them to cut through the cobwebby surfaces and see the new world and their people in a fresh way.

True, our world has become colder and emptier since our fathers, poets and teachers have left us. Most of them left before their time, cut down by anguish, privation and despair during the post years of the *plague* era. But their world, with its moral and ethical values, has not come to an end. It will be rediscovered in spite of Howe, not only by us, who carry it in our hearts and memories, but by all our future generations.

Two more things and I am finished.

One is a question, pure and simple! Where are our mothers, Mr. Howe? Did they not have a voice? Did they have nothing to say? What was their contribution, their will and heritage?

Two: Howe writes about the Bund in czarist Russia:

> Some of the younger Jewish radicals, convinced that the Bund was locked in a parochial impotence, decided to join their Russian comrades to build a Revolutionary movement that would encompass and then destroy the empire. This represented a personal solution that in relation to Jewishness was not very different from assimilation or conversion.

In the first place, it is not true that the Bundists were "locked in a parochial impotence." They played a major role in Russia, in Poland, in the establishment of socialist kibbutzim in Israel, and in America where they were instrumental in building the Arbeter Ring with its chain of Yiddish schools. And as to the slur of conversion and/or assimilation, it is precisely the same slur the Jewish establishment used and uses till this day against our younger generation who marched with Martin Luther King in the South, fought against the war in Vietnam, protest against the Chilean reign of terror, torture and murder and proclaim their Jewishness that is much different from the plastic Jewishness of their pompously modern parents, but much closer to the Jewishness of our fathers and mothers whom Howe places behind his final curtain that ends his "story" of our fathers.

Above: Winnipeg May Day Parade, 1932; photo: Jewish Historical Society of Western Canada (May 1985).

Right: Joshua (Joe) Gershman; photo: Searle Friedman (January-February 1986)

Union members of different nationalities unite to demand an eight-hour workday, circa 1910; photo: Brown Brothers Collection (May 1984)

May 1980

Incisive Analysis of the Jewish Left

JEWS AND THE LEFT by Arthur Liebman. New York: John Wiley and Sons, 704 pages, 1963.

REVIEWED BY ISAAC E. RONCH

It is a sign of the times that sociologists, historians and novelists have begun to probe the role which the Jewish immigrant has played and other Jews continue to play in helping build a secure and better life in our country.

Jews and the Left by Dr. Arthur Liebman, a professor of sociology at the State University of New York in Binghamton, is filled with valuable information on a time period beginning with the 1880s and extending almost to the present day. In a few instances, though, the author is about twenty years behind the times.

The author seeks to be as objective as is possible and yet he cannot be non-partisan. The period he describes was a stormy one filled with action and twists and turns.

When Dr. Liebman writes of the "lefts" such as Abe Cahan or Morris Hillquit, it is necessary to appreciate that he designates every opponent of the capitalist system as one who is on the left. It is only later in the book that he distinguishes between the left and the right in the labor movement.

He has delved into our past, beginning with those who arrived here from Germany and czarist Russia. It was no easy task for him to find his way between the various trends in the immigrant Jewish community, the conflicts in the unions, the splits in the radical socialist parties, the frictions among the leaders, the economic and ethnic reasons that contributed to changes in concepts from the right to the left, etc.

This book consists of nine chapters: 1) A Theoretical Overview; 2) The Left Parties and the Jews; 3) The Beginning: Czarist Russia; 4) American Roots; 5) The Garment Unions; 6) The Fraternal Orders and the Press of the Jewish Left; 7) Descent From the Heights: After the First World War, Developments that Weakened the Jewish Left; 8) How the Left Parties Responded to Jews and Jewish Problems; 9) The New Left and the Jewish New Left in the 1960s and '70s. The book ends with a summation, the author's personal conclusions and an epilogue.

Despite some shortcomings, the book is of great importance because of its many-faceted and first-hand information and even for the author's conclusions, with which one may or may not agree. It is a book which every serious reader should own.

Disputable Propositions

A great merit of this work is that at the conclusion of every chapter Dr. Liebman adds a brief summary which permits the reader to engage in a sort of dialogue with the author. For example, at the end of the third chapter, "The Beginning: Czarist Russia," he asserts: "The relation of the American Jews to the left was originally forged in czarist Russia." This statement may be disputed by other historians, but the author presents his facts and fortifies them with the source material from which they are derived.

Dr. Liebman emphasizes that anti-Semitism was undoubtedly a factor in the growth of Jewish leftism. The problem of anti-Semitism passes like a red thread through all the phases of the radical parties, in the socialist and communist movements and especially in respect to the Communist Party in America.

The Role of Yiddish and Yiddish Literature

It is noteworthy that the word "Yiddish" is frequently mentioned in the book. The Yiddish language and Jewish culture played a significant role in the Jewish left (the socialist and communist) movements.

Yet on this, one must pause and argue the point. It appears that the author's sources of information were English books and publications and interviews with authorities who are knowledgeable in the Yiddish language. But the author himself apparently does not know Yiddish and this is a considerable lack. One cannot write about the Yiddish radical movement in America without knowing Yiddish.

Dr. Liebman does credit the Yiddish language with being an important means of binding the left Jewish movements together. He carefully considers the role of *landsmanshaftn* (clubs of people from the same European town or city) in the structure of the Yiddish public life in this country. He discusses the ways in which conservative *landsmanshaftn* developed in progressive organizations, such as the *landsmanshaft* branches of the Workmen's Circle, the International Workers Order (IWO), etc. He also dwells on the children's camps, the choruses and the Yiddish children's schools of the Workmen's Circle and of the left movement.

What is conspicuously lacking in this massive work is a consideration of the role of Yiddish literature in the radical Yiddish movement. He mentions only in passing Sholem Asch's novel *Uncle Moses*, or Morris Rosenfeld's famous poem *My Little Son*.

One will not find any mention of the periodicals that educated the Jewish masses in the right-wing and left-wing movements. There is no mention of the role of such magazines as *Tzukunft* (Future) or the YKUF magazine, *Yiddishe Kultur*, or the quarterlies *Signal* or *Zamlungen*, or the writers' organizations Proletpen and the I.L. Peretz Writers Association. Similarly, no mention is made of the cultural organizations YKUF and CYCO and their publishing houses or the books that were issued by *The Forward* and the *Morning Freiheit*. Such a Yiddish work as Hertz Burgin's history of the Jewish labor movement would have been a great help to Dr. Liebman.

After all, it was the Yiddish radical literature that nourished the right- and left-wing Jewish movements. How can one leave out of account the poets Edelshtadt and Bovshover or the composers Jacob Schaefer, Lazar Weiner and Solomon Golub?

In the concluding portion of his book the author deals with the upheavals that occurred in the Jewish community in this country as a result of the events affecting Israel. He points out that many Jews suddenly voted for Nixon because of his "friendship" for Israel.

The final chapter of Dr. Liebman's book begins with this prediction:

> At this point I would like to offer a prediction about the future of socialism among the Jews in America. Socialism, I contend, contrary to popular impressions, will be on the future agenda of the American Jewish community. The conditions, the situations and the circumstances that led many Jews, particularly the best and the brightest, to socialism in the past will in various forms re-emerge to play a similar role for Jews in the future. I believe that, in America in the forthcoming decades, the Jewish community's harsh confrontation with capitalism will result in a renewed Jewish commitment to socialism.

This book deserves to be widely circulated, especially among the younger generation, among your children and grandchildren. It is a most important and necessary work.

—*Morning Freiheit*

January-February 1983

The Decline of the Jewish Left

ROZ USISKIN

The decline of the Jewish left, most perceptible in the 1950s, has been attributed by various authors to three main causes. Two of these causes have been noted in an interesting article by Rick Salutin, a Jew, Canadian playwright and a progressive thinker. The article, titled "The Conversion of the Jews," appeared in *Saturday Night*, January 1982 issue. The third cause is one I feel is an important element. Of crucial importance, of course, is that the decline of the Jewish left must be placed into a larger historical context. It was not only the Jewish left that declined in the 1950s, but the entire left declined simultaneously.

The first position taken by Salutin deals with a class analysis of the Jews and the upward mobility of a large segment of Canadian Jews from the working class to the middle class. Beginning with the war years, Salutin argues this mobility advanced rapidly with the economic prosperity of the 1950s. "From a working-class left-wing immigrant minority, Canadian Jews have evolved into a community pre-occupied with the middle-class ideal." For Salutin, the Jews have undergone a process of "bourgeoisification," or as some prefer, "the Jews have made it" syndrome.

In an answer to Salutin, both Joshua Gershman (former editor of the *Canadian Jewish Weekly/Vochenblatt*) and Morris Schappes (editor of *Jewish Currents*) have argued that "the majority of Jews are still on wages and salaries, though they are no longer industrial workers. They have not become reactionary in their politics." As evidence they point to the recent U.S. presidential election in which 39 per cent of Jews voted for Reagan as compared to 35 per cent that voted for Nixon. These figures, they argue, "are lower than for any minority except the blacks. If everyone had voted as the Jews did, Reagan would not be president." For Gershman, unlike Salutin, there has not been a major change in Jewish consciousness.

But let us suppose that Salutin is correct and there is a large preponderance of Jews in the middle class. Then the Jewish middle class, no less than other middle-class Canadians, are facing a very precarious future. Small businesses are in deep trouble due to high interest rates and the decline of buying power of many Canadians. Most bankruptcies in Canada have occurred precisely within this segment. The heightened insecurity of this group prompted one commentator to predict that "small business people may be won to an anti-monopoly coalition, a strategy some on the left now pursue."

The professionals and the intellectuals within the middle class are not as secure as in the 1950s. How many of our Jewish intellectuals are unemployed today, are working in other areas or are underemployed? As one commentator in *Jewish Currents*, Dr. William Tabb, economics professor at Queen's University, pointed out, "It is out of this professional strata that intellectuals may be drawn to participate in social change movements." In other words, Jews will neither be insulated nor protected from the current economic crisis. This reality will force Jews and others to consider socialism as an alternative to a capitalist economy. This entire question of class and the Jews must be given a great deal more attention by *Canadian Jewish Outlook*, specifically with regard to the changing nature of capitalism and the new forms of technology that are affecting every sector of the work place.

The second position dealing with the decline of the Jewish left in the 1950s is the position put forth by Joe Gershman. The 1956 Khrushchev revelations brought about a great deal of disaffection and disillusionment among many Jewish radicals. Gershman writes of the decline of socialist ideals due to the betrayal by Soviet anti-Semitism of socialist promises. He states: "Here I'm an old communist, and I stand completely or almost completely unarmed."

One cannot challenge the evidence of the rise of anti-Semitic literature in the Soviet Union. Neither can one challenge the right of all Soviet citizens or citizens of any other country to emigrate voluntarily. This must become the right of each and every citizen of the world. Yet what can one make of an article in the *Western Jewish News* of February 19, 1982, titled "Russian Jews converting to Christianity"? This most revealing article numbed readers in the North American Jewish community. One witness reported being shocked "at the number of conversion ceremonies for Russian Jews at a Manhattan Orthodox Church." These were not isolated cases as the article pointed out. (Forty in Manhattan, and now there is a Russian Christian Club in Chicago operated by a missionary Church.)

The article ends with a warning that "increased conversion among Russian Jews is a harbinger of what could eventually happen to the entire Russian Jewish community here" if American Jewry remains passive.

This article sharply brings into focus the argument that we heard on numerous occasions on our recent trip to the Soviet Union. Jews were leaving, some claimed, not because they were unable to live their lives as

Jews but rather they were leaving because of economics; because of the things that a consumer capitalist society could offer. I do not profess to know how to assuage Gershman's pain but this article brings to light another facet of the problem that must be examined.

A third cause for the decline of the Jewish radical movement not dealt with by either Salutin or Gershman cannot be ignored. It arose because of the Cold War in the 1950s. The fear that it engendered convinced many Jews to disavow their radical affiliations and move into the Jewish mainstream or into passivity. While noting the revival of the Cold War today, there is one crucial difference between the Cold War of the fifties and today's: the 1950s was a period of economic growth, the 1980s is a period of economic crisis, along with a concomitant rise of anti-Semitism, racism, etc. I strongly agree with Arthur Liebman's position in his book *The Jews and the Left*:

> I contend that significant segments of the Jewish community in America will be driven to the left in the future. Their economic decline and the general economic downturn of the American economy coupled with a rise in anti-Semitism will severely limit the political options open to them. They will move to the left because indeed there will not be many other political options open to them. When this movement occurs it will be the job of principled socialists in the Jewish community and outside of it to encourage this development and educate these new recruits...

While these three factors were reasons for the decline of the old Jewish left in the 1950s, in the 1980s I would suspect that to some extent these will be the factors which will trigger a revival of significant proportions of the Jewish left.

In conclusion, Mark Twain's comment seems appropriate: "The report of my death has been widely exaggerated." Similarly, I would contend that the report of the demise of the Jewish left is also widely exaggerated. The Jewish left in North America has still its major role to play and the progressive Jewish press has its most vital role to fulfil.

Let's get on with the task!

October-November 1985

Alejandro Lipschutz
His Vision for Indian Self-Determination

BERNARDO BERDICHEWSKY

Alejandro Lipschutz was a remarkable person, both as a human being and as a scientist. It is not by chance that the great Nobel laureate, Chilean poet Pablo Neruda, wrote in 1963 on the occasion of Lipschutz' 80th birthday: "The most important man in my country during the years that I have been writing is Don Alejandro Lipschutz from Santiago de Chile," and he continued: "the most universal of the Chileans was born far away from these lands, from these peoples, from these mountains. Nevertheless he taught us more than millions of those that were born here; he taught us not only universal science, systematic method, discipline of the intelligence, devotion for peace. He taught us the truth of our origins, showing us the national road to consciousness."

Lipschutz, already an old man, survived his good friend and admirer Neruda, who died about a week after the "Black September" military coup (September 11, 1973). He also survived his other good friend, the great Chilean statesman, President Salvador Allende, killed by the military during the coup. Lipschutz died quietly and alone in January 1980 at the Jewish Nursing Home in Santiago, Chile, at the advanced age of 96 years, surviving his wife, Dona Margarita, who died half a decade before at 92 years of age.

Lipschutz arrived in Chile in 1926 after a brilliant scientific career as a physiologist in Europe. He was born in August 1883 in Riga, capital of Latvia, where he studied until leaving for Switzerland and Germany where he received his M.D. in 1907 (University of Goettingen). By the time he left for Chile, he had published several books.

The Lipschutzes adopted Chile as their homeland, becoming citizens in 1941. They spent their first decade in the city of Concepcion, where Lipschutz was appointed to the physiology chair in the medical school. During this decade, he built a research institute, helped to establish the Chilean Biological Association and became Dean of the Medical School. He also got to know the Mapuche Indian people, native to that region of Chile. By the end of that decade he wrote his first book on the Indian question.

In 1937 Dr. Lipschutz and his wife moved to Santiago, the capital of the country, to establish and direct the first research institute on experimental medicine. He made this institute nationally and internationally known, and published important research works and studies. After more than a quarter of a century of dedicated work, Lipschutz retired, but continued working as emeritus researcher and professor. In the late sixties, when the National Scientific Prize was established in Chile, the first award went to Lipschutz. He received numerous awards and honors from important national and international institutions, including the Charles L. Mayer Cancer Award of the National Science Foundation, USA, 1944; Dr. Honoris Causa from the University of Havana, 1963; another from the Ethnology Institute of the Academy of Science of the USSR, 1973; and the Casa de las Americas Prize in Havana, 1974. He belonged to many prestigious scientific associations, both international and from particular countries, such as the USA, USSR, U.K., Spain, Chile, Argentina, Mexico, etc. He published more than 1,000 articles and scientific reports, and about 30 books.

He was a very hard working and incredibly prolific person, with a profoundly intelligent and sharply critical mind. But what impressed me most about Lipschutz, besides his strong personality and determination and his impressive prophet-like appearance, was his ideological consistency and his brilliant ability to deal not only professionally, but profoundly with both the biological sciences and the social sciences. What was also amazing is that he never confused the two fields. Even more important, he never reduced the sociological realm to the biological one, as was the practice of most biologists dealing with social problems. On the contrary, he opposed and criticized reductionism and social Darwinism and all forms of racism.

When looking at Lipschutz as a social scientist, it is difficult to classify him as sociologist, political scientist or anthropologist, although the latter was undoubtedly his favorite. However, Professor Lipschutz went beyond the natural sciences and the social sciences into the philosophy of science and of knowledge, dealing in particular with the work of Francis Bacon and Marx and Engels. He understood Marxism basically as a philosophy of practice. In spite of his respect for Engels and Lenin he didn't fall into the positivistic trap that permeated orthodox Marxism during his lifetime. Neither was he, as a biologist, impressed with Lysenko's mystified theory of heredity.

In his social science studies, Lipschutz was trying to creatively apply historical materialism, particularly in dealing with the Indian question. Lipschutz was impressed and influenced by Schweitzer's work in Africa. When he himself went to South America, he made personal contact with the exploited native people, particularly the Araucanians or Mapuche Indians, and dedicated his efforts to improving their lot. Having been involved since his early student days in political and revolutionary action (he participated in his home country in the 1905 Russian Revolution as a member of Lenin's Bolshevik faction), Lipschutz brought a socialist perspective to his crusade on behalf of the Indian peoples. He worked with the indigenist movements in Latin America, especially the Mexican movement. He was the central figure in the development of the Chilean Indigenist Movement and Institute. Through this he was able to influence several liberal and/or progressive governments in Chile in favor of more advanced Indian legislation. Lipschutz also influenced the strong Chilean working class parties, communists and socialists, and helped in drafting their political stands on the Indian question.

Dealing with Lipschutz' last published article, "The Law of the Tribe, the Law of the Nation and Double Patriotism in Latin America" (1979), I wrote the following in my book *Anthropology and Social Change in Rural Areas*:

> Latin American socioeconomic formation corresponds not only to a subcivilization, but to a pluralistic society as well—not only by virtue of its nearly twenty national states but also because almost every nation is a multiethnic society. Perhaps the most typical of these are the indigenous tribal societies at various degrees of incorporation into the predominant capitalist formation.
>
> Lipschutz deals with the problems of these ethnic communities in the contexts of the American continent and the world at large. The notion of "tribe" and "tribalism" is discussed here, analyzing the significance of the tribe in the history of social structure in Europe and in Latin America. The institution of lordship existed in Europe and Latin America as the unavoidable result of tribal evolution, especially in neolithic society with its agricultural surplus production. The result of lordship is the conquest of other tribes and the formation of empires. But the cultural values of conquered tribes may survive and become incorporated into the national culture. The nation in Europe and Asia has given recognition to tribal autonomy. The same will happen also in Latin America. Lipschutz deals with the changes which occur to the tribe as it moves to chiefdom or lordship. The ethnic identity of the tribe affirms itself through a conscious struggle for the survival of inherited cultural values. When this occurs in a nation in which the lord promotes the prominence of his own tribe's cultural values, this phenomenon is termed tribalism. Lipschutz points to examples in Europe, Asia,

Africa, and—the most salient example—the Soviet Union. In these areas the maintenance of tribal language and government recognition of the different ethnic groups achieves a "double patriotism"—of tribe and nation. The "Indianization" of Mexico, for example, is part of the formation of double patriotism. In Peru the potential for the affirmation of Indian cultural values is great, and in Chile such an affirmation was made by the Mapuche and the Allende government. When the national community has a consciousness of the nation, double patriotism may become an important force.

Within the Latin American Indigenist Movement, Lipschutz was aligned with the most advanced elements, such as Manuel Gamio and Vicente Lombardo Toledano in Mexico, and Luis E. Valcarcel and Jose Carlos Mariategui in Peru. "Indigenismo" is a social expression of advanced sectors of the progressive classes in Latin America. It is a product of important social transformation brought about by deep structural changes, such as the Mexican and the Bolivian Revolutions, truncated and unfinished as they were. Also the successful Cuban Revolution and the great reform processes, first in Guatemala, then in Peru and finally in Chile, also unfinished. Those processes unleashed massive popular movements, including major ones in Brazil and Argentina, with Vargas and Peron respectively. These events brought the popular masses —peasants, "pobladores" and Indians—into the political arena of their countries, in some sort of alliances with the national bourgeois and/or the working class.

The political struggles of the progressive classes against their countries' oligarchies brought these new popular masses—including the Indians—into the political scene as their allies. Thus the indigenist ideology and movement hoped to integrate the native population into the national life; that is to say, the peasantization, proletarianization and full incorporation in the capitalist process of "modernization," "urbanization" and "industrialization" of the Latin American countries. The liberal and social democratic sectors advocated equality under the law and individual opportunities for native peoples while the Marxist proletarian sectors also saw the opportunity to incorporate the native people into their country's class struggle. "Indigenismo" in Latin America, during its half century movement, from the 1920s to the 1970s, was a progressive movement developed by advanced social sectors of the non-Indian population to deal with the Indian question. Besides their internal differences and distinct degrees of progressiveness, all the indigenists' trends were basically similar regarding the main issue, i.e., the assimilation of the Indian tribes and communities into the national life. Lipschutz was one of the few exceptions. He went further than the most progressive figures of the movement, either in Mexico or in Peru.

That basic contradiction of the Indigenist Movement was sensed by Lipschutz, and he was one of the first to solve it, at least at the ideological level. He expressed the real trend and projection of the social and historical practice of the native people themselves. Already in the sixties—although he really started in the thirties—Lipschutz developed a model of tribal autonomy and Indian self-determination, when the Indian movements in the Americas had just slowly begun, almost unnoticed, to take shape.

Today the Indigenist Movement is being replaced by the Indian movement, and assimilationist ideology is being contested and rejected by the native people themselves. Following their own historical social practice, they are developing a movement of liberation from "internal colonialism." The old ideology of "Indigenismo" in Latin America, after more than half a century, is dialectically giving way now to its opposition—the Indian movement, toward autonomy, self-determination and liberation. Lipschutz was one of the first of the "Indigenistas" to understand the change, and to provide a foundation for the new ideology. In that sense, he was a real forerunner, and fulfilled plentifully and creatively a unique, progressive intellectual mission in social change.

May 1986

A True Man of the People
An Editorial

Progressive people all over Canada were saddened at the unexpected death of Joseph Zuken on March 25 after a brief illness. He was 73 years of age.

His funeral was attended by hundreds of Winnipeg citizens who paid tribute to his exemplary life. Thousands more across the country mourned his passing. His funeral oration was delivered by Ben Chud, co-editor of *Outlook*, a lifelong friend. Final graveside farewell was delivered by his colleague and co-worker, Mary Kardash, on behalf of the Communist Party of Manitoba.

Joe Zuken arrived with his family from the Ukraine in 1914, and spent all of his formative years in the working-class North End of Winnipeg. He never forgot his origins, but dedicated his life to defending the rights of working people, minority groups and the poor.

Neither did he forget his cultural roots. Joe was steeped in Yiddish culture and was its eloquent spokesman throughout his life. He was a lifelong member of the United Jewish People's Order and a member of the advisory board of *Outlook*.

Joe Zuken graduated with distinction from the Winnipeg Peretz Shule, where he subsequently taught for six years before he was able to open his law office. His law practice was unique as a model of dedication to service of common people.

But it was in public service that Joe Zuken made his mark, during a 42-year career in public office—twenty years on the school board and 22 years as a city councillor. From the time he was first elected in 1941 until his retirement in 1983 he lost only one election—in 1979 when he ran for mayor. Joe Zuken was a founder of the Labour Election Committee and continued to support its work even after his retirement from civic politics.

Amongst his many accomplishments were the establishment of kindergartens in the public school system, the naming of a school after Andrew Mynarski, V.C., Canadian war hero, the provision of free textbooks and increased salaries for teachers. He campaigned for low-rental housing; championed the establishment of the Seven Oaks Hospital and served as chairman of its board for many years. Joe received many honors, amongst which was an honorary degree from the University of Winnipeg, a community services medal from the University of Manitoba; he was a Queen's Counsel and a Bencher of the Manitoba Law Society.

Tributes have poured in from all over Canada from a wide spectrum, including public officials, educators, working people, professionals—from every ethnic group and different political persuasions.

Friends of Joe Zuken in Winnipeg are planning to set up a foundation which would fund future projects dear to Joe's heart. We wish them well. A foundation of this kind will help to keep alive Joe Zuken's ideals in the years to come.

December 1986

Rabbi Feinberg
Righteous Jew

HENRY M. ROSENTHAL

Once an outspoken rabbi of the Holy Blossom Synagogue in Toronto, Rabbi Abraham Feinberg died at his home in Reno, Nevada, after a brief illness. He was 87.

Rabbi Feinberg was born in Bellaire, Ohio, one of ten children of Nathan Feinberg, Cantor. He left school at the age of fourteen to work as a laborer, eventually managing to save enough money to enrol in the University of Cincinnati, where he won several scholarships. He was ordained a rabbi in 1924, and served several congregations before he was appointed by Temple Israel in New York. But in 1927, he abandoned organized religion for a music career, saying, "Organized religion, like Tutenkhamen, is full of material splendor, but dead—a deserted lighthouse. The tides of human energy beat on other shores."

There followed a spectacular career as a singer as Feinberg zoomed to national fame as "Anthony Frome, the Poet Prince" of the airwaves. But the coming to power of Hitler in 1933 wrought a change in Feinberg and he resolved to turn back to the pulpit. There he condemned the hypocritical non-intervention policy of the Western powers which delivered Spain into the hands of the fascists, and denounced the Duke of Windsor's flirtations with the Nazis. In 1943, he accepted the position of rabbi of the Holy Blossom Temple in Toronto, which had achieved, under liberal Rabbi Maurice Eisendrath, a continent-wide reputation as a defender of the weak and powerless.

Rabbi Feinberg's stewardship at the Holy Blossom Temple was marked with controversy from the beginning. He fought racism in all its forms, and spoke out forcefully for the exclusion of religious instruction from public schools, maintaining that "...there is no place in our public schools for the teaching of religion, and I mean any religion." His influence extended far beyond the pulpit, and he made the conservative leaders of the Canadian Jewish establishment very nervous by his outspokenness.

Retirement came in 1961, because of his failing eyesight, but his public career of challenging injustice and hypocrisy continued unabated.

He demonstrated his opposition to the Vietnam War by visiting Vietnam, where he was presented with a cane by Ho Chi Minh, which became almost a trademark of Rabbi Feinberg's from then on. More recently, Rabbi Feinberg identified strongly with the problems of the elderly, and conducted a popular radio program called Grey Lib. He has also written several books, including *Hanoi Diary* and *Storm the Gates of Jericho*, which achieved wide readership. His friendship with John Lennon and Yoko Ono of Beatles fame became a media event.

(Rabbi Feinberg wrote several articles for *Canadian Jewish Outlook*, with unique timeliness and eloquence. We prize our association with Rabbi Feinberg over the years, and mourn his passing. Would that there were more like him!—ed.)

The Contributors

MONA ELAINE ADILMAN is a widely published poet. She lives in Montreal.

TED ALLAN is the noted co-author of *The Scalpel and the Sword*. His short story in this collection later became part of the scenario for the film *Lies My Father Told Me*.

ABRAHAM J. ARNOLD has served as executive director of the Manitoba Association for Rights and Liberties.

WALTER BAUER, who taught at the University of Toronto, was the author of some 40 volumes of poetry.

LANNY BECKMAN is a freelance writer and publisher of New Star Books, Vancouver.

DR. BERNARDO BERDICHEWSKY, anthropologist and sociologist, was born in Chile. He teaches at Simon Fraser University in Burnaby and at Capilano College in North Vancouver.

S. CATHY BERSON is an anthropologist and freelance writer. She is also a member of the *Outlook* collective.

MICHAL BODEMANN is a sociology professor at the University of Toronto, currently on leave in Berlin.

DIONNE BRAND is a Trinidad-born CUSO worker now living in Canada. She is the author of several books of poetry.

MIKE CASS is a longtime journalist and European Correspondent for *Canadian Jewish Outlook*.

BEN CHUD was the co-editor of *Outlook* until his untimely death in October 1986. He was a Yiddish scholar, social work professor and an outstanding advocate of progressive Jewish values.

JACK COWAN is a founder of *Canadian Jewish Outlook* and honorary president of the United Jewish People's Order. He is the author of *My Outlook*.

IDA DAVID, originally from Montreal, is a writer now living in New York.

REVA DOLGOY is an art education consultant living near Ottawa.

DANIEL DRACHE is a political science professor at York University, Toronto. He co-edited *The Other Macdonald Report: The Consensus on Canada's Future that the Macdonald Commission Left Out*.

MARGARET ENNENBERG, formerly a teacher and social worker, is now a freelance writer living in Vancouver.

NORMAN EPSTEIN is a professor of chemical engineering at the University of B.C., and a member of the Engineers for Nuclear Disarmament.

ELIEZER FEILER is active on the Israeli peace front and is a member of Kibbutz Yad Hanna.

ABRAHAM FEINBERG was Rabbi Emeritus of the Holy Blossom Temple, Toronto. He challenged injustice and hypocrisy from his pulpit, on the streets of the community and in the several books he authored. He died at age 87 in 1986.

ZAYED GAMIET, born in South Africa, is a lawyer living in Vancouver. He is the chairman of the South African Coalition, B.C.

JOSHUA GERSHMAN was the editor of *Canadian Jewish Weekly* (*Vochenblatt*) and one of the founders of *Canadian Jewish Outlook*. He was Editor

Emeritus of *Canadian Jewish Outlook*. In his early years he was recognized as one of Canada's finest labor organizers.

ITCHE GOLDBERG is a Yiddish scholar and editor of the Yiddish literary magazine *Yiddishe Kultur*, published in New York.

KATHLEEN GOUGH is an anthropologist known internationally for her books and articles on India and Southeast Asia.

MORRIS J. GRANITE has written extensively for *Canadian Jewish Outlook*.

LARRY HAIVEN, formerly of Edmonton, is doing post-graduate studies in London, England.

RUTH HERMAN is a lawyer practising in Vancouver.

LEOPOLD INFELD was one of the world's outstanding mathematicians. He worked with Albert Einstein at Princeton University. He then taught at the University of Toronto for eleven years before returning to his native Poland in 1950.

SAMUEL L. KAGAN was a highly respected Canadian sculptor whose artistic credo was to emphasize human life and conditions.

ROSE KASHTAN was active in working-class theatre and progressive Jewish circles in Montreal and Toronto.

DAVE KASHTAN and the late ROSE KASHTAN were leaders in the Toronto movement to "Save the Rosenbergs."

ROCHL KORN was born in Galicia and settled in Montreal after World War II. She gained recognition as one of Canada's greatest Yiddish poets.

AARON KRAMER is the author of several books of poetry and is well known for his translations of Yiddish poetry. He teaches English at Dowling College in Long Island, N.Y.

GEORGE LEWIS (a pseudonym) is a freelance writer living in Toronto and is a regular contributor to *Canadian Jewish Outlook*.

JOEL LEXCHIN, M.D., is a member of the Medical Reform Group of Ontario and is author of *The Real Pushers: A Critical Analysis of the Canadian Drug Industry*.

LILITH (a pseudonym) is a freelance writer and the daughter of Holocaust survivors.

JOSEPH LIPSKI, Middle Eastern correspondent for *Canadian Jewish Outlook*, lives in Tel Aviv, Israel.

SOL LIPTZIN is an eminent Jewish scholar who resides in Israel.

PERETZ MARKISH was an outstanding Soviet Yiddish poet who fell victim to the Stalin-Beria terror. He was executed in 1952.

NORMAN MASSEY has written articles on historical Jewish intellectuals for *Canadian Jewish Outlook*. He was a regular Montreal correspondent for the *Canadian Jewish Weekly* (*Vochenblatt*).

JOHN MATE is active in the Forum for Peace in the Middle East Committee, Vancouver.

ASHER NEUDORFER is a lawyer living in Montreal. He is a member of the Regroupement Pour Un Dialogue Israel-Palestine and has been a contributing editor to *Canadian Jewish Outlook*.

MOISSAYE J. OLGIN (1878-1939) was a prolific Yiddish writer and the first editor of the *Morning Freiheit*. He was one of the foremost leaders of the Jewish left in North America.

EDWARD PARKER is former director of the School of Journalism at Ryerson Polytechnical Institute in Toronto.

The Contributors 381

STAN PERSKY teaches political studies at Capilano College in North Vancouver and is an active labour journalist and social critic.

RUTH PRESSMAN is a freelance writer and art critic living in Montreal.

ROBERT RATNER teaches sociology and criminology at the University of British Columbia.

PHILIP RESNICK teaches political science at the University of British Columbia and is the author of several books on Canadian politics.

SID RESNICK is the editor of the English section of the *Morning Freiheit*. He is an outstanding translator from Yiddish and a respected journalist.

ISAAC E. RONCH, who died in 1985, was a renowned American Yiddish poet, writer and essayist.

RITA L. ROSENFELD is a freelance writer and poet.

HELENE ROSENTHAL is a widely published poet and critic, now living in Vancouver.

HENRY M. ROSENTHAL was co-editor of *Canadian Jewish Outlook* from 1980 to 1986 and is now editor of *Outlook*.

STANLEY B. RYERSON is recognized as the dean of Marxist social sciences in Canada. He has authored several landmark books on Canadian history. He currently teaches at the University of Quebec.

GEORGE SCHEINMAN was a volunteer student who worked with Janusz Korczak at the famous Children's Home in Warsaw.

HILLEL SCHENKER is senior editor of the Tel Aviv-based Middle East monthly *New Outlook*.

PAUL SCHMIDT teaches English literature at the California College of Arts and Crafts in Oakland, Calif.

ED SHAFFER is professor of economics at the University of Alberta. He has published several books on Canada's energy policy and is widely recognized as an expert in this field.

SOLOMON SHEK worked for many years on the publication of the *Canadian Jewish Weekly* (*Vochenblatt*).

SHOLEM SHTERN is Canada's best-known Yiddish poet. He has published numerous volumes of poetry which have been translated into English and French.

MIRIAM SILVER is cultural director of the Emma Lazarus Federation of Jewish Women's Clubs in the USA.

REUBEN SLONIM is a rabbi, writer and broadcaster. Born in Winnipeg, he lives in Toronto and is the co-founder and president of the Association for the Living Jewish Spirit. He is the author of five books.

JAMES TORCZYNER, D.S.W., is an associate professor of social work at McGill University in Montreal.

ROZ USISKIN, who taught history at the University of Winnipeg, is recognized for her studies on early Jewish-Canadian settlement and on the Jewish left.

AVROM YANOVSKY was widely known for his trenchant political cartoons and other works of art.

JOSEPH ZUKEN, Q.C., was dubbed "Dean of the Winnipeg City Council" in recognition of his dedication during the 40 continuous years he served the people of Winnipeg.

RAJZEL ZYCHLINSKA is a Polish-born poet now living in Canada. She has published several highly acclaimed books of poetry.

Other recent New Star titles

SHRINK RESISTANT The Struggle Against Psychiatry in Canada *Edited by Bonnie Burstow and Don Weitz.* Through interviews, journal entries, poetry, graphics, and personal narratives, 40 current and former psychiatric inmates relate their experiences inside the walls of mental hospitals and at the hands of psychiatrists.
260 pages. **$11.95**

THE SUPREME COURT OF CANADA DECISION ON ABORTION *Edited by Shelagh Day and Stan Persky.* The complete text of the Supreme Court's historic decision in the Morgentaler case striking down Section 251 of the Criminal Code — Canada's abortion law. Includes a Commentary by Shelagh Day and an Introduction by Stan Persky.
225 pages. **$5.95**

FREE TRADE AND THE NEW RIGHT AGENDA *by John W. Warnock.* The Free Trade Agreement and how it fits into business's response to the crisis in the world's capitalist economies since the 1970's.
324 pages. **$11.95**

NO WAY TO LIVE Poor Women Speak Out *by Sheila Baxter.* Fifty women talk about their poverty. Includes statistical information on poverty and women, as well as a directory of anti-poverty and women's groups in Canada. 231 pages. **$9.95**

HASTINGS AND MAIN Stories from an Inner City Neighbourhood *Interviews by Laurel Kimbley; Edited by Jo-Ann Canning-Dew.* Reminiscences of twenty long-time residents of Vancouver's Downtown Eastside upset many of the stereotypes about "skid road". 158 pages. **$9.95**

AMERICA, GOD AND THE BOMB The Legacy of Ronald Reagan *by F.H. Knelman.* An updated, revised edition of the author's 1983 anti-nuclear arms classic *Reagan, God and the Bomb.* "Authoritative and frightening." — Linus Pauling. 478 pages. **$6.95**

CANADA IN THE EUROPEAN AGE *by R.T. Naylor.* A major reassessment of Canada's history to the end of World War I by one of the country's leading economic historians. 617 pages. **$19.95**

A PEOPLE IN ARMS *by Marie Jakober.* A dramatic novel of love and revolution, set in Nicaragua. Continues the story begun in her 1985 novel, *Sandinista.* 303 pages. **$9.95**

To order, send cheque or money order to New Star Books Ltd. Price shown includes shipping & handling.

For a free catalogue containing a complete list of New Star titles, write to the address below:

New Star Books Ltd.
2504 York Avenue
Vancouver, B.C.
CANADA V6K 1E3